George P. Merrill

Stones for Building and Decoration

George P. Merrill

Stones for Building and Decoration

ISBN/EAN: 9783743344174

Manufactured in Europe, USA, Canada, Australia, Japa

Cover: Foto ©Andreas Hilbeck / pixelio.de

Manufactured and distributed by brebook publishing software (www.brebook.com)

George P. Merrill

Stones for Building and Decoration

PLATE I.

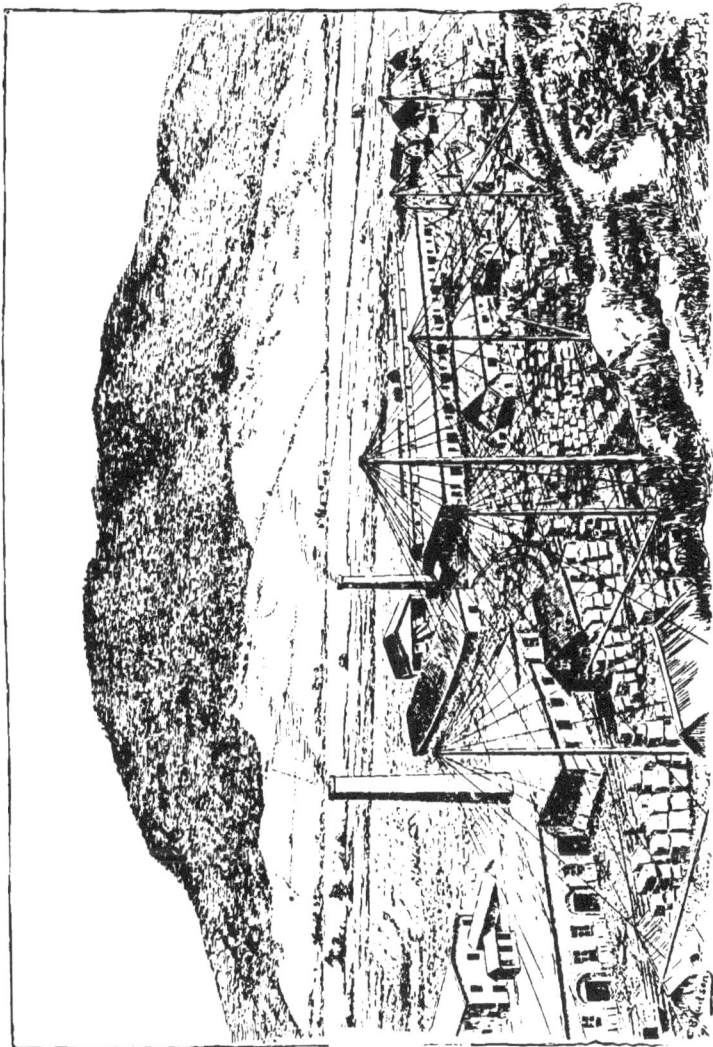

GENERAL VIEW OF MARBLE QUARRIES AND WORKS AT WEST RUTLAND, VERMONT.

Frontispiece.

STONES

FOR

BUILDING AND DECORATION.

BY

GEORGE P. MERRILL,

CURATOR OF GEOLOGY IN THE UNITED STATES NATIONAL MUSEUM.

NEW YORK:

JOHN WILEY & SONS,

53 EAST TENTH STREET.

1891.

PREFACE.

The work herewith presented is based upon the author's handbook and catalogue of the collect on of building and ornamental stones in the United States National Museum at Washington. It differs from that work, however, in many important particulars, several new chapters having been added, others rewritten and the whole so far as possible brought down to date. A portion of the added matter is essentially the same, though in a somewhat different form, as originally appeared in the columns of *Stone*, the *American Architect*, the *Scientific American Supplement*, and other of our industrial journals. The writer's experience in preparing the extensive collection in the National Museum, at Washington, as well as its partial duplicate in the American Museum in New York City, has afforded him ample opportunity for becoming acquainted with the quarry products of the country at large, while extensive field trips, particularly in the eastern and extreme western United States, have given him a practical insight into the resources of the regions as well as some knowledge concerning the usual methods of quarrying and working.

That there is a demand for a comprehensive and not too technical a work on this subject has been emphatically impressed upon the writer many times during the past few years. How far the pages herewith presented shall supply this demand, it is left for the public to decide. The alphabetical arrangement of States adopted in Part II. will very likely at

first be subject to criticism as unscientific. Such an arrangement for purposes of rapid reference, has however, been found
so much superior to the usual geographic method, that excuses
are not deemed necessary. The work, it should be stated, has
been written from an American standpoint, and treats principally of stones found within the limits of the United States, or
imported from other sources. In but few instances are stones
mentioned that are of purely historical interest.

The full-page plates illustrating quarry views, were, with a
single exception, drawn from photographs taken by the author.
They may, therefore, be considered as reasonably accurate.
Thanks are due the authorities of the Smithsonian Institution
for the privilege of electrotyping such of the engravings in the
original handbook as it was desired to reproduce here.

GEORGE P. MERRILL.

SMITHSONIAN INSTITUTION,
WASHINGTON, D. C., JUNE, 1891.

TABLE OF CONTENTS.

PART I.

PART II.

THE ROCKS, QUARRIES AND QUARRY REGIONS.

v

PART III.

PART IV.

APPENDICES.

LIST OF ILLUSTRATIONS.

FULL PAGE PLATES.

FIGURES IN THE TEXT.

STONES FOR BUILDING AND DECORATION.

PART I.

HISTORICAL.

The use of stone for purposes of construction dates from a very early period in human history. Within the limits of North America, however, except as practiced in a crude way by certain tribes in the arid regions of the West, its use necessarily dates from a period comparatively recent.

The early settlers in the eastern states found wood abundant and cheap. They were as a rule comparatively poor, and with little taste for architectural display, even had their means permitted its indulgence. But with the gradual increase in individual wealth and culture there was naturally developed a taste in architecture which could be gratified only in the employment of some less perishable material : for such, fortunately, the early settlers of eastern Massachusetts had not far to look. The first stones quarried in this State are thought by Professor Shaler to have been the clayslates in the vicinity of Boston. These, however, were worked only in a small way and the product used for grave- and mile-stones, and a few lintels.

According to Shurtleff * one of the first stone buildings in Boston was the house of Deacon John Phillips. This was erected about 1650, and continued to stand until 1864. It is supposed to have been built from granite bowlders found in the

---

* History of Boston, p. 589.

1

immediate vicinity. In 1737 was built of bowlders of Braintree granite the old Hancock house, since torn down, and in 1749-'54 King's chapel, which is still standing on the corner of School and Tremont Streets. This last was at the time the greatest stone construction ever undertaken in Boston, if not in America. Like those already mentioned, it was built from bowlders ; and, considering the method of cutting employed (to be noticed later), was a remarkable structure. The granite bowlders scattered over the commons had been very generally used in Quincy and vicinity for steps and foundations for some years previous to this, until at last, fearing lest the supply should become exhausted, the inhabitants assembled in town meeting and voted that, " no person shall dig or carry off " any stone " on the said commons or undivided lands upon any account whatever without license from the committee, upon penalty of the forfeiture of 10 shillings for every and each cart-load so dug and carried away."

It was not, however, until the early part of the present century that granite began to be used at all extensively in and about Boston, when the material was introduced in considerable quantities by canal from Chelmsford, 30 miles distant. It was from Chelmsford stone that was constructed in 1810 the Boston court-house ; in 1814 the New South church ; and about the same time the Congregational house on Beacon Street ; the old Parkman house on Bowdoin Square ; University hall in Cambridge ; and in 1818-'19 the first stone block in the city, a portion of which is still standing, on Brattle Street. In this year also a considerable quantity of the stone was shipped to Savannah, Georgia, for the construction of a church at that place. The greater part of this granite was, however, obtained from bowlders, and it was not until the opening of quarries at Quincy, in 1825, for the purpose of obtaining stone for the construction of the Bunker Hill monument that the business assumed any great importance.

In 1824 a Mr. Bates, of Quincy, went to Sandy Hook, in the adjacent town of Gloucester, and opened a granite quarry there. Not long after other quarries were opened at Anisquam, where an extensive industry was carried on for some years, though finally abandoned. Quarries were opened at Rockport, just beyond Gloucester, in 1827, and are still in active operation. In 1848 the quarries at Bay View were opened. These have since become the property of the Cape Ann Granite Company, and produce annually some 500,000 cubic feet of stone.

Although the Massachusetts quarries were the first systematically worked to obtain granite for building purposes, other States were not far behind. Thus we are told by Dr. Field * that as early as 1792 granite quarries were reported to have been opened at Haddam Neck, in Connecticut, and as many as ninety hands were employed in this and other quarries in the vicinity as early as 1819. This material is, however, a gneiss rather than a granite, and splitting readily into slabs, was used nearly altogether for curbing and paving, for which purpose it brought from 10 to 20 cents per cubic foot. The principal markets for the material were Rhode Island and the cities of Boston, New York, Albany, and Baltimore.

The rocky coast and adjacent islands of Maine are capable of furnishing immense quantities of granitic rock of a color and quality not to be excelled. The rare excellence of many of these sites for quarries, together with the ready facilities of transportation by water to all the leading cities, early made itself apparent to the shrewd and pushing business men of New England, and a very few years after the commencing of works at Quincy saw similar beginnings made at various points both on the coast and farther inland. The years 1836–'37 appear to

---

* Centennial address and historical sketches of Middletown, Cromwell, Portland, Chatham, and Middle Haddam.

have been peculiarly prolific in schemes for speculation in this industry.

It is stated by North * that during the latter year, out of one hundred and thirty-five acts of incorporation granted by the State legislature, thirty were for granite companies, three of which were located in Augusta. One was called the Augusta and New York Granite Company, and was for working, rending, transporting, and dealing in granite from the Hamlen ledge, situated about two miles from the river by way of Western Avenue. Another, named the Augusta and Philadelphia Granite Company, owned the Ballard ledge, a mile and a half from Kennebec bridge by way of Northern Avenue. A large portion of the granite for the state-house, court-house, and new jail was obtained from this ledge. The other company, called the Augusta Blue Ledge Company, purchased Hall's ledge, on the east side of the river, near Daniel Hewin's house, some $2\frac{1}{2}$ miles from the bridge.

It is further stated by this same authority that during the erection of the State-house blocks of granite for the colonnade, 21 feet long by nearly 4 feet in diameter, were obtained from the Melvin ledge, in Hallowell, about three miles away. Convenient and abundant as are these quarry sites, it seems a little singular that they should not have been earlier discovered and worked. In building the Kennebec bridge in 1797, the piers and abutments were constructed of stone split from drift bowlders, and the houses of Capt. William Robinson, Judge Bridge, and Benjamin Whitwell, all built about 1801, had for underpinning granite brought at great expense from near Boston, probably Quincy, or perhaps Chelmsford. Most of the stone of large dimensions of which the old jail was built in 1808 were also, it is stated, obtained with great labor from bowlders,

---

* History of Augusta, Maine, p. 582.

though an unsuccessful attempt was made to work the Rowell ledge at the time. Some of the top strata were broken off by means of wedges driven under the sheets, but the process was laborious and slow. The first successful attempt to work a ledge in town is stated to have been made by Jonathan Matthews on the Thwing ledge, in 1825. The Frankfort Granite Company, located at the base of Mosquito Mountain, Waldo County, began operations in May, 1836, and within the next two years took out and sold upwards of $50,000 worth of material. What is now the Hallowell Granite Company opened its quarries in 1838, and during the first ten years is stated to have sold $500,000 worth of stone.

It is stated by Professor Seely* that the earliest attempts at quarrying marbles in New England were those of Philo Tomlinson, who began operations at Marbledale, in the town of New Milford, Connecticut, about 1800. Other quarries were soon after opened, and in 1830 as many as fifteen were in active operation within a distance of three miles of this place. The product was sent to all parts of the country. Soon after this date, competition set in from other localities, particularly from Dover, New York, and Rutland, Vermont, and by 1850 the business had proved so unremunerative that the last quarry at Marbledale was abandoned. Marble quarries and mills were also put in active operation at West Stockbridge, in Massachusetts, as early as 1802 or 1803. Work was stopped here in 1855, owing to competition of Vermont and Italian marbles.

Of the many marble quarries in Vermont, those in East Dorset are believed to have been longest worked, Professor Seely stating one Isaac Underhill began operations here as early as 1785, the product being utilized for fire-jams, chimney backs, hearths, and lintels. Other quarries soon opened, and from 1785 to 1841, nine were in operation at this place. The

* Marble Border of New England, p. 27

first marble gravestone ever finished in the State is believed to have been the work of Jonas Stewart in 1790. Prior to the introduction of Italian and Rutland marble, about 1840, the supply of the Dorset stone was not equal to the demand. At West Rutland, works were first put in successful operation about 1838. At the present time not less than fifteen quarries are in operation, affording employment altogether to about 2,000 men.

The first stone quarried and used in Philadelphia is said to have been the micaceous and hornblendic gneiss which occurs in inexhaustible quantities in the immediate vincinity. This was at first used only for foundations and rough construction. The first house built within the city limits, that built in Letitia Court by order of William Penn, was constructed on a foundation of this stone about the year 1682. The Old Swedes church, built in 1698, Independence Hall, and numerous other structures are said to have had similar foundations. Later, entire walls were made of the material, as in the house of John Penn, erected in 1785, and which is still standing. The quarrying of marble in Montgomery County, Pennsylvania, is said to have been commenced by a Mr. Daniel about the time of the Revolution.* This stone seems to have immediately become a favorite for trimming purposes, and to have been used in Philadelphia to the almost entire exclusion of other material until as late as 1840. During this time many fine buildings were constructed from it, as will be noted later.

Sandstone quarrying in the United States doubtless began with the itinerant working of the extensive beds of Triassic brownstone in the vicinity of Portland, Connecticut. It is stated † that the first quarry here was opened " where the stone origin-

---

* First Geological Survey of Pennsylvania, Vol. 1.

† Centennial Address and Historical Sketches of Middletown, Cromwell, Portland, Chatham, and Middle Haddam, by D. D. Field, 1853.

ally rose high and hung shelving over the river." The value of the material was early recognized, and it began to be utilized for building and for monuments soon after the settlement of Middletown on the opposite side of the stream. The quarries were at this time regarded as common property, and were worked as occasion demanded both by people in the immediate vicinity and by those living at a distance, who carried off the material in scows or boats of some sort, nor thought of giving anything as an equivalent. This system of free quarrying had assumed such proportions as early as 1665, that on September 4 of that year, the citizens of Middletown assembled in town meeting and voted " that whoever shall dig or raise stone at ye rocks on the east side of the river (now Portland) for any without the town, the said digger shall be none but an inhabitant of Middletown, and shall be responsible to ye towne twelve pence pr. tunn for every tunn of stones that he or they shall digg for any person whosoever without the towne ; this money to be paid in wheat and pease to ye townsmen or their assigns for ye use of ye towne within six months after the transportation of the said stone."*

How soon the surface rock was exhausted and it became necessary, as now, to go below the level of the ground for suitable material is not stated, but the quarry thus opened was at length disposed of by the town and passed through various hands, among whom the names of Shaler & Hall are conspicuous. These parties pursued the business vigorously and made a handsome profit. For several years between 1810 and 1820 some thirty hands and from four to six teams were employed for the eight months comprising the quarrying season. Some 50 rods south of this quarry another was opened about 1783, and was owned by Messrs. Hulburt & Roberts. About 1814

---

* Freestone Quarries of Portland. Conn., by Prof. J. Johnson, National Magazine, 1853, p. 268.

this was purchased from the heirs of Aaron Hulburt and deeded to Erastus and Silas Brainard, who carried on the business conjointly until the death of the latter in 1847. The business is carried on under the name of Brainard & Co., to the present time. For some five years after this firm began work they employed but from seven to ten hands and two yoke of oxen. In 1819 a quarry was opened north of the Shaler & Hall quarry, by the firm of Patten & Russell. It was afterwards known as the Russell & Hall quarry, and finally in 1841 was united with that of Shaler & Hall, the firms combining to form the Middlesex Quarry Company. Some years later still another opening was made below the Brainard quarry near the ferry between Portland and Middletown. This also was known as the Shaler & Hall quarry; the original firm by this name having been incorporated with the Middlesex Quarry Company.

The three firms above enumerated continued until quite recently to monopolize the quarrying industry at this place. The quarries extend from a point near the ferry northward along the river for some three-fourths of a mile, and vary in depth from 50 to 150 feet. Their yield of stone of all grades during the time of their operation has been roughly estimated at 4,300,000 cubic feet. The rate of progress is given as follows: In 1850 the number of men employed at the three quarries was about 900 and 100 yoke of oxen; thirty vessels being regularly employed to convey the quarried material to the markets, each vessel conveying from 75 to 150 tons and making from twenty to thirty trips each season. Two years later the number of workmen regularly employed had increased to 1,200, while 200 more were engaged on contract work. The stone, even at this date, had found its way to markets as far west as Milwaukee and San Francisco. The census returns for 1880 showed the total number of men employed to be but 925, with 80 yoke of oxen and 55 horses and mules. The falling off in numbers may doubtless be considered due to the introduction of machinery and improved methods of working. The total product of the three quarries for this year was about 781,600 cubic feet, valued at not less than $650,000. A fleet of twenty-five vessels of various kinds was regularly employed in transporting this material to market.

The quarrying of slate for roofing purposes is an industry of comparatively recent origin in the United States, but few of the quarries having been operated for a longer period than thirty or forty years. The earliest opened and systematically worked are believed to have been those at West Bangor, Pennsylvania, which date back to 1835. The abundance of slate tombstones in many of our older church-yards, however, would seem to indicate that for other purposes than roofing, these stones have been quarried from a much earlier period. It is stated, moreover, that as early as 1721 a cargo of 20 tons of split slate was brought to Boston from Hangman's Island, in Braintree Bay, which may have been used in part for roofing purposes ; but the greater part of the material for this purpose was imported directly from Wales. It is also stated * that slates were quarried at Lancaster, Massachusetts, as early as 1750 or 1753, and were in extensive use in Boston soon after the close of the Revolution. The old Handcock house on Beacon street, already noted (*ante*, p. 2), was covered with slate from these quarries, as was also the old State-house and several other buildings. This quarry was worked more or less for fifty years and formed at one time quite an important industry, but which finally became unprofitable, and about 1825 or 1830 the works were discontinued, not to be again started till about 1877.

The first quarry opened in what is now the chief slate-producing region of the United States was that of Mr. J. W.

---

* Marvin's History of Lancaster, Massachusetts.

Williams, situated about a mile northwest of Slateford, in Pennsylvania. This dates back to the year 1812.*

The Vermont slate quarries are of still more recent development, work not being begun here till 1845, when Hon. Alason Allen began the manufacture of school slates at Fairhaven.† It is interesting to note, in this connection, that during the business depression of 1876–'80 almost the entire product of the American quarries was exported to England, where it sold for even less than the Welsh slates, though necessarily at very small profits. The return of more prosperous times, however, created a local demand, and the export trade has proportionally decreased, though considerable quantities are still sent to the West Indies, South America, England, Germany, and even New Zealand and Australia.

DISTRIBUTION OF BUILDING STONE IN THE UNITED STATES.

Since with material so weighty as stone, the matter of transportation is an important item, it may be well to devote a little space at the outstart to a consideration of the geographical distribution of stones of various kinds throughout the United States. This distribution, it will be observed, is a very unequal one, and since this is dependent upon geological causes a little attention must first be given to the various processes of rock formation.

The majority of stones used for any form of structural or decorative work may be roughly classed under three heads : (1) The crystalline silicious rocks, including the granites, gneisses and diabases, or trap-rocks ; (2) the calcareous rocks,

* Rep. D, 3, Second Geological Survey of Pennsylvania, p. 85.
† Geology of Vermont, Vol. II, 1861, p. 791.

including all limestones and dolomites, both the crystalline and compact common varieties ; and, (3) the fragmental or clastic rocks, including the sandstone and clay slates. Those of the first group result either as erupted molten matter from the earth's interior or from the metamorphism of silicious sediments. Those of the second group originate mainly as deposits of calcareous mud from the breaking up of shells, corals and the remains of other marine animals on an old sea bottom. Those of the third group result from the breaking up of older rocks, and the accumulation on the bottoms of lakes and seas of the resultant sand, clay, or mud in beds of varying thickness, to be subsequently hardened into stone.

Now the essential difference between a marble and a compact common limestone, like those of Ohio or Kansas, is that the first has undergone through the combined action of heat and pressure, just the right degree of change, or metamorphism as it is technically called, to develop in it crystallization and color ; the essential difference between a brick or fire clay and a cleavable slate suitable for roofing, is, as explained elsewhere, that the first named still retains its plastic condition as it was lain down in the form of fine silt on a sea bottom, while the slate has by geological agencies, by actual movements of the earth's crust, been so squeezed and compressed as to lose all resemblance to its former self, and become the cleavable article of commerce we now find it.

Now since the processes of change as noted above are dependent very largely upon the actual movements, warpings and foldings as one might say, of the earth's crust and the heat and chemical action which is thereby generated, and since these movements take place only with extreme slowness, whole geologic ages being occupied in their conception and completion, it follows as a matter of course that these metamorphic rocks, these gneisses, marbles and roofing slates, are found only among the older rocks and only in those portions of the country where this crust has been wrapped, compressed and folded as in the process of mountain making. In other words, one need expect to find these rocks in their best development only in States bordering along more or less extensive mountain ranges, while in the great interior plains and prairie regions they will be comparatively rare. It is of course probable, and perhaps may be regarded as a matter of certainty, that at great depths beneath the land surface in this interior region, are to be found the Archæan gneisses which seem to form the floor of the continent, and possibly other rocks metamorphosed by the heat and pressure of great depths. Being, however, covered by thousands of feet of later deposits they may for our purposes be left out of consideration. Let us then consider the physical features of the earth's crust as found within the limits of the United States, and discuss briefly the various rocks so far as they are dependent upon or controlled by these features.

Let one take a map of the United States and draw a straight line from a point near Montreal, Canada, to the middle of Alabama. East of this line will lie the entire Appalachian mountain system and with a few exceptions the States traversed by or bordering upon this system are the only States east of the Rocky mountains containing granites, gneisses, diabases, crystalline calcareous rocks (marbles) or roofing slates. These exceptions are to be found in northern Wisconsin ; in Minnesota, west of Minneapolis ; in small areas in southeastern Missouri, principally in Iron, Madison and St. François Counties ; the Black Hills in Dakota ; in a small area near Little Rock, Arkansas, and in a few small isolated areas in the Indian Territory and eastern Texas, as in Burnet County. The whole interior of the country, comprising all but the extreme eastern portions of West Virginia, Kentucky and Tennessee ; all of Ohio, Indiana, Illinois, Iowa, Nebraska, the Dakotas, Kansas, Mississippi,

Louisiana, Florida, Oklahoma, and with the exceptions above noted, all of Missouri, Arkansas and eastern Texas,* though containing sandstones and limestones of the common and oolitic types, produce neither granite, gneiss, trap-rocks nor slates, nor, except in small quantities, anything that can be called a marble. The earth's crust throughout this entire area has been little changed or disturbed by the eruption of molten rocks or by the processes of mountain making. The sedimentary rocks remain little altered, or if metamorphosed, they have been, and still remain, covered by later deposits.

It does not necessarily follow, however, that all the rocks east of this line, as drawn above, have undergone metamorphism. On the contrary there remain many areas of rock little changed, and in some cases it is possible to trace beds of unaltered limestone till they pass into the pure white marble. It has thus been shown that the pure white statuary marble of Carrara, Italy, was once a common fossiliferous limestone, but which has become converted into marble by the heat and pressure incident to the formation of the Apennine Mountains.

Hence it is that mountainous countries as a rule contain a greater variety of material than do the level prairie regions. Nature makes her own compensations, and if by mountain building or glacial erosion she has rendered a country unfit for cultivation, she has as a rule rendered an equivalent by furnishing and rendering accessible through the same agencies inexhaustible supplies of building stone, anthracite coal, copper, iron, and the ores of the precious metals.

He, then, who is seeking new supplies of any of these eruptive or metamorphic rocks, need not seek them in the interior States mentioned ; in the Southern States south of Mont-

---

* West of the Picos River are Archæan areas which will doubtless prove capable of furnishing valuable material.

gomery, Alabama; nor anywhere on the coast as in Maine and Massachusetts, south of Long Island. But in the Rocky Mountain regions we find once more a region of crumpling and folding, and here again begin to appear the eruptive and metamorphic rocks. These mountains, as is well known, enter the United States in Idaho and western Montana, and cross it in a southeasterly direction, passing through Wyoming, central Colorado, New Mexico, and thence into Mexico proper. The *core*, as we may say, of this range is largely granitic, sometimes of a red color and very coarsely crystalline, as may be seen where the Union Pacific railroad crosses it at Sherman, Wyoming. From here westward to the Pacific Slope occur granitic and trappean rocks innumerable, and undoubtedly many beds of fine marble and possibly slate. The regions are as yet too difficult of access, and cost of transportation too high; hence but little exploration for such materials has been actively carried on. The writer has seen very promising samples of marbles from Colorado and Wyoming, and doubtless other States are equally well provided. California has its Sierra Nevada, Cascade and Coast ranges, and with them granites and marbles of excellent quality. In this great western area are also immense developments of later volcanic rocks, or lavas, including basalts, andesites and liparites, which although in no case suitable for ornamental work, are comparatively light, soft, easily cut, as well as very durable.

In order to still further illustrate this distribution and the consequent resources of the various States, the following table is given. Only those stones are mentioned which it seems safe to assume occur in such quantities or under such conditions as to render them of present or prospective value for the purposes under discussion. For the purposes of easy reference the States are arranged alphabetically, an arrangement which is followed out in the descriptions of the quarry regions in Part II. A name in italics indicates that the stone is, or has been actively quarried within a comparatively recent period.

State or Territory.   Present and Prospective Resources.

Alabama..........Marble, limestone, granite, sandstone.

Arizona..........*Onyx marble*, limestone, granite, trappean and volcanic rocks, and *sandstones.*

Arkansas..........Marble, limestone, *syenite.*

California.........*Serpentine (verdantique marble), onyx marble, marble, limestone, granite, volcanic rocks* and *tuffs, sandstone, slate.*

Colorado..........Marble, *limestone, granite,* trappean and volcanic rocks, *sandstone, quartzite, rhyolite tuff.*

Connecticut.......Soapstone, serpentine (verdantique marble), marble, *granite* and *gneiss, diabase, sandstone.*

Delaware..........Marble, *gneiss.*

Florida...........Shell and oolitic limestone.

Georgia...........*Marble, granite, gneiss,* sandstone, *slate.*

Idaho............Limestone, *marble,* granite, trappean and volcanic rocks, sandstone.

Illinois............*Limestone* and *dolomite, sandstone.*

Indiana...........*Limestone* and *dolomite, sandstone.*

Indian Territory...Limestone, dolomite, sandstone.

Iowa.............*Gypsum, limestone, dolomite, sandstone.*

Kansas...........*Limestone, dolomite, sandstone.*

Kentucky.........*Limestone, dolomite, sandstone.*

Louisiana.........Limestone, sandstone.

Maine............Soapstone, serpentine (verdantique marble), limestone, *granite, gneiss, diabase,* norite, *gabbro,* quartz porphyry, sandstone, *slate.*

Maryland.........*Soapstone, serpentine (verdantique marble), marble, granite, sandstone, slate.*

Massachusetts.....*Soapstone,* serpentine (verdantique marble) *marble, granite, gneiss,* quartz porphyry.

Michigan..........*Limestone, dolomite,* granite, gneiss, *sandstone, slate.*

Minnesota.........*Limestone, dolomite, granite,* gneiss, sandstone, *slate.*

Mississippi.........Limestone, sandstone.

Missouri..........*Limestone, dolomite, granite, diabase,* quartz porphyry, *sandstone.*

Montana..........Limestone, dolomite, *granite,* gneiss, trappean and volcanic rocks, *sandstone.*

Nebraska.........*Limestone, dolomite, sandstone.*

State or Territory.	Present and Prospective Resources.

Nevada ... .Limestone, dolomite, granite, trappean and *volcanic* rocks, *sandstone.*

New Hampshire...*Soapstone,* limestone, *granite,* slate.

New Jersey.......Serpentine, limestone, dolomite, *marble,* granite, *gneiss, diabase, sandstone, slate.*

New Mexico.......*Serpentine* (*riccolite*) limestone, marble, trappean and volcanic rocks, sandstone, granite.

New York.........Soapstone, *serpentine* (*verdantique marble*), *limestone, dolomite, marble, granite, gneiss, norite, sandstone, slate.*

North Carolina....Soapstone, serpentine, limestone, dolomite, marble,*granite,* gneiss, diabase, *norite, sandstone.*

North Dakota.....Limestone, dolomite, sandstone.

Ohio.............*Limestone, dolomite, sandstone.*

Oklahoma.........Limestone, dolomite, sandstone.

Oregon..........Limestone, dolomite, granite, *trappean* and volcanic rocks, *sandstone.*

Pennsylvania......*Soapstone, serpentine, limestone, dolomite, marble,* granite, *gneiss, diabase,* quartz porphyry, *sandstone, conglomerate, slate.*

Rhode Island......Limestone, dolomite, *granite, gneiss.*

South Carolina....Limestone, *granite,* gneiss.

South Dakota.....*Limestone,* sandstone, *quartzite.*

Tennessee.........*Limestone, marble,* granite, diorite, sandstone.

Texas............*Limestone,* marble, *granite,* trappean and volcanic rocks, *sandstone.*

Utah.............Limestone, *marble, granite,* trappean and volcanic rocks, sandstone.

Vermont ....*Soapstone,* serpentine (verdantique marble) *marble, granite, gneiss, slate.*

Virginia..........*Soapstone,* limestone, marble, *granite, gneiss, diabase, sandstone, slate.*

Washington ....Limestone, marble, granite, trappean and volcanic rocks, *sandstone.*

West Virginia.....*Limestone, sandstone.*

Wisconsin.........*Dolomite,* granite, *gneiss,* quartz porphyry, *sandstone.*

Wyoming ....Limestone,*granite,* trappean and volcanic rocks, sandstone.

THE MINERALS OF BUILDING STONES.

A rock is a mineral aggregate ; more than this, it is an essential portion of the earth's crust, a geological body occupying a more or less well defined position in the structure of the earth, either in the form of stratified beds, eruptive masses, sheets or dykes, or as veins · and other chemical deposits of comparatively little importance as regards size and extent.

To fully comprehend, therefore, what is to be said on the subject of rocks, one must begin with a consideration of the minerals of which they are made up. As a rule the number of mineral species constituting any essential portion of a rock is very small, seldom exceeding three or four. In common limestone the only essential constituent is the mineral calcite ; granite, on the other hand, is almost invariably composed of minerals of at least three independent species. Upon the character of these, and the amount of their cohesion, is dependent to a very considerable extent, the suitability or desirability of any stone for architectural purposes. Microscopic examination will usually result in increasing the apparent number of mineral species, and it not infrequently happens that those present, even in minute quantities, are of great economic importance.

In the arrangement here adopted rock-forming minerals are divided into four classes : (1) Essential ; (2) accessory ; (3) original ; (4) secondary.

(1) The essential minerals are those which form the chief constituents of any rock, and which may be regarded as characteristic of any particular variety ; *e.g.*, quartz is an essential constituent of granite ; without the quartz the rock becomes a syenite.

(2) The accessory minerals are those which, though usually present, are of such minor importance that their absence does not materially effect the character of the rock ; *e.g.*, mica, hornblende, apatite, or magnetite, are nearly always present in granite, yet a rock in which any or all of these are lacking may still be classed as a granite. The accessory mineral which predominates is called the *characterizing* accessory and gives its name to the rock. Thus a biotite granite is one in which the accessory mineral biotite prevails.

(3) The original constituents of a rock are those which formed upon its first consolidation. All the essential constituents are original, but all the original constituents are not necessarily essential. Thus, in granite, quartz and orthoclase are both original and essential, while beryl and sphene, though original, are not essential.

(4) Secondary constituents are those which result from subsequent changes in a rock, changes due usually to the chemical action of percolating water. Such are the calcite, chalcedony, quartz, and zeolite deposits which form in the drusy and amygdaloidal cavities of traps and other rocks.

In the list on the following page is included all those minerals which ordinarily occur in such of our rocks as are used for building or ornamental purposes. In the first column are given those which compose any appreciable part of the rocks, and any one of which may at times become the principal ingredient or characterizing accessory. The second column contains those which, if present at all, occur only in small quantities.

As these are all fully described in the numerous works on mineralogy it is not deemed necessary to enter into any elaborate discussion of their properties here, excepting in the case of those few which from their abundance, or from other causes, have a pronounced effect upon the rocks in which they occur.

1. Quartz.
2. Feldspar.
   Orthoclase.
   Microcline.
   Albite.   ⎫
   Anorthite.   ⎪
   Labradorite.   ⎬ Plagioclase
   Andesite.   ⎪
   Oligoclase.   ⎭
3. Mica.
   Muscovite.
   Biotite.
   Phlogopite.
   Lepidomelane or Annite.
4. Amphibole.
   Tremolite.
   Actinolite.
   Common hornblende.
5. Pyroxene.
   Malacolite.
   Sahlite.
   Augite.
   Diallage.
   Enstatite.
   Hypersthene.
6. Olivine.
7. Epidote.
8. Elaeolite [Nepheline].
9. Calcite.
10. Aragonite.
11. Dolomite.
12. Gypsum.
13. Serpentine.
14. Talc.
15. Chlorite.

ELEMENTS.
Carbon.
Graphite.

SULPHIDES.
Galenite.
Sphalerite.
Pyrite.
Marcasite.

CHLORIDES.
Halite (common salt).

FLUORIDES.
Fluorite (fluor spar).

OXIDES.
Tridymite.
Hematite (specular iron).
Menaccanite (titanic iron).
Magnetite (magnetic iron).
Chromite (chromic iron).
Limonite (hydrous iron oxide).
Rutile.

ANHYDROUS SILICATES.
Acmite.
Beryl.
Danalite.
Garnet.
Zircon.
Zoisite.
Allanite.
Scapolite.
Sodalite
Tourmaline (shorl).
Titanite (sphene).

HYDROUS SILICATES.
Laumontite.
Natrolite.
Analcite.
Chabazite.
Stilbite.
Kaolin.

PHOSPHATES.
Apatite.

CARBONATES.
Ankerite.
Siderite.

QUARTZ.—*Composition :*   Pure silica, SiO₂.   Hardness, 7.*

This is one of the commonest minerals of the earth's crust, and is an essential constituent of granite, gneiss, mica schist, quartz porphyry, liparite, quartzite, and ordinary sandstone, occuring in the form of crystals, crystalline grains, and fragments of crystals.   It is usually easily recognized by its clear, colorless appearance, irregular, glass-like fracture, hardness, and entire insolubility in acids.   Its hardness is such that it scratches glass, and in this respect alone it differs from any other of the essential constituents.   It is, however, brittle, and hence, though the hardest mineral, is by no means the most refractory ; stones like granite, which are rich in quartz, working more easily than the trap-rocks, in which it is, as a rule, quite lacking.

Although ordinarily one of the most indestructible of minerals, and infusible in the hottest flame of the blow-pipe, yet highly quartzose rocks like granite are by no means fire-proof, but scale badly when subjected to the heat of a burning building.   This peculiar susceptibility of the rock to heat is thought by some to be due to the microscopic fluidal cavities which exist in the quartz, and which are at times exceeding abundant.

---

* For convenience in determining minerals the "scale of hardness" given below has been adopted by mineralogists.   By means of it one is enabled to designate the comparative hardness of minerals with ease and definiteness. Thus, in saying that serpentine has a hardness equal to 4 is meant that it is of the same hardness as the mineral fluorite, and can therefore be cut with a knife, but less readily than calcite or marble.

   1. *Talc.*—Easily scratched with the thumb-nail.

   2. *Gypsum.*—Can be scratched by the thumb-nail.

   3. *Calcite.*—Not readily scratched by the thumb-nail, but easily cut with a knife.

   4. *Fluorite.*—Can be cut with a knife, but less easily than calcite.

   5. *Apatite.*—Can be cut with a knife, but only with difficulty.

   6. *Orthoclase feldspar.*—Can be cut with a knife only with great difficulty and on thin edges.

   7. *Quartz.*—Cannot be cut with a knife ; scratches glass.

THE FELDSPARS. Hardness, 5 to 7.

The feldspars are essentially silicates containing alumina together with potash, soda, or lime. There are six varieties that are common constituents of building stones, viz., orthoclase, microcline, albite, oligoclase, labradorite, and anorthite. Of these, albite, oligoclase, labradorite, and anorthite are usually indistinguishable from one another by the eye alone, especially in fine-grained rocks, and are therefore designated by the convenient term *plagioclase feldspars* or simply *plagioclase.* Orthoclase is the prevailing feldspar and most important constituent in granites and gneisses, and is usually accompanied by albite or oligoclase, or frequently microcline. Anorthite and labradorite are equally important constituents of basic eruptive rocks, such as diabase, basalt, and andesite.

The physical condition of the feldspar in a building stone is a matter of the greatest importance. In those rocks which withstand the effect of the weather through long periods of years without change or disintegration, the feldspars, if examined with a microscope, will be found hard, compact, and fresh, containing but few cavities or impurities. On the other hand, the feldspars of many rocks, if thus examined, will be found filled with minute cavities and flaws, which are often so filled with impurities and products of decomposition as to be quite opaque (Hawes). Such rocks will not for any length of time withstand the weather, since infiltrating waters containing minute quantities of carbonic and other acids, aided by heat and frost, can not fail to produce the dire result of disintegration.

The feldspars have also an important influence upon the cutting of a stone. The hardness and toughness of many granites and other crystalline siliceous rocks are due, not to the hard and brittle quartz, but to the feldspathic constituent, which is quite variable. The soft granites consist of the same constituents, but the feldspars are porous and therefore offer less resistance to the cutting tool. The feldspars also possess a distinct cleavage, that is, they split or cleave in one or two directions much more readily than in others. It, therefore, sometimes happens, especially in coarse-grained and por-phyritic rocks, that it is very difficult to obtain the perfect surface necessary for polishing, since little particles of the feld-spars are constantly splitting out, leaving small cavities or " nicks."

The color of a rock frequently depends largely upon its feld-spathic constituent. If the feldspar be clear, transparent, and glassy, the light enters it and is absorbed, giving to the stone a dark color, as is the case with the Quincy granites and many quartz porphyries and diabases. If the feldspar is soft and porous, the light is reflected from the surface and the rock appears white. In all the pink and red granites and gneisses the color is due to the pink and red orthoclase they contain. It sometimes happens that the orthoclase and plagioclase —when both are present in the same rock—are differently colored, the orthoclase being pink or red, while the plagioclase is nearly white.

THE MICAS. Hardness 2.5 to 3.

. Two kinds of mica occur as prominent constituents of build-ing stones, especially the granites and gneisses. These are black mica or biotite, and white mica or muscovite. Both kinds occur in small shining scales which are sometimes hexagonal in outline, though more frequently of quite irregular form.

The composition of the micas is complex, but the black variety is essentially a silicate of iron, alumina, magnesia, and potash, while the white variety is a silicate of alumina and pot-ash with small amounts of iron, soda, magnesia, and water.

Other micas common in such stone as are used for building are lepidomelane and phlogopite. The first of these is black in color and closely resembles biotite, from which it differs in containing smaller proportions of the protoxide of iron and in the folia being opaque and inelastic. For all practical purposes this mica is, however, identical with biotite, and no distinction has been attempted in the present work. Phlogopite is more nearly colorless, like muscovite, from which it can often be distinguished only with difficulty. It is a common constituent of many limestones, dolomites, and serpentinous rocks.

The kind, amount, and disposition of mica in a building stone has a very important bearing upon its working and weathering qualities as well as general fitness for architectural purposes. If it occurs in any abundance and the folia are arranged in parallel layers the rock splits much more readily in a direction parallel to the mica laminæ than in that at right angles to them. Mica is itself moreover " soft and fissile, and hence is an element of weakness." It also receives a polish only with difficulty and which is soon lost upon exposure to the weather. Black mica, moreover, owing to its large percentage of iron, is liable to succumb to atmospheric agencies.*

The finest grades of building stone should contain mica only in small flakes evenly distributed throughout the mass of the rock.

From the marked contrast in color of the two micas it follows

---

* Dr. P. Schweitzer while studying the superficial decomposition of the gneiss of New York Island, discovered that the black mica, after getting first coated with a brown film of oxide of iron, " rapidly disintegrated and disappeared," while the white mica possessing greater powers of endurance remains fresh and intact.—Chem. News, IV., 1874, p. 444.

The same phenomena may be noticed in the mica schists about Washington, D. C.

that they have a decided influence upon the color of the rock containing them. Folia of black mica in any abundance naturally give the rock a dark-gray hue, while the white mica, being nearly colorless, has a neutral effect. Hence, other things being equal, muscovite granites are much lighter in color than those in which biotite is the characterizing accessory.

AMPHIBOLE. Hornblende.   Hardness 5 to 6.

Two principal varieties of this mineral are recognized : (1) The non-aluminous, including the white, gray, and pale green, often fibrous forms as tremolite, actinolite and asbestus, and (2) the aluminous, which includes the dark-green, brown, and black varieties. The aluminous variety, common hornblende, is an original and essential constituent of diorite, and of many varieties of granite, gneiss, syenite, schist, andesite and trachyte, and is also present as a secondary constituent in many rocks, resulting from a molecular alteration of the augite. The non-aluminous varieties occur in gneiss, crystalline limestone, and other metamorphic rocks.

The hornblende in such rocks as are used for building purposes can be readily recognized by its dark-green or almost black color and the compactness and tenacity of its crystals which are not easily separable into thin leaves or folia as is black mica, with which it might otherwise be confounded. Hornblende acquires readily a good and lasting polish and as the mineral itself is strong and durable, its presence in a rock is thought to be preferable to that of mica.

THE PYROXENES.   Hardness 5 to 6.

Two principal varieties of this mineral are recognized, as with the amphiboles, (1) the non-aluminous, including the light-colored varieties malacolite, sahlite, and diallage, and (2) the aluminous, including the dark variety, augite.

The lighter-colored non-aluminous varieties, malacolite and sahlite, are common in mica and hornblendic schists, gneiss, and granite, though seldom in sufficient abundance to be noticeable to the naked eye. The foliated variety, diallage, is an essential constituent of the rock gabbro, and is also common in serpentine. The darker colored aluminous variety, augite, is an essential constituent of diabase and basalt, and also occurs in many syenites, andesites, and other eruptive rocks.

In such rocks as are used for building purposes the pyroxene cannot usually be distinguished by the unaided eye from hornblende. With the exception of the Quincy granites and the New Castle, Delaware, gneisses, pyroxenes do not occur in any of our granitic rocks now quarried, but in the diabases and basalts the augite is a very important constituent. It is usually a compact and tough yellowish-green or nearly black mineral, and, like hornblende, readily acquires a good and lasting polish. The pyroxene of the Quincy granite, however, proves an exceptionally brittle variety, and the continual breaking away of little pieces during the process of dressing the stone makes the production of a perfectly smooth surface a matter of great difficulty.

CALCITE. Calc-spar. *Composition:* Calcium carbonate, $CaCo_3$ = carbon dioxide, 44 per cent.; lime 56 per cent. Hardness 3.

This is an original constituent of many rocks, such as limestone, ophiolite, and calcareous shale, and is the essential constituent of most marbles, of stalactites, travertine, and calcsinter. It also occurs as a secondary constituent resulting from the decomposition of other minerals, filling wholly, or in part, cavities in rocks of all ages, such as granite, gneiss, syenite, diabase, diorite, liparite, trachyte, andesite, and basalt.

Calcite when pure is white in color, and soft enough to be be cut with a knife. It can be readily distinguished from other minerals, excepting aragonite, by its brisk effervescence when treated with a dilute acid.

ARAGONITE.—*Composition:* Same as calcite.   Hardness, 3.5 to 4.

This mineral has the same chemical composition as calcite, but differs in its crystalline form and specific gravity. It sometimes occurs in deposits of sufficient extent to be quarried as marble. The beautiful " onyx marble " of San Luis Obispo is nearly pure aragonite.

DOLOMITE.—*Composition:* (CaMg) CO_3 = Calcium carbonate, 54.35 per cent.; magnesium carbonate, 45.65 per cent.   Hardness, 3.2 to 4.

This mineral closely resembles calcite, but can be readily distinguished from the same by its greater hardness and from its being acted upon but little, if at all, by a dilute acid. Like calcite, it frequently occurs in compact crystalline massive forms, and is quarried for building material or for making lime. Many of our marbles are dolomites, as for instance those of Cockeysville, Maryland, and Pleasantville, New York.

GYPSUM. Calcium Sulphate.—*Composition:* $CaSO_4 + 2aq$ = sulphur trioxide, 46.5 per cent.; lime, 32.6 per cent.; water, 20.9 per cent.   Hardness, 2.

Gypsum rarely occurs in crystalline rocks, but forms extensive beds among stratified rocks such as limestones and beds of clay. The fine translucent variety is used for ornamental purposes, and is known as alabaster. It is soft enough to be readily cut with a knife or scratched with the thumb-nail, and is not at all acted on by acids. It is therefore readily distinguished from calcite, which it somewhat resembles.

SERPENTINE.—*Composition:* A hydrous silicate of magnesia, $Mg_3Si_2O_7 +$ $2aq$ = silica, 43.48 per cent.; magnesia, 43.48 per cent.; water, 13.04 per cent. Hardness, 4.

This mineral occurs mixed with calcite or dolomite, forming the so-called verdantique marble or ophiolite. As a secondary product it is sometimes found resulting from the alteration of olivine and other magnesian minerals in various eruptive rocks, such as basalt, diabase, and the peridotites. It often occurs in extensive deposits, usually mixed with more or less chromite, magnetite, enstatite, or similar minerals, and is of value as a building or ornamental stone, as will be noticed later.

Serpentine can usually be recognized by its green or yellowish color, slightly soapy feeling, lack of cleavage, and softness, it being readily cut with a knife. It is, however, not so soft as talc, with which it might possibly be confounded by any but a mineralogist.

TALC. Steatite.—*Composition :* A hydrous silicate of magnesia = silica, 63.49 per cent.; magnesia, 31.75 per cent.; water, 4.76 per cent. Hardness, 1.

This is a common mineral, occurring as an essential constituent of talc schist or as an alteration product, replacing hornblende, augite, mica, and other magnesian minerals. The common form is that of small, greenish, inelastic scales. It often occurs massive, and is known by the name of soapstone, and is used extensively in stoves and furnaces. The finely *granular crypto-crystalline* variety is known as *French chalk*, used by tailors and others. In its common form this mineral might be mistaken for a mica, but for its soapy feeling and softness, which is such that it can be readily scratched by the thumb-nail.

OLIVINE. Chrysolite. Peridot.—*Composition :* Silicate of iron and magnesia. Hardness, 6 to 7.

Olivine is an essential constituent of basalt, and the peridotites and is prominent in many lavas, diabases, gabbros, and other igneous rocks, where it occurs in the form of rounded blebs of a bottle-green color. It also occurs occasionally in metamorphic rocks and is a constituent of many meteorites. Olivine is subject to extensive alteration, becoming changed

into serpentine. Many beds of serpentine result from the alteration of olivine-bearing rocks.

GARNET.—*Composition :* Variable ; essentially a silicate of alumina, lime,
iron, or magnesia.   Hardness, 6.5 to 7.5.

This mineral is an abundant accessory in mica schist, gneiss,
granite, crystalline limestone, occasionally in serpentine, in
liparite, and other lavas.

The presence of garnets in stones designed for finely finished
work is always detrimental, since, owing to their brittleness and
hardness, they break away from the matrix in the process of
dressing and render the production of smooth surfaces a matter
of difficulty.   Those garnets which are found in such stone as
are used for building are nearly always of a red color and
rounded form.

EPIDOTE.—*Composition :* Silica, 37.83 per cent.; alumina, 22.63 per cent.;
iron oxides, 15.98 per cent.; lime, 23.27 per cent.; water, 2.05 per cent.
Hardness, 6 to 7.

This mineral is a common constituent of many granites.
gneisses, and schists, especially the hornblendic varieties.   It is
also found as a secondary constituent in the amygdaloidal cavities of many trap rocks, and is readily recognizable from its
green color.   Although a common constituent in small proportions of many rocks, those cases in which it is sufficiently
abundant to give them a specific character are extremely rare.
Certain of the New Hampshire and Massachusetts granites contain it in such quantities as to be recognizable as greenish specks
on a polished surface, as does also the melaphyr quarried at
Brighton, in the latter State.

CHLORITE.   Viridite.—Hardness, 2 to 3.

Under the general name chlorite are included several minerals occurring in fibres and folia, closely resembling the micas,

from which they differ in their large percentage of water, and in their folia being inelastic. The three principal varieties recognized are ripidolite, penninite, and prochlorite, any one of which may occur as the essential constituent of a chlorite schist. Chlorite as a secondary product often results from and entirely replaces the pyroxene, hornblende, or mica in rocks of various kinds, and also occurs filling wholly or in part the amygdaloidal cavities of trap rocks. In this form it is frequently visible only with the microscope, and owing to the difficulties in the way of an exact determination of its mineral species is called *viridite*, from the Latin *viridis*, green, this being its usual color. The characteristic greenness which gave the name *greenstone* to the diorites and diabases is due in large part to the secondary chlorite contained by them.

IRON PYRITES.—*Composition :* Iron disulphide, $FeS_2 =$ sulphur, 53.3 per cent.; iron, 46.7 per cent. Hardness, 6 to 6.5.

A very common accessory in rocks of all kinds and all ages, usually occurring in small cubes or irregular masses of a brassy yellow color.

It may be set down as a rule that rocks containing this mineral should not be used for ornamental work that is to be exposed to the weather, since it is very liable to oxidation in time, staining the stone and perhaps causing the more serious result of disintegration. This form of the iron disulphide is, however, less objectionable than that known as *marcasite* or the gray iron pyrites. For some unexplained reason this form of the mineral decomposes even more readily than the pyrite, and hence its presence is always objectionable in rocks where permanency of color or durability is desired.

A microscopic study of pyrite-bearing rocks has shown that there are many important considerations bearing upon the weathering properties of this mineral. Thus it is found, as in many of the Ohio limestones and dolomites, occurring not only in well defined cubes of a brass-yellow color, but also in an amorphous granular condition in a very fine state of subdivision which appears almost black under the microscope. Experience has shown that in the latter form it is much more liable to oxidation than when in cubes, and hence we see the necessity of a microscopic examination of a stone as one of the guides to its probable weathering qualities. In this finely amorphous condition the pyrite is stated by Hawes to have an important effect upon the color of the stone. Thus the Springfield and Covington (Ohio) dolomites present in different layers two well defined colors—a blue and a yellow. An examination with the microscope shows that they differ only in that the blue variety contains the pyrite in the finely disseminated unoxidized state, while in the yellow it has become changed into the hydrous oxide. This change having taken place while the stone lies in the quarry, is unaccompanied by results of a serious nature, unless the uniform change in color be so considered. Had the change taken place in the quarried stone after being laid in the walls of a building, the results would in all probability have proved more undesirable. Pyrite when imbedded firmly in rocks of a close, compact nature is less liable to oxidation that when contained in one of a loose and porous texture. In the magnesian limestones of Dayton, Ohio, the microscope reveals many minute cubes of pyrite which are imbedded so firmly in its mass as to be not at all deleterious, since beyond the reach of atmospheric agencies. In many close-textured rocks, as the slates, pyrite is proverbially long-lived, and hence as a rule we can only regard it with suspicion, as an ingredient whose presence can result in little that is good and perhaps a great deal that is bad. It should be noted that pyrite on decomposing, may give rise to sulphates and perhaps to free sulphuric acid, which in themselves aid in the work of disintegration.

" In limestones or dolomites the presence of iron pyrites operates disastrously ; for, if magnesia be present, the sulphuric acid from the decomposing iron pyrites produces a soluble efflorescent salt, which exudes to the surface and forms white patches, which are alternately washed off and replaced, but leaving a whitened surface probably from the presence of sulphate of lime. If the limestone be entirely calcareous, the salt formed (a sulphate of lime) is insoluble, and therefore produces less obvious results. In some cases, however, the lime of which the mortar or cement is made may contain magnesia, and the decomposition of the iron pyrites in the adjacent stone produces an efflorescent salt which exudes from the joints. This condition is not unfrequently observed in buildings constructed of the bluestone of the Hudson River group. As an example, we may notice the efflorescent patches proceeding from some of the joints between the stones of St. Peter's Church, on State street, in Albany."*

MAGNETITE. Magnetic Iron Ore.—*Composition:* $FeO + Fe_2O_3 =$ iron sesquioxide, 68.97 per cent.; iron.protoxide, 31.03 per cent. Hardness, 5.5 to 6.8.

This occurs as an original constitutent in may schists and granites; in the latter usually in minute crystals visible only with the microscope. It is almost invariably present in igneous rocks such as diorite, diabase, and basalt. When present in considerable quantities it sometimes becomes converted

---

* Hall, Report on Building Stone, p. 50. The white efflorescence so frequently seen on stone and brick buildings, seems, according to good authorities, to be, in most cases, due to the mortar in which the stone is laid, and is not an inherent quality of the stone itself. The subject is, therefore, not more fully dwelt upon in the present work.

entirely into the sesquioxide of iron through taking oxygen from the atmosphere. It then stains the rock a rusty red color, as is observable in many diabases.

HEMATITE. **Specular Iron Ore.**—*Chemical composition:* Anhydrous sesquioxide of iron, Fe_2O_3 = iron, 70.9 per cent.; oxygen, 30.20 per cent.

This mineral occurs in varying proportions in rocks of all ages. In granite its usual form is that of minute scales of a blood-red color. In an amorphous condition it often forms the cementing material of sandstones, when it imparts to them a red or reddish-brown color. This form of iron oxide is, however, less common as a cementing substance than the hydrous sesquioxides *turgite* and *limonite*, which are the forms occurring in the Triassic sandstones of the eastern United States.*

THE PHYSICAL AND CHEMICAL PROPERTIES OF BUILDING STONE.

The physical properties of a rock—the manner in which its various constituents are grouped together—is a matter of perhaps even greater importance than is the character of the minerals themselves. This will become more plainly evident as we proceed. We will therefore devote a few pages here to a consideration of those properties of rocks which may be grouped under the heads of density, hardness and structure, together with notes on their color and chemical composition.

(1) DENSITY AND HARDNESS.

Density.—This is an important property, since upon it are dependent to a large extent the weight per cubic foot, the strength, and the absorptive powers of the stone. Among

---

* Julien, Proceedings American Association for the Advancement of Science, 1888.

rocks of the same mineral composition, those which are the densest will be found heaviest, least absorptive, and usually the strongest.

To ascertain the weight of a rock it is customary to compare its weight with that of an equal bulk of distilled water, in other words to ascertain its specific gravity. The specific gravity multiplied by 62.5 pounds (the weight of a cubic foot of water) will thus give the weight per cubic foot of stone. The weights given in the tables have been thus computed. (See p. 404.)

Hardness.—The apparent hardness of a rock is dependent upon (1) the hardness of its component minerals and (2) their state of aggregation. However hard the minerals of a rock may be, it appears soft and works readily if the particles adhere with slight tenacity. Many of the softest sandstones are composed of the hard mineral quartz, but the grains fall apart so readily that the stone is as a whole soft. (See under State of Aggregation.)

(2) STRUCTURE.

Under this head are considered those characters of rocks which are dependent upon the form, size, and arrangement of their component minerals.

All rocks may be classified sufficiently close for present purposes under one of the three heads (1) crystalline, (2) vitreous or glassy, and (3) fragmental. Of the first, granite and crystalline limestone may be considered as types; of the second, obsidian and pitchstone, and of the third, sandstone. Many structural properties are common to all, others are confined to rocks of a single type. Accordingly as the structure is or is not readily recognizable by the unaided eye, we have:

(1) *Macroscopic structure, or structure which is distinguishable in the hand specimen and without the aid of a microscope.*— Under this head are comprehended structures designated by

such names as *granular, massive, stratified, foliated, porphyritic, concretionary*, etc.; terms the precise meaning of which is given in the glossary, and which, with perhaps one or two exceptions need not be further considered here ; and

(2) *Microscopic structures.*—Many rocks are so fine grained and compact that nothing of their mineral nature or structure can be learned from study with the eye alone, and recourse must be had to the microscope. In such cases it is customary among lithologists to grind a small chip of the rock so thin as to be transparent, and then, when properly mounted in Canada balsam, to submit it to microscopic study. By this method many important points of structure and composition are brought out that would otherwise be unattainable. The physical condition of the minerals of a rock, their freedom from decomposition, and methods of arrangement can often only be ascertained by this method. By it the presence of many minute and perhaps important constituents is made known, the presence of which would otherwise be unsuspected. This subject is further treated under the head of Rock-forming Minerals and the descriptions of the various kinds of rocks.

In Fig. 1 of Pl. 11 is shown the structure of the muscovite biotite granite of Hallowell, Maine, drawn as are the other figures on this plate from thin sections and under a magnifying power of about twenty-five diameters. This is a granite of quite complex structure, consisting of (1) orthoclase, (2) microcline, (3) plagioclase, (4) quartz, (5) black mica, or biotite, and (6) white mica or muscovite. There are also little needles of apatite, scattering grains of iron ore, and occasionally small garnets present which do not show in the figure. The quartz, moreover, is pierced in every direction by minute hair-like crystals which are supposed to be rutile. The structure, as in all granites and gneisses, is crystalline throughout, as in the marbles (Fig. 3) and diabase (Fig. 4). The crystals are, however,

PLATE II.

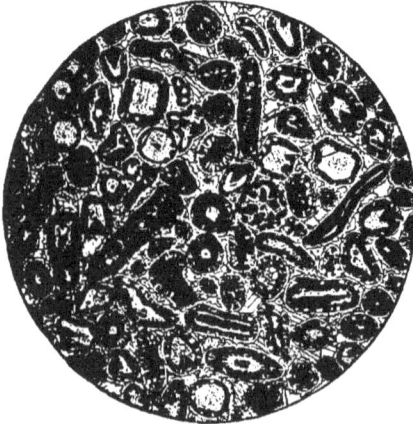

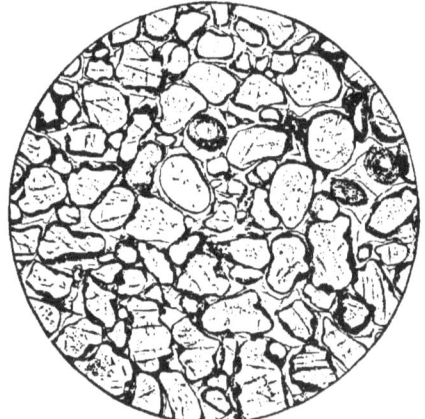

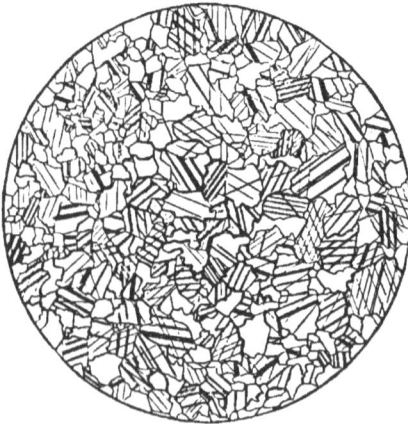

MICROSCOPIC STRUCTURE OF BUILDING STONES.

To face page 35.

very imperfect in outline, owing to mutual interference in process of formation. Although the rock contains a very large
proportion of the hard minerals quartz and feldspar, these do
not interlock so thoroughly as do the augite and feldspars in
the diabase. As, moreover, quartz is a brittle substance, these
rocks work much more readily and will crush under less pressure
than those of which Fig. 4 is a type.

In Fig. 2 of the same plate is shown the structure of an oolitic
limestone from Princeton, in Caldwell County, Kentucky. It
will be noticed that the first step in the formation of this stone
was the deposition of concentric coatings of lime about a nucleus
which is sometimes nearly round, but more frequently quite
angular and irregular. After the concretions were completed
there were formed in all cases about each one narrow zones of
minute radiating crystals of clear, colorless calcite ; then the
larger crystals formed in the interstices. An examination of
the section in polarized light shows that while the concentric
portions are nearly always amorphous the nuclei (and always
the interstitial matter) is frequently crystalline. The nuclei are
composed in some cases of single fragments, or, again, of a
group of fragments. Certain of the oolites present no distinct
concentric structure, but appear as mere rounded masses merg-
ing gradually into the crystalline interstitial portions. On the
application of acetic acid to an uncovered slide of this rock a
brisk effervesence at once set in, which, when the slide was
again placed on the stage of the microscope, was seen not to
arise from all portions of the slide alike, but to be confined
almost exclusively to the outer non-crystalline portions of the
oolites, so that in time these almost completely disappeared,
leaving the crystalline nuclei and cementing material till the
very last. Some of the outlines thus left are peculiarly de-
ceptive, having almost the appearance of a cross-section of
coral or a crinoid stem. This structure is common, so far as I

have observed, to all the oolitic limestones of both Kentucky and Indiana. In the weathering of these stones then we would have produced an effect precisely the opposite of that produced in fragmental siliceous rocks. In the latter case the cement is removed and the grains themselves are but slightly acted upon ; in the former, the grains themselves disappear and the cementing material remains. It should be remarked, however, that we have as yet no proof that the action of an acid atmosphere on one of these oolites would proceed with other than extreme slowness. In fact, their compactness, freedom from cleavage, fractures, and flaws would seem to indicate just the contrary. Further investigations on this point are necessary before one can speak definitely.

The microscopic structure of ordinary white crystalline limestone is shown in Fig. 3, drawn from a magnified section of a West Rutland marble. The entire mass of the rock, it will be observed, is made up of small calcite crystals of quite uniform size closely locked together, and with no appreciable interspaces. The dark stripes across the crystals are caused by twin lamellæ and cleavage lines. All traces of its fossil origin, if such it had, have been obliterated by metamorphism.

Fig. 4 is that of a diabase from Weehawken, N. J. The elongated, nearly colorless crystals, shaded with long parallel lines, are plagioclase feldspar, the very irregular ones augite, while the perfectly black and opaque are magnetite. The figure, however, is given to show the structure rather than the mineral composition of the rock. It will be noticed that every portion of available space is occupied, there being no residual spaces to be filled by cement, as in the sandstone ; also that the feldspars and augites so closely interlock that they can not be forced apart without breaking. As both of these minerals are quite tough and hard, the great strength, durability, and hard-working qualities of the rock can readily be understood, although the constituents themselves are not harder than those that go to make up some of the most friable sandstones.

As showing the differences in structure and composition of the sandstones, Figs. 5 and 6 are given, drawn from thin sections of the brown Triassic stone from Portland, Connecticut, and a reddish Potsdam stone from quarries in the town of Potsdam, New York. In the first mentioned, Fig. 6, the stone, it will be noticed, is composed of (1) clear, angular grains of quartz, (2) clouded grains of orthoclase and plagioclase, the latter being recognized by its parallel banding, and numerous irregular and contorted shreds of black and white mica. These are all crowded into a loosely compacted mass and the interstices filled by a cement composed of an amorphous mixture of iron oxides, carbonate of lime, and clayey matter. These are represented in black in the figure. It will be observed that only the quartzes and a few of the feldspars are in a fresh and undecomposed condition, nearly all of the latter being badly kaolinized. The Potsdam stone (Fig. 5) shows, however, a markedly different structure. Here the granules are wholly of quartz, and very much rounded in form. No feldspars, mica, or other minerals are present. The original rounded outline of the quartz granule is shown by the dotted lines and deeply shaded portions, while every portion of the interstices is occupied by a clear, coloress, siliceous cement binding the rock into a hard, compact, and impervious quartzite almost absolutely unaffected by chemical and atmospheric agencies.*

* This rock shows to beautiful advantage the secondary enlargement of quartz granules by deposition of interstitial silica having the same crystallographic orientation as the granules themselves, a peculiarity first noted by the Swedish geologist Tornebohm, later by Sorby (Quar. Jour. Geol. Soc., 1880, p. 58), and since described in great detail in American Rocks by Irving and Van Hise, (Am. Jour. of Sci., June, 1883); also Bull. No. 8, U. S. Geol. Survey). I may say further here that the red and brown colors of our Triassic sandstones seem to be due not merely to the thin pellicle of iron oxides with which each

The cause of the wide variation in relative durability of stones of these two types becomes now at once apparent. In the first case the abundant amorphous cement is not only slightly soluble, and liable to partial removal by the water from rains, but it also facilitates the absorption of a proportionally large amount of moisture. On being subjected to repeated freezing and thawing while in this saturated condition, the grains gradually become loosened and the characteristic scaling results. Stones of the Potsdam type, on the other hand, are practically non-absorptive and insoluble, and are susceptible to no other natural influences than the constant expansion and contraction caused by changes in temperature. They are consequently vastly more durable. Unfortunately they are also much harder, and hence can be utilized only at greatly increased expense.

(3) STATE OF AGGREGATION.

This is one of the most important properties of building stone, since is dependent upon it very largely the hardness or softness of a rock and its consequent working qualities. Many rocks composed of hard materials work readily because their grains are but loosely coherent, while others of softer materials

granule is surrounded, but the feldspathic grains—often badly decomposed—are stained throughout by the same material, and which also occurs mixed with clayey, calcareous and silicious matter forming the cement. This is never the case, so far as I have observed, in the Potsdam stones, in which the oxide occurs only as a thin coating around each granule, as shown by the shaded portions in Fig. 5. My own experience, also, is to the effect that the fragments of which the Triassic stones are composed, are much less rounded by attrition than seems ordinarily supposed, or as they are represented when figured. Fig. 4 is very typical of the Portland stone, but it does not in the least resemble that given in Fig. 6, Plate xii, Lith. & Min. of New Hampshire. Naturally, however, samples selected from different beds, or from different localities, will be found to vary greatly.

are quite tough and difficult to work owing to the tenacity with which their particles adhere to one another. Obviously a stone in which the grains adhere closely and strongly one to another will be less absorbent and more durable under pressure than one which is loose textured and friable. A rock is called *flinty* when fine grained and closely compacted like flint; *earthy* when partially decomposed into earth or loam; *friable* when it falls easily into powder or crumbles readily under the tool. Upon the state of aggregation and the fineness of the grain is dependent very largely the kind of fracture possessed by a rock. Fine grained, compact rocks like flint, obsidian, and some limestones, break with concave and convex shell-like surfaces, forming a conchoidal fracture; such stones are called *plucky* by the workmen and they are often quite difficult to dress on this account. Others break with a rough and jagged surface called *hackly* or *splintery*. When as in free-working sandstone and granite the broken surface is quite straight and free from inequalities they are referred to as having a *straight* or *right* fracture.

(4) RIFT AND GRAIN.

The rift of a rock is the direction parallel to its foliation or bedding and along which it can usually be relied upon to split with greatest ease. It is best represented in mica schist, gneiss, and other rocks of sedimentary origin. It is a property, however, common to massive rocks, though usually much less pronounced. The *grain* is always in a direction at right angles with the rift.

These are two most important qualities in any stone that it is desired to work into blocks of any regularity of shape. Without them the production of rough blocks for street paving or for finely finished work would be possible only with greatly increased expense, and only the very softest stones could be worked with any degree of economy. With them the hardest rocks are sometimes most readily worked. Thus the Sioux Falls (South Dakota) quartzite, one of the hardest known rocks, is as readily broken out into square blocks for paving as a granite or soft sandstone.

(5) COLOR.

The color of a stone is as a rule dependent more upon its chemical than its physical properties. As will be noted, however, the color of the granites and similar rocks is sometimes varied in shades of light and dark, accordingly as the feldspars are clear and glassy and absorb the light, or white and opaque and reflect it. The chief coloring matter in rocks is iron, which exists either in chemical combination with the various minerals or in some of its simpler compounds such as the sulphide, carbonate, or oxide disseminated in minute particles throughout the mass of the rock. The free oxides of iron impart a brownish or reddish hue, the carbonates or sulphides a bluish or gray. A very light or nearly white color denotes the absence of iron in any of its forms. On the condition of the iron is dependent also the permanency of color. Either the sulphide, carbonate or other protoxide compounds, are liable to oxidation, and hence stones containing it in these forms fade or turn yellowish and stain on exposure. The sesquioxide on the other hand can undergo no further oxidation, and hence the color caused by it is the most durable. As a rule, therefore, the decidedly red colors may be considered most permanent.

The blue and black colors of marbles and limestones are due largely to carbonaceous matter.

The effects of the various mineral constituents in varying the shades of colors are mentioned in the chapter on rock-forming minerals and in the descriptions of the different kinds of stones. Great care and judgment is needed in the selection of proper colors in building. Heavy rock-faced walls of dull brown sandstone, dark gneiss, or diabase always impart an appearance of gloom, while warm, bright colors are cheering and pleasing to the eye. The late Architect Richardson owed a considerable share of his success to his power of selecting for any particular piece of work stone of such color as to be most effective and harmonious in the finished structure.

(6) THE CHEMICAL CHARACTERS OF ROCKS.

This naturally varies with the mineral composition and their ever-varying proportions. Nevertheless, it is possible to obtain general averages from which the stones of each particular kind will not be found to vary widely. It is customary to consider rocks which, like granite, are rich in silica as *acidic*, while those in which, as in basalt, the average percentage falls below fifty are called *basic*. Various descriptive adjectives are applied to the names of rocks according as they vary in composition. *Calcareous* rocks consist principally of lime, or contain an appreciable amount; *argillaceous* contain clay, which can usually be recognized by its odor when breathed upon; *siliceous* contain some form of silica; *ferruginous*, iron in the form of oxide; *carbonaceous*, more or less carbon; *bituminous* contain bitumen, which can often be detected by the odor of petroleum given off when the rock is freshly broken. Calcareous rocks can always be detected from their effervescing when treated with a dilute acid. The chemical composition of a stone is often a guide to its suitability for structural purposes. Those containing much lime are more liable to be unfavorably affected by the acid gases of cities, and the various forms of iron present are of importance both regarding the weathering properties of the stones and their colors, as will be

noticed later under special cases. A table of rock composi-
tions is to be found near the close of this volume.

ROCK CLASSIFICATION.

The rocks now in use for constructive purposes may be
classified sufficiently close for present purposes under the following heads:

A.—CRYSTALLINE AND VITREOUS.

I.—*Simple Rocks.*

(1) Silicates :
    (a) Talc (including Steatite and
        Soapstone).
    (b) Serpentine. (In part.)
(2) Sulphates :
    (a) Gypsum (including Alabas-
        ter and Satin Spar).
(3) Carbonates :
    (a) Limestone and Dolomites.

II.—*Compound Rocks.*

(1) Massive with Quartz and Ortho-
    clase ; acidic :
    (a) Granites and Granite Por-
        phyries.
    (b) Quartz Porphyries.
    (c) Liparites.
(2) Massive, without Quartz :
    (a) Syenite.
    (b) Quartz-free Orthoclase Por-
       phyries.
    (c) Trachytes and Phonolites.

(3) Plagioclase rocks; basic :
    (a) Diorites and Diorite Por-
       phyrites.
    (b) Diabases, Gabbros, Mela-
       phyres, and Basalts.
    (c) The Andesites.
(4) Rocks without feldspars :
    (a) The Peridotites. (Serpen-
       tines in part.)
(5) Schistose or foliated rocks :
    (a) Gneiss (included here with
       the Granites).
    (b) The Schists.

B. FRAGMENTAL.

    (a) The Psammites, including
       Sandstone, Conglomer-
       ate, Breccia, and Gray-
       wacke.
    (b) Pelites including Clayslates
       and Pipe Clay.
    (c) Volcanic fragmental rocks,
       Tuffs.
    (d) Fragmental rocks of organic
       origin (included here un-
       der the head of Lime-
       stones).

The order in which the rocks are mentioned above will be adhered to in the descriptions given in the following pages. For the benefit of those not familiar with the order of succession of the various rock formations in the earth's crust, the following table is also given :

GEOLOGICAL RECORD ;

OR ORDER OF SUCCESSION OF THE ROCKS COMPOSING THE EARTH'S CRUST.

Quaternary, or Post-tertiary.	The age of Man.	Recent, or Terrace. Champlain. Glacial, or Drift.	
Tertiary, or Cenozoic.	Age of Mammals.	Tertiary.	Pliocene. Miocene. Eocene.
Secondary, or Mesozoic.	Age of Reptiles.	Cretaceous.	Laramie. Upper. Middle. Lower.
		Jurassic.	Wealden. Upper oolite. Middle oolite. Lower oolite. Upper Lias. Marlstone. Lower Lias.
		Triassic.	Keuper. Muschelkalk. Bunter Sandstone.

Primary, or Paleozoic time.	Carboniferous age.	Permian.	Permian.
		Carboniferous.	{ Upper Coal-measures. { Lower coal-measures. { Millstone Grit.
		Subcarboniferous.	{ Upper. { Lower.
	Devonian, or age of Fishes.	Catskill.	Catskill.
		Chemung.	{ Chemung. { Portage. { Genesee.
		Hamilton.	{ Hamilton. { Marcellus.
		Corniferous.	{ Corniferous. { Schoharie. { Cauda-galli.
	Silurian, age of Invertebrates.	Upper Silurian.	Oriskany. Lower Helderberg. Salina.	Oriskany. Lower Helderberg. Salina.
			Niagara.	{ Niagara. { Clinton. { Medina.
	Lower Silurian.	Trenton.	{ Cincinnati. { Utica. { Trenton.
		Canadian.	{ Chazy. { Quebec. { Calciferous.
	Cambrian, or Primordial.	Upper. Middle. Lower.	{ Potsdam. { Georgian. { St. John's.
		Archæan, Pre-Cambrian.	{ Huronian. { Laurentian.

PART II.

STEATITE :—SOAPSTONE.

This, although not properly a building stone, is of sufficient economic importance to merit attention.

(I) COMPOSITION AND USES.

The name soapstone is properly applied to a compact, dark bluish gray rock composed essentially of the mineral talc. It is therefore, like serpentine, a hydrous silicate of magnesia, consisting when pure of 65.49 per cent of silica ; 31.75 per cent of magnesia, and 4.76 per cent of water. As a matter of fact few, if any known varieties, are chemically pure, but nearly all contain admixtures in the form of mica, chlorite, amphibole, quartz (popularly called flint), magnetite, pyrrhotite and pyrite. The stone is soft enough to be cut readily with a knife, or even with the thumb nail, and has a pronounced soapy feeling ; hence the name soapstone ; from the fact that it has in years past been used—particularly by the aboriginal tribes—for making rude pots, it has also received the name potstone. Steatite is the name commonly applied by mineralogists to these rocks, particularly the fine and compact light-colored varieties, while the eminently foliated or micaceous varieties are known as simply talc.

45

The soapstones are suited for a considerable range of application. Although so soft they are among the most indestructible and lasting of rocks, but are too slippery and perhaps of too sombre a color for general structural purposes. At present the chief use of the material in the United States is in the form of thin slabs for stationary wash-tubs. At one time it was extensively used throughout New England in the manufacture of stoves for heating purposes, and to some extent for fire brick, the well seasoned stone being thoroughly fire-proof. The putting upon the market of unseasoned materials, or of material with bad veins which caused the stone to crack or fly to fragments when subjected to high temperature, aroused a prejudice against the employment of the material, and the manufacture is stated to have been to a considerable extent discontinued as a consequence. In the manufacture of either stoves or washtubs, slabs of considerable size, free from segregation nodules of quartz, pyrite or other minerals, or from dry seams, are essential. As but few of the now known outcrops can furnish material of this nature, the main part of the business of the country is in the hands of but two or three companies. The waste material from the quarries, or the entire output in certain cases, is pulverized and used as a lubricant or a white earth. Rubbed between the thumb and finger, the powder is smooth and oily, without a particle of grit, and its lubricating power is in some cases very remarkable. It is also used in soap making, for which purpose it can, however, be considered only as an adulterant, increasing the weight but not the cleansing properties of the article. It is further used as a " filler " in the manufacture of paper, and as a dressing for fine leathers. Small quantities are used in the powdered form by shoe and glove dealers also. The pure creamy white talc, such as is obtained from North Carolina, is used for crayons and slate pencils, while the still finer, cryptocrystalline varieties such as are at present obtained almost wholly from abroad, are used by tailors under the name of " French chalk," and for making the tips for gas burners. Fine compact grades of a somewhat similar rock (agalmatolite) are used extensively in China and Japan for small ornaments. The stone is readily carved in fine sharp lines, and is a general favorite for making the grotesque images for which these countries are noted.

Soapstone occurs associated with stratified rocks only in the older formations, and hence the principal beds now known lie in the Appalachian regions in the Eastern United States. The beds, as a rule, are not extensive but occur as lenticular shaped masses of uncertain area intercalated with other magnesian and hornblendic or micaceous rocks, frequently more or less admixed with serpentine. The rock, like serpentine, is as a rule traversed by bad seams and joints, and the opening of any new deposit is always attended with more or less risk, as there is in many cases no guarantee that sound blocks of sufficient size to be of value will ever be obtainable.

(2) SOAPSTONES OF THE VARIOUS STATES AND
TERRITORIES.

Arkansas.—A fine, compact, brecciated steatite occurs some 12 miles north of Benton, Salina County. The supply is stated to be abundant.*

California.—Soapstone of fine quality is said to occur near Placerville, in El Dorado County; also in Tuolumne County, near Sonora and Buchanan.†

Maine.—A large bed of soapstone is stated by Jackson ‡ to

---

* Agriculture and Mineral Resources of Arkansas, 1887.
† Eighth Annual Report State Mineralogist of California, 1888.
‡ First Annual Report Geology of Maine, 1837 p. 79.

occur on Orr's Island in Cumberland County. The stone is interstratified with micaceous and talcose schists, the strata running N.N.E. and S.S.W., with a dip of 80° W.N.W. The bed is exposed in an outcropping 14 feet wide on the southeast side of the island. The stone is stated to be hard to saw, yet capable of being wrought into excellent slabs for the construction of stoves and firegrates, being very refractory, and not cracking when exposed to intense heat. This bed, so far as the author is aware, has never been worked. Other beds are stated to occur at Jaquish and Harpswell, and which have been wrought to some extent.

Maryland.—Small areas of soapstone resulting from the alteration of an eruptive enstatite rock are common in Carroll and Montgomery Counties in this State, and have for many years been quarried in a crude and itinerant manner near Sykesville, in Carroll County. The rock on the surface here, as is usual, is badly jointed, and the openings are not of sufficient depth to afford much encouragement. The quarried material is sawn up into slabs of small size for foot-warmers and grillers.

Massachusetts.—Quarries of soapstone have been worked from time to time in Lynnfield and North Dana, in this State. The Lynnfield stone occurs in connection with serpentine. It is soft enough to be readily cut with an ordinary hand-saw when first quarried, but hardens on exposure. When quarried, it was used chiefly for stove-backs, sills, and steps. At North Dana the soapstone quarries were opened as early as 1846, and have at times been quite extensively worked.

New Hampshire.—An extensive bed of fine quality soapstone was discovered in 1794 at Francestown, in this State, and was worked as early as 1802. Up to 1867 some 2,020 tons had been quarried and sold. In this latter year some 3,700 stoves were manufactured by one company alone. The business has been conducted upon a large scale ever since. The bed has been followed some 400 feet, and the present opening is some 40 feet wide, 80 feet long, and 80 feet deep Other beds constituting a part of the same formation occur in Weare, Warner, Canterbury, and Richmond, all of which have been operated to a greater or less extent. Five beds of soapstone also occur in the town of Orford, and an important quarry was opened in Haverhill as early as 1855. It has not, however, been worked continuously.*

New York.—Soapstone or talc occurs in abundance in Fowler and Edwards, Saint Lawrence County, in this State. It is said to be of good quality, remarkably tough, and very refractory in fire.†

North Carolina.—Soapstone of fine quality occurs in several localities in the southwestern part of this State, the national collection showing specimens from 7 miles northeast of Murphy, Cherokee County; from 4½ miles from Greenborough, Guilford County; from Alamance County; from Nantehala River, Cherokee County; and from Deep River, Moore County. Of these the Nantehala stone is a pure, nearly white, compact talc, said to be fully equal to the best French chalk. It has been much used as a white earth. The Deep River "soapstone" is a compact variety of the mineral pyrophylite. This is also used as white earth. Both these stones are shipped in bulk to New York, where they are ground and bolted. The stones from the other localities are of the ordinary type of soapstones, but apparently of good quality.

Pennsylvania.—In the southern edge of Montgomery County, " extending from the northern brow of Chestnut Hill between the two turnpikes, across the Wissahickon Creek and

---

* Geology of New Hampshire, Vol. III., p. 86–88.
† Geology of New York, 1838, p. 206.

the Schuylkill to a point about a mile west of Merion Square," occurs a long, straight outcrop of steatite and serpentine. The eastern and central part of this belt on its southern side " consists chiefly of a talcose steatite," while the northern side contains much serpentine interspersed in lumps through the steatite. Only in a few neighborhoods does the steatite or serpentine occur in a state of sufficient purity to be profitably quarried. On the east bank of the Schuylkill, about two miles below Spring Mill, a good quality of material occurs that has long been successfully worked. It has also been quarried on the west bank of the river about a third of a mile away, and to a less extent on the west bank of the Wissa-hickon, opposite Thorp's Mill. The material is now used principally for lining stoves, fire-places, and furnaces, though toward the end or the last century and the early part of the present one, before the introduction of Montgomery County marble, it was in considerable demand for door steps and sills. It proved poorly adapted for this purpose, however, owing to the unequal hardness of its different constituents, the soap-stone wearing rapidly away, while the serpentine was left pro-jecting like knots or " hob-nails in a plank." *

South Carolina.—Steatite or soapstone is said to occur in this State in the counties of Chester, Spartanburgh, Union, Pickens, Oconee, Anderson, Abbeville, Kershaw, Fairfield, and Richland. The Anderson County stone is said to have been much used for hearthstones. That of Pickens County is con-sidered of value, but it has been quarried to a very limited extent.†

Texas.—Soapstone of good quality and inexhaustible in quantity is stated to occur in large veins on the Hondo and

---

* Rep. C⁴. Second Geological Survey of Pennsylvania, pp. 95, 96.
† South Carolina, Population, Resources, etc., 1883.

Sandy Creeks, about midway of their courses through Llano County.*

Vermont.—Most of the steatite of this State is found on the east side of the Green Mountains and near the eastern line of the talcose slate formation, beds of it extending nearly the entire length of the State. The rock occurs usually associated with serpentine and hornblende. The beds are not continuous and have, as a rule, a great thickness in comparison with their length. It not infrequently happens that several isolated outcrops occur on the same line of strata, sometimes several miles apart, and in many cases alternating with beds of dolomitic limestones that are scattered along with them.

At least sixty beds of this rock occur in the State in the towns of Readsboro, Marlborough, Newfane, Windham, Townsend, Athens, Grafton, Andover, Chester, Cavendish, Baltimore, Ludlow, Plymouth, Bridgewater, Thetford, Bethel, Rochester, Warren, Braintree, Waitsfield, Moretown, Duxbury, Waterbury, Bolton, Stow, Cambridge, Waterville, Berkshire, Eden, Lowell, Belvidere, Johnson, Enosburgh, Westfield, Richford, Troy, and Jay.

Of the beds named those in Grafton and Athens are stated to have been longest worked and to have produced the most stone. The beds lie in gneiss. The quarries were profitably worked as early as 1820. Another important bed is that in the town of Weathersfield. This, like that of Grafton, is situated in gneiss, but has no overlying rock, and the soapstone occurs in inexhaustible quantities. It was first worked about 1847, and during 1859 about 800 tons of material were removed and sold. The Rochester beds were also of great importance, the stone being peculiarly fine-grained and com-

---

* Second Annual Report Geology of Texas, 1876, p. 26.

pact. It was formerly much used in the manufacture of refrigerators. The quality of the stone is represented to be unusually good and free from impurities.* The bed at New-fane occurs in connection with serpentine, and is some half a mile in length by not less than twelve rods in width at its northern extremity. The soapstone and serpentine are strangely mixed, and the general course of the bed being like that of an irregular vein of granite in limestone.

Virginia.—Soapstone occurs in this State, according to Professor Rogers,† near the mouth of the Hardware River, both in Fluvanna and Buckingham Counties. There is also a bed of it associated with the talcose slates in Albemarle County, a little west of the Green Mountain. The beds from here extend in a southwesterly direction, passing through Nelson County, where they are associated with serpentine ; thence they cross the James River above Lynchburgh, and present an outcrop about two miles westward of the town on the road leading to Liberty ; also one about two and a half miles westward of New London. Continuing in the same direction it is seen at the meadows of Goose Creek, where it has been quarried to some extent. Continuing in the same general direction the soapstone again appears in several nearly parallel ranges, of which the most eastern makes its appearance near the Pigg River, in Franklin County. A second belt occurs in the same vicinity near the eastern base of Jack's Mountain ; a third still farther west, about one mile from Franklin Court-house, and a fourth yet more to the west, on the eastern slope of Grassy Hill. The material from near Franklin Court-house is stated to be the best of any of the above. About thirty miles southwest from Richmond, at Chula,

---

* Geology of Vermont, Vol. II., p. 783–91.
† Geology of the Virginias, p. 79.

in Amelia County, there are outcrops of soapstone said to be of fine quality, and which in former times were quite extensively operated by the Indians. They have been re-opened within a few years, and the material is now in the market. Specimens of the stone examined by the writer are by no means pure talc, but carry abundant long brownish fibers of some amphibolic mineral.

SERPENTINE, OPHICALCITE, VERD-ANTIQUE MARBLE.

(1) COMPOSITION, ORIGIN, AND USES OF SERPENTINE.

THE rock serpentine is essentially a hydrous silicate of magnesia, consisting when pure of nearly equal proportions of silica and magnesia with from 12 to 13 per cent of water. The massive varieties quarried for architectural purposes are always more or less impure, containing frequently from 10 to 12 per cent of iron oxides, together with varying quantities of chrome iron (chromite), iron pyrites, hornblende, olivine, minerals of the pyroxene group, and the carbonates of lime and magnesia. The reason for this great diversity in composition lies mainly in the fact that serpentine rarely if ever occurs as an original deposit, but as noted below, is always secondary, a product of alteration of either eruptive or sedimentary rocks rich in magnesian minerals. As, however, these rocks in no case consist of pure magnesian silicates, but carry in addition lime, alumina and various metallic oxides, these constituents separate out during the process of change, and recrystallize in veins, streaks and blotches as calcite, dolomite, magnetite, etc., thus producing the common variations in color. The purer varieties are uniformly green or light yellowish, while the commercial forms, as is well known, are variously streaked and blotched and sometimes brownish, almost black or even of a blood-red color, the different shades, according to Delesse, being dependent upon the amount and state of oxidation of the included ferruginous substances.

The name *Serpentine* as applied to this class of rocks is from the Latin *serpentinus*, a serpent, in allusion to the colors and their spotted or mottled arrangement. The name *ophiolite* or *ophite* as sometimes applied to the spotted green and white varieties is from the Greek word ωφίτηs, also meaning a serpent, or serpent-like. These rocks are also called *ophicalcite* by various writers. Precious serpentine is the pure translucent, massive variety of a rich oil green color, like that from Montville, New Jersey. Chrysotile and Amianthus are the names applied to fibrous and silky varieties ; these are utilized as a substitute for asbestus, being less brittle and of finer fiber. The name *verd antique* (verte antique, or verde antique), antique green, it should be stated, is not applied to the rock of any particular locality, but to any of the green serpentinous marbles used by the ancient Romans, and which were obtained originally from Italy, Greece, or Egypt.

The origin of serpentine rocks has long been a matter of dispute among geologists. Recent investigations tend to show that in many cases they result unmistakably from the alteration of igneous eruptive rocks, especially the olivine bearing varieties, such as the peridotites. In the varieties ophicalcite, consisting of intermingled serpentine and calcite or dolomite, the serpentine is apparently in all cases derived by a process of hydration from a non-aluminous pyroxene. The theory long ably advocated by Dr. Hunt to the effect that the serpentine occurring intercalated with beds of schistose rocks and limestones, resulted from metamorphism of silico-magnesian sediments deposited by sea waters is now very generally abandoned, and it is doubtful if the substance ever occurs as an original deposit even in the eozoonal forms, but is presumably always secondary.*

The following analyses will serve to illustrate the change in composition which takes place in the conversion of (1) olivine, and (2) pyroxene in to serpentine.

	I		II		III
	a	b	c	d	
Silica	41,32%	42,72%	54,215%	42,38%	43,48%
Magnesia	54,69	42,52	19,82	42,14	43,48
Lime			24,71		
Alumina	0,28	0,06	0,59	0,07	
Ferric Oxide			0,20	0,97	
Ferrous Oxide	2,39	2,25	0,27	0,17	
Water	0,20	13,39	0,14	14,12	13,04

(a) Olivine, Snarum, Norway; (b) Serpentine derived from the same; (c) Pyroxene, Montville, New Jersey; (d) Serpentine, derived from the same; and (III) the theoretical composition of serpentine.

This change it will be observed is in the case of the olivine simply a process of hydration—an assumption of some 13% of water. In the pyroxene the process is more complex and consists of a loss in silica, of all the lime which crystallizes out as calcite, and an assumption of nearly 14% of water.

Owing to its softness, which is such that it can be readily carved or turned on a lathe and its beautiful colors when polished, serpentine has long been a favorite with all civilized nations for ornaments and interior decorative work. The rock, however, occurs almost universally in a badly jointed condition, so that blocks of small size only can be obtained, or if large, they are liable to break under pressure or even in process of dressing. (See plate III.) No stone with which the quarry-

---

* The reader is referred to British Petrography by J. J. H. Teall (Dulan & Co., Soho Square, London,) p. 104 for a most excellent historical sketch of this subject. Also to Becker's report on the quicksilver deposits of the Pacific Slope, monograph XIII., U. S. Geological Survey, p. 117.

men have to deal is, as a rule, so full of defects as these serpentinous rocks.   It is in most cases practically impossible to
obtain slabs of more than a few feet in diameter which will not,
through flaws or dry seams, fall apart if sawn at all thin, and it
can in no case be used in blocks or pillars of any size where
more than a very moderate degree of strength is required, since
the prevalence of these seams so weakens it as to render it
worse than valueless.   Every line or vein of different color with
which the stone is traversed but marks an old flaw and is a line
of weakness.

The almost universal characteristic of the stone is one in-
vestors will do well to carry in mind ; a total disregard of this
trait, due presumably to ignorance, has led to no end of quarry
failures.   Still another fact worthy of being mentioned, is that
however high a lustre the stone may take, or however beautiful
it may appear in small pieces, the color is not one that accords
readily with its surroundings, and the demand for it for purely
decorative work must always be more limited than that for
other marbles whose colors are more harmonious.   Moreover,
the stone is not adapted for polished work in exposed situations, since the different substances composing the body of the
stone and filling the veins, and imparting beauty by contrast,
will, on exposure, weather unequally.

The white and yellowish veins lose their lustre and crumble
away, or turn dull yellow, while the whole block becomes
seamed and the serpentine itself takes on a greasy lustre making it as unsightly as it once was beautiful.   This unfortunate
property of veined stones is further alluded to in the chapter
on the Selection of Building Stones (p. 382).   For small ornaments, and in slabs of moderate dimensions for interior decorations, serpentine is capable of producing good affects.   Too
much has been and still is expected from it, and in this, largely,
lies the failure that has fallen to the lot of nearly every quarry
that has been opened in America.

(2) SERPENTINES OF THE VARIOUS STATES AND TERRITORIES.

California.—Inexhaustible quantities of serpentine of a deep green or yellowish color occur in the region round about San Francisco, and often in such situations as to be easily available, as at the head of Market street. So far as observed none of the material is of such a quality as to render it of value for ornamental work, while its gloomy color renders it equally objectionable for purposes of general construction.

The rock is also abundant in other parts of the State, but the writer having seen little of the material excepting as displayed in small fragments in the State museum at San Francisco, is obliged to reply mainly upon the statements of others regarding their economic value.

A body of serpentine varying from dark green to dark mahogany is stated * to occur six or seven miles north-east of Ione, near Dry Creek, in Amador County. Other deposits are stated by the same authority to occur near Benicia in Solano County. According to Becker, † serpentine occurs in irregular areas throughout the quicksilver belt of California sometimes in comparatively pure masses and sometimes as one of the mineral constituents of altered sandstones and granular metamorphic rocks. The entire area covered by the rocks of this class is estimated as not less than 1000 square miles, between Clear Lake and New Idria. These Mr. Becker regards not as altered olivine rocks, but as derived from a variety of minerals including even the quartz and feldspar granules in silicious sandstones.

* Report State Mineralogist of California, 1888, p. 104.

† Geology of the Quicksilver Deposits of the Pacific Siope. Monograph XIII., U. S. Geological Survey, p. 108.

Near the town of Victor, San Bernardino County, are extensive beds of a serpentinous limestone which perhaps may as well be described here. According to the reports of the State Mineralogist * the stone occurs in inexhaustible quantities and blocks of large size are obtainable free from flaws. Samples of the stone examined by the writer vary from light yellowish and greenish to deep green, variously mottled and streaked. The stone has apparently a similar origin to the verdantique of New York State (see p. 65) and is therefore a mixture of calcareous and serpentinous matter. It is of fine grain, close texture, and acquires a high polish. It is possible that owing to its general lighter and more harmonious colors this stone may prove more successful in our markets than have the majority of verdantique marbles.

Connecticut.—The serpentine deposits of Connecticut are thus described by Professor Shepard :† " Connecticut prospers, however, in the green marbles of Milford, a material for decoration much more beautiful and highly prized than white marble. These were first detected in 1811. Two quarries were soon after opened, one near the village of Milford, and called the Milford quarry; the other 2½ miles west of New Haven, and called the New Haven quarry. They were wrought with considerable activity for several years, and furnished an abundance of very rich marble ; but as the working of them was attended with heavy expense from the difficulty of obtaining blocks of large dimensions that were perfectly sound, and from the labor required in sawing and polishing, they were in a few years abandoned, and have for a long time been in a neglected condition. The experiment proved an un-

---

* 10th Annual, 1890, p. 528.
† Report on the Geological Survey of Connecticut, by C. U. Shepard, 1837, pp. 101-103.

fortunate one, therefore, not from any deficiency of marble or its lack of beauty—for these were both fully admitted—but from a want of wealth and taste in the country to sustain the price.

It was perhaps an unfortunate thing that the whole of the marble afforded by these quarries was denominated *verde antique*, whereas but a small part of that furnished is entitled to this name.

The quarry at Milford is capable of furnishing abundant supplies of this highly valued marble (*i.e.*, the verde antique variety), although, from the circumstance that it occupies narrow and irregular seams among the veined marble, blocks or slabs of any size must always be dear compared with pieces sawn as formerly, without any regard to its separation from the more common kind. . . . Whenever the attempt to work it is made, it is to be hoped that the same experience of the past will prevent its use for monuments exposed to the weather, for besides the incongruity of its colors compared with the marbles usually employed for this purpose, it soon loses its lustre and emits color from the action of the weather on the grains of magnetic iron ore it contains.

The New Haven marble, though destitute of the accidental and in some measure classical value which pertains to the Milford variety, is nevertheless a beautiful thing for decoration. In vivacity of colors and the delicacy of their arrangement it is hardly capable of being surpassed. It may be described as a bluish gray or dove-colored limestone clouded with greenish yellow serpentine, the latter containing black grains and sheet veins of magnetic iron ore. The disposition of the colors is cloud-like, flamed, and veined. It polishes with difficulty in consequence of the magnetic iron it contains, which, though it heightens its beauty, unfits it for exposure to the weather." So far as the present writer is aware these quarries have not been worked since the time mentioned by Professor Shepard ; *i.e.*, since a few years subsequent to 1811.

Delaware.—Serpentine of various shades of green is stated to occur about 6 miles northeast from Wilmington, New Castle County, and also to the westward, near the State line, where Brandywine Creek enters the State line from Pennsylvania.* So far as the writer is aware it has never been quarried.

Maine.—A large bed of serpentine occurs on the northern end of Deer Isle, in Penobscot Bay, in this State. The rock is very massive, and of a dark green, almost black color, sometimes streaked and spotted by veins of amianthus and diallage crystals. It is indeed almost too dark and somber for ornamental work, but seems very durable and well adapted for general building purposes. A company was formed some years ago for working this stone, and a shop erected for saws and grinding beds. A considerable amount of material was quarried, but the work was soon discontinued, and had not been resumed at the time of the writer's visit in 1884. The company seem to have fallen into the error of supposing that the stone could be used in long pieces and slabs for window trimmings, and door-posts, but for which, owing to its jointed condition, it is entirely unfitted. The deposit covers a nearly level area of many acres in extent, and lies within a short distance of the shipping wharf.

Maryland.—In the vicinity of Broad Creek, in Harford County, in this State, occurs a very large deposit of serpentine, which is described by Professor Genth † substantially as follows :

---

* Geology of Delaware, 1841, p. 35.
† Geological Report of the Maryland "Verde Antique" marble, etc., in Harford County, Md., by Prof. F. A. Genth, 1875.

" The outcrop of the first or upper bed of green serpentine, of about 500 feet in thickness, can be traced by its outcrop almost the whole distance between the upper ford on Broad Creek and over the hill in a northeasterly direction to a ravine on the same creek, a distance of about 1,800 feet; it also crosses the creek in a southwesterly direction, but it has not been ascertained how far it extends. The outcrop of the second bed was measured on the top of the hill between the horseshoe of Broad Creek, and found to be about 180 feet, and it is very conspicuous on the west side of the creek. Its full extent was not determined. The rock is a variety of massive serpentine somewhat resembling *williamsite*, and shows sometimes a slightly slaty structure. It occurs in various shades from a pale leek-green to a deep blackish green, and from a small admixture of magnetic iron, more or less clouded ; rarely with thin veins of dolomite passing through the mass. It is translucent to semi-transparent, exceedingly tough and its hardness is considerably greater than that of marble." An analysis of the deep-green variety gave the following results :

	Per cent.		Per cent.
Silicic acid	40.06	Magnesia	39.02
Alumina	1.37	Water	12.10
Chromic oxide	0.20	Magnetic iron	3.02
Niccolous oxide	0.71		
Ferrous oxide	3.43		00.00
Manganous oxide	0.09		

Specific gravity 2.668, which denotes a weight of 166$\frac{3}{4}$ pounds per cubic foot, or practically the same as granite. Specimens of this stone received at the National Museum admitted of a very high lustrous polish, the colors being quite uniformly green, slightly mottled with lighter and darker shades. It is not a true verde antique in the sense in which this name was originally employed. So far as can be judged from appearances, this is a most excellent stone, and admirably suited for interior decorative work.

About 6 miles north of the city of Baltimore, at a locality known as the Bare Hills, occurs an outcrop of a coarse light-green serpentine covering many acres. The rock is quite porous, of a dull light-green color, and unfitted for any kind of ornamental work, but admirably suited for general building, especially in rock-faced and rubble work.

At the time of the writer's visit, in the summer of 1885, but a single quarry had been opened, and this was not at the time in operation. The material had been used with excellent effect in the construction of a school-house in the immediate vicinity. The stone occurs in the form of low rounded masses or bosses, and is regarded by Dr. G. H. Williams as an altered peridotite.* The supply is inexhaustible. Portions of the rock carry a very considerable amount of chrome iron, which was at one time mined here quite extensively. In the quarry the rock occurs in a very badly jointed condition, and the blocks are rounded and irregular. Firm blocks several feet in length, which cut up readily into sizes suitable for house walls and similar purposes, can, however, be obtained.

Massachusetts.—Serpentine exists in Massachusetts in great abundance, particularly in the Hoosac mountain range. " The most extensive bed occurs in Middlefield, in the southern part of the town. This bed can not be less than a quarter of a mile in breadth and 5 or 6 miles long. The colors of the rock are various and its hardness unequal. If wrought, it might supply the whole world. It yields both the precious and the common varieties. There is another bed in the same town, associated with steatite or soapstone. In the west part of Westfield and extending into Russell is found another extensive bed of this

---

*Bulletin U. S. Geological Survey, No. 28.

rock of a much darker color and containing green talc. This has been used in a few instances for ornamental architecture, and has a rich appearance when wrought.

" Three beds of serpentine are found in Blanford and another in Pelham, in the southwest part of the town. The color of this last is dark, and the quantity of the talc is considerably large. A large bed occurs in connection with soapstone on the north side of Deerfield River, in Zoar, near the turnpike from Greenfield to Williamstown. Specimens from this place resemble those from the celebrated localities of this rock at Zoblitz, in Saxony." Two beds of serpentine exist also at Windsor, in this State.

" A locality of noble or precious serpentine has long been known to exist in Newbury, 2½ miles south of Newburyport, at an abandoned lime quarry called the ' Devil's Den.' Only small masses can be here obtained, but when polished they will compare with any in the world for beauty. Perhaps the most interesting and important bed of this rock that has as yet been found in the State is that at Lynnfield, in Essex County. The bed has been traced from a point near the center of the town some 2 or 3 miles in a northeasterly direction."* When first quarried the stone is said to be so soft that it can be cut with a handsaw and very readily turned on a lathe.

New Jersey.—A beautiful deep-green and oil yellow, often translucent serpentine, occurs, associated with dolomite, at Montville, in this State. Only pieces of small size are obtainable, and though of exceptional beauty the stone has never been utilized except for cabinet specimens.

The stone has been shown by the writer to result from the alteration of segregation masses of a non-aluminous pyroxene imbedded in the dolomite.†

---

* Hitchcock's Geology of Massachusetts, Vol. I., p. 158.
† Proceedings U. S. National Museum, 1885, p. 105.

New Mexico.—A banded and mottled light and dark green impure serpentinous rock occurs in the form of a narrow dike just north of the Gila River, about half way between Silver City and the Arizona line in this territory. The colors are good, and the stone seems well adapted for both ornamental work and general building. It is known commercially as *ricolite*, from the Spanish word *rico*, rich, in allusion to its rich green color. The following analysis, if correct, shows the the stone to be much more impure than one would be led to suppose from a casual inspection:

Silica	43.72%
Alumina	16.86%
Magnesia	23.78%
Water	11.10%
Lime	2.22%
Soda and Potash	2.30%
Iron oxides	traces.
Total	99.98%

A closely related and very unique rock which may answer well for certain forms of ornamentation also occurs in this vicinity. The main mass of this rock, so far as the writer has seen it, is composed of a finely granular pyroxenic mineral of a delicate light blue color. Throughout this are scattered irregular sporadic areas of yellowish green serpentine resulting from the hydration of the pyroxene. The effect is decidedly unlike anything I have seen elsewhere, and the developments of the quarry may be awaited with interest.*

New York.—At Moriah and Port Henry, in Essex County, in this State, there has been quarried from time to time under

---

* The writer is indebted to Mr. J. H. Huntington for whatever information he possesses relative to these stones.

the name of ophite marble, a peculiar granular stone consisting of an intimate mixture of serpentine, dolomite and calcite interspersed with small flecks of phlogopite. This stone, which is an altered dolomitic and pyroxenic limestone,* seems nearly free from the numerous dry seams and joints that prove so objectionable in most serpentines, and can be obtained in sound blocks of fair size. The serpentinous portions are deep green in color, while the calcareous granules are faint water blue, or whitish, affording a very pleasing contrast. In certain of the outcrops a mineral of the pyrite group occurs, which is of course deleterious, as liable to oxidation, and it is said to be the presence of this mineral that led to the abandonment of some of the older quarries. Other reasons have doubtless contributed. Among these may be mentioned the fact that at few of the openings, as seen by the writer, can blocks of large size and homogeneous texture be obtained, every few feet showing large and irregular nodules of deep greenish and yellowish serpentine, calcite, or white pyroxene, and often large scales of graphite, which would prove nearly as objectionable on a polished surface as do the dark patches in many of our granites. Blocks being quarried at the time of my visit (1888) showed, however, a very even granular texture of nearly equal parts of serpentine, calcite and dolomite in grains of from one eighth to one-fourth of an inch in diameter, forming an aggregate quite granitic in appearance at a slight distance. The stone polishes well, and is said to be durable. In the quarry bed, where the stone had been exposed for ages, it was noticed that the calcite had weathered out on the surface, leaving the serpentine protruding in small greenish knobs. The stone has been quoted in some of the older quarry price-lists at $6.00 a cubic foot for the best monumental stock.

---

* Proceedings U. S. National Museum, Vol. XII., 1889, p. 595.

In Warren County a stone of this same general nature occurs, and which has in times past been quarried near the town of Thurman. This stone, as shown by samples in the National Museum, is composed of about equal parts snow-white calcite and light yellowish-green serpentine in flecks and patches from one-sixteenth to one-fourth of an inch in diameter. The texture, as in the Essex County stone, is, however, by no means uniform, and the large blocks frequently show large and very irregular patches of deep lustrous green serpentine with snow-white, and still unaltered pyroxenic nuclei, the serpentine here, as is the case with that of Montville, (New Jersey,) and the last mentioned, being secondary after a non-aluminous pyroxene. Geologically these beds are of interest as having furnished fragmental remains of the once-problematic organism, the so-called Eozoon Canadense.[*]

It is stated [†] that the largest and most valuable deposit of serpentine in the State is found in the towns of Gouverneur, Fowler, and Edwards, in St. Lawrence County. The rock is said to be massive and sound, and remarkably free from the checks and flaws usually so profusely developed in rocks of this class. In Pitcairn, in the same county, there is also a fine deposit of serpentine of the variety commonly called precious. The calcareous spar is white or grayish-white, and forms a handsome background for the translucent serpentine. The quality of the rock is said to be excellent and free from natural flaws and fissures.

Serpentine also forms the main range of hills on Staten Island, and extends from New Brighton to a little west of Richmond, a distance of 8 miles. The rock assumes a variety of colors, from almost black to nearly white.

---

[*] See on the Ophiolite of Thurman, Warren County, New York, with remarks in the Eozoon Canadense, by the writer in American Journal of Science for March, 1889.

[†] Geology of New York, 1838, p. 205.

North Carolina.—The massive varieties of serpentine are found in many localities. The best appears to come from the neighborhood of Patterson, Caldwell County. It has a dark, greenish-black color, and contains fine veins of the yellowish-green fibrous and silky chrysotile, and admits of a fine polish; greenish-gray massive serpentine, also with seams of greenish and grayish white chrysotile is found at the Baker mine in Caldwell County, at which place are also found the varieties marmolite and picrolite; this last also occurs abundantly in the Buck Creek corundum mine, Clay County. Dark green serpentine has been observed in the neighborhood of Asheville, in Buncombe County, in Forsythe and Wake Counties. A grayish or yellowish green serpentine occurs in Caldwell, Wilkes, Surry, Yancey, Stokes, Orange, and Wake Counties, and in the chryso-lite beds of Macon, Jackson, Yancey, Mitchell, Watanga, Burke, and other counties. It results from the decomposition of the chrysolite.*

The writer has seen but a single sample of these rocks, and hence can express no opinion regarding their value.

Pennsylvania.—Serpentine is a common rock in several counties in the southeastern part of this State, but so far as the writer is aware none of the outcrops furnish material of such a nature as to be suitable for decorative work. A small area of the stone occurs in the extreme southeastern part of Bucks County; three lines of outcrops occur in the southwestern part of Montgomery County, passing through Lower Merion into Delaware County near Radnor. From the southern corner of this township numerous isolated outcrops occur throughout a broad belt extending southwesterly through the townships of Marble, Newtown, Middletown, Providence, Aston, Concord, and Birmingham. In the words of the State Geologist, "A serpentine belt extending from Chester Creek, at Lenni (or

---

* Geology of North Carolina, 1881, p. 57.

Rockdale), past Media to Darby Creek in Radnor township (nine miles) has been quarried for building stone. It consists of separate and parallel outcrops; at least twenty-seven other local exposures of serpentine in various townships are marked upon the map, all of them in the *Chestnut Hill schist area*, and apparently belonging to the upper part of that series."* A long range of serpentine is also found in Williston and East Goshen townships· in Chester County, and a still more extensive belt in the extreme southern part of the county, in Elk and Nottingham townships. This last extends over into Lancaster County, where there are two belts separated by a belt of schist, the southernmost "running along the Maryland line and holding the famous Woods chrome mine, which at one time produced all the chrome in the world, and in busy times as high as 500 tons a month. The serpentine is here unstratified, 1000 yards wide, striking N. 78 E. with sandy chloritic slates north of it and hornblendic gneiss and syenite south of it."

In Lower Merion township (Montgomery County), the serpentine has been quarried from exposures near the Philadelphia and Reading Railroad. The rock here is compact, dark greenish in color, and suited only for general building. It is associated with steatite and is regarded by Mr. T. D. Rand † as resulting from the alteration of an enstatite rock as is also that of Radnor township.

Of the areas above mentioned those of Chester County have so far proven most important from our standpoint, and extensive quarries have for some years been worked near the town of West Chester. The stone here, as usual, occurs only in a badly jointed condition (see illustration plate III.), but owing to its softness, and consequent readiness with which it

---

* Geol. Surv. of Penna., Rep. x., Geol. Atlas and Counties, p. xlvii.

† Annual Report Pennsylvania Geological Survey, 1886, Part iv.

PLATE III.

SERPENTINE QUARRIES, CHESTER COUNTY, PENNSYLVANIA.

To face page 68.

can be worked, it has come into very general use for building purposes, particularly in New York, Philadelphia, Baltimore, Washington and Chicago. The buildings of the University of Pennsylvania, the Academy of Sciences, and some twenty churches in Philadelphia, are of this stone. The use of the stone in cities has not been long enough continued to furnish accurate data regarding its durability, but it is stated that houses erected in the vicinity of the quarries one hundred and fifty years ago show the color of the stone to-day as fresh as when first quarried. The writer's personal observations are, however, to the effect that in a majority of cases many of the blocks exposed in a wall turn whitish, or at least fade to a lighter green. Such a change can scarcely be considered detrimental.

Although the stone has been upon the general market only about ten years it has acquired an excellent reputation. To the writer it seems that in the majority of cases very poor taste has been shown on the part of the designers, very many of the buildings being anything but beautiful from an architectural standpoint. The almost universal practice of using a light, yellowish-gray sandstone for the trimmings in houses of this material should also be condemned, since the contrast is not sufficient nor satisfactory.

The origin of the Chester County stone, as with serpentines in general, has been a subject of considerable discussion. As long ago as 1862 Dr. Genth* advanced the opinion that the Texas, Lancaster County, stone originated by the alteration of asbestus. Prof. Frazer,† in his work on the geology of southeastern Pennsylvania considered it as a modification of the Huron-

---

* American Journal of Science (2) 33, p. 202.

† Theses Presentées a la Faculté des Sciences de Lille, Université de France, 1882; also Rep. C⁴ Second Geol. Survey of Penna., 1883.

ian schists of the region. Prof. Chester, however, who has since studied the rock with the aid of the microscope and thin sections, regards it as derived from a tremolite rock carrying accessory olivine, the tremolite itself being secondary after pyroxene, and the rock mass as a whole eruptive through the Azoic schists, rather than an integral part of that formation.*

A beautiful and deep lustrous green variety susceptible of a high polish and known as *Williamsite* was found in abundant small pieces during the working of the Fulton township chromite mines. Excepting as polished specimens for mineral cabinets the material was never utilized.

A narrow belt of a light oil yellow to deep green serpentine occurs associated with the beds of limestone on the southwestern flank of Chestnut Hill, near Easton, in Northampton County. The stone evidently originated from the alteration of a white tremolite rock with which it is associated.† The serpentine as here found never occurs in masses of such size as to be of economic value, though of considerable interest to mineral collectors.

Texas.—Serpentine of a dark green color and fitted for either building or ornamental work is stated to occur on Crab Apple Creek in Gillespie County.‡

Vermont.—The bed of talcose schist that extends in a general northern and southern direction throughout the entire length of central Vermont bears numerous outcrops of serpentine or of serpentine in combination with dolomite, but which, so far as the writer is aware, have been quarried only in Roxbury and Cavendish. The quarry at Cavendish was worked very early, having been opened about 1835, before

---

* Annual Report Geological Survey of Penna. for 1887.
† Proc. U. S. National Museum, Vol. XII., 1889. p. 599.
‡ First Report Geological and Mineralogical Survey of Texas. 1888, p. 63.

there were adequate means of transportation of the quarried stone or there was any sufficient demand for so expensive a material. The methods of working and polishing the stone were, moreover, so little understood that very poor results were obtained and the works were shortly discontinued as a consequence.

In Roxbury the American Verdantique Marble Company early opened quarries and erected a mill for sawing. The business was pushed quite vigorously for a time ; but, owing to several causes, probably the same as the first enumerated, the works were shut down in 1858, and have not since been reopened. A considerable quantity of the material was taken out for the interior decorations of the United States Capitol extensions, but for some reason it was never used.

The Roxbury stone is one of the most beautiful of all our serpentines and the best adapted for all kinds of interior decorative work. The colors are deep, bright green, traversed by a coarse net-work of white veins. It is designated by Hunt* an ophiolite, and is stated by him to be a mixture of serpentine, talc, and ferriferous carbonate of magnesia. It acquires a smooth surface and beautiful polish, and it is a serious comment upon American taste that there is not sufficient demand for the material to cause the quarries to be re-opened. At Cavendish the railroad now passes within one-half mile of the quarry and good water-power is close at hand, while the Roxbury quarry is within 30 rods of the railway station. The rock lacks the brecciated structure characteristic of most foreign verd-antique, but compares more closely with the variety known as Verde di Genova than with any other with which the author is acquainted. Among the other localities in this State

---

* T. S. Hunt, on Ophiolites, American Journal of Science, vol. XXV. p. 239 ; second series, p. 226.

in which serpentine occurs may be mentioned Richford, Montgomery, Jay, Troy, Lowell, Middlesex, Wailsfield, Warren,
Rochester, Ludlow, Windham, Wadsborough, and Dover.

Of the Lowell stone it is stated * that two ranges of serpentine occur, commencing near the headwaters of the Missiseo
and extending nearly to Canada. "For the richness and number of the varieties it would not seem possible that they can
be surpassed, while their extent, amounting to 20 or 30 square
miles, is beyond the possible demand of all future ages. They
are exhibited in several precipitous ledges, which are easy of
access and of being worked."

Concerning the locality at Troy, the same authority states:
"Elegant varieties are numerous, among which are most conspicuous the very bright green noble serpentine, which covers
most of the numerous jointed faces with a coat of one-eighth
to one-half of an inch thick, and the spotted varieties. Numerous seams may render it difficult to obtain large slabs, but
smaller pieces, suitable for a great variety of ornamental purposes, may be obtained, of great beauty and in any quantity."

(3) FOREIGN SERPENTINES.

Canada.—Serpentine of a pale green color, marked with
spots and clouds of a rich brown due to disseminated iron protoxide, and forming a fine ornamental stone occurs in Grenville and in Burgess in the Province of Quebec. Other rocks
of this class occur in the towns of Melbourne, Orford, St.
Joseph, and at Mt. Albert in Gaspé.† So far as the author is
aware, these have been as yet but little quarried, though seemingly very promising.

England.—None of the American serpentinous rocks now

---

* Geology of Vermont, 1861, vol. I. p. 544.

† Geology of Canada, 1863.

known can compare in point of beauty, in variety and elegance of colors, with those of the Lizard district in Cornwall,
England. A series of polished blocks of these in the national
collections at Washington show the prevailing colors to be
dark olive green with veins, streaks, and blotches of greenish
white, chocolate brown, and blood red. The green varieties
are often spotted by ill-defined flakes of a "silky bronzitic
mineral."

The rock is softer than the serpentine of Harford County,
Maryland, but takes an equally good surface and polish, and
works much more readily. It is stated by Hull * to be obtainable in blocks from 7 to 8 feet in length and from 2 to 3 feet
in diameter. According to this same authority, the stone is
admirably adapted for interior decorations and is now being
used for ornamental fonts, pulpits, small shafts, and pilasters,
as well as for vases, tazza, and inlaid work.

Considering the remarkable beauty and the variety of
colors displayed by this stone, it seems strange that it should
not have found its way more extensively into American markets.

The rock is regarded by Bonney † as an altered intruded
igneous rock, rich in olivine (peridotite).

Ireland.—The only Irish serpentines which have achieved
any notoriety in America, are the so-called Connemara greens
and which occur according to Mr. G. H. Kinahan‡ only in the
west of County Galway. These are classed by this authority
as ophiolites and ophicalcites. They vary in color from light
to dark green, either uniform or clouded, the majority being
variously mottled, streaked, and variegated. The rocks occur

---

* Building and Ornamental Stones, p. 102.

† Quar. Jour. Geol. Soc. of London, 1877, p. 884.

‡ Economic Geology of Ireland. Jour. Royal Geol. Society of Ireland.
vol. VIII. (new series), part II. p. 152.

in one group of strata, once continuous, but now more or less disconnected and isolated by faulting.   In Streamstown Bay Valley is a continuous narrow band of the rocks over three miles in length, and which furnishes a great variety of beautiful material utilized in the manufacture of brooches and various articles of *vertu.*

The stone found in the American market seems to have been brought from quarries near Lissoughter, in this county. The rock here is in general uniform or clouded green, some of it being dark, but at the same time translucent.   Very good-sized stones are obtainable, but in rough unshapely blocks. The largest column yet obtained from these quarries measured nine feet nine inches in length, and is in the mansion of Lord Ardilann, at St. Anne's, County Dublin.

Writing of these stones Mr. Kinahan says that at one time there was a considerable demand for the Connemara greens, " but unfortunately for the reputation of the stone, architects would insist on using them for outside decorations, and consequently, not through any real inferiority in the stones, they soon weathered and became unsightly.   Thus was generated a most undeserved prejudice against the green marbles, which when used in their proper sphere as inside work, cannot be surpassed in beauty or elegance."

Italy.—The principal serpentinous rocks of Italy are the ophicalcites of Pegli and Pietra Lavezzara, near Genoa, and of Levante, and the true serpentine of Tuscany.   The Verde di Pegli is a breccia consisting of deep green fragments of serpentine cemented by light green calcite.   The contrast of colors thus produced is said to be very pleasing.   The Verde di Genova stone from quarries at Pietra Lavezzara is also a breccia consisting of green, blackish green, brown, or red serpentine fragments with an abundant cement of white or greenish calcite.   It has been quarried from time immemorial, and is largely used in France where it is known as *Vert de Gênes.* Its selling price at Turin is about 20 cents per cubic foot. The ophicalcite of Levante is a breccia like the preceding, the frag-ment being of a violet or wine red color. It is difficult to work but acquires a good polish. The Italian name for the stone is *rosso* or *Verde di Levante;* though sometimes called *granito di Levante.* The Tuscany serpentine from quarries near Prato is known commercially as *Verde di Prato.* The stone is of a deep green color, carrying crystals or nodules of diallage and is traversed by a net-work of fine lines giving it a brecciated appearance. It contains also veins of noble serpen-tine of a clear greenish or whitish color. It is softer than ordinary serpentine and acquires only a dull polish, but works very readily. The dark green variety is most valued, and having been used in ancient monuments is frequently called the *Nero antico di Prato.** This stone is stated by Hull to be subject to rapid decay when exposed to atmospheric influences.

GYPSUM : ALABASTER.

This can scarcely be considered a building-stone, and it is used only to a small extent for ornamental purposes. We may, however, devote a little space to the subject.

(1) COMPOSITION AND USES OF GYPSUM.

Pure gypsum is composed of the sulphate of lime and water in the proportions of about 79.1 per cent of the former to 20.9 per cent of the latter (ante, p. 26). Three varieties are com-mon : (1) crystallized gypsum or selenite, which occurs in broad, flat, transparent plates sometimes a yard in diameter and of value only as mineral specimens and for optical pur-

---

* Delesse, pp. 77–79.

poses ; (2) fibrous gypsum, which includes the variety satin spar used for making small ornaments ; and (3) massive gypsum, which includes the common white and clouded varieties used in making plaster, and the pure, white, fine-grained variety alabaster.*

(2) LOCALITIES OF GYPSUM IN THE UNITED STATES.

The principal localities of gypsum in the United States as given by various authorities are in New York, Ohio, Illinois, Iowa, Michigan, Virginia, Tennessee, Arkansas, and Texas, where it occurs in extensive beds and usually associated with salt springs. It is also found associated with Triassic deposits in the Rocky Mountain region. Handsome selenite and snowy gypsum are also stated to occur near Lockport and Camillus, N. Y., in Davidson County, Tennessee, and in the form of rosettes in the Mammoth Cave of Kentucky.

According to G. F. Kunz† the ornaments of satin spar sold at Niagara Falls and other " tourist places " are nearly all imported from Wales, through some few of the common white variety are cut from the beds of this stone found in the vicinity. The Italian alabaster is used extensively in making statuettes, but the common varieties found in this country and Nova Scotia are used chiefly for land plaster and as plaster of paris, or stucco. So far as the writer is aware the gypsum quarried at Fort Dodge, Iowa, is the only one that has been at all used for structural purposes in this country.

According to Dr. White ‡ several residences, a railway station, and other minor structures, including a large culvert, have been built of gypsum at this place. In the construction

---

* Much of the material popularly called alabaster is in reality travertine (see p. 116).

† Min. Resources of the United States, 1883–84, p. 77.

‡ Geol. of Iowa, vol. ii. p. 302.

of the culvert the lower courses that came in contact with the water were of limestone, as the gypsum had proven slightly soluble and hence less durable in such positions. The stone is regarded by Dr. White as very durable in ordinary situations, and the ease with which it can be worked renders it preferable to the limestones in the immediate vicinity. The method of quarrying is to bore holes with a common auger and then blast by means of powder. The blocks are then trimmed to the proper size and shape by means of common wood-saws and hatchets or axes.

(3) FOREIGN GYPSUM AND ALABASTER.

England.—An English alabaster, white, variously clouded and streaked with dull brownish red has been introduced into the New York markets, and has been used in the bank counters of the Equitable Building on lower Broadway. The stone is altogether too soft for use in such exposed situations. It is said to be from quarries in Devonshire.

Italy.—Alabaster of the finest quality occurs in several parts of Italy, particularly at Miemo, in Tuscany, Fontibagni, and Castellina, and at Aosta, in Piedmont. The purest and best variety is, however, from Valdi Marmolago, near Castellina.* Some of these are very extensively worked, the clouded varieties being made into vases and other objects, while the pure white varieties are made into statuettes. In this form they are sold in considerable quantities in this country, passing under the name of *Florentine marbles*. As prepared for the market these are indistinguishable from true marble by any but an expert, and it is safe to say a large number of people are yearly imposed upon. Should one have reason to suppose that this article is being imposed upon him for true marble he has but to try

---

* Hull, *op. cit.* p. 165

the object in some obscure part with the thumb-nail. Alabaster is readily scratched or indented in this manner while marble is not affected. Another test is to apply a dilute acid. True marble will dissolve and effervesce briskly, while the alabaster remains unchanged. Besides being softer, and hence more liable to injury, these alabaster objects are inferior to those of marble in that they are more easily soiled and are difficult to cleanse.

It is stated* that the Italian alabaster is, when first quarried semi-transparent, and that it is wrought while in this state. It is then rendered white and opaque (like marble) by placing the objects in a vessel of cold water which is slowly raised to the boiling point. It is then allowed to cool to a temperature of about 70° or 80° Fahr. when the objects are moved and wiped dry. At first they appear little changed by their baptism, but gradually assume the desired color and opacity.

Spain.—Beautiful white and variegated alabaster occurs in the province of Guadalajara and Saragossa.

LIMESTONES AND DOLOMITES.

(1) CHEMICAL COMPOSITION AND ORIGIN.

The name limestone as commonly applied is made to include a large and widely varying group of rocks, differing from one another in color, texture, structure and origin and with but the one property in common of consisting essentially of carbonate of lime. A pure limestone should consist only of carbonate of lime. In point of fact, however, none of our natural stones are chemically pure, but all contain a greater or less amount of foreign material either chemically combined or as admixed minerals. The more common of these foreign sub-

---

* Appleton's Dictionary of Mechanics, vol. II. p. 387.

stances are carbonate of magnesia, carbonates and oxides of iron, silica, clay, bituminous matter, mica, talc and minerals of the hornblende or pyroxene groups. The presence of these substances gives rise to a variety of shades and colors among which water-blue, green, yellow, pink, red, and all shades of gray to black are common. The yellow, pink and red colors in such cases are due, as a rule, to iron oxides, while the various shades of blue-gray, gray and black are due to the carbonaceous matter derived from organic remains. The green color of some of the Vermont marbles appears to be due to the presence of talc.

Limestones are ordinarily regarded as originating as chemical deposits, or from the consolidation of calcareous remains of marine animals. Many beds, as for instance the Indiana oolites, are products of a combination of these processes. The shells of dead mollusks, corals and crinoids were tumbled about by the waves until ground into grains of calcareous sand, about and around each of which were subsequently deposited from solution the successive coats of lime as shown in Fig. 2 on. Plate II. It is very probable that few of our limestones were wholly derived directly from organic remains, but are in part at least chemical deposits. The alternation of beds of snow-white, blue-gray, greenish and almost black layers, as in the Vermont quarries may perhaps be best explained on the assumption that the white layers resulted as deposits from solution, while the darker layers are but beds of indurated shell mud and sand colored by the organic impurities they contained at the time they were first laid down.

Limestones occur in stratified beds among rocks of all geological ages, from the Archæan to the most recent. The majority of those used for building and ornamental work belong either to the Cambrian, Silurian, Devonian, or Carboniferous ages.

(2) VARIETIES OF LIMESTONES AND DOLOMITES.

The following list includes all the principal varieties of limestone popularly recognized, the distinctions being founded upon their structure, chemical composition, and mode of origin :

Crystalline limestone. Marble.—A crystalline, granular aggregate of calcite crystals. The crystals are usually of quite uniform size in the same marble, but often vary widely in those from different localities. The fine grained white varieties which appear like loaf sugar are called *saccharoidal.* Common statuary marble is a good example of this variety.

Compact Common Limestone.—A fine-grained crystalline aggregate which to the eye often appears quite homogeneous and amorphous. It is rarely pure, but contains admixtures of other minerals, giving rise to many varieties, to which particular names are given. *Lithographic Limestone* is an extremely fine-grained crystalline magnesian limestone, with a small amount of impurities, and of a drab or yellowish hue. *Bituminous limestone* contains a considerable proportion of bitumen, caused by decomposing animal or vegetable matter. Its presence is easily recognized by the odor of petroleum given off when the rock is freshly broken. *Hydraulic limestone* contains 10 per cent and upward of silica, and usually some alumina. When burned into lime and made into mortar or cement it has the property of setting under water. *Oolitic limestones* are made up of small rounded concretionary grains that have become cemented together to form a solid rock. These little rounded grains resemble the roe of a fish ; hence the name, from the Greek word ωόν, an egg. Where the grains are nearly the size of a pea the rock is called *pisolite.*

· *Travertine,* or *Calc Sinter,* is limestone deposited by running streams and springs. It occurs in all gradations of texture from light flaky to a compact rock fit for building. A light porous calc sinter has been deposited by the Mammoth Hot Springs of Yellowstone National Park, some of which is nearly pure carbonate of lime and snowy white in color. Travertine occurs in great abundance at Tivoli, in Italy, from whence it was quarried in building ancient Rome. The exterior of the Amphitheatrum Flavium, or Colosseum, the largest theatre the world has ever known, was of this stone, as was also the more modern structure of St. Peter's, in the same city.* The Latin name of the stone was *lapis Tiburtinus*, of which the word travertine is supposed to be a corruption.

Stalactite and *stalagmite* are the names given to the deposits of limestone on the roofs and floors of caves. Such are often beautifully crystalline and colored by metallic oxides, giving rise to beautiful marbles, which are incorrectly called onyx, as are also the travertines from which they differ only in method of deposition.

Fossilferous Limestones.—Many limestones are made up wholly or in part of the fossil remains of marine animals, as is shown in the accompanying figure (p. 82), which is drawn from a magnified section of a limestone of the Cincinnati group from near Hamilton, Ohio.

In some cases the remains are retained nearly perfect ; again the entire fossil may have been replaced by crystalline calcite. In other instances stones are found which are made up only of casts of shells, the original shell material having decayed and disappeared, as in the Eocene limestone from North Carolina. Many of the most beautiful marbles belong to the group of fossil limestones, as, for instance, the red and white variegated Tennessee marbles. *Crinoidal limestones* are made up of fossil crinoidal fragments.

---

† Hull, Building and Ornamental Stones, pp. 279, 281.

Shell limestones or *shell sand-rocks* as they are called by some authorities, are made up of shells usually much broken, though sometimes almost entire. The well-known *coquina* from Saint Augustine, Florida, is a good illustration of this variety. *Coral*

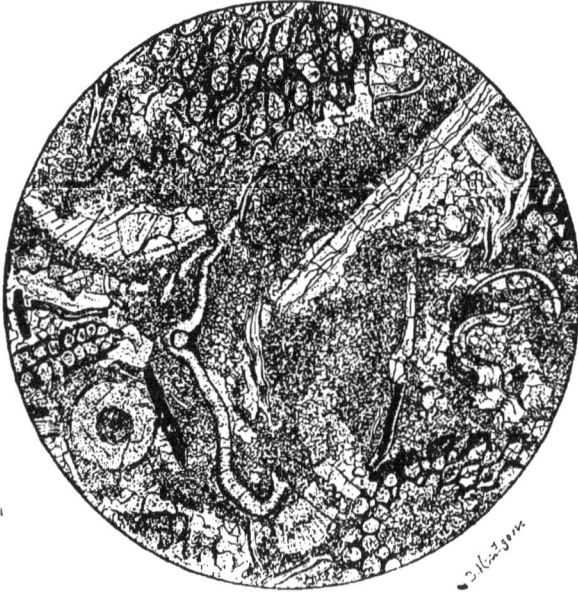

rock is of the same nature, excepting that it is composed of fragments of corals. *Chalk* is a fine white limestone composed largely of the minute shells of foraminifera.

Magnesian Limestones; also called Dolomitic Limestones.— Under this head are included those limestones which contain 10 per cent and upwards of carbonate of magnesia. They may be finely or coarsely crystalline ; light, porous, or com- pact ; fossiliferous or non-fossiliferous ; in short, may show all the variations common to ordinary limestones, from which they can usually be distinguished only by chemical tests. Many marbles are magnesian, as will be noticed by reference to the tables. When the carbonate of magnesia in a limestone rises as high as 45.65 per cent the rock is no longer called magnesian limestone, but—

Dolomite.*—This in its typical form is a crystalline granular aggregate of the mineral dolomite, and is usually whitish or yellowish in color. It can in its typical form be distinguished from limestone by its increased hardness (3.5–4.5) and specific gravity (2.8–2.95). It is also less soluble, being scarcely at all acted on by dilute hydrochloric acid. Dolomite shows all the peculiarities pertaining to limestones, both in color and texture, and a chemical analysis is often required to distinguish between them. The pure white marble from Cockeysville, Maryland, is a dolomite, but by the eye alone can scarcely be distinguished from the white crystalline limestones (marbles) of Vermont. The red-mottled marbles of Malletts Bay, Vermont, are also dolomites, as are the white marbles of Lee, Massachusetts, and Pleasantville, New York.

In composition there is no essential difference between a limestone or dolomite and what is popularly called a marble, but for convenience sake the subject will be here treated in two parts, the first to include such of this class of rocks as are put upon the market as marbles, and the second the rocks of the same composition, but unfit for finer grades of building and ornamental work and known popularly as simply limestones.

(3) LIMESTONES AND DOLOMITES. MARBLES.

Under the head of marbles, then, are here included all those rocks consisting essentially of carbonate of lime (limestone) or

---

* So called after the French geologist, Dolomieu.

carbonate of lime and magnesia (magnesian limestone and dolomite) that are susceptible of receiving a good polish and are suitable for ornamental work.

Alabama.—Beds of marble of great beauty are stated to occur along the Cahawba River in Shelby County of this State. The colors enumerated are gray with red veins, red and yellow, buff with fossils, white crystalline, clouded with red and black. A black variety veined with white occurs on the road from Pralls Ferry to Montevallo and on Six Mile Creek. Other good beds are stated to occur on the Huntsville road about 19 miles from Tuscaloosa and at Jonesborough, the latter rock being compact and of a red and white color ; the same strata occurs at Village Springs. On Big Sandy Creek good marbles occur similar to those on the Cahawba.* None of the above are actively quarried, and the writer has had the opportunity of examining but a single specimen, that a small block of fine and even texture, pure white color and excellent quality, said to be from near Talladega.

Arkansas.—According to Professor Branner† marbles occur throughout the northern part of this State. They are of Lower Silurian age, and vary in color from red to light pink, mottled and white. The beds are from ten to one hundred or more feet in thickness. They begin in Independence County about twenty miles northeast of Batesville, and cross the State westward and northward in a belt nearly or quite three miles wide. This belt passes just north of Batesville, north of Mountain View, north of Marshall and on west by way of St. Joe into Boone and Carroll Counties.

On the banks of some of the streams traversing this region great perpendicular walls of these marble beds are exposed.

---

* Geology of Alabama, First Biennial Report, 1849, p. 45.
† Stone, Indianapolis, Indiana, Oct. 1880.

Such exposures occur on White River where the stone might be quarried advantageously and loaded upon boats. These stones can be obtained in blocks as large as can be handled, while their colors make them desirable both for architectural and ornamental purposes. The ease with which they can be quarried and dressed is also in their favor.

At present railroad facilities for transportation are almost entirely lacking.

California.—It has been stated that owing to the violent geological agencies that have been in operation since the formation of the marble deposits in this State the stones are found to be so broken and shattered in nearly every case, that it is impossible to obtain blocks of large size free from cracks and flaws.* The State is nevertheless not lacking in desirable material.

Near Indian Diggings, in Eldorado County, there occurs a fine-grained white, blue-veined marble that closely resembles the Italian bardiglio, from the Miseglia quarries, but that the groundmass is lighter in color. It has been used only for grave-stones and to but a slight extent at that. In Kern County are deposits of marble of various shades, but all so broken and shattered on the surface as to be very difficult to work.

Near Colfax, in Placer County, are also beds of a dark blue-gray mottled magnesian limestone that takes a good polish and might be utilized as marble. Other deposits occur in Los Angeles, Monterey, Nevada, Butte, Humboldt, Tuolumne and Plumas Counties. At Colton, in Los Angeles County the marble beds are described by Prof. Jackson† as affording pure white clouded with gray and grayish black finely mottled with

---

* Report of Tenth Census, 1880, vol. x. p. 279.
† Seventh Annual Report State Mineralogist of California, 1887, p. 212.

white varieties, the clouded white being the most abundant. This is stated to be a medium grained granular stone, homogeneous in texture quite sound and strong and taking a good polish. Chemical tests show that the stone is composed of a mixture of calcite and dolomite granules. This not only renders the production of a perfect surface and polish more difficult than would otherwise be the case, but will also cause it to weather unevenly (see p. 381). The clouding of the marble and the dark gray colors are here due to scales of graphite.

At the foot of the Inyo Mountains in Inyo County, about five miles north of the town of Keller, there occurs an extensive bed of dolomite in which within a few years marble quarries have been opened. The strata here are upturned at an angle of 75° to 80° and the beds superficially seamed and cracked to such an extent that large blocks on the immediate surface are unobtainable. Although the quarry openings are as yet shallow the indications are, however, that these defects soon disappear, and at no great depths sound blocks of any size that can be handled may be obtained.*

The stone at the various outcrops now exposed is quite variable. At one of the openings it is pure snow white, fine grained and equal in texture to Italian marble, but much harder, firmer and more compact. But a few hundred yards from this is an opening which seems destined to furnish some of the most unique and yet beautiful stone thus far produced in America. In texture this is of the same quality as the last, but the white groundmass is injected in every direction with blotches, streaks and finely divided branching and feathery dark brown nearly black dendritic or fern-like markings— presumably caused by oxide of manganese—and which added to occasional blotches of Siena yellow produce an effect that

---

* Tenth Annual Report State Mineralogist, 1890.

must be seen to be appreciated.   Still a third variety is Siena yellow of varying shades.   This last while nearer the true Italian Siena than any now produced, differs in being distinctly granular in texture, and can perhaps be more correctly compared with the well-known Estremoz, or so-called Lisbon yellow from Alemtejo Province, Portugal.

A fine grained black marble is also found in the near vicinity, which, while it does not polish well may answer for floor tiling.

The Inyo marbles are perhaps among the most promising the west has as yet produced.   Chemically they are a very pure dolomite, close grained and compact, and equally well adapted for exterior and interior work.   Their superior hardness will cause a greater expense in working than in the eastern or Italian marbles, but whether these items will not be more than counterbalanced by cost of transportation the future only can decide.   The quarries are on steep hillsides quite devoid of timber or soil, and cost of fuel necessitates the transportation of the rough blocks to Essex, Nevada, a distance of some miles, before they can be sawn.

Chemical analysis made at the laboratories of the State Mining Bureau yielded 54.25% carbonate of lime, 44.45% carbonate of magnesia, and but 0.60% of iron and silica.   Specific gravity 2.80, which is equal to a weight of 179½ pounds per cubic foot.

Near Plymouth in Amador County there are said to be white and variegated marbles suitable for general building, but of too coarse a grain for decorative work.

White marble occurs in the mountains near San Jacinto in San Diego County.   Good stone is described* as occurring in San Bernardino County, near Slover Mountain.   This last has

---

* Eighth Annual Report State Mineralogist of California, 1888, p. 504.

been worked for the San Bernardino market. Massive aragonite suitable for ornamental work also occurs here. It is described as most beautifully striped and banded in various colors.
This and other of the so-called onyx and serpentinous marbles
are more fully described elsewhere.

Colorado.—No marbles are as yet quarried in this State, but
the National collections show a small piece of a black, white-
veined breccia from Pitkin that might rival the imported
" Portoro " from the Monte d'Arma quarries in Italy, if occurring in sufficient abundance. Concerning the extent and character of the formation the author knows nothing. In the
marble yards of Denver the author was shown during the summer of 1886 a fine chocolate-colored stone, somewhat resembling the more uniform colors of Tennessee marble, which was
stated to have been brought from near Fort Collins, in Laramie
County, where it occurred in great quantities ; also a fair grade
of white blue-veined marble from Gunnison County. A beautiful breccia marble is stated * to occur in abundance a few
miles north of Boulder City.

Prof. Newberry states † that on Yule Creek, a branch of
Crystal River, in a series of massive gray Palaeozoic limestones
there is a belt of white marble apparently superior in quality
to anything found elsewhere in the United States. The marble belt is stated as being about 100 feet in thickness, and not
less than six miles in length. The prevailing colors are pure
white or white slightly clouded with gray. On the east side
of the belt some of the layers are of a very beautiful blue or
dove color. " So far as can be judged from exposures, much
of this deposit deserves to be classed as statuary marble, and
some of it is apparently equal to that taken from the quarries
at Carrara, Italy, or the Grecian Parian or Pentellic marbles."

* Biennial Report of State Geologists of Colorado, 1880, p. 33.
† School of Mines Quarterly, vol. X. No. 1, 1888, p. 71.

Connecticut.—In the northern part of Litchfield County, near the Massachusetts line, in the town of Canaan, East Canaan, and Falls Village, there occur massive beds of a coarsely crystalline white dolomite, which have in years past furnished valuable building marbles, though recently they have been but little worked. The stone is said to weather well and to be obtainable in large blocks eminently suited for building, but like the Lee (Mass.) dolomite it frequently contains crystals of white tremolite, which weather out on exposure. It is therefore not so well suited for finely finished or monumental work. The State-house at Hartford is the most important structure yet made from this material.

As elsewhere noted it was at Marble Dale, in the town of Milford in this State, that marble quarrying was first systematically undertaken in this country, and at one time (1830) not less than fifteen quarries were in active operation in the vicinity. So far as can be learned not a single one of these is now being worked.

Delaware.—No marbles are at present quarried in this State, but a coarse white dolomite is found near Hockessin, New Castle County. This, so far as can be judged from the single specimen examined, might be used for general building, though not well suited for ornamental work.

Georgia.—An important belt of marble is said to extend through the counties of Cherokee, Pickens, Gilmer, and Fannin in the northern part of this State, the material varying in color from pure white through blue and variegated varieties, some of which are remarkably beautiful. Variegated marbles also occur in the counties of Polk, Floyd, Whitfield, Catoosa, Chattooga, Gordon, Murray, Barton, and Walker; chocolate-red varieties similar to the marbles of Tennessee are said to occur in abundance in Whitfield County, the bed in Red Clay Valley extending in uninterrupted continuity for 10 miles, and varying from one-fourth to one-half a mile in width.* Of the beds above mentioned those in Pickens and Cherokee Counties are at present the most important and the only ones that have been worked to any extent, quarrying having quite recently been commenced here by various companies. These marbles are of uniform texture, but much coarser than the Vermont marble, which in other respects they resemble. They are soft, work readily, and acquire an excellent surface and polish. In color they vary from snow white and pink to black and white mottled. The pink variety is unique as well as beautiful, and there is at present nothing like it produced in other parts of the country, though in color it closely resembles the pink marble from Cherokee and Macon Counties, North Carolina, to be noticed later. It is, however, coarser.

Chemical tests show these stones to be nearly pure calcium carbonate, quite free from admixtures of other minerals. They can apparently be depended on to weather uniformly. Pressure tests made at the Watertown arsenal on six-inch cubes gave maximum results of 12,078 lbs. per square inch.

The ready working qualities of these stones, the fact that owing to the mildness of the climate the works can be in operation at all seasons of the year, together with the remoteness of regions where similar marbles are produced, all point to a rapid development of an extensive quarrying industry in this part of the country.

Idaho.—Marble sufficient to supply the local demand for cemetery work is stated to be quarried at Spring Basin, Cassia County, in this State.

Iowa.—The calcareous rocks of Iowa are, as a rule, noncrystalline, dull in color, and with few qualities that render them desirable for ornamental purposes. But few of them are

---

* Commonwealth of Georgia, p. 135.

pure limestone, but nearly all contain more or less magnesia, iron, or clayey matter ; very many of them are true dolo- mites.

Near Charles City, in Floyd County, on the banks of Cedar River, are extensive quarries in the Devonian (Hamilton) beds of magnesian limestones, certain strata of which furnish a coral marble at once unique and beautiful. The prevailing color of the stone is light drab, but the abundant fossils vary from yel- lowish to deep mahogany brown. These last, which belong to the class of corals called Stomatophora, are very abundant and of all sizes up to 18 inches in diameter. As seen on a pol- ished surface imbedded in the fine, drab, non-crystalline paste of the groundmass, they present an appearance totally unlike anything quarried elsewhere in America—an appearance at once grotesque and wonderfully beautiful. The stone admits of a high polish, and would seem excellently adapted for all manner of interior decorations, if obtainable in blocks suffi- ciently uniform in texture. A small amount of argillaceous matter and scattering particles of amorphous pyrite, which are occasionally visible, render its adaptability to outdoor work decidedly doubtful. The stone is known commercially as Madrepore marble. A polished slab 2 by 4 feet is in the collections of the National Museum.

The light yellowish, buff, or brown sub-Carboniferous mag- nesian limestone, quarried near Le Grand in Marshall County, also contains massive layers beautifully veined with iron oxide, and which are suitable for ornamental purposes, though it is not considered suitable for monuments and other work subject to continuous exposure. I have not seen samples of this ma- terial, though it is well spoken of by White.* It is popularly known as Iowa marble. The only other stone which, so far

---

* Geology of Iowa, vol. II. p. 313.

as I am aware, has ever been utilized for ornamental purposes is the so-called " Iowa City," or " Bird's-eye marble." This is nothing more than fossil coral " (*Acervularia Davidsoni*) imbedded in the common Devonian limestone and often perfectly consolidated by carbonate of lime so that it may be polished like ordinary marble. When so polished its appearance is very beautiful, for the whole internal structure of the coral is as well shown as it is in living specimens, and yet it is hard and compact as real marble." The stone would be valuable could it be obtained in blocks of large size. Unfortunately it occurs in pieces of but a few pounds' weight ; it is used therefore only for paper-weights, and small ornaments of various kinds.

Maryland.—The principal marble quarries of this State are located near Cockeysville and Texas, some 16 miles north of Baltimore, on the Northern Central Railroad. Here there occurs a small and isolated area of Lower Silurian (?) dolomite of medium texture and white color that has been very extensively used for general building purposes in Baltimore, Washington, and the neighboring towns, and to a less extent in Philadelphia. In the quarries the stone lies in large horizontal masses, and blocks 28 by 10 by 3 feet have been quarried entire. This stone was used in the construction of Christ Church in Baltimore, the Washington Monument and the columns and heavy platforms of the Capitol extensions at Washington, D. C.

Near Union Bridge, in Frederick County, there occurs a fine-grained and compact white magnesian limestone, but which has not been quarried to any extent.

The only true conglomerate or breccia marble that has ever been utilized to any extent in the United States is found near Point of Rocks, Frederick County, in this State. The rock, which belongs geologically to the Triassic formations, is composed of rounded and angular fragments of all sizes, up to several inches in diameter, of quartz and magnesian limestone imbedded in a fine gray calcareous groundmass. This composition renders the proper dressing of the stone a matter of some difficulty, since the hard quartz pebbles break away from the softer parts in which they lie, leaving numerous cavities to be filled with colored wax or shellac. It should therefore never be worked with hammer and chisel, but only with saw and grinding material, and no attempt made at other than plain surfaces. The stone was used for the pillars in the old Hall of Representatives in the Capitol at Washington, and a polished slab 34 inches long by 20 inches wide, may be seen in the National Museum at Washington. The pebbles forming the stone are of so varied shades that to state its exact color is a matter of difficulty. Red, white, and slate-gray are perhaps the prevailing tints. On account of its locality this stone has been popularly called "Potomac" marble, or sometimes calico marble, in reference to its structure and spotted appearance. The formation from whence it is derived is said to commence near the mouth of the Monocacy River, and to extend along the Potomac to Point of Rocks, and along the valley on the eastern side of the Catoctin Mountain to within 2 miles of Frederick. The writer is informed, moreover, that the same formation occurs in Virginia, near Leesburgh, and that here the quartzose pebbles are almost entirely lacking, thereby rendering the stone much less difficult to work.

Massachusetts.—Crystalline limestones and dolomites of such a character as to assume the name of marble are now or have been in times past quarried in various towns of Berkshire County, in this State. The stones are all white or some shade of gray color, medium fine-grained in texture, and are better adapted for general building than for any form of ornamental work.

The quarries at **Lee** were opened in 1852, and the stone has

been used in the Capitol extension at Washington and the new
city buildings in Philadelphia; but little of it has been used for
monuments. In the quarries the stone lies very massive, and
it is stated cubes 20 feet in diameter could be obtained if
necessary. The Sheffield quarries were opened about 1838.
The rock here is massive, with but little jointing. Natural
blocks 40 feet square, and 3 feet in thickness can be obtained.
The Alford stone is used mostly for monumental work, and appears very durable. Much of the marble from these localities
contains small crystals of white tremolite which weather out on
exposure, leaving the rock with a rough pitted surface. This
is very noticeable in the exterior walls of the Capitol building
at Washington, already noted.

Missouri.—The writer has seen but few true marbles from
this State, though colored marbles of fine quality equalling the
variegated varieties of Tennessee are reported by Professor
Broadhead as occurring in Iron, Madison, and Cape Girardeau
Counties. The Iron County stone is reported as light drab in
color, with buff veins. The outcrop occupies an exposure of
several hundred feet of a low bluff on Marble Creek near the
east line adjoining Madison County. The Madison County
marble occurs near Fredericktown, and is described as the best-
appearing marble in the State, both in regard to color and texture, the colors being red, peach-blossom, and greenish, beautifully blended. The stone is represented as very durable, but
liable to tarnish on a polished surface when exposed to the
weather. The Cape Girardeau stone is represented as of a
variety of colors—purple, yellow, red, pink, gray, and greenish
all being enumerated; the supply is unlimited. None of these
marbles are at present systematically worked, owing to lack of
capital and distance from market. Professor Broadhead further
states that few of the marble beds of southeastern Missouri are

thick enough to be economically worked, as there would be too large a portion of waste material.

No pure white crystalline marbles are as yet known to occur within the State limits. Other stones capable of receiving a polish and suitable for marble are stated to occur in the counties of Saint Louis, Saint Charles, Warren, Montgomery, Ralls, Calloway, Lincoln, Cooper, Pettis, Cass, Jackson, Livingston, and Clay.*

Montana.—This State as yet quarries no marble of importance. There were exhibited, however, at the Centennial, in Philadelphia, 1876, and since then in the National Museum at Washington, two samples from Lewis and Clarke County that are worthy of note, since they form the nearest approach to the imported Italian black and gold marble from the Spezzia quarries of any at present found in America. The rock is very close and compact, of a dark blue-gray color, and traversed by irregular wavy bands of varying width of a dull chrome-yellow color. So far as observed the stone is far inferior in point of beauty to its Italian prototype, and apparently would prove more difficult to work.

Nevada.—Practically no attempts have as yet been made toward working the marble deposits of this state, and indeed very little is known regarding their extent and qualities. Prof. Newberry† states that in the Tempiute Mountains, in the southeastern part of the State, there are beds of limestone of a great variety of colors and textures, susceptible of a high polish and scarcely inferior in point of beauty to any marble imported from the old world.

New Jersey.—At one time extensive marble quarries were worked in the outcrops of Devonian limestone at Lower Har-

---

* See also Bulletin No. 1, Missouri Geological Survey, 1890.
† School of Mines Quarterly, No. 1, vol. X. 1888, p. 70.

mony in Warren County. The stone is of a grayish hue, in places banded owing to alternate lines of light and dark minerals. Nodules of hornblende and steatite are scattered through the rock, and rarely there is pyrite and some graphite. The stone was worked mainly for the Pennsylvania market.

A very beautiful stone known commercially as the " Rose Crystal Marble" has been quarried on a subordinate ridge of the Jenny Jump Mountain range in this county, at the corner of the Hope and Danville road, and the road running northward along the Great Meadows.

The stone consists mainly of large white, flesh pink, and rose colored crystals of calcite interspersed with black mica, a green pyroxene and occasional black tourmalines.

Its texture is such that it must be handled with some care, but it polishes well and makes a beautiful ornamental stone for interior work. It is said to have been obtainable in blocks 8 x 3 x 2 feet without seams or flaws.* The fact that the quarries were situated seven miles from the nearest railroad may account in part for its being no longer worked, but it is a great pity that so beautiful a stone should not be utilized.

New York.—The belts of Archæan dolomite which lie to the north of New York City and cross the State in a northeasterly direction furnish a very fair quality of white and gray marbles that have at various times been quiet extensively utilized. Of these belts, one reaches New York Island, crossing the Harlem River at Kings' Bridge ; another outcrops on the Sound near New Rochelle ; others still strike the Hudson above New York, at Hastings, Dobbs Ferry, Sing Sing, etc. Several of these beds furnish good marbles for building stone, gray, blue, or white, but none that is fine for decorative purposes. The best marbles yet obtained from the series of deposits are those of

---

* Annual Report State Geologist of New Jersey, 1872.

Tuckahoe and Pleasantville in Westchester County. The Tuckahoe marble is pure white in color, and coarser than those of New England in general, notice elsewhere. It is somewhat irregular in quality, but the better grades are highly esteemed for architectural purposes, and have been used in some of the finest buildings in New York City. By exposure to the impure atmosphere of the city, its color changes to a light gray. This is apparently due to its coarseness of texture, which gives a roughness to the surface, and causes the smoke and dust to adhere to it more closely than they would to a finer stone.

The dolomite belt in which the Pleasantville marble quarries are situated is one of the broadest known, being more than half a mile wide. It consists chiefly of beds of impure dolomite, white or banded, which contain too much siliceous matter to be available for building or ornamental purposes, with some layers, often of a considerable thickness, of pure white marble, in part similar to that of Tuckahoe, and partly still more coarsely crystalline. These beds are more or less interstratified with layers of granite or gneiss, the whole series standing nearly on edge. The belt which furnishes the snowflake marble is about one hundred feet wide, standing vertical, and consists throughout of pure white dolomite, almost without cloud or stain, and with no foreign matter.*

On account of its coarseness this stone is not well adapted for carved work or for use in long columns. The Tuckahoe stone is not quite so coarse in texture and has been more extensively employed for building purposes. At Sing Sing and Dover Plains are other quarries of rather coarse white dolomite marble, but which are not extensively worked.

A very coarsely crystalline light-gray magnesian limestone of Archæan age occurs at Gouverneur, in St. Lawrence County.

---

* Newberry, Report of Judges, vol. III. International Exposition, 1876.

Although too coarse for carved work it answers well for massive structures, and, as it acquires a good surface and polish, is used largely for monuments as well as for building and for ornamental work. It is believed to be durable, since gravestones in the vicinity which have been set upwards of seventy years still present clean and uniform surfaces, and are free from lichens and discolorations of any kind.

Two excellent varieties of colored marbles occur in the Lower Silurian formation at Plattsburgh and Chazy, in Clinton County, in this State, and which are commercially known as "Lepanto"* and French gray. The first consists of a close fine-grained gray groundmass with pink and white fossil remains, which are evidently crinoidal. The second is more uniformly gray and bears larger fossils. It is an excellent stone, and, with perhaps the exception of those of Tennessee, has been used more extensively for mantels, table tops, tiling, and general interior decorative work than any other of our marbles.

At Glens Falls, on the Hudson River, occurs an extensive deposit of dark blue-black magnesian limestone, certain strata of which furnish the finest varieties of black marble at present quarried in this country. The stone is very fine-grained and compact, and, when polished, of a deep, lustrous black color, though the uniformity of the surface is sometimes broken by the presence of a small white fossil. A two-foot cube of this stone is in the National collections. The finest quality of this marble occurs in a single stratum some 12 feet in thickness. The poorer qualities are burned for lime, of which they furnish material of exceptional purity. Black marble is also quarried to some extent at Willsborough, in Essex County. At Port Henry, in this same county, there is quarried a green and

---

* The Lepanto marble is figured in Pl. xxxii. of the Census Report, where it is wrongly set down as from Isle La Motte, Vermont.

white speckled marbled, composed of an intimate mixture of serpentine, calcite, and dolomite that has been used for interior decorative work. The stone has been noticed more fully under the head of serpentine.

At Lockport there is extensively quarried a soft gray crinoidal Upper Silurian limestone in which the fossils are frequently of a pink or bluish opalescent color. It is used to some extent for mantels and other ornamental purposes.*

In the town of Warwick, in Orange County, there is found a beautiful, coarsely crystalline marble of a carmine-red color, sometimes slightly mottled or veined with white. But little of it has been used and the supply is reported as small.

North Carolina.—Although no quarries of marble are at the present time worked to any extent in this State, there occur within its limits numerous deposits of most excellent material that only require enterprise and capital to bring to a ready market. One of the most important of these is near Red Marble Gap, in Macon County. The rock is a beautiful bright flesh pink, sometimes blotched or striped with blue and yellow. The texture is fine and even, and it acquires an excellent surface and polish. The stone is stated by Professor Kerr to occur in the side of the mountain in cliffs 150 feet or more in height, and blocks of almost any size can be obtained. It is quite different from anything now in the market, and would doubtless find a ready sale if once introduced. Other marbles of white or blue-gray color occur in Murphy, and Valley Town, Cherokee County; Warren Springs, Madison County, and near Marion, in McDowell County. Lack of transportation facilities at present is a serious drawback to the introduction of any of these into our principal markets. I have seen, also, small

---

* J. S. Newberry in report on building and ornamental stones, vol. III. International Exhibition Reports, p. 158.

pieces of very compact deep blue-black crystalline limestone, taking a high polish and suitable for the finest grades of ornamental work from near Nantehaleh, Swain County, in this State. Portions of the stone are traversed by a coarse network of pure white calcite veins that greatly add to its beauty.

Pennsylvania.—The belt of Lower Silurian limestone that extends from Sadsbury and Bart Townships, in Lancaster County, in a general easterly direction through Chester County, and through the western half of Montgomery County, includes within its area the only quarries of merchantable marble at present worked within the State limits. According to Professor Rogers* this belt forms the bed of a narrow valley some 58 miles in total length, extending from near Abington, in Montgomery County, to the source of Big Beaver Creek, in Lancaster County. The prevailing colors of the stone throughout the larger portion of this area are yellowish or bluish, and it is, as a consequence, suitable only for making quicklime or for ordinary rough building purposes. On the southern side of the valley, however, between Brandywine and Wissahickon Creeks, the stone has become highly metamorphosed and converted into a crystalline granular marble, white or some shade of blue in color, though often variously veined or mottled. All the quarries as yet opened are situated in Montgomery County, on the steeply upturned or overturned edges of the outcrops within half a mile of the southern edge of the formation between Marble Hall and the Chester County line.

It is stated that quarries were first opened here about the time of the Revolutionary war, and that up to 1840 this stone was the favorite and almost only material used in the better class of stone buildings in and about Philadelphia. At about the latter date increased facilities for transportation brought

---

* Report of First Geological Survey of Pennasylvania, vol. I. p 211.

the better varieties of eastern marbles and other stones into competition with it and its use has as a consequence considerably diminished. Among the important buildings constructed of the stone during its popularity were the United States Custom-house and Mint, the Naval Asylum and Girard College, while the seemingly endless rows of red brick houses with white marble steps, door and window trimmings, are even now as characteristic of Philadelphia as are the brown-stone fronts of New York City. The sarcophagi for General and Martha Washington, at Mount Vernon, are also of this material.

While the Montgomery County stone has shown itself to be very durable, in point of beauty it falls far short of the marbles from the more Eastern States, and hence its use for any form of ornamental work has almost entirely ceased. There were, however, on exhibition at the Philadelphia Exposition of 1876 (and since then transferred to the National Museum) samples of this limestone from along the Lebanon Branch of the Philadelphia and Reading Railroad, some of which gave promise of great utility. I would mention especially two samples from Myerstown and Mill Lane. These are very fine-grained and compact, of a drab or bluish color on a polished surface, and traversed by wavy and very irregularly anastomosing, nearly black lines. They seem in every way admirably adapted for decorative work, though I am not aware that they have as yet been at all used for this purpose. Newberry states* that a fine variety of black marble occurs in or near Williamsport, Lycoming County. I have never seen the stone and know nothing further regarding it. A black limestone that takes a fine polish and appears well suited for interior work is stated also to occur near the east end of Mosquito Valley, in the same county. For exterior work it is stated to be unsuited, as it splinters up badly on exposure.

---

* Op. cit. pp. 138, 139.

Tennessee.—The valley of East Tennessee is underlaid by limestone of Lower Silurian age that furnishes some of the finest and most beautiful grades of colored marbles at present quarried in the United States.

At the present time the most extensive quarries are situated in Knox and Hawkins Counties. The prevailing colors found here are chocolate red and white, often coarsely variegated and fossiliferous, though finely and evenly crystalline varieties of a beautiful pink or strawberry color, with scarcely a trace of fossil remains, also occur. All of them cut to a sharp edge and acquire a beautiful and lasting polish not excelled and rarely equalled by any foreign or domestic marbles. Of foreign marbles, so far as the writer is aware, they have no exact counterpart, but perhaps resemble the Rosso de Levanto from Spezia, or the Persian fiorto, more closely than any other that can be mentioned.

Besides the localities above mentioned, colored marbles occur in the following counties in this part of the State: Hancock, Grainger, Jefferson, Roane, Blount, Monroe, McMinn, and Bradley; some also occur in Meigs, Anderson, Union, and Campbell Counties. The Hawkins County marble is part of a comparatively short belt of Trenton and Nashville rocks lying west of Rogersville. It is some 16 or 17 miles long, and from 50 to 300 feet in thickness. The supply is therefore practically unlimited and inexhaustible. The best variety of the stone is used only for ornamental work, owing to its high price, being valued at from $2 to $3 per cubic foot delivered at the nearest railway station.

The Knox County quarries are mostly situated within a few miles of the city of Knoxville. According to Dr. Safford the entire thickness of the marble bed here is some 300 feet, the different layers of which vary from chocolate red and white variegated varieties through grayish white, pinkish, and more rarely greenish colors. The most esteemed variety has when polished, a brownish red color, with white spots and clouds, due to fossil corals and crinoids. The grayish white variety, which is the nearest approach to a truly white marble of any now found in the State, is greatly esteemed for tombstones, monuments, tiling, etc., and is said to be very durable, tombstones which have been exposed for upward of thirty years showing no signs of disintegration or wear. Both the Hawkins County and Knox County stones are very strong and heavy, weighing about 180 pounds per cubic foot, which is some 14 pounds heavier than granite. Quite similar variegated marbles are said to occur in many of the counties of the Cumberland table-land, as in Franklin County, on the Elk River and at the Oil Springs, on Leipor's Creek, in ˙ ·ury County. Some of the marbles of this latter place have ˙ᵼ grayish groundmass, with fleecy clouds of red and green.*

A beautiful olive-green fossiliferous marble is also found in the eleventh district of Davidson County, though the extent of the deposit is not known by the writer. Near Calhoun, in McMinn County, just south of the Chilhowee Mountain, occur breccia marbles of exceptional beauty, of pink and olive green colors. One quite unique stone from this locality is composed of a grayish-ground mass, with large rounded and angular fragments of a lemon-yellow color. These same marbles also occur in Greene, Cocke, Sevier, and all counties of the Unaka range, but they are not much worked, on account of the hardness of the included fragments.†

Dove-colored marbles are stated by the same authority to occur a few miles south of Manchester, Coffee County, and in

---

* Tennessee and its Agricultural and Mineral Wealth, by J. B. Killebrew, page 149.

† Geology of Tennessee, p. 221.

Wilson and Davidson Counties. Dark limestones, almost black when polished, and often traversed by veins of calcite, forming a good black marble, are not uncommon. Such occur in the vicinity of Jonesborough, Washington County; at Greeneville and Newport, Cocke County; on the Pigeons, in Sevier County; and also in McMinn and Polk Counties. They are at present but little used.

Colored marbles are also said to occur in the Western Tennessee Valley. These, though somewhat inferior in point of beauty to those of the East Valley, are still valuable stones. Perry, Decatur, Wayne, and Hardin Counties are mentioned as offering the best facilities. On Shoal Creek, in Lawrence County, are said to be beds of fawn-colored or brownish-red marbles, some 40 feet in thickness and extending on both sides of the creek for a distance of fifteen miles. The stone is often variegated by fleecy clouds of green or red, green and white colors. Owing to lack of transportation facilities it is not now in the market. In Wilson and Davidson Counties other beds of bluish or dove-colored marble occur, and in Rutherford County is a bed of pale yellow marble with serpentine veins of red and black dots. The extent of the deposit is not known, and at present the stone is seen only in the form of small objects for paper-weights and curiosities.

Texas.—The resources of this State are as yet but little known. There are on exhibition in the National Museum at Washington several samples of compact, light-colored Cretaceous limestones, from the vicinity of Austin, Travis County, a few of which are of such quality as to be used as marbles. There was on exhibition at the New Orleans Exposition in 1884–85 a marble fire-place and mantel of Austin marble that was worthy of more than passing notice. The stone was compact, very light drab in color, and interspersed with large fossil shells and transparent calcite crystal. This composition would

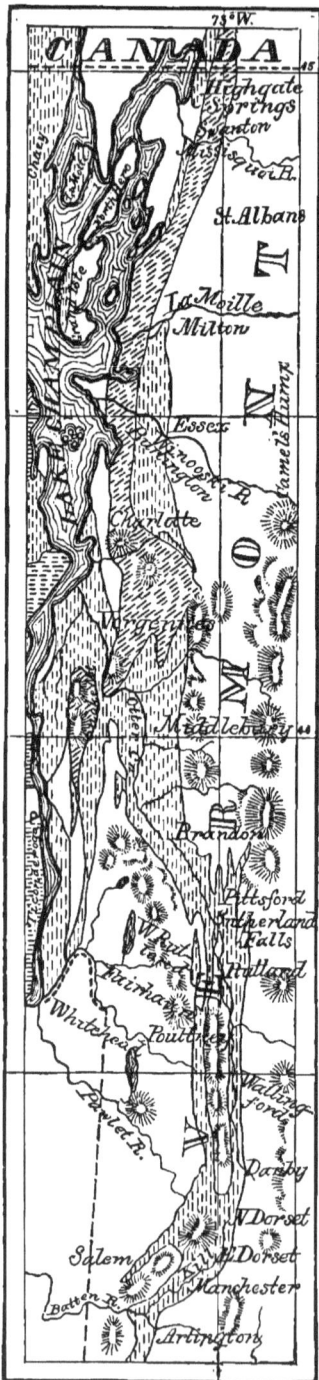

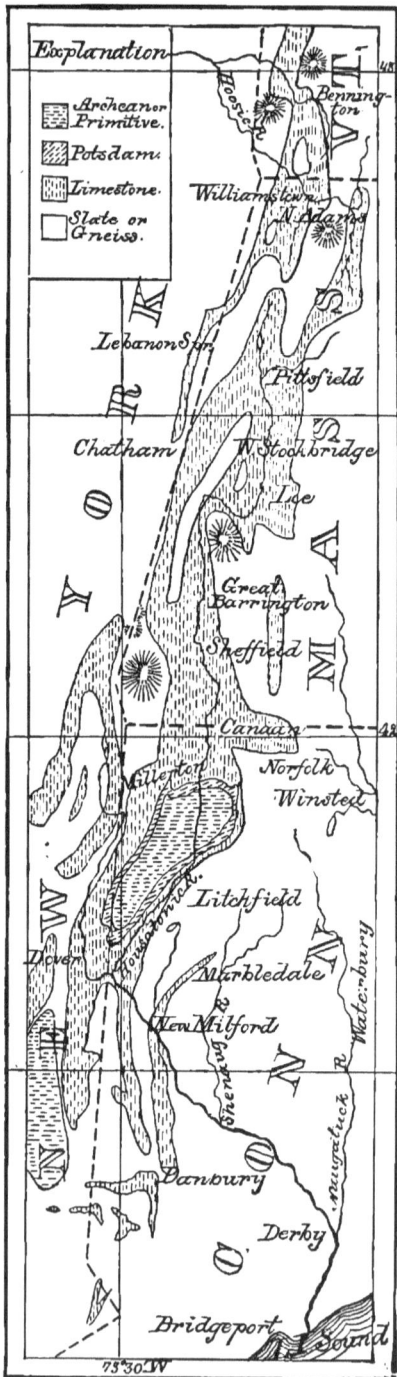

PLATE IV.

THE MARBLE REGION OF WESTERN NEW ENGLAND.

[The marble is indicated as limestone on the map.]

To face page 105.

render some care necessary in cutting, but the final result would seem to justify the outlay. Other marbles from Burnet and vicinity present a variety of colors, some of which are very pleasing. They range from blue-gray and distinctly crystalline to very fine and compact forms, designated as "mahogany-red," "red and white," "purple variegated," etc. The mahogany-red is dull in color, and traversed by a net-work of lighter lines. It is too hard and brittle to work economically. The most promising variety is the purple variegated. This presents an extremely compact base of a grayish, or light lavender-tint, which is traversed by fine, irregular lines of a red and purple color. The stone acquires an excellent surface and polish, but is so hard as to work with great difficulty.

Utah.—A yellowish white crystalline limestone, that can scarcely be called a marble, occurs near Payson, in this Territory, and a compact nearly black stone, interspersed with numerous white fossil shells, in the San Pete Valley. Neither stone can lay any claim to beauty, though possibly the last mentioned might be made to do as marble under certain circumstances.

Vermont.—Since this is the leading marble-producing State of the Union a brief description of the chief geological features of the marble formations may not be out of place here. According to Professor Brainard* this formation extends along the western borders of the States of Connecticut, Massachusetts, and Vermont, between the Green Mountain elevation, which extends from the Canada line nearly to Long Island Sound, and the intermittent Taconic Mountains, which extend south of Lake Champlain, and in places admit the marble veins within the border of New York. Of these immense for-

---

* The Marble Border of Western New England, p. 9.

mations, which are from 1,000 to 2,000 feet in thickness, the lower portion, known to geologists as the Calciferous (300 to 400 feet in thickness), is for the most part siliceous, partaking of the nature of the sandrock that underlies it. The upper portion, known as the Trenton (500 to 600 feet in thickness), is impure from the presence of clayey matter, partaking of the nature of the slate formation that overlies it. Only certain layers of the middle portions seem to have been fitted by their original constitution for the production of marble.

The limits of the formation may be best understood by reference to the accompanying map (Plate IV), redrawn from Professor Brainard's report.*

Professor Hitchcock† conveniently divides the marbles of this Sate into four groups or classes: (1) the common white and bluish or Eolian marble, so called from its occurring extensively on Mount Eolus; (2) the Winooski; (3) the variegated of Plymouth, and (4) the dark, almost black, of Isle La Motte. We will consider these in the order here given.

The beds of the Eolian variety as described by Prof. Hitchcock are not restricted to one locality, but are distributed over a large portion of western Vermont, the formation in which it occurs extending the entire length of the State, and usually interstratified with siliceous and magnesian limestones. The strata vary in thickness from a few inches to 6 or 8 feet, the thickest beds being usually found where the marble is coarse-grained and friable.

In texture this variety of the stone is as a rule fine-grained, and often saccharoidal, though less so than the Italian marbles. In color it varies from pure snowy white through all shades of bluish, and sometimes greenish, often beautifully mottled and

---

* By permission of the Middlebury Historical Society.
† Geology of Vermont, vol. II. p. 752.

veined, to deep blue black, the bluish and dark varieties being as a rule the finest and most durable. Many quarries have first and last been opened along this belt, and the industry has added materially to the prosperity of the towns here situated. Among those towns in which the quarry industry has been particularly active may be mentioned (beginning with the southernmost), Dorset, and East Dorset, Wallingford, West Rutland, Sutherland Falls (Proctor), Pittsford, Brandon, and Middlebury. As a rule the best marbles are said to occur where the beds or strata stand at a high angle, as at West Rutland.

The quarries in Dorset are mostly situated upon the sides of Mount Eolus, or Dorset Mountain, as it is also called, a section of which, after Hitchcock, is here given.

The thickness of the slaty cap rock is estimated at 498 feet, and the various beds of limestone below at 1,970 feet. Although but a small portion of this is suitable for quarrying, still the supply is readily seen to be inexhaustible. The prevailing colors of the stone, as at Rutland, are white and bluish, variously mottled and veined. According to Professor Seely, the first quarry opened in Dorset was by Isaac Underhill, in 1785, the stone being used chiefly for fire-jambs, chimney-backs, etc. The first marble grave-stones ever furnished here were the work of Jonas Stewart, in 1790.

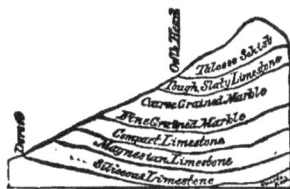

From Dorset the beds thin out toward the north, the more northerly beds, though thinner, usually furnishing the finer grained and more compact stone.

The marble strata in Rutland and Addison Counties appear in two parallel lines about 2 miles apart, stretching from the north line of Middlebury to the south line of Rutland, and are from 100 to 200 feet in thickness. These strata are not how-

ever homogeneous throughout, but as seen in the quarry openings the stone occurs in beds usually but a few feet in thickness
which vary considerably in color, so that several grades, from
pure white through greenish, bluish, and almost black, may be
taken from the same quarry.

Professor Hitchcock gives the following figures relative to
the marble-beds at one of the West Rutland quarries, beginning at the eastern side or top layer :

1. Upper blue layer, 4 feet thick.
2. Upper white layer, 3 feet 6 inches thick.
3. Gray limestone layer, 5 feet thick.
4. White statuary layer, 3 feet thick.
5. Striped layer, 1 foot 8 inches thick.
6. New white layer, 4 feet thick.
7. Wedged white layer, from 8 inches 2 feet 6 inches thick.
8. Muddy layer, 4 feet thick.
9. Striped green layer, 4 feet thick.
10. Camphor-gum layer, 3 feet thick.
11. White layer, 9 feet thick.
12. Blue layer, 3 feet 6 inches.

The quarries themselves at this village lie along the western
base of a low range of hills, which, to the ordinary observer,
give no sign of the vast wealth of material concealed beneath
their gray and uninteresting exteriors. In quarrying, the best
beds are selected, and upon their upturned edges excavation is
commenced, first by blasting, to remove the weathered and
worthless material, and afterward by channeling, drilling, and
wedging ; no powder being used lest the fine massive blocks
become shattered and unfit for use. The quarry thus descends
in the form of a rectangular pit, with almost perpendicular,
often overhanging, walls, to a depth of sometimes more than
200 feet, when the beds are found to curve to the eastward and
pass under the hill, becoming thus more nearly horizontal ; in
following these the quarry assumes the appearance of a vast
cavern from whose smoke-blackened, gaping mouths one would
little suppose could be drawn the huge blocks of snow-white
material lying in gigantic piles in the near vicinity (see Plates
I and V). Some of the quarries have been partially roofed
over to protect them from snow and rain, and seem like mines

PLATE V.

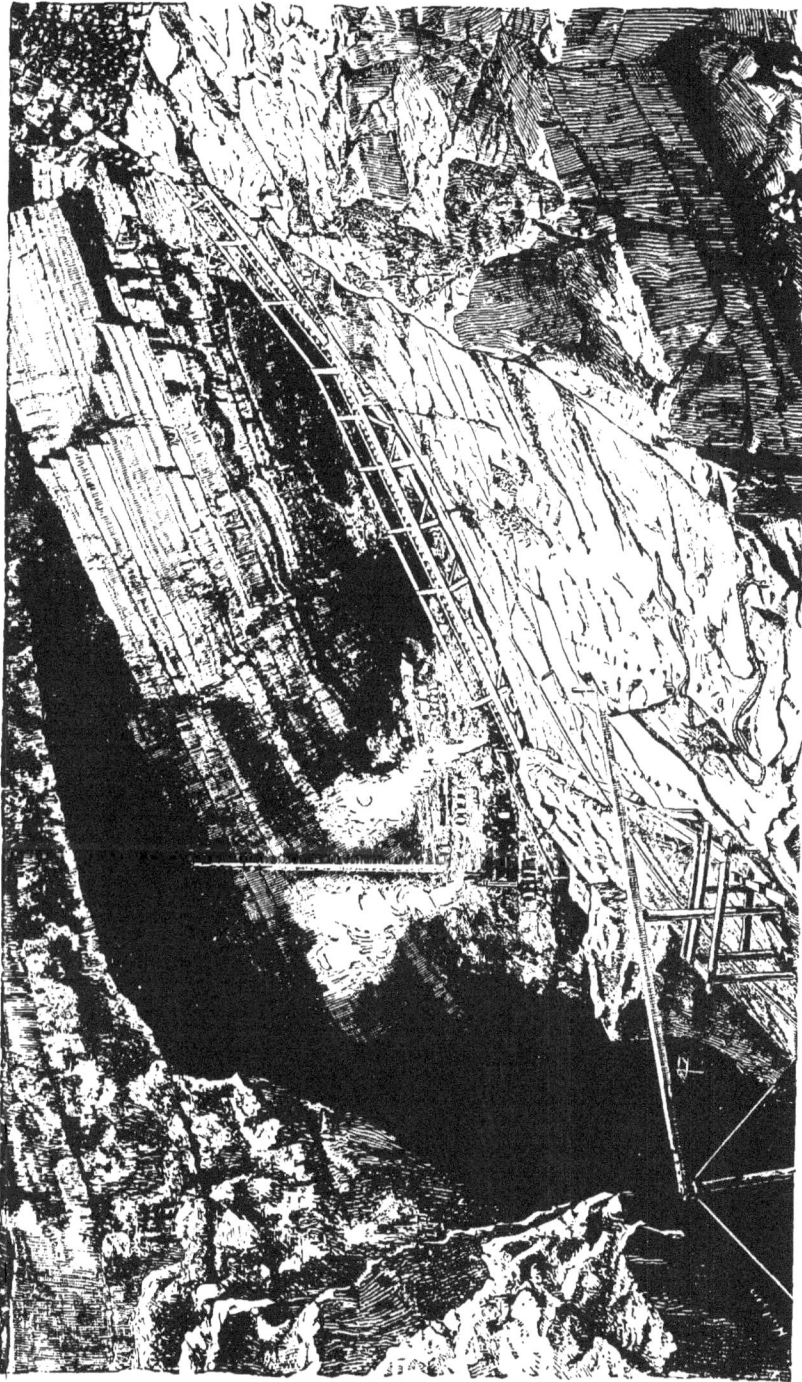

INTERIOR VIEW OF MARBLE QUARRY AT WEST RUTLAND, VERMONT.

To face page 108.

rather than quarries. The scant daylight at the bottom is scarce sufficient to guide the quarryman in his work. As one peers cautiously over the edge into the black and seemingly bottomless abyss, naught but darkness and ascending smoke and steam are visible, while his astonished ears are filled with such an unearthly clamor of quarrying machines, the puffing of engines, and the shouts of laborers, as is comparable with nothing within the range of our limited experience, and the reader is at liberty to make his own comparisons.

The stone taken from the quarries is worked up in the companies' shops in the immediate vicinity or shipped in the rough as occasion demands. The supply is used for monumental, decorative, or statuary work and general building.

At Sutherland Falls the stone is very massive, and large blocks are taken out for building purposes. Some of the most valuable marbles, according to Professor Seely, are here known as the dark and light mourning vein varieties. The dark mourning vein has a ground of deep blue, while lines, nearly black, run through it in a zigzag course, presenting a beautiful appearance. The light mourning vein has similar veins, but the ground is lighter. The quarries at this place are described by Professor Seely as being in the form of a hollow cube cut into a hill, with perpendicular walls on the north and west rising to a height of nearly 100 feet, open to the sky, and with an acre of rock forming its horizontal marble floor. Over this floor are run channeling machines, cutting out long parallel blocks which are afterwards cut up into convenient size, lifted from their beds, and taken to the mills to be sawn.

It is stated * that Pittsford has the honor of having one of the earliest quarries in the State, if not the earliest, Jeremiah Sheldon having worked marble here as early as 1795. There

---

* The Marble Border of Western New England, p. 46.

are three beds of marble running through the town, north and
south. The most easterly has a breadth of some 200 feet, and
the stone is of the same character as that at Sutherland Falls
or Proctor, as the town is now called. The middle bed is separated from the first by about 200 feet of lime rock. The bed
itself is some 400 feet wide, and the stone varies in color from
pure white to dark blue. The third or west bed which is
thought to correspond to that of West Rutland is about half
a mile west of the central and is about 400 feet wide. The
stone is dark-blue and often beautifully mottled. Some of the
beds here, as at West Rutland, furnish a beautiful snow-white
saccharoidal stone suitable for statuary purposes, for which it
has been used to a slight extent. The Vermont statuary marble, however, differs from its Italian prototype, in being of a
dead white color and lacking the mellow, waxy lustre so characteristic of the Italian stone.

Several outcrops of marble occur in Middlebury, and which
have been worked for many years past ; but in consequence of
the thinness of the beds, their badly jointed structure, and the
interstratification of a magnesian slate that produces numerous
" rising seams," it is said to be quite difficult to obtain perfectly sound blocks of large size. Nevertheless much valuable
material has been taken out here, both for architectural and
monumental work.

The bed of primordial rock known to geologists as the
" red sand-rock," which occurs in the northwestern part of the
State, bordering on Lake Champlain, is, as a rule, a hard, dark-
red sandstone, containing some 8 or 9 per cent of potash, with
about the same amounts of iron and lime. The entire formation, which is some 2,000 feet in thickness, is, however, by no
means uniform in composition, but includes considerable beds
of limestone, dolomite, slate, and shale. It is the dolomitic
layer which furnishes the peculiar red-and-white mottled stone

popularly known as Winooski marble. According to a writer in the American Naturalist,* the beds of this marble appear first one or two miles north of Burlington, and extend in a somewhat interrupted series north through St. Albans, and end between that place and Swanton. More than thirty years ago a quarry was opened in this rock about 6 miles from Burlington, but owing to the hardness of the stone the enterprise proved a failure and the quarries were abandoned. Later, quarries were opened at St. Albans, and still more recently were re-opened at Burlington, the stone being used largely for flooring-tiles, wainscotings, and general interior decorative work. As a rule the stone is crystalline and very hard, much harder than ordinary marble. Its color is quite variable, though some shade of red mottled with white usually predominates. Some varieties are beautifully light pink and white, or pink and deep blue-gray or greenish. The very common chocolate-red and white variety is put upon the market as *Lyonaise marble*, and is used largely for tiling, its natural color being often rendered darker by oiling.

Chemically the stone is a dolomite, though varying widely in composition in samples from different localities. Some samples show a very decided brecciated structure, while in others this entirely disappears. It is, as a rule, very hard to work, and, as exhibited in the capitol building at Albany, New York, the surface is often disfigured by irregular cavities and flaws which are rather unsightly. The color is said to fade on exposure to the weather, and hence the stone is used mostly for interior work.

An excellent outcrop of this marble occurs on the shore of Mallet's Bay, in the town of Colchester. The strata at this point are nearly horizontal, and in many places form the banks

---

* George H. Perkins, American Naturalist, Feb. 1881.

of the lake. One of the quarries is so situated that a vessel can be brought up alongside and loaded with blocks with as much ease as they are usually loaded upon carts or cars at inland quarries. The stone occurs in beds varying in thickness from 1 to 6 feet, and blocks of almost any size can be obtained. It is hard to work, but as a consequence is very durable when once finished, being not easily scratched or scarred.

The best developments of the rock for marble quarrying are at Colchester, as already mentioned, Milton, Georgia, Saint Albans, and Swanton. At the last-named place there also occurs a beautiful gray marble, with angular fossil fragments of a white and pink color, identical with the " Lepanto " marble of New York. There is also a fine and compact dove-colored marble here, admirably adapted for decorative work, but the quarries are now abandoned.

The Plymouth marble, so called, is a quite pure dolomite, an analysis by Dr. Hunt resulting as follows :

	Per cent.
Carbonate of lime	53.9
Carbonate of magnesia	44.7
Oxides of iron and alumina	1.3
	99.9

The stone occurs in the talcose schist formation near the centre of the town of Plymouth, at an elevation of 250 feet above the Plymouth pond. Quarries were opened here about 1835, but were soon abandoned, as the demand at that time was almost altogether for white marble. The beds dip 60° to the east, and the quarry walls, which have been exposed to the weather for twenty years, seem unaffected. In color the stone is blue or bluish-brown, diversified with long stripes and figures of various shapes in white. It is fine grained and compact, splitting with equal facility in every direction.*

The Isle La Motte marble derives its name from Isle La Motte, in Lake Champlain, where it occurs in considerable abundance. It also occurs on several other islands in this lake and upon its banks in many places. According to Professor Hitchcock this was the first marble worked in the State, quarries having been opened prior to the Revolutionary war. The stone, which is largely used for flooring-tiles, is very dark, almost black in color, and highly fossiliferous, having undergone less metamorphism than the marble in the interior of the State. So far as the author has observed, its color and texture are such as to preclude its obtaining a high rank for purely decorative purposes, but for floor-tiling is much esteemed and very durable. Fossil shells of great beauty are not uncommon, and, being snowy white in color, show up in strong contrast to the dark paste in which they are embedded.

Virginia.—The extensive area comprehended under the title of the Valley of Virginia embraces " all the portion of the State having for its eastern boundary the western slope of the Blue Ridge and its inflected continuation the Poplar Camp and Iron Mountains, and for its western the Little North and a portion of the Big North Mountain, with the southern prolongation of the former, Caldwell and Brushy Mountains; and near its southwestern termination the line of knobs forming the extension of Walker's Mountain."†

The central portion of the valley as thus outlined is underlaid largely by limestones of Silurio-Cambrian age, which are in several places, according to the authority above quoted, capable of yielding good marbles. The special varieties men-

---

* Geology of Vermont, vol. II. p. 776.

† Rogers, Geology of the Virginias, pp. 203, 204.

tioned are : (1) a dun-colored marble met with near New Market and Woodstock, and on the opposite side of the Massanutten Mountain in Page County; (2) a mottled bluish marble to the west of New Market ; (3) a gray marble occurring some three-fourths of a mile in a southeasterly direction from Buchanan, in Botetourt County; (4) a white marble of exquisite color and fine grain about 5 miles from Lexington, in Rockbridge County ; (5) a red marble occurring only in the Cambrian formations lying among the mountains in the more southwestern counties ; and (6) a shaded marble found in Rockingham County. This last is said to be compact, susceptible of a beautiful polish, and of a yellowish gray and slate color. None of the above have as yet received more than a local application.

At Craigsville, in Augusta County, there occurs a gray, sometimes pink-spotted encrinal limestone which acquires a good polish, and though in no way remarkable for its beauty is capable of extensive application for furniture and interior decoration. The Archæan area to the eastward of the Valley of Virginia also includes sundry areas of workable marble. It is stated by Rogers that " near the mouth of the Tye River (in Nelson County) and the Rockfish, a true marble is found, of a beautiful whiteness and of a texture which renders it susceptible of a fine polish as well as being readily wrought with the chisel. A few miles from Lynchburg, in Campbell County, a good marble is likewise found." " The Tye River marble and one or more analogous veins " are further stated to " have all the characters of a statuary marble of fine quality, and should not some peculiarity, as yet unperceived, prevent their application for the purposes of the sculptor, they will no doubt be looked upon as very valuable possessions." The writer has seen none of the material from this locality. White and pink marbles of excellent quality also occur in the vicinity of Goose

Creek, in Loudoun County. I have seen samples of the white, which for purity of color, fineness of grain, and general excellence, are not excelled by any marble now quarried in the United States, but the extent of the deposit is as yet unknown.

These same beds also produce a green or verdantique marble of great beauty. The stone is an impure magnesian limestone admixed with a large amount of serpentinous matter. The prevailing hue is green, but the stone is streaked and blotched in various shades and often brecciated. It is well adapted for interior work, but the presence of abundant pyrite renders it unfit for exterior application.

The stalagmitic deposits upon the floors of the caverns at Luray, in Page County, furnish, when cut, occasional fine pieces of the so-called onyx marble, but the stone is too easily fractured and too uneven in texture to be worked economically as is noted elsewhere, even were the deposits of sufficient extent to warrant the opening of quarries.

Wyoming.—The resources of this State are not as yet fully known. White and greenish marbles of good quality have been stated * to occur on Cedar Creek in the extreme eastern part of the Platte River valley and the Savary section in the extreme west. In the collections of the National Museum are to be seen samples of a fine-grained and compact reddish marble variegated with white and drab, from quarries in Muskrat Cañon in township 30 west, range 65 west. The stone acquires a good polish and is somewhat harder than a majority of the marbles now worked.

The published returns of the eleventh census give the following figures relative to the marble industry of the United States for the year 1889 :—

---

* Stone, April 1889.

| States. | Product. | |
	Cubic feet.	Value.
California.................	33,792	$87,030
Georgia................. ..	250,000	196,250
Maryland...................	333,305	139.816
New York.................	1,171,550	354,197
Tennessee.................	309,709	419.467
Vermont	1,068,305	2,169,560
All other states............	150,552	121,850
Total	3,320,213	$3,488,170

(4) THE ONYX MARBLES, OR TRAVERTINES.

The so-called onyx marbles, although of the same composition, differ from those of the common type in being chemical
deposits rather than altered sedimentary beds. Like the
stalagmitic deposits in caves, they are formed by the evaporation of water holding carbonate of lime in solution, and owe
their banded structure and variegated colors to the intermittent
character of the deposition, and the presence or absence of
various impurities, mainly metallic oxides. The term onyx,
as commonly applied is a misnomer, and has been given merely
because in their banded appearance they somewhat resemble
the true onyx, which is a variety of agate. The stone is properly a travertine. It is an interesting illustration of the mis-
leading character of popular names that the onyx marbles, and
particularly those from Algeria and Egypt, are so universally
known as alabaster, while true alabaster is a pure white and
compact variety of gypsum; in fact the alabaster boxes mentioned in the scriptures, as used for holding precious ointments,
are said to have been in reality constructed of travertine.

Owing to their translucency, delicacy and variety of colors, the readiness with which they can be worked and the high polish which they admit of, these marbles have long been favorites for smaller ornamentation and highly decorative work, and will doubtless long so continue. As with the red granites of Syene, and the green and red porphyries, the ancient Egyptians knew their value, and utilized them as long ago as the time of the Rameses ; the ancient Romans, too, appreciated their beauty and utilized them in the construction of their monuments and the interior decorations of their houses.

The only onyx marble until recently of any commercial importance within the limits of the United States, is found at San Luis Obispo, California. The stone as I have seen it in the dealers' shops in San Francisco, and as shown in the National collection, is nearly white, finely banded, translucent, and takes a beautiful surface and polish. It lacks the variety of colors of the Mexican onyx, but is nevertheless a beautiful stone and if it can be obtained in any abundance will find a ready market.

According to Mr. Angell,* the San Luis Obispo onyx quarries are situated in the heart of the Santa Lucia Mountains. There are two openings on sections 9 and 16, township 31 south, range 15 east, Mount Diablo meridian.

The two out-croppings so far discovered are about half a mile apart, one on the northern and one on the southern slope of a hill which rises about 80 feet between them. Whether or no they are portions of the same bed is yet to be determined. The strike of the two is not the same. The rock of the northern outcrop is milky white. That of the southern variegated in yellow, green, pink, blue, golden and red colors beautifully

---

* Tenth Annual Report State Mineralogist of California, 1890, p. 584.

blended.   The enclosing rock is sandy slate, the ledges of the
onyx standing nearly perpendicular and having a thickness of
about 16 feet.

The stone is stated to be worth about $100.00 a ton in San
Francisco, and when polished about $10.00 a square foot.

A dull red resinous, or yellow travertine, but which occurs
only in small masses, has been quarried in times past at Suisin
in the same State, and a beautiful light emerald green variety
in Siskiyou county, but neither deposit, so far as can be learned, is sufficiently extensive to have any great commercial value.
Other onyx marbles are mentioned in the various reports of the
the State mineralogist as occuring in the State, but not having
seen samples, the writer is obliged to quote wholly from other
authorities.   An orange and blue variety is stated to occur in
the southeast quarter of section 9, township 32 south, range 15
east, Mt. Diablo meridian.

An onyx marble is also stated to occur in the form of veins
and bunches in the limestone of Slover Mountain near the town
of Colton in San Bernardino County.   The stone is described
as beautifully striped and banded with various shades of yellow
and brown.   It is regarded as a promising stone.*

The serpentines and other marbles occuring here are noted
elsewhere.

A recent find of high grade onyx is reported from near
Prescott, in Yavapai County, Arizona.   The colors are given as
green, white, black and white, milky, red, old gold and brown.
At the time this work goes to press the writer has had no
opportunity of personally inspecting the stone, and hence attempts to give no detailed description of its qualities.

Quarries of the oynx marbles have on sundry occasions been
opened in the stalagmitic deposits of caves in Missouri, but the

---

* Annual Report of State Mineralogist, 1888, p. 509.

stone is stated by dealers to be soft and of too dull a color to be greatly desirable. The similar deposits in the Luray caves of Virginia have furnished occasional blocks of considerable beauty, but the rock is, as a rule, too coarsely crystalline and too friable, to be of value, even when the colors are good. At least this is the case with a majority of the blocks in the National collections at Washington. I am told by Dr. G. Brown Goode, however, that it is a common thing to find in the country mansions of Virginia, very handsome mantels of this stone, but which have as a rule been cut from stray blocks found loose in the fields. As above noted, the San Luis Obispo stone is the one of chief commercial importance at present. The Mexican onyx differs from that of California, in presenting a greater variety of colors. Creamy-white, amber yellow, streaked or blotched with green or red, to uniformly light green or green with red blotches are common. Cut across the grain the stone often presents a beautifully banded structure like the grain of wood. Cut in this way, however, it is very weak, and needs always to be backed by slabs of stronger and cheaper material. The stone occurs in such abundance at Tecali, State of Puebla, Mexico, that it has been used in rough blocks for building the native houses, and I am informed by M. Ferrari, of the Mexican Geological Commission, that the name Tecalli was given the locality on this account, the word being derived from two Aztec words *tetl*, stone, and *calli*, house. When cut into thin slabs the stone is quite translucent, and I am informed by this same authority that it has been used in this form for window panes in some of the public buildings of the City of Mexico. M. Mariano Barcena, who read a paper describing the stone and its mode of occurrence before the Philadelphia Academy of Science, at the time of the Exposition in 1876, reported on it as having a specific gravity of 2.90 (equal to a weight of 181 pounds to the cubic foot), and consisting of 96.36 per cent carbonate of lime and magnesia, some 3.54 per cent sulphate of lime and 0.10 per cent water, oxides of iron and manganese, the higher colored varieties showing larger percentages of the metallic oxides.

This stone is by far the most beautiful and variegated of the onyx marbles, and is now imported into the United States at the rate of many tons annually. It is used wholly for interior decorations, and is to be seen in the form of turned columns, and tops for small tables and stands, in any of the leading house-furnishing shops. Slabs of 1 inch in thickness are valued according to color at the rate of from $2.50 to $6.00 per square foot in the New York market.

The only other onyx marbles of any great commercial importance now quarried are from Algeria and Egypt in northern Africa. Some slight confusion among authorities seems to exist regarding these localities. Hull, in his work on Building and Ornamental Stones published in 1872, speaks of the Egyptian onyx as found at Blad Recam near the Ravine of Oned Abdallah. Delesse,* however, puts down Oned (or Oued) Abdallah as in Algeria, and states that the Egyptian onyx is from quarries situated at Benisouef, about twenty-five leagues south of Cairo, on the Nile, and at Syout (or Sivat) still farther south. The Syout stone is said to be distinguishable from that of Benisouef by its paler, slightly grayish color. As the African onyx now imported is almost universally known as Egyptian onyx, it seems probable that it is from either the Benisouef or Syout quarries, possibly both. The Egyptian stone lacks the variety of colors displayed by that of Mexico, varying only from whitish to amber yellow. It is nevertheless a beautiful stone, and is utilized for furniture tops, clocks, and a

---

* Materiaux de Construction de L'Exposition 1855, p. 158.

variety of smaller ornamentations. The quarries were first worked by the Egyptians and later by the Romans.

The Algerian stone is stated by Delesse* to occur at Ain-Tembaleck, near the river Isser, and to lie in irregular beds varying from a few inches to nearly ten feet in thickness. The stone is translucent, and of faintly white color, with a compact at times somewhat fibrous structure, and is stated to weigh about 170 pounds to the cubic foot. The Algerian, like the Egyptian quarries, are said to have furnished material for the embellishment of ancient Rome and Carthage, but for over a thousand years the quarries were completely lost sight of—to be rediscovered by M. Delmont, about 1849. Samples of the Algerian stone, received at Washington from the Musée Nationale de France, are nearly white or of a faint yellowish color, and in no way remarkable for their beauty.

Travertines or stalagmitic marbles (*L'albatre Calcaire*) are stated by Delesse † to be abundant in many parts of the province of Tuscany, Italy, notably at Serravezza, Vignone, San-Filippo, Grosseto, and Castel-Nuovo. None of these, so far as I can learn, are regularly imported into the United States. Small samples in the National collections, and marked as from Civita Vecchia and Montalto, are of a yellowish or dull white color, and not remarkably beautiful. Other stalagmitic marbles in this same collection, but not of sufficient beauty to be of great value, are from Jura in France, and Stuttgardt, Germany. The various cavities and caves in the limestone forming the rock of Gibraltar often furnish small masses of a handsomely banded brownish stalagmite which is cut into small ornaments and widely circulated. The National collections show a small mounted canon and several irregular blocks

---

* Materiaux de Construction de L'Exposition Universelle, 1855, p. 155.
† Op. sit., 176.

and slabs of this material, which, however, ranks rather as a curiosity than as a commercial article.

The above list includes all the travertines, onyx marbles, calcareous alabasters, or whatever they may be called, that, so far as the writer is aware, occur in such form as to be of any commercial value. A quarry within the limits of the United States, good in quality and in quantity, will prove a rich " find " for somebody.

(5) LIMESTONES AND DOLOMITES OTHER THAN MARBLES.

Alabama.—A dark compact limestone occurs near Calera, in Shelby County, and a light-colored, finely fossiliferous one near Dickson, in Colbert County. The last mentioned closely resembles in general appearance the celebrated limestone from Bedford, Indiana, to be noticed later. It appears of good quality, and works readily.

Arkansas.—Oolitic limestone suitable for building, and having the reputation of being very durable, is stated by Mr. Owen* to occur near Batesville, in Independence County. Prof. Branner also reports † a cream-colored magnesian limestone of good quality as occurring in the vicinity of Eureka Springs in Carroll County.

Colorado.—The National collections from this State show a coarse, reddish limestone from Jefferson County, and also a very compact, finely crystalline black stone, traversed by a coarse net-work of very fine white lines, from Pitkin in Gunnison County. This last stone takes a polish, and might almost be classed as a marble. Neither stone is now quarried to any extent.

---

* Geology of Arkansas, vol. 1. p. 220.
† Stone, Oct. 1889, p. 93.

Florida.—This State at present furnishes scarcely anything in the line of building stone, nor is there much demand for any other form of building material than wood. On Anastasia Island, about two miles from Saint Augustine, there was formerly quarried to a considerable extent a very coarse and porous shell limestone which was used in the construction of the old city of Saint Augustine and of Fort Marion, which was built about the middle of the eighteenth century. The rock is composed simply of shells of a bivalve mollusk, more or less broken and cemented together by the same material in a more finely divided state. Fragments of shells an inch or more in diameter occur. The rock is loosely compacted and very porous, but in a mild climate like that of Florida is nevertheless durable. The quarries were opened upwards of two hundred years ago, but the stone is not now extensively used, owing in part to the dampness of houses constructed of it, and in part to the cheapness of wood. The rock, which is popularly known as *Coquina* (the Spanish word for shell), is of Upper Eocene age. In the quarries the stone lies within a few feet of the surface, and can be cut out with an ax, in sizes and shapes to suit.

The oolitic limestone occurring at Key West has been quarried and used in the construction of numerous private and public buildings in that vicinity. It is of too loose and porous a texture to be of value for other than local use.

Illinois.—No siliceous crystalline rocks of any kind are to be found within the State limits, almost the entire product being limestone or dolomite, with a few quarries of sandstone, which are noticed on p. 260. According to Professor Conover* the State embraces rocks representing most of the epochs of the Silurian, Devonian, and Carboniferous ages. Over the

---

* Report of Tenth Census, vol. x. 1880.

greater part of its area these rocks have been but little disturbed, and occur with beds approximately horizontal or inclined at a small angle to the horizon.

The surface of the State is almost everywhere covered by a
variable depth of the looser deposits of the Tertiary and Qua-
ternary ages. Owing partly to the nature of the rock, but
most largely in all probabilities to these subsequent deposits,
a very large portion of the country presents a very level or
slightly undulating prairie surface, within the limits of which
are few rock exposures. This is true of the whole central and
eastern part of the State, the larger portion of its territory.

Skirting this great area on all sides except the east, is a
country of very different character, though the change is
gradual—a valley country with very marked water courses,
which cut through the beds of clay and sand to and into the
rock formations below. Throughout the greater part of this
area the rocks immediately underlying are Silurian, Devonian,
or Sub-carboniferous, all of which furnish excellent building
materials, and but few localities of considerable area are found
where at least a fair building material cannot easily be
obtained.

The most notable of the limestones of this State is the fine
grained, very light-colored Niagara stone, quarried in the vicinity of Lemont and Joliet, in Will County. The Lemont quarries lie on both sides of the Illinois and Lake Michigan Canal,
and the beds of stone are quarried to their lower limits through
a variable thickness of from 12 to 40 feet. The stone here is
uniformly a fine-grained, homogeneous, light-drab· limestone,
occurring in beds from 6 to 24, and sometimes 30 inches in
thickness. The beds are divided vertically by seams occurring
at intervals of from 12 to 50 feet, and continuing with smooth
faces for long distances, and also by a second set running
nearly at right angles with the first, but only continuous be-

tween massive joints and at irregular intervals. This structure renders the rock very easily quarried and obtainable in blocks of almost any required dimensions. The stone is soft and easily worked, taking readily a smooth surface, but no polish. It can be turned on a lathe, and is made into balustrades and other forms of ornamental work. It can be carved in bas relief, but is not sufficiently tough for high reliefs that are to be exposed to the weather. To produce smooth surfaces for flagging, the stone is planed by machines somewhat similar to those used in planing iron. The stone from the immediate vicinity of Lemont is said to contain less iron and to tarnish less readily than that a few miles distant at Joliet.

The stone in the quarry contains much moisture, and during cold weather care has to be taken to avoid injury by freezing before the quarry water has evaporated. This causes a considerable annual expense in making earth protections, except in those few quarries that are so situated that they can be flooded with water during the winter months.

The quarries extend for nearly 4 miles below Lemont, where a gap occurs, to just below Lockport, from which point a line of closely-adjoining quarries extend to below Joliet. The finer varieties of the stone do not seem well fitted for heavy masonry in damp situations. Fine clay seams abound, which are invisible when the stone is first quarried, and which under favorable circumstances do not develop at all, but when exposed to heavy pressure or to alternate moisture and dryness, accompanied by frost, they are soon developed, and often render the stone worthless. Even the best varieties of the stone tarnish after a short exposure, especially in cities where soft coal is burned.

The Joliet quarries extend from a point about a mile below Lockport to the same distance below Joliet. Two distinct varieties of stone occur. That quarried from the lower beds on the right bank of the river is as a rule rougher, more coarsely textured, and tarnishes more readily than that from the higher levels. It is now but little used, except for heavy masonry. In the quarries back from the river, on the higher levels, the stone is fine grained, more homogeneous, and in this respect fully equal to the Lemont stones. The beds now worked are from 3 to 4 feet in thickness, and large blocks are obtainable. Most of it seems to weather-stain rather more than that from Lemont. The value of the stone quarried at these two places is probably fully equal to that of all the other stone quarried in the State.*

Three large quarries are worked in these same formations at Batavia, but as a rule the stone is coarser and more difficult to work than those just described. Other quarries occur at Thornton and Blue Island, Cook County, and other parts of the State. Within the city limits of Chicago there is quarried from this same formation a coarser somewhat cellular stone, that from its unique character perhaps merits a special description. According to Hunt† this stone when pure is a nearly white granular crystalline dolomite, containing 54.6 per cent carbonate of lime. It, however, contains so large a portion of bituminous matter, that blocks sometimes become quite black on exposure. The color fades somewhat in time, but the petroleum odor is often perceptible for long distances. The stone has been used to some extent for building purposes, as notably in the First Presbyterian Church in Chicago. The

---

* These beds were formerly described as composed of light buff stone, while the deeper portions of the quarries now furnish "bluestone." The difference results from the difference in amount of oxidation of the small quantity of iron disseminated through the whole mass, the change having resulted from atmospheric influences. The same change must ultimately take place in all the bluestone which is brought to the surface. (Geology of Illinois, vol. IV. p. 220.)

† Chemical and Geological Essays, p.172.

gummy bituminous matter causes the dust from the streets to adhere to exposed surfaces, thus giving the buildings a peculiar antique appearance. We are informed by Mr. Batchen that this pseudo-antique appearance is greatly admired by some. The presence of the bitumen is beneficial in at least one respect, in that it renders the stone less pervious to moisture, and hence less liable to disintegration by freezing.

Lower Silurian (Trenton) limestones and dolomities are quite extensively quarried in Jo Daviess County, and make a handsome and very durable building material. Calhoun, Alexandria, and Ogle Counties also furnish good material, but which, for the lack of space, cannot be described here in detail. At various points in Whiteside and Hopkins Counties there are outcrops of limestones belonging to the Cincinnati group, a part of which will furnish durable building material. The stone needs, however, to be selected with the greatest care, since all the beds are not of equal quality.

At Jonesborough, in Union County, there occurs a fine, even-grained, compact, beautifully oolitic stone that cuts to a sharp even edge, and seems admirably adapted for carved work and general building purposes as well. Specimens in the National Museum are of a lighter color than the Bedford (Ind.) oolitic and take a better polish. We have had no means of ascertaining its lasting qualities, but it is stated* to be liable to injury from frost when exposed in damp places. The stone is of Carboniferous age. Other oolitic stones occur at Roseclair, in Hardin County. They are of a dark bluish-gray color and take a good polish.

There are many other localities in the State which furnish excellent varieties of building stone. These can not be mentioned here for lack of space. Interested parties are therefore

---

* Report of Tenth Census, vol. x. p. 225.

referred to the National Museum collections and to the report of the Tenth Census.

Indiana.—The limestones of Indiana, such as are quarried for architectural purposes, belong either to the Upper Silurian or sub-Carboniferous formations in the central and southern part of the State. Few quarries of any importance lie north of Indianapolis, and of such as do the output is used mainly for the manufacture of quicklime. According to Prof. Collett* the southeastern part of the state supplies a large quantity of stone for foundations and rubble masonry from the bluffs along the Ohio River and which extend through Wayne, Union, Fayette, Franklin, Dearborn, Ohio, and Switzerland, west to Clark County, besides being found to some extent in the counties adjoining these to the west, which are included in the Lower Silurian geological range.

Close-grained, compact, magnesian limestones are largely quarried in the counties bordering the above on the west, forming a belt extending northward from the Ohio to the Wabash River in Carroll, Cash, Miami, Wabash and Huntington, and to some extent in the counties to the northeast of these. The stone lies in even beds, having a thickness of from a few inches to two or more feet, and is especially adapted to work in foundations, piers, abutments and massive range work where great strength is required. The thinner strata furnish, at a low cost, excellent slabs for flagging and curbstones.

From Warren County at the extreme west of the State, southwesterly to the Ohio River, in a gradually widening range, the valuable limestones of the Keokuk group, (sub-Carboniferous), the sand stones of the Chester, and oolitic limestones of the intermediate St. Louis group, are quarried. By far the most beautiful and valuable of this stone for architectural pur-

---

* Twelfth Annual Report State Geologist, 1882, p. 20.

poses, is the oolitic variety from Lawrence, Monroe, Owen, Crawford, Harrison and Washington Counties. The supply is inexhaustible, as it lies in massive strata of twenty to seventy feet thick, over an area of more than seventy square miles.

The Lawrence County stone is extensively quarried near Bedford and is popularly known as " Bedford stone " or " Bedford oolite." The rock is of fine even texture, and is composed of small rounded concretionary grains of about the size of a grain of mustard seed compactly cemented together by crystalline lime or calcite. The stone is soft, but tenacious (specimens having borne a pressure of 12,000 pounds per square inch), and works readily in every direction. It is therefore a great favorite for carved work, and is used more extensively for this purpose than any other of our limestones. No better example of the adaptability of the stone for this purpose can be given than the elegant mansion of Mr. C. J. Vanderbilt, on Fifth avenue, in New York City. Unfortunately, as is usually the case with light limestones, this stains badly in cities where there is a great amount of manufacturing, as is only too well illustrated in the case referred to.

Although the quarries have been worked systematically for but a few years, the stone is already widely known, and is coming into very general use in nearly every city of importance in the country. At the locality above referred to the stone occurs in a solid bed, that has been worked to a depth of 40 feet without reaching the bottom.

Stones from the other counties mentioned are very similar in general appearance, but not always so distinctly oolitic and often contain a considerable percentage of bituminous matter. Samples exhibited at the Museum from near Corydon in Harrison County are of a beautifully fine and even oolitic structure, very light color, firm and compact. They resemble the oolitic stone from Princeton, Kentucky, more closely than any other, but are much more compact. The stone is stated to occur in inexhaustible quantities.

The Washington County deposit at Salem is said to be an exceptionally fine one, there being a solid bed of the oolite 30 feet in thickness, with only about 5 feet of cap rock.

Near Silverville, in Lawrence County, there occurs a very fine-grained compact stone of a drab color, that acquires readily a smooth and even surface. An attempt has been made to utilize this for lithographic purposes, but, it is stated, with indifferent success. It bears a close resemblance to the darker variety of the well-known Bavarian lithographic stone, but is somewhat harder.

At Anderson, in Madison County, a light-colored, fine-grained stone occurs in beds of from 4 to 12 inches in thickness, which is used locally for flagging and general trimming purposes.

Iowa.—Although this State abounds in limestones and dolomites to the exclusion of almost all other varieties of building stone, but little of the material now quarried is of such a nature as ever to acquire more than a local reputation. Though having altogether more than three times the number of quarries found in Illinois, these are mostly small affairs, and the value of the total product is but little more than one-half that of the latter State. At the time of the taking of the Tenth Census the whole number of quarries in the State was 131, of which 128 were of limestone and dolomites, and the remaining three of sandstone, which are mentioned on p. 261.

At the present time the most important quarries are situated in the Niagara·division of the Upper Silurian formations, in the vicinity of Stone City, Jones County ; Farley, Dubuque County, and in various portions of Jackson, Cedar, Clinton, and Scott Counties. The Jones County stone is a very light-colored, fine-grained and compact bituminous dolomite. That from Farley is very similar in general appearance, but contains less bituminous matter. In the small blocks displayed at the National Museum the stones appear of good quality, but we have had no opportunity of learning their weathering qualities. A finely crystalline light-colored limestone of sub-Carboniferous age is quite extensively quarried near Burlington, in Des Moines County. According to Professor McGee * this stone, which is practically identical with that of Keokuk, in Lee County, is used chiefly for common masonry, and only occasionally for dressed work. The upper beds are " nearly white in color, fine, compact, homogeneous, and hard, with a conchoidal or splintery fracture, like the so-called lithographic limestone of nearly the same geological age. This stone has been used to some extent for ornamental purposes, but contains too many incipient fractures, and is too liable to unexpected disruption to be of special value."

Near Le Grand and Montour, in Tama County, there occurs a magnesian limestone of the same age as that just described, which is fine-grained, compact, and generally buff or whitish in color. The coarser portions are extensively used for heavy masonry, while the finer grades, which are often beautifully veined with iron oxidies, are used for ornamental work under the name of Iowa marbles. Some of the stone from this locality is oolitic. Similar stones are extensively quarried at Iowa Falls, and at Humboldt and Dakota, in Humboldt County. Limestones and dolomites belonging to the St. Louis epoch of the sub-Carboniferous age are quite extensively quarried in various parts of Lee, Des Moines, Henry, Washington, Van Buren, Jefferson, Keokuk, Wapello, Manhaska, Marion, Story, Hamilton, and Webster Counties. That from near Farmington, Van Buren County, varies from light buff to nearly white in color, is fine-grained, and has been quarried for

---

* Report of Tenth Census, vol. x. p. 261.

lithographic purposes. It is, however, no longer used, having been found to contain too many dry seams often cemented by crystalline carbonate of lime. At Chequest the limestone takes a fair polish and is known as Chequest marble.

In the Devonian limestones near Iowa City and Roberts Ferry there frequently occur masses of fossil coral (*Acervularia davidsoni*) which, when cut and polished, form beautiful ornaments and paper-weights, though of small size. They are known popularly as bird's-eye and fish-egg marbles, and have already been noticed (*ante*, p. 92).

Kansas.—The limestones and dolomites of this State are, as a rule, of a light color, soft and porous, and incapable of receiving a polish such as will fit them for any form of ornamental work. Many of them are cellular and loosely compacted, being made up in large part of a small fossil rhizopod about the size of a grain of wheat and known under the name of *fusulina.* Such stones are obviously unfitted for exposed work in localities subject to great extremes of temperature, although they may be very durable in mild or dry climates. Those at present quarried are almost without exception of Carboniferous or Permian age, and occur only in thin beds, varying from a few inches to 8 or 10 feet in thickness.

Near Irving their occurs a light-colored, soft, thin-bedded stone, which has in times past been used for building purposes in Atchison and Kansas City. It is soft and easily quarried and for ordinary construction requires but little dressing. At Frankfort a similar stone occurs which has been used to some extent for buildings, though principally for foundations. Some of the stones from these localities are of very poor quality, being soft and quite cellular through the breaking away of the small fossils above referred to. Atchison, in the same county, has quarries of a darker, more compact stone, which are worked for local use.

In the vicinity of Topeka there are quarried light-colored, compact, finely fossiliferous dolomites and limestones which work very readily, and which have been used in the construction of about thirty-five common buildings in that city, besides a church, school, and opera houses in Emporia. They have also been used in Parsons, in Labette County, and neighboring towns in Missouri.

Near Lane, in Franklin County, gray and buff limestones are quarried and used quite extensively in Ottawa and Garnett, in the same State, though some have been shipped to Chicago. The buff variety is sometimes oolitic, resembling to some extent the Bedford (Indiana) stone. The texture is firm and compact, and it acquires a good surface and polish. The gray variety is coarser, and often somewhat cellular, owing to the imperfect filling of the spaces between the fossil particles of which it is composed. A section of the quarry shows the gray stone to occur in a bed about 4 feet in thickness, and the buff oolitic about 6 feet in thickness, the layers of which vary from 18 to 24 inches each.

Near Marion Center, in Marion County, there is quarried a light-drab cellular magnesian limestone of Permian age, that has been used in the construction of the asylum for the blind and insane at Wyandotte and Topeka, in this State. Similar stones are quarried at Cottonwood, in Chase County. The stratum of quarry rock here is some 6 feet in thickness and blocks of any desired size and of thickness not exceeding $2\frac{1}{2}$ feet can be obtained. The principal markets for these stones are Kansas City, Missouri; Lincoln and Omaha, Nebraska; Pueblo and Denver, Colorado, and Atchison, Topeka, and Leavenworth, Kansas.

In the vicinity of Fort Scott are some half a dozen irregularly worked quarries which furnish stone for building foundations and pavements in the near vicinity. The stone is dark-colored, fine-grained, and semi-crystalline, and is said to stand the wear of from ten to fifteen years' exposure very well. It turns to a brownish color on long exposure and is strong enough for ordinary structures. The stone quarried at Winfield is a light-colored, fine-grained cellular rock and so soft as to be quarried by means of plug and feathers only, the holes being first bored by means of a common auger without point. It is a handsome stone and has a good reputation for durability. It is used mostly in this State, though some is shipped to Kansas City, Missouri.

Many of the towns in Butler County produce fine-grained, light-colored limestones suitable for rough building in the immediate vicinity, but not at all suitable for ornamental work.

Kentucky.—Although the building stones of this State are entirely unknown in our principal markets, and but few of them have more than a strictly local reputation, it by no means follows that there is any lack of material or that it is at all inferior in quality. While it is true that no marbles or granites of importance are found, yet there abound limestones of the finest quality and in inexhaustible quanities. The oolitic limestones of this State are without superiors, if indeed they have equals. In Todd, Grayson, Meade, Simpson, Christian, and Caldwell Counties oolitic stones occur of very light, almost white color, and excellent quality. The varieties from Litchfield and Princeton are especially worthy of mention. The oolitic character is very pronounced in these stones, and while in some cases the production of a perfect surface is impossible, owing to the breaking away of these minute rounded grains, still in the better qualities the sharp edges and smooth surfaces are as readily acquired as on the celebrated Bedford (Indiana) or other stones of this character. These are superior to the Bedford stone, moreover, in their clear and uniform colors; never, so far as observed, being blotched with oil, as is the latter. Professor Proctor informs the writer that the stone is quarried with ease, is easily wrought, stands pressure well, and is considered one of the most reliable stones in the State.

Compact fine-grained limestones of a dark drab color, taking a smooth surface, but not suited for marble, are found in the towns of Franklin, Simpson County; Lebanon, Marion County; Russellville, Logan County, and others. A part of the Franklin County stone is fine-grained and suitable for lithographic purposes, though inferior to the imported Bavarian stone. Very light-colored compact limestones are found also in Simpson, Logan, and Franklin Counties, but the writer has no information regarding their availability or the extent to which they are quarried.

Maine.—Limestone is an abundant and common rock in this State, especially in the southeastern part, in the counties of Knox and Lincoln, where it is very extensively burnt into quicklime. So far as I am aware none of the stone is utilized for building, as its colors—blue and blue-black, veined with white—are poorly adapted for such purposes. No stone suitable for marble is yet known to occur in the State, though Hitchcock * expresses the opinion that such may yet be found in "the belt of Helderberg limestone running from Matagamon (east branch Penobscot) River northeasterly."

Many samples of so-called white marble have been taken from the limestone formations about Rockland, in Knox County, but, so far as observed by the present writer, they are all too coarsely crystalline or too distinctly granular in structure to be of value.

Michigan.—Limestone or dolomites of a character suitable for building purposes are at present but little quarried in this State, the entire value of the output during the census year of 1880 being but about $26,000. A fine-grained fossiliferous

---

* Second Annual Report Geology of Maine, 1862, p. 428.

dolomite of a drab color is worked at Sibley's Station, in Wayne County, and a very light colored granular rock, of similar composition, near Raisinville, in Monroe County. Near Alpena light-colored limestones are quarried which are hard, compact, and said to be durable. They are not obtainable anywhere in large quantities nor in blocks of large size, but there are numerous small openings sufficient to supply the local demand. Other localities where stone can be obtained are at Trenton, near Detroit, and upon Macon Creek, both in Monroe County. The stone is apt to contain dry seams and requires care in selecting. These are all of Devonian age.

Minnesota.—The Lower Silurian limestones and dolomites of this State, which are at present the only ones quarried, are nearly all of a light buff, drab, or blue color, fine-grained and compact, though in some cases cellular and semi-crystalline. According to Professor Winchell * the stone appears in the bluffs of the Mississippi River and St. Croix Valley, and is quarried at all points (except Lake City) where there is any demand between Stillwater and Winona, along the Mississippi Valley on the Minnesota side, and also at several places farther west, as at Caledonia, in Houston County, Lanesborough and Rushford, in Fillmore County, and at points in Winona County.

At Stillwater the rock is a silicious dolomite of a light buff color. In the ledge, which is about 45 feet thick, it occurs in alternate bands of compact and cellular rock varying from 3 to 6 feet in thickness. The coarser variety is most durable and is used in heavy masonry, as bridges and foundations. The finer variety is used for house trimming, ashlar work and tombstones.

At St. Paul the rock is a fine light-bluish semi-crystalline

* Report Tenth Census, p. 249, and Geology of Minnesota, vol. 1.

magnesian limestone. It is usually quite regularly stratified, and occurs in beds from 3 to 24 inches in thickness, with joints from 10 to 30 feet apart. Blocks 10 by 5 by 2 feet can be obtained if desired. It is used only locally. At Minneapolis the rock is quite similar, though sometimes slightly fossiliferous or mottled with argillaceous spots. It was formerly used almost exclusively in Minneapolis, but is now being gradually replaced by stone from the neighboring States.

In speaking of these stones Professor Winchell says: *

" In the use of the Trenton limestone quarried at St. Paul and Minneapolis regard should be had constantly to its laminated structure. The beds quarried now are as they were originally deposited, and as cut for use embrace in every block many layers of from one-half to two inches in thickness. These consist of alternating clayey and calcareous portions, the latter constituting the hard and enduring part of the stone. These layers are not always distinct and continuous over large surfaces, but they blend or shade into each other every few inches. Yet in process of time, under natural weathering, they get separated so as to fall apart, the clayey matter disintegrating first and causing the calcareous structure which sustains the whole to break up into small sheets or fragments. Hence this stone should never be placed on edge, but in the same position it occupied in the quarry. It should never be allowed to occupy projecting or exposed parts of a building. More especially if it be on edge and in a projecting cornice or capital it is the source of weakness to the structure, as well as of danger to all passers, from the dropping of sheets or fragments as the weather, by wet or frost, separates them from each other. Its color is also against its being put in the exposed and ornamental parts of a structure. . . . The color of the Trenton

---

* Preliminary Report on Building Stone, etc., 1889, p. 33.

makes it very suitable for foundations and for the ranges below the water-table, but even there it should be well bedded in mortar and protected by the water-table in order to keep out the water."

At Red Wing, in Goodhue County, the stone is quarried only for local building and for burning into quicklime. Blocks as large as can conveniently be handled can be obtained. At Frontenac, in the same county, the stone is of buff or gray color, medium fine, and quite cellular. This rock is considered one of the best in the State, and is used for all varieties of building purposes, as well as for bases and tombstones. Blocks 11 by 7 by 5½ feet and weighing 18 tons have been taken out, which is about as large as the quarries will furnish. It is said to work with comparative ease, and to withstand the weather well. Although having been in use longer than any other stone in the State, it has not as yet shown any change whatever from atmospheric influences. Its powers of resistance to pressure vary from 5,000 to 7,000 pounds per square inch.

At Kasota and Mendota, in Le Seuer County, the dolomite is of a buff or rusty pink color, of homogeneous texture, and very strong and durable. It withstands a pressure of 10,000 pounds per square inch without crushing. Blocks 10 by 11 by 1 foot in thickness can be obtained. It is quite generally used throughout the State, the pink variety being most admired and bringing the highest price.

At Mankato, in Blue Earth County, the rock is also a dolomite, buff in color, fine, compact, and semi-crystalline, sometimes cellular. Blocks 20 by 10 by 6 feet can be obtained from the quarries.

At Winona the dolomite is quarried for general building purposes, flagging, and burning into lime. It is of a buff color, usually fine and uniform in texture, though sometimes containing cherty lumps, and porous. Blocks of any size that can be handled may be taken from the quarries.

Missouri.—As stated by Professor Broadhead,* the limestone quarries of this State have not as yet been much developed, and few have the dignity of a merchantable product. It is probable that under 25,000 square miles of the State of Missouri there may be found good quarries of limestone. A third of this area may include beds of lower Carboniferous limestone, and two thirds may include the magnesian limestone series of the upper Cambrian.

Good quarries of the lower (or sub-) Carboniferous limestones, very suitable for building purposes, may be opened in the counties from Cape Girardeau to Clark, and from St. Charles to Howard, as well as in Saline, Pettis, Henry, Cedar, Lawrence, Green, Jasper, Newton, MacDonald and Barry. Excellent quarries of the Burlington beds have been opened at Louisville, Hannibal, Sedalia, and other places. These stones are usually of a bluish, gray, or brown color, somewhat coarse in texture, and most of them have proven very durable. The chief objection to the stone is said to be the rough bedding plane and, in quarrying, the frequent occurrence of chert beds.

The Keokuk group of the sub-Carboniferous is also an important source of quarry rock and material for lime. The best beds are found in Green, Lawrence, Newton and Jasper Counties. Like the stones just described they are coarse grained but of a deeper blue-gray color. There are well developed quarries in Greenfield, Ashgrove, Springfield, Pierce City. Carthage and Neosho. At the latter place the stone is beautifully oolitic. The St. Louis limestone, well exposed in the city of St. Louis and at St. Charles, is also a useful stone.

---

* Building Trades Journal, July, 1888.

Ordinarily it is strong, and looks well in structure, reflecting a more uniform light drab color, which is permanent on exposure. The beds of this limestone as found at St. Genevieve are oolitic.

An attempt was made about fifteen years ago to introduce stone from the Upper Trenton beds into the St. Louis market, but experience proved the rock to be wanting in continued elements of beauty. The stone would polish well and present a pleasing appearance at first, but it was not sufficiently uniform in texture, and a certain fossil which was abundant was too soon disintegrated by atmospheric agencies. The quarry was therefore abandoned.

A very fine-grained and compact limestone of a dark drab color occurs near Saverton, in Ralls County, which has been used to some extent for lithographic purposes. Stones from other localities are mostly compact, and of light or dull red color. A very light encrinital stone is quarried in the vicinity of Hamilton and Bear Creek, in Marion County.

Nebraska.—According to Professor Aughey,* Carboniferous limestones of such quality as to render them suitable for building purposes are to be found in Richardson, Pawnee, Gage, Johnson, Nemaha, Otoe, and Cass Counties. Many of these as those of Johnson County, are made up almost wholly of minute fossils of the size and shape of a grain of wheat, and known technically as *fusulina.* In Nemaha and Otoe Counties the beds are exposed along the Missouri River and are here quarried and used for building. One of the best and most massive limestones of the State occurs below Plattsmouth in Cass County, on the banks of the river. Unfortunately, the great thickness of the superficial deposits here renders the quarries very expensive in working. At La Platte, in Sarpy County, near

---

* Physical Geography and Geology of Nebraska, p. 311.

the line of the Burlington and Missouri Railroad there is also a
fine bed of siliceous limestone, which has been used in the construction of the United States post-office and court-house in
Lincoln. The stone contains innumerable fusulina impressions
and is adapted to only general building, not monumental work.
Another exposure of this same stone occurs farther up the
Platte River and which has been worked on the river bank
opposite South Bend. This stone has been used in the wing
of the Capitol building at Lincoln. At Syracuse, in Otoe
County, are quarries of impure, variously colored limestones,
from whence large quantities of building material have been
taken.

The Cretaceous limestones of this State are stated to likewise furnish a quantity of excellent stone. So far as the present writer has had opportunity of examining, few, if any, of
these or the other stones described are of such a nature as to
ever be in great demand outside of the limits of the State.

New York.—According to Professor Smock,* the limestones
quarried for building stones in this State belong to the following named formations, beginning with the lowest in the geological scale : Calciferous, Chazy, Trenton, Niagara, Lower
Helderberg, Upper Helderberg or Corniferous and the Tully
limestones. These will be here considered in the order
given.

Rocks of the Calciferous formation may be traced along the
Mohawk valley, in Montgomery, Herkimer and Oneida Counties, and are quarried in numerous instances, as at Little Falls,
Canajoharie and Sandhill. The rock is a more or less siliceous
magnesian limestone, of a drab, blue-gray or blue-black color,
and said to be, as a rule, strong and durable. It is largely
used for general building.

---

* Bulletin No. 3, New York State Museum, 1888, p. 20.

The Chazy limestone is seen in Clinton in its typical development, and affords strong and heavy stone at various quarries in the Champlain valley, as at Willsboro Point and near
Plattsburgh. The Trenton formation occupies the Mohawk
and Champlain valleys, a broader zone around the western sides
of the Adirondack region, and the St. Lawrence valley from
the Canada line southwest to Lake Ontario. The counties of
Montgomery, Fulton, Herkimer, Oneida, Lewis, Jefferson, St.
Lawrence, Hamilton, Clinton, Essex, Warren and Saratoga all
have outcrops of limestone referable to this age. The stone
varies greatly in different localities, or at times, even in the
same outcrop, the same quarry sometimes yielding both
marble and coarse common rock suitable only for building.
The Niagara limestone has its greatest development near the
Niagara River and is quarried at Lockport and Rochester. At
Lockport the stone is gray, thick bedded and subcrystalline ; it
has been widely used for building purposes. The Lower Helderberg group includes a wide variation in its limestones.
The formation may be traced from the Helderberg mountains
westward, south of the Mohawk river nearly to Syracuse. The
lower beds are dark colored, compact, thick, and afford a stone
which may be polished ; the upper beds furnish a gray, heavy
bedded and strong stone which answers for heavy masonry.
Quarries in the rocks of this group have been opened in the
Schoharie valley at Cobbleskill, Cherry valley and at Springfield, Otsego County ; also near Hudson, in Becrafts mountain,
and near Catskill. Rocks of the Upper Helderberg group also
display a great diversity throughout the areas they occupy.
The formation outcrops in Onondaga, Cayuga, Seneca, Monroe, Genesee, Erie and Ulster Counties, and is quarried at
Union Springs, Waterloo, Seneca Falls, Auburn, Leroy, Wil-
liamsville, Buffalo and Kingston.
    Only a few of the more important stones of the above-

named formations can be here described in full, owing to lack of space ; for further information the reader is referred to the work quoted.

At Greenport, Columbia County, a stratum of Lower Silurian limestone upward of 60 or 70 feet in thickness is extensively worked for ornamental and building purposes. The quarry proper is said to cover an area of 40 acres, and a face 30 feet high and half a mile in length has been opened. The stone is of medium texture, semi-crystalline, highly fossiliferous, and of a water-blue or gray color. It is said to have been used to some extent under the name of Coral-shell Marble for interior decorative work in Boston and other cities. On both sides of the Hudson River, at the gorge of Glens Falls, the Trenton magnesian limestones are worked both for black marble and for ordinary limestone for burning into quicklime. According to Professor Smock, the quarry on the right bank— the Saratoga County side of the stream—shows the following section :

1. Black slate rock in thin layers........................ 15 feet.
2. Gray limestone.................................... 10 "
3. Black thin-bedded limestone....................... 12 "
4. Gray limestone................................ 2 "
5. Black *Marble*................................... 12 "
6. Limestone.................................. 4 "

Of these the marble has already been described on p. 98. The gray limestone is used for heavy masonry and general building, while the main output is used for lime making. At Willsborough and Crown Point, in Essex County, there are also extensive quarries of blue-black magnesian limestone of good quality. In various towns in Montgomery County a gray or blue-gray semi-crystalline limestone is worked for building material. The stone is said to be strong and durable, though care needs to be used in its selection. At Tribes Hill the stone is gray or blue-gray, in some cases almost black on a polished surface. It is used for house trimmings and ashlar work as well as bridge construction. Several churches in Amsterdam are of this material. At Canajoharie, in this same county, are beds that furnish a blue-gray finely crystalline stone, which has been used in mill buildings at Utica, and in the churches of Fort Plain and Canajoharie. At the Indian reservation in Onondaga County a gray, compact, semi-crystalline limestone, said to possess great strength and durability, was formerly extensively quarried, but the work has of late fallen off somewhat, owing to lack of transportation facilities. A gray crinoidal stone that takes a fair polish is also found at Onondaga, in the same county.

Professor Smock describes this gray variety as resembling the best varieties of the Maine granites when finely cut. It has been used in many of the finest structures in Syracuse, including the new U. S. Government building, the Hall of Languages, Syracuse University, and several churches.

At Auburn, in Cayuga County, the Upper Helderberg beds furnish large amounts of gray and blue-gray magnesian limestone, which has been used extensively in the public and private buildings of that place.

At Lockport, in Niagara County, a fossil-bearing calcareous dolomite has been quarried for many years for general purposes of construction in New York and Rochester. The stone does not take a good surface and consequently does not polish readily, but some portions make quite showy mantels, owing to the presence of red crinoidal remains. According to Professor Julien* this stone, as used in New York city, has not proved durable. The fault, however, he regards in part due to

---

* Report of Tenth Census, vol. x. p. 369.

the manner in which the stone is used, about 40 per cent. of the blocks being set on edge.

North Carolina.—Limestones and dolomites of good quality for building purposes occur in abundance in this State, but are not extensively quarried for lack of a market or transportation facilities. Near New Berne, Craven County, there occurs a very coarse cellular shell-stone of Eocene age that has been used for underpinnings and fences, but it is said not to weather well. Material of the same nature, but much finer in texture and more compact, occurs at Rocky Point, in Pender County, and which has been used in the construction of breakwaters and other harbor improvements at Wilmington, in this State. A coarse, dull red dolomite occurs at Warm Springs, in Madison County, and also light blue-gray varieties, but neither are worked, as there is little demand for the material.

Ohio.—The limestones and dolomites of this State are almost altogether of a dull, uninteresting color, and though in many cases durable and strong, are entirely unfit for any sort of fine building and ornamental work. They are therefore used chiefly for the rough work of foundations, street paving, and flagging, and to a very large extent for making quicklime. In many instances they have been used locally for building purposes, but their qualities are not such as to cause them to be sought from a distance.

At Point Marblehead, in the northern part of the State, dull, light-colored compact dolomites of Carboniferous age have been quarried for making lime and for building purposes for the past fifty years. Many buildings in the vicinity have been constructed from it, and it has also been largely used by the Government for light-houses and other structures along the lake front. Of late years its use for building has very considerably diminished. Near Sandusky, in Erie County, the same formations have been extensively worked, not less than

12 acres in the vicinity having been quarried over to a depth of 8 feet. The stone is of a dull, bluish-gray color, and is used for building, flagging, and making lime ; about one hundred and eighty houses_ in the city have been constructed from it. Near Columbus, in Franklin County, the Devonian limestones are extensively quarried, and the product has in a few instances been used for building purposes. By far the greater part of the product is, however, used as a flux for iron and for making quicklime. A dolomite from the same formations is quarried for rough building and lime burning at and near Marion, in Marion County.

In Allen, Miami, Clarke, Greene, Montgomery, Preble, and several other counties the dolomites and limestones of Upper Silurian age are extensively worked, but so far as the author can learn but a small part of the quarry product is utilized for building. At Springfield the stone is buff in color and somewhat porous, though it is said to be strong and durable.

Near Greenfield, Ross County, and Lexington, Highland County, there are extensive quarries of a bituminous dolomite, which is largely used in Cincinnati for flagging, steps, and in the manufacture of lime. Specimens in the National Museum from these places show the stone to vary from dark grayish, distinctly laminated, to fine, compact, and homogeneous of a yellowish or buff color. The buff stone can be cut to a sharp edge, and acquires a good surface, but takes only a dull polish. So far as the author has observed this is one of the finest appearing and best working stones in the State.

The Montgomery County stone is a magnesian limestone, and it is said to have acquired a good reputation. It is not now used as much as formerly, however. The stone quarried in the other localities mentioned present so little diversity of character as to need no special description. Those interested are referred to vol. x. of the Reports of the Tenth Census, and to vol. v. of the Reports of the Geological Survey of Ohio.

Pennsylvania.—The lower Silurian formations in Montgomery, Lancaster, and Chester Counties, which furnish the supply of marble already referred to on page 100, furnish also large quantities of gray or bluish-gray stone of the same composition, but owing to its color and texture unsuited for any form of ornamental work. It is, however, extensively quarried for general building, for foundations and bridge abutments. Besides in Montgomery County, limestone is quarried for local use in Easton, Tuckerton, and Reading, Berks County, and in Annville, Lebanon County; also near Harrisburg, Dauphin County; Leaman Place, Lancaster County; York, York County; Bridgeport, Shiremanstown, and Carlisle, Cumberland County. The stone from the Lancaster quarries breaks with an irregular fracture; is "plucky," as the stone-cutters say, and is hence hard to work. It is, however, very durable, exposure for many years having no other apparent effect than that of a slight fading of the color.

The York stone is very fine-grained, compact, and of a deep blue-black color. It takes a high polish, and but for its uneven texture might make a fine marble. In Wrightsville, in this same county, a white or bluish crystalline granular stone is quarried, which takes a fair polish, and which might perhaps be used for marble.

At Chambersburg and in other parts of Franklin county the stone is a calcareous dolomite, dark in color, fine-grained, and very durable; buildings which have stood for a century showing only a slight fading. It is used locally for rough building and lime burning.

At various localities near South Mountain, a limestone breccia similar to that of Frederick, Maryland, occurs, and which perhaps can be made to yield good stone for ornamental work. At none of the localities mentioned does the stone, so far as the writer is aware, possess such characters as to make it of value for building excepting in the immediate vicinity of the quarries, where it can be had cheaply owing to slight cost of transportation. The output as above indicated is used mainly for foundations, street paving, a flux in iron furnaces or for making quicklime.*

Tennessee.—A compact, finely fossiliferous, light pink spotted limestone occurs in the vicinity of Nashville, in this State, and which is quite extensively quarried for use in the near vicinity. The stone is said to be of rather poor quality, but is used on account of its accessibility. Near Chattanooga, in Hamilton County, a magnesian limestone of bluish-black color is quarried for local use. The quarry is said to be very favorably located, and the stone cheap and very durable.

Light pink, finely fossiliferous, semi-crystalline limestones occur at Columbia, Maury County; light-colored, similar-textured stones at Carter's Creek; light, almost white, at Morristown; red, compact fossiliferous at Springville; and compact drab and almost black dolomites near Charlotte Pike. A fine grained, compact, and light-colored oolitic stone occurs at Sherwood Station, which cuts to a sharp, smooth edge and seems a most excellent stone. So far as the author is aware, none of these are quarried for anything more than local use.

Texas.—Compact, fine-grained Cretaceous (?) limestones of excellent quality occur near San Saba in this State. A portion of these are entirely crystalline and acquire an excellent surface and polish, such as fits them for interior decorative work.

Light-colored, fine-grained limestones also occur in the vicinity of Austin, in Travis County; and dark mottled varieties near Burnet, in Burnet County.

---

*Details of quarries are to be found in vol. x. Report Tenth Census, pp. 149 to 156.

Wisconsin.—The more thickly settled portions of this State are underlain by Silurian rocks so disposed that there are but few regions where rock fit for ordinary purposes of construction can not be obtained in quantities sufficient to supply the local demand. Previous to 1880, however, with a single exception, no quarries had been worked for export beyond the state limits, and but few that had been worked for other than local markes. As a whole the stones belonging to this class are characterized by their light colors, compact textures, and hardness. Many of them will take a good polish and might be used for ornamental work, but that the colors are dull and uninteresting. Such occur and are quarried to a considerable extent at Byron, Fond du Lac, and Eden, in Fond du Lac County, but although the stone seems very durable, its hardness is such that it has not been used for facings or any kind of ornamental work. Coarse drab dolomites are quarried for general building at Ledyard and Kaukauna, in Outagamie County; at Neenah and Oshkosh, Winnebago County, and at Duck Creek Station, in Brown County. In various parts of Waukesha County there occurs a light drab, sometimes almost white, dolomite, which though a hard stone to cut, has been quite extensively used and with very good effect for general building. At Eden, Oak Centre and Sylvester, Green County, a similar stone occurs, which also crops out in Calumet County. Here it is of a white mottled color, takes a good polish, and is locally called marble.

Near Racine there occur beds of dolomite, varying from coarse, porous, and irregularly bedded to a fine, compact, and homogeneous rock, eminently adapted for fine building material, though not well suited for ornamental work. The quarries are very extensively worked. Other quarries in the same formation occur at Milwaukee, Cedarburgh, Grafton, Sheboygan, and Manitowoc. The Milwaukee quarries furnish several grades of building material, and of almost any necessary size. These are said to be remarkable for the great depth of excellent building stone which their working has developed.

Numerous other quarries occur in Rock, Dane, and La Crosse Counties, but which can not be mentioned here for lack of space.

(6) FOREIGN LIMESTONES AND MARBLES.

Bermuda.—The building stones of Bermuda are altogether calcareous and fragmental. Although popularly known as coral limestones, they contain as a rule fully as large a proportion of shell as of coral fragments. Nearly all the quarried material belongs, according to Professor Rice,[*] to the drift sand-rock or Æolian variety, *i.e.*, rocks made up of fragments blown inland from the beach and subsequently cemented by calcareous matter in a crystalline or subcrystalline state. The rock varies in color and texture from chalky white, fine-grained, and porous (somewhat like the French Caen stone), to a darker, coarser, but tough and compact form, in which the individual fragments, often of a pink color, are one-fourth of an inch or more in diameter.

According to the authority above quoted the rock is usually very soft, and is quarried out in large blocks by means of a peculiar long-handled chisel, and afterward sawn up in sizes and shapes to suit individual cases. The harder varieties, as found at Paynter's Vale and elsewhere, are, however, worked like " any ancient limestone or marble."

Most of the houses of Bermuda are stated by Professor Rice to be built of this soft, friable variety, and even the roofs are covered with the same material sawn into thin slabs.

---

[*] Geology of Bermuda, Bull. 25, U. S. National Museum, 1884.

When covered with a coating of whitewash the stone is found sufficiently durable for ordinary buildings in that climate, but if exposed to the rigors of a New England winter it would crumble rapidly. The hard rock, such as is found at Paynter's Vale and Ireland Island, "has been used in the construction of the fortifications and other government works" on the islands. "The quarry of the Royal Engineers, near Elbow Bay, appears to be in beach-rock."

British Columbia.—Marbles of excellent quality for general building and to some extent for ornamental work occur on Taxada Island. The colors range from gray to white, sometimes handsomely mottled.* White, gray, and pinkish varieties are also reported from White Cliff Island ; gray, handsomely variegated varieties from Beaver Cove, on the east coast of Vancouver's Island ; gray and mottled varieties from White Cliff Island ; gray mottled from Nimpish Lake, and a considerable variety from Horne Lake.

Canada.—An outcrop of deep red marble, veined with white calcite occurs associated with red shales and sandstones a short distance east of the Calway River in the Province of Quebec. The bed is stated to be from ten to forty feet thick, and to be exposed for a distance of half a mile along the strike.†

The beds of crystalline Laurentian limestone in Hastings County, Ontario Province, are capable of furnishing at various points marbles of the ordinary granular type, varying in color from white through shades of gray to nearly black. Quarries are worked in the village of Madoc, where the limestone band is some 900 feet across with a north and south trend, and also

---

* Ann. Rep. Geol. Survey of Canada, 1887–88.
† Ann. Rep. Geol. Survey of Canada, 1887–88, vol. iii., part 2, pp. 113, 114. K.

in the township of Hungerford, where there is a bed some 500 feet in width. This last stone is described as pure white in color, clouded bluish and greenish in places, and with bands of pinkish or salmon color in other parts.

The town of Renfrew is also situated on a wide band of crystalline limestone which furnishes a good marble for general building purposes. Other bands occur at Arnprior and Echo Lake.*

Africa.—Within a very few years there have been reopened in Algeria and Tunis the famous quarries of Numidian marbles, from whence the ancient Romans are stated to have obtained the celebrated Giallo Antico and other stones for the decoration of their houses and temples.

According to Playfair, the name *Numidian* is incorrect, as the marbles are not found in Numidia proper, but in the provinces of Africa and Mauritania. " Most of the Giallo Antico," says this authority, " used in Rome was obtained from Simittu Colonia, the modern Chemtou, in the valley of Medjerda, the quarries of which are now being worked by a Belgian company ; but the most remarkable and valuable marbles are found near Kleber, in the province of Oran, in Algeria.

At this point there rises an imposing mountain marked on the maps as Djebel-er-Roos, or Mountain of the Capes, but commonly called *Montagne grise*, from its gray, arid appearance. On the summit of this is an elevated plateau of an oblong form, running in an east and west direction. The soil, where any exists, is of a deep red color, and there are traces of iron everywhere, but more especially on the western side. The original color of the rock was creamy white ; in the extreme eastern part where the amount of iron is small, it exists very much in its natural condition, only somewhat stained with

---

* Mineral Resources of Ontario.   Report of Royal Commission, 1890.

iron, which communicates to it a tint resembling ivory. In conjunction with this is a rose-colored variety which is capable of being worked either in large masses or in the finest ornamentation. Here all the rock is of a uniform structure ; in the west of the plateau, however, there appears to have taken place some great earth movement. The whole of this side of the mountain has been crushed by pressure into fragments varying in size from large angular masses to the merest dust. The disintegrated mass has subsequently been cemented together ; the fragments have retained to a certain extent their original rose or yellow color, while the matrix has been stained of the deepest brown or red, owing to the metallic oxides which have been carried through the fissures, the whole thus forming a beautiful breccia of endless variety and color. The matrix is as hard as the fragments it contains, so that the stone takes a beautiful polish throughout its whole surface.

Between these two extreme varieties, namely, the white and rose marble on the east, and the breccias on the west, there are many others, such as the well-known yellow or *giallo antico*, a cippolino of almost indescribable beauty, a variety called *paonazza*, from its resemblance to a peacock's plumage, and a deep red species, somewhat brecciated, and resembling if not identical with the celebrated *rosso antico*. All of these owe their color to the iron, and the crushing force to which they have been subjected.*

The National collections contain a series of these marbles, which range in color through many shades of gray, drab, siena yellow, and rose-red, and which are designated in our markets under the names of *jaune, antique doré, paonazzo rosso, jaune chiaro ondate, jaune rosé, rose clair, breche sanguin,* and *jaspe rouge.* All are extremely compact and hard and acquire a sur-

---

* Geological Magazine, Dec. 1885, p. 562.

face and polish of wonderful beauty. The United States, at present, produces nothing that can compare with them for interior decorations.

Nummulitic limestone.—The celebrated nummulitic lime-stone of Eocene age from Northern Africa, and which was so extensively used by the Egyptians in the construction of their pyramids, is represented in the collections of the National Museum by a 7-inch cube, the gift of Commander Gorringe, U. S. Navy. This particular block was formerly a portion of the steps leading to the obelisk at Alexandria, and was brought away at the same time as the obelisk itself. Hull states that this stone was used in the construction of Baalbec, Aleppo, and some of the cities of the Holy Land. The pyramid of Cheops in Egypt is of the same material.

England.—The English marbles are rarely to be met with in the American markets. The country is, however, by no means deficient in materials of this nature well suited for decorative purposes, although the white statuary varieties are stated by Hull to be wholly lacking. According to this authority beds belonging to the Devonian and Carboniferous formations furnish a good supply of colored marbles. Beds belonging to the lower Cretaceous and upper Jurassic (Purbeck and Wealden) formations have also in times past furnished small blocks used mainly in the form of slender shafts in ecclesiastical building.

The National collections show a series of colored marbles, from quarries in Petitor, Ogwell, and Ashburton in Devon which compare very favorably with other and better known stones. They are as a rule of a very fine and compact texture, highly fossiliferous, and acquire an excellent surface and pol-ish. The Petitor stones vary in color from light yellowish, white and clouded, through pink and gray, light and dark band-ed, to dove, mottled with deep red. An Ashburton variety known as bird's-eye marble, is a dark gray stone thickly studded with small white fossil favosites. The stone is further variegated with small white and dull red veins. Another dark mottled variety is made up of distorted fossil corals of varying sizes up to two inches in diameter imbedded in a cement so impregnated with iron oxides that a polished surface is covered with an irregular network of dull, deep red lines, forming a beautiful contrast with the gray, rounded fossil forms. The Ogwell stones vary from light pinkish, mottled with gray, through dull red, and red spotted and veined with gray.

The well-known Bath stone or Bath oolite is a light, almost white or cream-colored oolitic limestone from quarries in the Jurassic formations which extend from the coast of Dorset, in the south of England, in a northeasterly direction through Somersetshire, Gloucestershire, Oxfordshire, Northamptonshire and Lincolnshire, to Yorkshire.

In texture it is distinctly oolitic, soft, and very easy to work. Its durability when exposed in the trying climate of America is a matter of great doubt. Nevertheless, churches and cathedrals erected in the west of England as long ago as the eleventh, twelfth, and fifteenth centuries, are stated by Hull to be still in a state of good preservation.

As yet the stone has been but little used in this country, though a movement has of late been on foot for its introduction.

Portland stone.—This stone, which has been in use in England since the middle of the seventeenth century, is a lightcolored Jurassic limestone from quarries on the Isle of Portland, near Weymouth. In composition it is a nearly pure carbonate of lime, but its texture is too uneven to recommend it for other than massive structures. It was used in the construction of St. Paul's Cathedral (London), and many churches erected during the reign of Queen Anne.

Ireland.—The so-called " Irish-black " is one of the best
known of the black marbles and has in times past been extensively imported into this country. The Angliham and Men-
lough quarries from whence the stone is taken are situated
about three miles north of Galway. As long ago as 1868 there
were 40 feet of clearing over the beds, and at the present date
the amount of clearing and pumping have greatly increased,
thereby adding much to the cost of the stone. In the Angliham quarry there were three beds of marble, one 9 inches
thick : one 12 inches thick : and one 14 inches thick. The 9
inch bed furnished the purest stone : the 12 inch bed was
known as the London bed, the product being held wholly for
the London market, preference being given to it on account of
its capability of being cut most economically. The historic
Kilkenny marble is from the quarries lying close to the river,
near Archers Grove, about half a mile south east of the town
of Kilkenny. The stone occurs in three varieties : shelly
black, pure black and dark gray. The shelly black is the best
known variety, the black background thickly studded with
white shells giving it a world wide reputation. Other black
marbles are found in the town of Carlow, in Donegal, Ferm-
auagh, Kerry, Limerick, Mayo, Monaghan, Sligo, Tipperary
and Waterford. According to G. H. Kinahan, who is authority for the above, * the Irish black marbles were at one time in
great request, quarries in various counties being worked in
great measure for exportation to England and elsewhere. The
pure black varieties were used mainly for monumental purposes. Although in late years the best " blacks " were most
in requisition, yet the black mottled or white spotted, like the
famous Kilkenny stone, were much sought, as were also the

---

* Economic Geology of Ireland. Journal Royal Geological Society of Ireland, vol. VIII. (new series), part II. 1886-87, p. 137.

inferior varieties, used mainly for tombstones. At present the trade is very low, only the best black varieties being now in demand.

EUROPE.

Belgium.—This country is stated by Violet * to be exceptionally rich in colored marbles, though white varieties are entirely wanting. They are mostly of a somber or dull color, and, like the marbles of Northern France, belong, according to Delesse, † to the Carboniferous and Devonian formations. The principal varieties now quarried for exportation, as represented in the collections of the National Museum, are the black of St. Anne, from Biesme, province of Namur, the blue from Couillet, near Charleroi, province of Hainaut, the reds from Cerfontaine and Merlemont, near Philippeville, province of Namur, and the well-known " Belgian black " from quarries in Golzines, and the environs of Dinant, also in the province of Namur.‡ All of these are very fine grained and compact, admitting of smooth surfaces and high polish.

The St. Anne marble is of a deep blue-black color with many short and interrupted veins of white ; those of Couillet are much lighter in color and with more white ; some of the varieties are breccias composed of fragments of compact blue-gray limestone imbedded in a white crystalline matrix. The red marbles of Cerfontaine and Merlemont are known as *rouge griotte, rouge griotte fleuré, rouge impérial* and *rouge royal.* All

---

* Les marbres, p. 44.

† Matériaux de construction, p. 194.

‡ Violet gives the full list of Belgian marbles as follows : "Le marbre Saint Anne, le rouge royal, le rouge impérial, la griotte de Flandre, le griotte fleurée, le granite belge, le bleu belge, la Florence belge, bizantin belge, bleu antique, le grand antique, le petit antique, et les marbres noirs de Golzinnes et de Dinant."

.

are dull red, of light and dark shades, variously spotted, flecked, and veined with white and gray ; none of them are as brilliant in color as the French griottes. The variety *rouge royal* is
very light, and somewhat resembles certain varieties of the
Tennessee marbles, but is inferior. The well-known Belgian
black is of a deep black color, hard, and difficult to work, but
takes a high polish, and is considered the best of its kind now
in the market.

France : Griotte, or French Red Marble.—This beautiful
stone takes its name, according to Violet,* from the griotte
cherry, owing to its brilliant red color. When, as frequently
happens, the uniform redness is broken by small white spots,
it is called " bird's-eye griotte " (*griotte œil de perdrix*). Some
varieties are traversed by white veins, but these are regarded
as defects and are avoided in quarrying. The stone is found
in several localities in the French Pyrenees, notably in the
valley of the Barousse, of the Pique, at the bridge of the
Taoulo, and in the environs of Prades. It is used for all manner of interior decorative work in France, and is exported to a
very considerable extent to this country. This is by all odds
the most brilliant in color of any marble of which the author
has knowledge. In the small slabs usually seen in soda fountains and counters it appears homogeneous and free from
flaws. As displayed in the halls of the capital building at
Albany, New York, however, it is full of flaws and has been so
extensively " filled " as to give the whole surface a gummy
appearance, in striking contrast with that of the Tennessee
marble with which it is associated. The price in France as
given by Violet is from 400 to 500 francs per cubic metre, or
about $2.75 to $3.50 per cubic foot, according to quality.

Another marble of a brilliant scarlet color, blotched with
white and known as Languedoc marble or French red, is stated

* Les Marbres, etc. Rapports sur L'Exposition Universelle, 1878, XXVIII. p. 15.

.

by Violet to occur at various points in the Pyrenees, but in masses of exceptional beauty and compactness at *Montagne Noire* (Black Mountain), where it has been quarried since the sixteenth century. It is obtainable here in blocks of considerable size, which bring in the market of Carcassone prices varying from 250 to 350 francs per cubic metre, or, roughly speaking, from $1.75 to $2.20 per cubic foot. Other French marbles, though which are but little used in this country, are the rose marble from Caunes, the *vert-moulin*, also called *griotte campan*, the *campan vert*, or the *campan mélangé*. The wrongly so-called Italian griotte is, according to Chateau, obtained from quarries at La Motte de Félines d'Hautpoul, Department of Herault. Violet states that this name was given it simply that it might command a higher price.

Caen stone.—This is one of the most noted limestones of modern history. It is a soft, fine-grained stone, very light colored, and admirably adapted for carved work, but so absorbent as to be entirely unfitted for outdoor work in such a climate as that of the United States. Egleston* states that in the climate of New York City the stone does not endure longer than ten years unless protected by paint.

The stone takes its name from Caen, in Normandy, where the principal quarries are situated. It was probably introduced into Great Britain soon after the Norman conquest, where it was largely used in cathedrals and other buildings down to the middle of the fifteenth century. The cathedral of Canterbury and Westminster Abbey are of this stone.

Brocatelle.—This is a very beautiful marble and much used for mantels and other interior decorations. The body of the stone is very fine and compact, and of a light yellow color, traversed by irregular veins and blotches of dull red. It is

---

* Transaction American Society of Civil Engineers, xv. 1886.

further variegated by patches or nodules of white crystalline calcite. It takes an excellent polish and requires less filling than many marbles. Its source is stated by Violet to be Jura, in southern France. The stone is difficult of extraction and brings a high price.

The name brocatelle is stated by Newberry to signify a coarse kind of brocade used for tapestry.

The National collections show a variety of coarsely mottled white, gray and almost black stones of fine grain and susceptible of a high polish, from Scherneck, near St. Die, and from Framont in the Department of Vosges; also a stone of similar structure but with a chocolate red base from the same locality. A compact black stone thickly studded with small white asterisks is found in the valley of the Hogneau. A coarse conglomerate marble taking a fair surface and polish, and composed of dull pink, yellowish and drab pebbles in a pinkish base, is found in the valley of Tholonet, near Aix, and is known commercially as *Breche d' Alet.*

Germany.—The two principal marbles now imported from this country are known commercially as *Formosa* and *Bougard.* Both are very beautiful stones, ranking among the finest now in general use. The first named is dark gray and white mottled and blotched with red; it is slightly fossiliferous. The Bougard has about the same colors, but is lighter and the tints are more obscure They are said to come from Nassau.

Austria.—The marbles of Austria stand in strong contrast with those of the United States, in that with few exceptions they have undergone less metamorphism, and are, therefore, of an extremely fine and compact, microcrystalline texture and often highly fossiliferous. Stones of this type of structure and varying from dark chocolate, through creamy white, pinkish, dull red and yellowish variegated, dark siena yellow or drab, and often beautifully brecciated, occur in the Jurassic formations in the vicinity of Castione, in the Tyrol. Drab and white mottled fossiliferous stones are also found in the Lias formations of this same district. Dark chocolate red and variegated, and gray and black highly fossiliferous stones are found near Saltzburg, and also pure white crystalline forms resembling those of Massachusetts and Connecticut. By far the most beautiful of the above are the pink, yellowish, and white brecciated varieties from Castione.

Many of these stones are hard and plucky, but can be worked down to a smooth surface and acquire a high polish such as is obtainable only on stones of such dense and compact structure. It is a matter of regret that similar stones are not as yet to be found on the markets of the United States.

Chalky white, buff and gray limestones suitable for building and carved work, but which do not polish, are obtained from the Miocene formations of Margarethen, Oszlopp, Mannersdorfer, Hundsheimer and other towns in Lower Austria. The so-called lumachelle marble is a fossiliferous limestone in which the shells still retain their nacre, or pearly lining, and which when polished gives off in spots a brilliant iridescent lustre with rainbow tints ; the finer varieties being seemingly set with opals. It is a beautiful stone for inlaid work and elaborate ornamentation, but is usually found only in small slabs. A variety quite commonly seen in mineral cabinets is of a dark grayish-brown color and with occasional brilliantly iridescent spots and streaks like those of the fire opal. It is brought from Bleiberg and Hall in the Tyrol.

Spain and Portugal.—These countries possess a great amount and variety of stone suitable for building and ornamental work, but, so far as the writer is aware, only a few of the marbles and limestones are exported to this country, and need be referred to here.

There is stated to be a zone of crystalline marbles of white,

yellow, and flesh color, which extends through the provinces of
Estremoz, Borba, and Villa Viçosa ; a black variety with white
veins also occurs at Monte Claros.   These are all susceptible
of a good polish, and blocks of large size can be obtained.
The beds belong to the Laurentian formations.   In Vianna,
Alrito, Portei, and the mountains of Ficalho other marbles are
found of the same general character.   The rocks of the
Jurassic and Cretaceous formations also furnish a large quantity of material for building and ornamental use.   This is
especially the case at Coimbra, Figueira da Foz, Cintra, and
Pero Pinheiro.   At Cintra the limestones have been metamorphosed by the adjoining granites, while those of Pero
Pinheiro were likewise metamorphosed by the volcanic rocks
of the suburbs of Lisbon.*

One of the finest of the above-mentioned marbles, and one
which is much used in the United States, is the yellow, from
Estremoz.   This is known commercially as *Lisbon* marble.   In
color and texture it is almost identical with the celebrated
Italian Siena, with which it favorably compares.   A peculiar
stone from this same locality is white with streaks and blotches
of a blood-red color.   It is more peculiar than beautiful.   The
marbles of Pero Pinheiro are of mottled white and pink—
almost red—color, fine grained and compact.   They are said
to have been extensively used in Lisbon, where they have
proved very durable.   Other marbles that perhaps need
especial mention are the breccias from Serra de Arrabida and
Chodes, Saragossa Province.   The first named is composed
of rounded and angular pebbles of a gray, drab, black, and red
color, embedded in a dull red paste.   In a general way it resembles the breccia from Montgomery County, Maryland, but

---

* Portuguese Special Catalogue, Departments, I., II., III., IV., and V.; International Exhibit, 1876, pp. 29, 30.

has less beauty. The Chodes stone is composed of very angular fragments, of a black color, in a reddish brown paste. The proportion of paste to the fragments is very large and much filling is necessary in polishing. Fine, compact marbles of dull reddish hues, often veined with drab, occur in Pannella Province. Others that may be mentioned are the red and yellow mottled marbles of Murcia Province, the black of Alicante Province, and the black white-veined breccias of Madrid. A fine translucent alabaster is also included among the productions of Saragossa Province.

A very full series of these stones was exhibited at the Centennial Exposition at Philadelphia in 1876, and from there transferred to the National Museum at Washington.

Italy.—The quarries of the Apennines in northern Italy, near Carrara, Massa, and Serravezza, furnish marbles of a great variety of colors of the finest qualities and in apparently inexhaustible quantities. To give a full description of these quarries and their various products would be to transcend the limits of this work. I shall therefore confine myself to a brief description of only those stones which are imported to any extent into this country.

White statuary marble.—This is a fine grained saccharoidal pure white stone, without specks or flaws. On a polished surface it has a peculiar soft, almost waxy appearance, entirely different from the dead whiteness of the Vermont statuary marbles, to which it is considered greatly superior. It is brought principally from the Poggio Silvestro and Betogli quarries, that from the first named locality being considered the best. The price of the stone in Italy varies from 15 to 40 lires per cubic foot in blocks of sufficient size for an ordinary statue 5 feet in height.

Ordinary white or block marble.—This is usually white in color, though sometimes faintly bluish and veined. It is largely imported into this country, and used for monumental work. The variety from the Canal Bianco quarries is white, with faint bluish lines ; that from Gioja quarries is fine-grained, and uniformly white and somewhat translucent, sometimes resembling gypsum on a polished surface. The variety from the Ravaccione quarries is faintly water-blue, while that from the Tantiscritti quarries is of similar color, but traversed by fine, dark-bluish veins. These stones sell for from 4 to 10 lires per cubic foot, in blocks containing not over 20 cubic feet each.

The veined marbles from the Vara and Gioja quarries are of a white color, but often blotched with darker hues, and traversed by a coarse irregular net-work of faintly bluish lines. The Bardiglio marbles of the ordinary type from the Para and Gioja quarries are of a water-blue color, blotched irregularly with white, and far inferior in point of beauty to the justly famed *Bardiglio veined* marbles from the Seravezza quarries. These are of a light-blue color, traversed by an irregular net-work of fine dark-blue lines, intersecting one another at acute angles. This stone is used very extensively in soda-water fountains, counters, and for panellings.

The red mixed marble from quarries at Levante is also much sought, but works with difficulty and requires much filling. It is properly a breccia, composed of irregular whitish and red fragments embedded in a reddish paste. It does not take a high polish, nor are its colors brilliant. The so-called *Parmazo* marbles, from the Miseglia, Pescina, and Bocca del Frobbi quarries, are all white or whitish, and traversed by a very coarse net-work of black or blue-black veins.

The yellow or Siena marbles are, next to the white statuary, probably the most sought and widely known of Italian marbles. Like the majority of foreign colored marbles, they are exceedingly fine-grained and compact in texture, and take a high lustrous polish. The prevailing color is bright yellow, though often blotched with slight purplish or violet shades. When these darker veins or blotches prevail to a considerable extent the stone is called *Brocatelle.* The most beautiful variety of the Siena marble is obtained, according to Delesse, from Monte Arenti, in Montagnola. It is of a uniform yellow color, but blocks of large size can be obtained only rarely, and these often bring a price as high as $6 per cubic foot. The Brocatelle variety from the same locality is worth only about two-thirds this sum.

The Portor or black and gold marble.—This is, according to Delesse, a black silicious limestone, traversed by yellowish, reddish, or brown veins of carbonate of iron. It is brought chiefly from the Isle of Palmaria, in the Gulf of Spezia, and from Porto Venere. A small amount is also produced at Carrara and Serravezza. Blocks of this stone in the National Museum show a good surface and high polish. It is a beautiful stone, and the name black and gold well describes it. The Portor marble, from the Monte d'Arma quarries, is a breccia of fragments of black limestone with a yellowish cement. This is inclined to break away in the process of dressing, thus rendering the production of a perfect surface impossible without much filling.

Black marble.—A fair variety of this material is brought from the Colonnata quarries. The stone is not as dark as the Belgian black, nor does it admit of so high a polish.

Breccia marble.—The breccia marbles from Gragnana and Serravezza I have never seen in use in this country, though they are stated to be imported to a slight extent. The first-named consists of small bluish-white fragments cemented closely by a chalk-red cement, while the second variety has both white and red fragments similarly cemented.

The yellow marbles of Verona and Gragnana are quite different in appearance from those of Siena, being rather of a brownish hue, and taking only a dull polish. They are compact rocks, excellently adapted for decorative work. The so called red marble from the Castel Poggio quarries is rather a chocolate color, dull in polish, but pleasing to the eye.

Ruin marble.—This is a very compact yellowish or drab limestone, the beds of which appear to have been fractured in every conceivable direction by geological agencies, after which the resultant fragments have become recemented by a calcareous or ferruginous cement. The rock is therefore really a breccia, although the proportional amount of cement is very small, and the actual displacement of the various particles but slight. When cut and polished the slabs have somewhat the appearance of mosaics, representing the ruins of ancient castles or other structures. Hence the name of "ruin marble." The locality as given by Delesse, is the bridge of Rignano, Val de Sieve, in the environs of Florence, Italy.

Greece.—The celebrated Parian marble of the ancients was brought from Paros, a small island of the Grecian Archipelago. It is stated * that the southern part only of the island consists of crystalline limestone, the pure white statuary marble forming beds of from five to fifteen feet in thickness intercalated with other layers of coarser texture and traversed by dark veins, the coloring matter being oxides of iron and manganese. It is further stated that the marble beds are much disturbed and folded, and often dip at high angles. The ancients avoided the stone lying near the axis of this elevation, as being of poorer quality than that in other parts. A recently formed Greek company instead of profiting by this experience attempted quarrying in these parts, but the poor character of the material obtained soon discredited the marble in the market, and the company failed as a consequence after expending some $800,000 in their plant.

* Robert Swan in Report British Association, Sept., 1889.

SOME MINOR ORNAMENTAL STONES.

It may be well to mention here, briefly, a few of the rarer stones used for ornamental purposes, particularly for inlaid and finely decorative work. Such stones as are used merely as gems will not be included, since they are sufficiently well described in other available treastises. (See bibliography, p. 428).

Agalmatolite.—This is a somewhat general name given to a not well defined class of rocks of varying composition but having in common a fine compact texture free from grit, a serpentinous or talcose look and feel, and which owing to their physical rather than chemical properties are readily carved into a variety of forms. The more important substances here included are the minerals pyrophyllite and pinite. The first is an aluminous bisilicate of the composition, silica 64.82%, alumina 24.48, water 5.25%, with traces of iron, magnesia and lime. A nearly white schistose rock of this nature occurs in the Deep River region, and at Carbonton, Moore County, North Carolina, but is utilized only as a white earth and for slate pencils. Near Washington in Wilkes County, Georgia, is a deep lustrous green and white variety of the same mineral, and which though soft could be used advantageously in certain forms of ornamentation. On a polished surface the stone shows a gray groundmass mottled with irregular streaks and blotches of pea green and occasional shreds of silvery white mica.

Pinite is, according to Dana, a hydrous alkaline silicate, containing silica 46%, alumina 30%, potash 10%, water 6%. Rocks of this general class are much used in China, Corea and Japan for making a variety of objects including ornamental dishes, miniature pagodas, and grotesque images. The name agalmatolite, according to the the above authority, being from the Greek αγαλμα, an image, and pagodite from *pagoda*, on

account of the use to which the stone is put.   A common color
of the Chinese rock is faint greenish mottled with red.   A similar stone from the State of Sonora, Mexico, is exhibited in the
collections of the National Museum, but there are no records
to show that it has here ever been put to any use.

Catlinite, or *Indian Pipestone.*—Although frequently found
in the collections of amateur mineralogists this substance cannot be considered a true mineral, but as shown by analyses is
rather an indurated clay of quite variable composition.   The
usual color is a deep though dull red, often beautifully flecked
with small yellowish dots.   The stone is soft enough to be
readily cut with a knife, but is sufficiently firm and compact to
retain the sharpest edges and lines that may be carved upon it.
There is, in fact, an entire absence of granulation and its texture
is as fine and close as that of the Bavarian lithographic stone.

The material first derived its notoriety from the fact that
the Sioux Indians utilized it for the manufacture of their pipes
and various other articles, and at the present time these same
people living in the vicinity of Flandreau, Dakota, derive a
considerable income from the manufacture and sale of these
articles.   The substance is found in various places in Minnesota and Wisconsin, but the principal quarry, if such it can be
called, is situated a little north of what is now Pipestone City,
in Pipestone County, Minnesota.   The country is low prairie
land, and the stone occurs as a layer of only about eighteen
inches thickness, interstratified with a hard, tough quartzite.   It
can therefore be obtained in pieces of only very moderate
dimensions, and this too at a very considerable outlay of time
and labor.*

The color and textural qualities of the stone are such that

---

*See Geology of Minnesota, vol. II.; also American Journal Science, 1867,
p. 15, and American Naturalist, 1868–69.

it might, in proper combinations, be used to excellent advantage in interior decorative work.

On the Sweetwater branch of the Ruby River south-west from Virginia City, in Madison County, Montana, there occurs a peculiar rock, in many respects similar to that just described.

Whatever may have been the origin of the rock it now has the aspect of an indurated clay. Its prevailing colors are gray, drab, yellow and red sometimes pinkish, or bluish, the colors being always arranged in concentric zones varying from the dimensions of a mere line to an inch or more in width. The rock occurs only in small jointed blocks, and the zonal banding is in all cases approximately parallel to the outline of the blocks, being a product of the oxidation of the ferruginous constituent of the rock.

In texture the rock is as smooth, fine and homogeneous as is the catlinite above described. It hence is susceptible of a fine surface and good polish. In proper combination the stone could be used to good advantage for interior decorations. At present the nearest railroad shipping point is at Dillon some twenty-five miles away.

Fossil Coral.—The masses of fossil acervularia from the Devonian limestones of Iowa furnish very beautiful material for small ornaments, as already described on p. 92.

Labradorite.—The name Labradorite is given to a mineral belonging to the feldspar group, and which owes its claims to recognition as an ornamental stone to a beautiful and sometimes actually gorgeous iridescence in every shade of blue, green and yellow. The stone is of a gray color, quite hard, and as a rule the iridescent portions occur only in small areas. As moreover the polished surface needs be turned at various angles with the light in order to bring out its full beauty, it is not well suited for stationary objects, but

rather for vases and other small ornaments. The present supply comes mainly from Labrador and Russia. It is the presence of this feldspar that gives rise to the bluish iridesence
sometimes seen on the so-called *Au Sable* granite, quarried at
Keeseville, New York.

Lapis–Lazuli.—This is a hard, tough and compact rock of
a rich, azure-blue color, and vitreous lustre. It is not a homogeneous mineral, but an intimate mixture of granular calcite,
ekebergite and a blue mineral, the exact chemical nature of
which has not been fully made out. The chemical composition, as given by Dana, shows it to be composed mainly of silica
and alumina, with smaller percentages of lime, soda, iron, and
sulphur.

The stone is much esteemed for highly ornamental inlaid
work, but is very expensive, so that as a rule it is used only in
the form of a thin veneering.

The stone occurs in granular limestone and syenitic rocks
according to Dana. The commercial supply is brought from
Persia, Siberia and China.

Malachite and Azurite.—These are the names given to the
green and blue carbonates of copper, and which occur at times
in sufficient abundance and compactness of texture to permit
of their being utilized for table tops, vases and other small
ornaments. Both forms of the carbonate are common as ores
of copper, though it is but rarely that they occur in such
abundance as to be of value for decorative purposes.

The most noted source of malachite is Nijni Tagilsk, in the
Russian Urals. The mineral occurs in stalagmitic masses of a
beautiful banded structure and of various shades of green.
Solid blocks of a cubic yard in dimensions are stated to have
been obtained here.

Another source is the Burra Burra Mine, near Adelaide,
Australia. Smaller masses have been found in the copper
mines of Arizona.

The deep azure blue carbonate *azurite* is less common than malachite. It occurs not infrequently interbanded with the latter in stalagmitic masses, which show, therefore, beautiful blue and green concentric bands when cut across.

Nephrite, or *Jade.*—The name nephrite, or jade, has been given by mineralogists to a very compact and tough, light greenish to whitish mineral of the amphibole group, and which has been used for making cutting-implements and ornaments by numerous widely-scattered barbarous or semi-barbarous nations. The attention of scientists was first drawn to the substance by the finding of implements of it, not only among the tribes still living, but among prehistoric ruins, such as the Swiss lake dwellings. The constant recurrence of objects of this nature among perhaps widely separated tribes was a very striking fact, and it was thought at one time that this might indicate a means of inter-tribal intercourse, or trade, or even perhaps a common origin, since it at first seemed scarcely probable that a stone so difficult to work and of so similar an appearance should be found and utilized for similar purposes the world over. This idea has, however, been now shown to be fallacious. It is, however, none the less interesting a fact that the mineral occurs in comparative rarity among so many nations, and that moreover it should have quite independently been in all cases adopted for similar purposes.

The localities from whence objects of nephrite have from time to time been reported by collectors, are as follows: Brittany, Switzerland, Silesia, New Zealand, New Caledonia, China, Turkestan, Siberia and Alaska.

The finding of nephrite objects, as knives, beads, etc., among natives of the last-named place, after it was known to occur in Siberia, gave rise to the erroneous supposition that there was tribal communication between the two localities. Within a few years, however, various United States exploring parties have brought in samples of the rough jade found *in situ* in Alaska, proving again the oft-proved fact that as a means of tracing migration or communication, the occurrence of the substance is of no value.

The Chinese seem to have been the great masters in working this refractory material, and their delicate carvings of jade are famous the world over, and sometimes bring almost fabulous prices among collectors. A thousand dollars for a finely carved vase or ornament, perhaps but a few inches in length, is, as I am informed, no uncommon figure. It is stated that in the Indian museum, in London, there is a beautiful white jade object which it required three generations of jade workers eighty-five years to complete. As with many other stones, jade or nephrite was once believed to possess medicinal virtue, and its name, nephrite, is from the Greek word *nephros*, signifying kidney, in allusion to its supposed efficacy in diseases of these organs.

It is stated that jade was in use among the Chinese fully 2,737 years before Christ, or more than 4,600 years ago.

Obsidian.—The possibilities of this rock will be mentioned under the head of liparites, and it need not be further described here.

Pegmatite—Graphic Granite. This a granitic rock consisting mainly of quartz and orthoclase, but in which the constituents instead of crystallizing in the usual granular condition are in the form of long parallel and imperfect prisms as will be later noted, so that a cross section shows the clear glassy quartz rudely imitative of letters of the ancient Grecian or Phœnician alphabet, set mosaic-like in a groundmass of white orthoclase.

The prevailing color is nearly white, the stone is hard and can be worked only in comparatively small pieces.

Quartz.—The various forms of silica, known as quartz

agate, jasper, etc., are almost too well known to merit special mention.

The ordinary limpid quartz and the amethystine variety is used in the cheaper forms of jewelry and is carved into beautiful images or polished spheres by the Japanese, but it is not used for large ornamentation. The name jasper is given to an impure crypto-crystalline variety colored, blotched and streaked with shades of red, brown and yellow by iron oxides. The heliotrope or bloodstone, a green jasper blotched with blood red, is one of the most prized varieties. The name agate is given to the banded nodular masses of chalcedony that form in the cavities of trap rock or sometimes replace the organic matter in fossil wood. Nearly all agates as sold are colored artificially by first boiling them in honey or an organic oil and then heating them, whereby the carbonaceous matter absorbed unequally by the various layers is turned various shades of brown and black, thereby rendering more conspicuous the banding. Wood is not infrequently fossilized by silica, the organic matter being replaced atom by atom by the siliceous matter until a more or less complete cast of the woody structure remains. Such are often variously colored, mainly in red tints by iron oxides and when cut and polished are very beautiful.

In the so-called fossil forest near Corriza, Apache County, Arizona, have been found many tree trunks thus fossilized, which, when cut and polished, have furnished small columns and tops for stands, of exceptional beauty.

The great toughness of the material renders it very expensive to work.

Rhodochrosite.—This mineral is chemically a carbonate of manganese. Its claim as an ornamental stone lies in its compact texture and delicate pink color. Unfortunately it has never been found in uniform masses of large size; and as, moreover, it is stated to fade slightly on exposure to strong light, its utility is perhaps doubtful. It occurs commonly in veins along with ores of gold, silver and copper. Fine massive blocks are taken out of the silver and copper mines at Butte, Montana.

Rhodonite.—This is a silicate of manganese of a red or pink color and frequently more or less streaked and spotted. It is hard and tough, with a close texture, and admits of a high polish. It has been as yet but little used, the main supply being brought from the Urals of Siberia. Boulders of the material have frequently been found at Cunningham, Massachusetts, and it has been stated * that the parent ledge is also now known. As the mineral here is of exceptionally fine color, there is, perhaps, a prospect that it may become of some commercial value.

Like rhodochrosite it is stated to change color on prolonged exposure.

Thulite stone.—The name thulite is given to a red manganese epidote, and hence the name thulite stone to a rock in which this mineral is the essential constituent. So far as the author is aware rocks of this nature have as yet been found in any abundance only in Norway, at Hinderheim about 21 kilometers north of Trondhjem, on the north side of the Trondhjemfjord. As above noted the essential constituent is thulite ; there is also a little quartz, piedmontite, and common epidote.

The texture is finely granular and the color a pleasing rose red. It has as yet been little used, owing to the difficulty of obtaining large blocks of uniform color, its brittle nature, and the difficulty of polishing. The rock is described as occurring in sporadic areas, rarely more than 5 or 6 feet across, in a granitic gneiss.†

---

* Mineral Resources of the United States. 1887.
† H. Reusch. Geologiske Iagttageleer Fra Trondhjems Stifft. 1890.

THE GRANITES AND GNEISSES.

(I) COMPOSITION AND GENERAL PROPERTIES.

Granite from the Latin *granum*, a grain, in allusion to the granular structure.

The essential constituents of granite are quartz and a potash feldspar (either orthoclase or microcline) and plagioclase. Nearly always one or more minerals of the mica, hornblende or pyroxene group are present, and in small, usually microscopic, proportions, the accessories magnetite, apatite, and zircon; more rarely occur sphene, beryl, tourmaline, topaz, garnet epidote, allanite, fluorite and pyrite. Delesse* has made the following determination of the relative proportion of the principal constituents in two well-known granites.

RED EGYPTIAN GRANITE	PORPHYRITIC GRANITE, VOSGES.
Red orthoclase............43%	White orthoclase...........28%
White albite.............. 9%	Reddish oligoclase.......... 7%
Gray quartz..............44%	Gray quartz...............59%
Black Mica.............. 4%	Mica........... .... 6%
100%	100%

The average chemical composition is as follows :

	Per cent.
Silica....	72.00
Alumina.......................................	15.07
Iron peroxide...................................	2.22
Magnesia	5.00
Lime..	2.00
Potash..	4.12
Soda..	2.90
Loss by ignition..............................	1.19

* Prestwich Chemical and Physical Geology, vol. I. p 42.

The average specific gravity of granite is 2.66, which is equal to a weight of 166½ pounds per cubic foot, or practically 2 tons per cubic yard. According to Professor Ansted* granites ordinarily contain about 0.8 per cent. of water, and are capable of absorbing some 0.2 per cent. more. In other words, a cubic yard would in its ordinary state contain 3.5 gallons of water. The crushing strength of granite is quite variable, but usually lies between 15,000 and 20,000 pounds per square inch, as will be seen by reference to the tables.

Structurally the granites are holocrystalline granular rocks without trace of amorphous interstitial matter. As a rule none of the essential constituents show perfect crystal outlines, though the feldspathic minerals are often quite perfectly formed. The quartz has in all cases been the last mineral to solidify, and hence occurs only as irregular granules occupying the interspaces of the other minerals. It appears always fresh and glassy, but on microscopic examination is found to contain numerous inclosures, such as rutile needles and little prisms of apatite. A most interesting fact is the presence of minute cavities within the quartz, usually filled wholly or in part with a liquid, though sometimes empty. This liquid is commonly water containing various salts, as the chloride of sodium or potassium, which at times separates out in the form of minute crystals. Carbonic acid is frequently present, giving rise to a minute bubble like that of a spirit-level, and which moves from side to side of its small chamber as though endowed with life. So minute are these cavities that it has been estimated from one to ten thousand millions could be contained in a single cubic inch of space.† The rocks vary in texture almost indefinitely, presenting all gradations from fine and evenly granu-

---

* Hull, Building and Ornamental Stones, p. 30.
† Judd, Volcanoes ; What they are and what they teach, p. 64.

lar to coarsely porphyritic forms, in which the feldspars, which are the only constituents porphyritically developed, are several inches in length. The prevailing color is some shade of gray, though greenish, yellowish, pink and deep red are not uncommon. The various hues are due to the color of the prevailing feldspar and the abundance and kind of the accessory minerals. Granites in which muscovite is the prevailing mica are nearly always very light gray in color : the dark gray colors are due largely to abundant black mica or hornblende : the greenish, pink or red colors to the prevailing greenish, pink or red feldspars. The varying effects of the predominating constituents upon the physical and enduring qualities of the stone have already been referred to under the head of rock-forming minerals and need not be repeated here.

Gneiss differs from granite in that its various constituents are arranged in more or less paralled layers, giving the rock a banded or schistose structure and causing it to split in a direction paralled with the bands much more readily than across them. Chemically and from a mineral standpoint the rock is identical with granite and is used so far as these structural peculiarities will allow for the same purposes. It is therefore in the following pages included with the granites. The word *gneiss*, it should be stated, is of German origin and pronounced as is our word *nice*, not as though spelled *nees*.

These rocks are often called *stratified* or *bastard* granites by the quarrymen.

(2) GEOLOGICAL AGE AND MODE OF OCCURRENCE.

The granites are massive rocks, occuring most frequently associated with the older and lower rocks of the earth's crust, sometimes interstratified with metamorphic rocks or forming the central portions of mountain chains. They are not, as once supposed, the oldest of rocks, but occur frequently in eruptive masses or bosses invading rocks of all ages up to late Mesozoic or Tertiary times. Thus Professor Whitney considers the eruptive granites of the Sierra Nevada to be Jurassic. Zirkel divides the granites described in the reports of the 40th Parallel Survey into three groups ; (1) Those of Jurassic age ; (2) those of Paleozoic age, and (3) those of Archæan age. The granites of the eastern United States, on the other hand, have, in times past, been regarded as mainly Archæan, though Dr. Wadsworth* has shown that the Quincy, Massachusetts, stone is an eruptive rock of late Primordial or more recent age, while Professor Hitchcock regards the eruptive granites of Vermont as having been protruded during Silurian or perhaps Devonian times.

(3) VARIETIES OF GRANITE.

In classifying granites the varietal distinction is based upon the prevailing accessory minerals. The more common varieties are *muscovite* granite, *biotite* granite, *muscovite-biotite* granite, *hornblende* granite and *hornblende-biotite* granite ; more rarely occur *augite, epidote, tourmaline, cordierite,* and *chlorite* granites. The variety without any accessory minerals is sometimes called *granitell. Protogine* is the name given to granites which have talc or chlorite as the characterizing accessory. Pegmatite or graphic granite is a vein rock containing little if any mica, but consisting nearly altogether of quartz and orthoclase. It owes its peculiar structure to the crystallization of these two constituents in long parallel and imperfect prisms, so that a cross-section shows peculiar triangular and polygonal figures comparable to the letters of the ancient Greek or Phœnician alphabets.

---

* Proceedings Boston Society of National History, XXI. 1881.

Aplit is a name used by the Germans for a granite quite poor in mica, and consisting essentially of quartz and feldspar only. The name *greisen* is applied to a quartz-mica rock with accessory topaz occurring associated with the tin ores of Saxony, and regarded as a granite metamorphosed by exhalations of fluoric acid. *Luxullianite* and *Trowlesworthite* are tourmaline-fluorite granites occurring at Luxullian and Trowlesworth in Cornwall, England.

By far the larger proportion of the granites at present quarried in the United States have mica, either muscovite or biotite, as the characterizing accessory, and hence can be spoken of as mica granites.

(4) USES OF GRANITE.

Owing to their great hardness granites have, until within a few years, been used only in the more massive forms of architecture. It is true that in past ages the cheapness of human life and labor in great part counterbalanced this difficulty, and that Egyptian civilization has left a profusion of temples, obelisks, pyramids and statues with surfaces or interiors often carved and polished in the finest and most delicate manner. With the present high valuation set upon labor such work could never be executed but by the aid of improved machinery and methods of workmanship.*

It is perhaps only within the last dozen or possibly twenty years that granite has begun to be considered an ornamental stone. Buildings antedating this are massive, and in only too many instances sombre and unpleasing. One's attention need,

---

* Granite came into early use for building purposes in America probably more on account of its ready accessibility than from any desire on the part of the people for so refractory a material, the matter of transportation then, as now, being an important item in deciding what material was to be used.

however, but be called to the highly ornate character of the State, War and Navy Department building in Washington, the polished granite stairways and pilasters in the new City Hall in Philadelphia, and the thousands of granite tombstones and monuments in our cemeteries to be convinced that the stone not merely possesses all the requisite qualities of an ornamental stone, but that its use as such is also eminently practicable. There are, indeed, few stones fitted by nature for so wide an application. Ranging in colors from nearly white to dark gray, from the most delicate pink to deep red, from fine and evenly granular to coarsely porphyritic, the stone more nearly meets the universal need than any other that can be mentioned. It has well been called the noblest of rocks.

(5) GRANITES OF THE VARIOUS STATES AND TERRITORIES.

California.—It is stated that the first stone house erected in San Francisco was built of stone brought from China, and at the present day the granites most employed are brought from Scotland and the Eastern United States. However this may be, it is obvious that this condition of affairs need not long continue to exist, since granites of good quality occur in inexhaustible quantity in the near vicinity. As early as 1853 a granite quarry was opened in Sacramento County, and since then others have been opened and systematically worked in Penrhyn and Rocklin in Placer County. The Penrhyn works are some 28 miles east from Sacramento on the line of the Central Pacific Railroad. The first quarries were opened in 1864, and are now said to cover some 680 acres at Penrhyn and Rocklin,* the latter point being some 6 or 8 miles distant from the former in a westerly direction.

---

* Samples of stone said to be from Rocklin, and which the writer has examined, are rather quartz diorites than true granites.

The rock varies in color from light to dark gray, one variety, which contains both hornblende and biotite, being almost black on a polished surface. They are, as a rule, fine grained, and take a good polish. Blocks more than 100 feet long, 50 feet wide, and ten feet thick have been quarried out and afterwards broken up.

The Penrhyn stone is designated a hornblende granitite by Jackson,* who gives its mineral composition as quartz, orthoclase, plagioclase, hornblende, and biotite, with microscopic apatite and magnetite. Submitted by the above authority to the action of a carbonic acid gas solution, a sample of this stone lost 0.05 per cent in weight; by disintegration in acid fumes it lost 1.09 per cent. In this latter treatment every mica scale on the surface of the exposed fragments bleached to a pearly whiteness. The iron was dissolved out, staining the rock slightly, while the feldspar grains became a trifle duller in lustre. On being heated in a muffle to somewhat above a bright redness, the stone developed a complete network of deep-seated cracks, and after emersion in water could be readily crushed to powder in the hands.

The Rocklin stone is described by the same authority as a fine-grained white stone, carrying abundant small scales of black mica and occasional granules of pyrite. The composition is given as essentially the same as the Penrhyn stone, but that muscovite replaces the hornblende. Submitted to the same tests as above the stone lost in the carbonic acid gas solution 0.1 per cent; and by decomposition and disintegration in the strong acid fumes 0.68 per cent. In this, as in the last case, mica scales bleached white, and the rock became slightly stained. Heated in the muffle the stone behaved like the Penrhyn granite, though not cracking quite so deeply; it,

---

* Eighth Annual Report State Mineralogist of California. 1888.

however, could be readily crushed to powder after immersion. Reports on crushing strength and ratio of absorption of these stones, and also that of a very similar granite from Mount Raymond is Fresno County are given in the table, on p. 404. A fine quarry of granite is stated to occur some eight miles northeast of Sonora in Tuolumne County.

A fine-grained, very light-gray granite of excellent appearance, said to be found on the line of the California Southern Railroad between Los Angeles and Cucamonga, is beginning to be used in Los Angeles. In texture it is as fine as the finest Westerly, (Rhode Island), or Manchester (Virginia) stone, and of a uniform light gray color. A coarser stone, carrying abundant hornblende and black mica, is found also at Sawpit Cañon, in the same county. It works readily, but contains too much hornblende, and also too many small crystals of sphene, to be of value for fine monumental work.

Colorado.—Until within a comparatively recent period granites have been but little worked in Colorado, although the State contains great quantities of this material. A coarse red granite has been quarried to some extent from bowlders at Platte Cañon, Jefferson County, but the rock is poor in color and possesses but little tenacity. Fine gray granite of good quality occurs at Georgetown and Lawson, in Clear Creek County, and there are inexhaustible quantities of equally good material all through the mountains, but which are not quarried owing to the cost of transportation.

· *Connecticut.*—Extensive quarries of granite and gneiss are located at various points in this State, especially near Thomaston and Roxbury, in Litchfield County; on Long Island Sound, Fairfield County: near Ansonia, Bradford, and Stony Creek, New Haven County; Haddam, Middlesex County, and near Lyme, Niantic, Groton, and Mason's Island, New London County. The Connecticut granites and gneisses are usually fine-grained and light gray in color, and the appearance is, as a rule, so characteristic as to distinguish them from other granites of the Atlantic States.

The most of these stones are, however, quarried only for local use, and but few find their way into markets outside of the State. A beautiful light gray muscovite-biotite granite is quarried at Thomaston and Reynolds Bridge, which for evenness of grain and clearness of color cannot be excelled. The stone from Roxbury is a trifle darker, but though of fine and even grain and acquiring a good polish, is used only for curbings, foundations, and pavings. The Ansonia rock is a very fine-grained muscovite biotite gneiss, and has been used for general building purposes in New Haven and Bridgeport. The Leetes Island and Stoney Creek rocks are of a pink color, the first mentioned being sometimes very coarsely porphyritic. A turned column of the Leetes Island rock in the National Museum shows large pink orthoclase crystals two inches or more in length embedded in the finer gray groundmass of the rock. A beautiful and very coarsely crystalline red granite occurs near Lyme, but the stone is not in the market, being too expensive to work. It has been used to some extent in Newport, Rhode Island, and some of the material may be seen in the Chaney Memorial Church at this place. Contrary to the general rule in red granites, the feldspars of this rock are not opaque but quite clear and transparent, and in point of beauty the rock far excels the celebrated Scotch granites from Peterhead. The Haddam, Greenwich, and Bridgeport gneisses are all hornblendic, very dark gray, and split readily in the direction of their lamination; their uses are strictly local.

Delaware.—This State produces scarcely anything in the way of granitic rocks. A few quarries of a dark gray gneissoid rock are worked near Wilmington, and are used for general building purposes in this city. One church and several private dwellings have been constructed of this stone.

Georgia.—Although this State is known to contain inexhaustible quantities of building stones of the finest quality, but little systematic quarrying is done, and none of the rocks have more than a local reputation. A fine grade of muscovite granite, light gray in color, occurs, at Stone Mountain, near Atlanta, and also a dark gray hornblendic gneiss. A hornblendic granite resembling that of Quincy, Massachusetts, is said to occur in Oglethorpe County, though the author has never seen any of the material.

Maine.—The large extent of coast line of the State of Maine, composed of granitic rocks of a kind suitable for building purposes, renders possible the shipment and transportation of the quarried rock at rates much lower than would otherwise be attainable, the quarries being frequently situated so near the water's edge that little, if any, handling is necessary prior to loading upon the vessel. This favorable circumstance, together with the excellent quality of the rock obtainable, led to the early opening of very numerous quarries both on the mainland and the adjacent islands, and hence at the present time Maine granites are found in very general use in nearly every city of importance in the country, even as far west as California, and frequently to the almost entire exclusion of perhaps equally good material close at hand.

The granitic areas of the State are outlined as follows by Prof. Hitchcock : * First is the Katahdin area, exclusively in the forest region. This is generally a fine grained rock, that on Mount Katahdin is tabular, and the sheets have a dip like sedimentary strata. The summit rock is red, capping a white variety of granite. The divisional planes seem, however, to be

---

* Geology of Northern New England.

joints. Neither this nor any of the granite areas appear like gneiss, though patches of gneiss may occasionally be seen close at hand. Between Penobscot Bay and Schoodic Lake (in Washington County) there is probably a continuous band of granite, which extends through New Brunswick northeasterly a distance of two hundred and ninety miles, and a width varying from ten to twenty miles. Between Elsworth and Holden, eleven miles, this range is porphyritic. In Topsfield, Washington County, it is hornblendic. Protogene (chlorite granite) composes green mountain in Eden, on Mt. Desert. Elsewhere on the island, there is common granite, and a red compact variety, with feldspars predominating. This granitic area seems to be connected with the one just described on the west. Another large granite area extends from Jonesport to Calais in Washington County, and thence into New Brunswick.

According to the returns furnished by the special agents in the employ of the building-stone department of the Tenth Census, there were during the census year some eighty-three quarries of various kinds of building stone in the State, situated chiefly either immediately on the coast or within easy reach of tide-water. Of these eighty-three quarries seventy-four were of granite or gneiss. The different varieties of these stones produced may be classed under the following heads: Biotite granite, biotite-muscovite granite, hornblende granite, hornblende-biotite granite, biotite gneiss, and biotite-muscovite gneiss. The great majority of the stones now quarried belong to the first-named variety. They vary in color usually from light to dark gray, though pinkish and red varieties are quarried in a few instances. At Red Beach, near Calais, and at Jonesborough there is quarried a pink or reddish rock, very compact and hard, which from a simple examination with the unaided eye is seen to be composed of pink or cream-colored feldspars, smoky quartz, and a few small shreds of mica. An examination of a thin section with the microscope does not greatly increase the number of constituent minerals. The mica, which is usually of a greenish color, is very evenly disseminated throughout the rock and in very small shreds, bearing numerous inclosures of magnetite. A few small apatite crystals are as usual present, but are visible only with a microscope.

The evenness of the grain of these rocks, and the occurrence of the mica only in small amount and in minute flakes are matters of great practical importance, since they allow the production of a more perfect surface and lasting polish than would otherwise be possible. The texture is much finer than is that of the red Scotch granite, and the color a more delicate pink. They are, in fact, the most beautiful of any of our pink or red granites now in the market, and are used very extensively for monuments, ornamental work, and general building purposes. The largest blocks ever taken out from these quarries was 7 by 7 feet and 2 feet thick. It is said, however, that blocks 30 by 15 by 2½ feet could be obtained if desired. The principal markets of the stone are Boston, Providence, New York City, Baltimore, Philadelphia, Buffalo, Cincinnati, Cleveland, and Columbus, Ohio, Springfield and Chicago, Illinois, Milwaukee, St. Louis, Charleston, South Carolina, Washington, D. C., and San Francisco, California.

At West Sullivan, in Hancock County, a light gray, sometimes slightly pinkish, granite of medium texture is extensively quarried for paving blocks and general building purposes. The stone corresponds closely with that quarried in the town of Franklin. At Somesville, on Somes Sound, near Southwest Harbor, Mt. Desert, is quarried a granite of rather coarse texture and of a slightly pinkish tinge, the color being due to the orthoclase which is often present in crystals of such size as to give the work a slight porphyritic structure.

This stone was used in the construction of the Brooklyn approaches to the East River Bridge, and in the arches and foundations of the new bridges in Back Bay Park, Boston. Blocks 150 by 50 by 18 feet have been loosened in the quarry. The position of these quarries is peculiarly good for shipping, as they lie near the head of Somes Sound, along a narrow and very deep fiord, running several miles inland from Southwest Harbor, between the mountains. One of the quarries is situated on the side of a hill and at the water's edge. The sheets of stone are very thick in some cases, one being 18 feet in thickness.

A coarse dull red, very tough and strong hornblende granite is also quarried on the island at Otter Creek, between Somes Sound and Bar Harbor. The stone is of finer texture than are the red Scotch granites, and more closely resembles the red granites of the Bay of Fundy than any other with which the writer is acquainted. Its value for purely monumental purposes is often lessened by the presence of black patches of finer grain, and which are objectionable either on fine cut or polished surfaces.

In the vicinity of East Blue Hill, in this same county, are quarried some of the most beautiful gray granites at present in the market. The rock varies from fine, even-grained gray or slightly pinkish to coarsely porphyritic. A foot cube of this granite in the National collections is composed of a fine even-grained gray groundmass, carrying very many snow-white crystals of orthoclase an inch or more in length. This is one of the most beautiful gray granites for monumental work with which the author is acquainted. Blocks 90 by 80 by 6 feet have been moved out in some of these quarries. Specimens of this granite tested at the Centennial Exposition at Philadelphia in 1876, showed a crushing strength of 22,000 pounds per square inch. In the quarries the stone lies in sheets from 3 to 10 feet in thickness. A portion of the granite from this region is of a pinkish cast, similar to that of Mt. Desert. On the southern end of Deer Isle, also in Hancock County, and on the smaller islands in the immediate vicinity, are inexhaustible supplies of coarse gray granite, sometimes porphyritic, with pinkish orthoclase crystals from two to three inches in diameter. There is not, however, sufficient contrast in color to make the stone desirable for monumental work, and its coarse texture is against it. Much of the rock here closely resembles that of Vinalhaven and Hurricane Island, for either of which it might readily be mistaken.

Two varieties of granite are quarried at Mount Waldo, in the town of Frankfort. Both are light-gray rocks, frequently porphyritic with large white orthoclase crystals. Both varieties are of the same mineral composition, the difference being simply one of texture, one being quite coarse and somewhat porphyritic, while the other is much finer and of more even texture. The mica occurs in large flakes, which the microscope shows to be frequently pierced by small crystals of apatite. A part of the mica is greenish in color and contains a few small grains of epidote. An occasional flake of white mica was noticed in this rock, and there is present the usual sprinkling of magnetite granules, together with an occasional cube of pyrite. Quarries were opened at Mt. Waldo in 1853, and single blocks 80 by 40 by 20 feet have been taken out and afterward cut up. It is estimated that blocks 150 by 50 by 12 feet could be obtained if desired. The rock has been used largely in the building of forts on the coast of Maine, but is also used for all purposes, both ornamental and otherwise, to which granite is usually applied, and has been shipped as far South as Mobile and New Orleans. The principal quarry is situated on Mt. Waldo, overlooking the Penobscot River, at an elevation of some 320 feet above high tide.

At Vinalhaven or Fox Island, in Penobscot Bay, are the

most extensive quarries at present in operation in this country. Quarries were first opened here about 1850, and the annual product has averaged upwards of 200,000 cubic feet, valued at some $110,000. Upwards of six hundred men are regularly employed at the works, though the number has at times risen as high as one thousand five hundred. The capabilities of the quarries can be best illustrated by stating that during a visit of the writer to these quarries in the summer of 1883 he was shown the remains of a huge block of granite 300 feet long, 20 feet wide, and varying from 6 to 10 feet in thickness, that had been loosened from the quarry in a single piece and afterward broken up. The largest block ever quarried and dressed was the General Wool monument, now in Troy, New York, which measured, when finished, 60 feet in height by 5½ feet square at the base, or only 6 feet 7 inches shorter than the Egyptian obelisk now in Central Park.

In texture the Vinalhaven rock is rather coarse and the general color gray, although the prevailing feldspar is sometimes of a light flesh color. Besides biotite, the rock contains small amounts of hornblende and microscopic apatite and zircon crystals. It takes a good and lasting polish, and is well adapted for all manner of ornamental work and general building purposes. The stone has been used so extensively, all over the country, that to cite special cases seems superfluous.

A granite closely resembling that of Vinalhaven is extensively quarried at Hurricane Island, some 3 miles distant, in a south-westerly direction, and is used for similar purposes. The structure of the stone here differs in different parts of the quarry. In one portion it lies in comparatively thin sheets, while in another there occur immense masses of solid rock, extending downward for 50 feet without perceptible jointing. A block of 80 tons has been moved, and a mass 80 by 40 by

25 feet was loosened in the quarry.   Natural blocks 500 feet
long, 20 feet wide, and 50 feet deep occur.

The celebrated quarries on Dix Island, in Knox County,
from whence was obtained the granite for the United States
Treasury building at Washington, including the monolithic
columns, 31½ high by 3 feet in diameter, are at the present
writing abandoned.   Nearly the whole island has been quarried
over, and the large bluffs entirely removed.   The rock is rich
in quartz, and therefore quite hard, but is a good and safe
working stone.   It has been very extensively used in New
York City, Philadelphia, and Washington, D. C.

The granite of Augusta and Hallowell has long been justly
celebrated for its beauty and fine working qualities.   It is a
fine, light-gray rock, the uniformity of texture being often
broken by the presence of large white crystals of microcline,
which inclose small, rounded grains of quartz.   Biotite and
muscovite occur in abundance, and in about equal proportions,
but in small flakes, the muscovite appearing as silvery-white
glistening particles on a broken surface of the rock.   The rock
is therefore classed as a *biotite-muscovite granite.*   Under the
microscope three feldspars are readily distinguished, orthoclase
in imperfect crystals and irregular grains, an abundance of
plagioclase, and microcline in large plates filled with cavities
and inclosures of muscovite and quartz.   In the thin sections
the quartz inclosures are usually circular in outline and are
pierced in every direction by minute thread-like crystals of
rutile, in polarized light showing up in strong contrast with the
beautiful basket-work structure of the inclosing microcline.
All the feldspars are quite fresh and pure.   A few apatite
crystals are present, together with occasional garnets, which in
thin sections are destitute of crystalline form, appearing as
rounded or oval nearly colorless bodies traversed by many
irregular lines of fracture.   They are quite free from impuri-

PLATE VI.

GRANITE QUARRY AT HALLOWELL, MAINE.

To face page 191.

ties, though occasionally containing inclosures of biotite. As is usual in muscovite-bearing rocks but little magnetite is present ; in two cases only grains of pyrite were noticed.

This is one of the best working of the Maine granites, and is used very extensively, not only for building and monuments, but is carved into statues, like marble. The rock is considered a gneiss, by Hitchcock, but showing no signs of stratification in the hand specimen, is classed here as a granite. As illustrative of the great extent of the quarries, it is stated that blocks 200 feet in length, by 40 feet in width and 8 feet in thickness, can be broken out in a single piece if so desired. There is no gap between the sheets, and little or no pyrite to cause discoloration. The sheets, as is usually the case, increase in thickness downward, being about 1 foot thick at the surface and 10 feet thick at the bottom of the present openings, which are from 50 to 60 feet deep. (See Plate VI.)

This stone is in such demand for statuary and monumental work that an Italian designer, who served his apprenticeship in Roman studios, is employed constantly by the company. Many of the workmen are also said to be Italians who worked on marble in Italy, but have learned to cut granite since their arrival in Hallowell. Among the prominent structures and monuments constructed, wholly or in part, of this stone, are the new capitol, Albany, N. Y.; Bank of Northern Liberties, Philadelphia ; State capitol, Augusta, Me.; Emory Block, Portland, Me.; Odd Fellows' Memorial Hall, Equitable Building, and part of the old Quincy Market, Boston ; Ludlow Street Jail, the Tribune Building, and the old Tombs Prison, New York City ; the statues of the Pilgrims' Monument at Plymouth, Mass. ; Soldiers' and Sailors' Monuments at Marblehead, Mass., Portsmouth, Ohio, Augusta, Boothbay, and Gardiner, Me.; Odd Fellows' Monument, Mount Hope, Boston, and the Washington Artillery Monument and Hernandez tomb, New Orleans. The statues on the Pilgrims' Monument are said to be the largest granite figures in America. The standing figure is 38 feet in height, while the four in sitting posture are each fifteen feet in height.

A granite quite similar to that described above is also quarried, though less extensively, at North Jay, in Franklin County. Similar rocks but of a gneissoid structure occur in Waldo and Lincoln Counties.

Other granites, in many cases fully equal to those above described, occur in various parts of the State, and which can be but briefly noticed for lack of space. Mention may be made of the fine dark-gray biotite granite quarried at Swanville in Waldo County; the fine and coarse gray stone of St. George and Spruce Head Island, in Knox County; those from Wayne in Kennebec County; Canaan and Norridgwock, in Somerset County; Sebec Lake, in Piscataquis County; Brunswick and Pownal, in Cumberland County; Biddeford, South Berwick and Kennebunkport, in York County; and from Bryant's Pond, in Oxford County. Also of the darker gray hornblende mica granites of St. George and of Lincoln, in Penobscot County. The so-called "black granites" of Addison, Vinalhaven and Tenants Harbor are diabases and gabbros, and will be mentioned in their proper places. (See p 231.)

Very many of the biotite granites of this State contain numerous masses or nodules of a darker color and finer texture than the rock itself, they frequently appearing as black patches on a polished surface. These are of all sizes up to a foot in diameter. They sometimes occur with sharp, distinct outlines, or again merge gradually into the surrounding rock with no definite line of demarkation. Some of them possess a fine, even texture, while others are rendered slightly porphyritic in structure through included crystals of plagioclase of considerable size. Under the microscope they are all found to consist essentially of the same minerals as the rocks in which they occur, although in a more finely crystalline state and different proportions; biotite usually prevails and causes the dark color of the patch. Very many of them, however, are penetrated in every direction by innumerable, minute, colorless, needle-like crystals, an exact determination of which, on account of their small size, is impossible. Many of the included larger crystals of feldspar, which, so far as observed are always triclinic, have their angles rounded away, and are reduced to mere oval grains. Such nodules are usually regarded as of concretionary origin.* The finer texture and darker color of these patches render them very conspicuous and in some of the quarries many fine blocks of granite are rendered quite unsuited for finely finished or polished work on account of their abundance.

Maryland.—The Archæan area of Maryland lies northwesterly of an extremely sinuous line drawn through Havre de Gras, Baltimore and Washington, D. C. It includes, therefore, large parts of the counties of Cecil, Harford, Baltimore, Howard, Montgomery, Frederick and Carroll.†, Throughout this area are numerous outcroppings of granitic and gneissic rock of a character suitable for general structural purposes, and in a few instances for monumental work as well.

The most noted quarries in the State are situated in Baltimore County, near Woodstock. The rock is a biotite granite, varying from light to dark gray in color, and of about medium texture. It is used extensively for general building purposes

---

* See "On Concretionary Patches and Fragments of other Rocks contained in Granite," by J. A. Phillips, Quarterly Journal of the London Geological Society, vol. xxxvi. 1880, pp. 1-22. Also, " On the Black Nodules in the Maine Granites," by G. P. Merrill. Proceedings U. S. National Museum vol. 6, 1883, p. 137.

† G. H. Williams. Johns Hopkins University Circular, vol. vii. No. 65. 1888.

and for monumental work in Báltimore, Washington and some of the Western States. At Mount Royal and opposite Ellicott City fine-grained, dark-gray gneiss is quite extensively quarried for general building purposes, curbstones, etc. A part of this rock is beautifully porphyritic through large feldspars an inch or more in length.

A dark-gray gneiss, which is extensively used in Baltimore for rough work, is quarried in the immediate vicinity of the city.

At Port Deposit, in Cecil County, a gray biotite gneiss is extensively quarried, and is used chiefly for bridge building, docks, harbor improvement and general building work. It has been used in the construction of Haverford College, Maryland, St. Dominick's Church, Washington, and several churches in the immediate vicinity. Other locations where good quality of granite is exposed, are Gwynn's Falls, in Baltimore County, and 3 miles east of Rockville, in Montgomery County.

All of the Maryland granites and gneisses at present quarried have biotite as their chief accessory, are of a gray color and of medium fineness of grain. They appear, however, better adapted for general building than for ornamental work.

Massachusetts.—As Massachusetts was the earliest settled of the New England States, it is but natural that here the systematic quarrying of granite should first be undertaken. As already noted, granite from the bowlders on the Quincy Commons and from Chelmsford began to be used in and about Boston as early as 1737, but it was not until the early part of the present century that its use became at all general. Indeed, it may be said that it was not until the opening of the quarries at Quincy in 1825 that the granite industry assumed any importance. From this time the use of the stone for general building purposes increased in a marked degree, and the history of granite quarrying in the United States may properly begin with this date.

This early opening of quarries at Quincy was due largely to the demand for stone at Charlestown for building the Bunker Hill monument, but the attention of capitalists being thereby called to the extent of the granite ledges in this vicinity other works were soon established, and at the present time the two.towns of Quincy and West Quincy contain upwards of thirty quarries. Altogether these produce not less than 700,000 cubic feet annnally, and give employment to nearly a thousand men.

The Quincy granites are, as a rule, dark blue-gray in color, coarse grained, and hard. A pinkish variety is quarried to a slight extent. They are all hornblende pyroxene granites, and their general appearance so characteristic that once seen they are always easily recognizable wherever met with. As already mentioned, these rocks contain besides hornblende a brittle variety of pyroxene, which makes the production of a perfect surface somewhat difficult. Nevertheless, they are very extensively used both for rough and finished work. The United States custom-houses at Boston, Massachusetts ; Providence, Rhode Island ; Mobile, Alabama ; Savannah, Georgia ; New Orleans, Louisiana, and San Francisco, California, are of this stone, as are also the new Masonic Temple and Ridgeway Library buildings, in Philadelphia. In Boston alone there are one hundred and sixty-two buildings constructed wholly or in part of this material. Its suitability for interior decorative work cannot be better shown than by reference to the polished stairways and pilasters in the new city buildings at Philadelphia.

Other very extensive quarries of hornblende-granite are located at Cape Ann, in the town of Gloucester, where it is stated* that quarrying was commenced as early as 1824 by a Mr. Bates, of Quincy. The largest quarries in the State, and, with the exception of those at Vinalhaven, Maine, the largest works now in operation in the United States, are situated at this place. Like that of Quincy, the rock is hornblendic, though frequently considerable·black mica is present.† The texture is coarse and the color greenish, owing to the orthoclase it contains. Some varieties are, however, simply gray. It is a hard, tough rock, eminently durable, and well suited for all manner of general building and ornamental work. The stone has been used in the construction of the post-office and several churches and private buildings in Boston, and the Butler house on Capitol Hill at Washington.

Other hornblendic granites, somewhat similar in appearance, are quarried at Rockport, Peabody, Wyoma, Lynn, and Lynnfield. The Rockport stone is the most important of these, and has been quarried since 1830. In color and texture it is indistinguishable from much of the Gloucester stone, but, if anything, is of a more decided greenish hue. In the quarries it is extremely massive, and blocks 100 feet long by 50 feet wide and 16 feet thick have been loosened from the bed in a single piece, while it is estimated a block 200 feet long, 50 feet wide and 20 feet thick could be obtained if desired. The principal markets are New York, Boston, New Orleans, and Cuba.

Several important quarries of coarse biotite granite are worked in this State, but their product is mostly used in the near vicinity. Light pink varieties admirably adapted for rock-faced work occur at Brockton, Milford, and North Easton. The

---

* History of Gloucester, Cape Ann, by J. J. Babson, p. 577.

† The black mica of the Gloucester and Rockport granites has been shown by Professors Dana and Cooke to be lepidomelane or annite. (Text-book of Mineralogy, p. 313).

Milford stone is particularly effective when used in this manner, as is well illustrated in the new city hall at Albany, New York, and also in the new railway station at Auburndale, Massachusetts. At Framingham, Leominster, Fitchburg, Clinton, Fall River, and Freetown are also quarries of coarse gray but apparently strong and durable granites of this class.

Epidote granite.—This is a rare variety of granite in this country, the quarries of Dedham producing all that is now upon the market. The stone is fine-grained and of a light pink color. Besides epidote, which is visible to the naked eye as small greenish specks, it contains numerous flecks of chlorite, resulting from the alteration of a black mica. The stone works readily and gives very pleasing effects either in polished or rock-face work. It is of this stone that was constructed the new Trinity Church in Boston, and which is considered by good authorities to be, from an architectural standpoint, the finest building in America.

Gneiss.—A fine-grained very light gray, sometimes pinkish, muscovite gneiss of excellent quality has been quarried more or less for the past thirty-five years near the town of Westford. Other quarries of gneiss are at West Andover, Lawrence, Lowell, Ayer, several towns in Worcester County, at Becket, Northfield, and Monson.

Being in most cases distinctly stratified, these gneisses are not adapted to so wide a range of application as the massive granites, but at the same time the ease with which in many cases they can be quarried makes them particularly valuable for foundations, bridge abutments, curbing, paving and rock-faced building. At the Monson quarries, for instance, the rock is divided by a series of joints, approximately parallel to the surface of the hill on which the quarries are situated, into immense lenticular sheets from 6 inches to 10 feet in thickness. By taking advantage of these natural facilities a block was split out in 1869 which measured 354 feet in length by 11 feet in width and 4 feet in thickness. An analysis of the Monson stone from the Flint quarry is given in the tables.

As a general rule it may be stated that while the granites and gneisses of Massachusetts are good and safeworking stones they are coarse and with a few prominent exceptions in no way remarkable for their beauty. In the matter of color and texture they bear a striking contrast to the fine and even grained stones of her sister States, Connecticut and Rhode Island.

Minnesota.—According to Professor Winchell more than half the State of Minnesota is underlaid by that general class of rocks—the crystalline—to which granite belongs. In the northern part of the State there are large exposures of very fine light-colored granites, but being beyond the limits of settlements and roads those in the southern and western part, in the country bordering along the Mississippi and Minnesota Rivers, are of more especial interest and importance. These last have been somewhat quarried and the materials can be seen in some of the principal buildings in various parts of the State, as well as in cities beyond the State limits. The first quarry in these rocks in Minnesota was that now owned by Breen & Young, at East St. Cloud, Sherburne County.

This was opened in 1868, and the stone first taken out was used in the corners, steps, and trimmings of the United States custom-house and post-office in St. Paul. Three kinds of stone were taken out and used indiscriminately, and all of them may be seen in the building first erected. The variety now more generally used is of a gray color and uniform texture. The crystalline grains are rather fine, so that the texture is close. The color, however, is sometimes disturbed by the appearance of greenish spots of the size of butternuts or even as large as 6 inches in diameter, caused by segregations of a green chlorite. " About one-third of the whole rock is made up of quartz, and two-thirds of the remainder of orthoclase. About one-half the remainder is hornblende and the residue is divided between the other minerals, the chlorite predominating." An occasional grain of a triclinic feldspar is present together with magnetite and pyrite in minute crystals.*

"The red granite from East St. Cloud is not very different from the foregoing, but the feldspar is mainly flesh red and all the grains are coarser." It also has a higher per cent of silica, a fact that has been discovered practically by the owners, who had given up the general use of it because of its being more costly to work. " . . . In the winter of 1874–5 a block weighing ten tons was taken out of the red-granite quarry, about 3 miles west of St. Cloud, for a monument base. . . . It was very fine, and greatly resembled the Scotch granite in color, grain, and polish. At the point where this was taken out the granite rises about 20 feet above the general surface and spreads over more than an acre. A similar red granite occurs at Watab (in Benton County), and has furnished several handsome monuments." A light gray granite also occurs here.†

At Sauk Rapids, in the same county, there is found a fine-grained gray granite closely resembling the gray variety from East St. Cloud. It has been quite generally used, and is one of the best-known granites in the State.

Missouri.—Although there are inexhaustible quantities of granite in the northern part of Iron and Madison Counties and

---

* See Geology and Natural History Survey of Minnesota, vol. I. pages 142–148.

† These rocks are designated in Professor Winchell's report above referred to as "Syenites." According to the system of classification now generally adopted, they are rather hornblendic or hornblende-biotite granites, as designated by the author in the census report, p. 90. The name *syenite*, as already noted, is applied to a quartzless rock (see pp. 42 and 223).

the southern portion of St. François, there are but few quarries of the material systematically worked.

At Graniteville, Iron County, and in Syenite, St. Francois County, there occurs a coarse red granite, quite poor in mica, which is now extensively quarried for the St. Louis and Chicago markets. It is somewhat lighter in color than the well-known Scotch granite, but is admirably suited for massive structural purposes, as is well illustrated in the lower stories of the fine business blocks erected during the season of 1886 on Adams street, between Fifth avenue and Franklin, and on the corner of Adams and La Salle streets, in Chicago. The enormous blocks of rock-faced granite and large polished columns of this stone as here displayed* would indicate that this is destined to be one of the leading granites of this portion of the country. It admits of a high lustrous polish and is coming into use for monumental work.

Professor Broadhead states† that the Archæan granites are exposed to view over an area of over 150 square miles in Madison County, with as large an area in St. Francois, a smaller one in Iron County, a few square miles in St. Genivieve, and a limited area in Wayne. The colors are various shades of gray and red. Exposed strata show evidence of continuous weathering through many years. Since opening, the interior beds show favorable characters for durability. At the Knob Lick quarries, St. Francois County, there are three varieties, as to color, red, gray, and red and whitish. Of these the gray

---

* The window-sills in the first of the above-mentioned buildings are rough blocks of granite, each 3 feet square by 17 feet 4 inches in length, and weighing about 10 tons each. The polished columns of the building corner of Adams and La Salle streets are ten in number, each 18 feet high by 4½ feet in diameter, and weighing not far from 18 tons. The largest single block of polished granite yet produced at these works is the Allen monument, in St. Louis, which is 42 feet in height by 4½ feet square at the base. The weight is about 45 tons.

† The Building Trades Journal, July, 1888.

is considered the best. A dark colored but handsome stone is quarried near Piedmont, in Wayne County. A dark grayish-brown porphyritic rock is quarried in the northern part of Madison County, and a similar rock occurs at Fredericktown; also one of like composition and appearance covers several square miles of Stone mountain in St. Francois County. Gray granite is also found eight miles southwest of Ironton in Iron County, and in the northern part of Madison; a coarser feldspathic granite is also found in the northwestern part of this same country.

Montana.—There is a plenty of good granite within the limits of the State, but for lack of a market scarcely any quarrying is at present carried on.

A cube of a fine-grained light gray biotite granite is in the collections of the National Museum from Lewis and Clark Counties, but so far as the writer is aware the quarry has never been worked to any extent. A coarse hornblende mica granite of a greenish-gray color and somewhat resembling the celebrated Quincy and Gloucester (Massachusetts) stone forms the country rock in the region of the celebrated silver and copper mines of Butte, and is beginning to be used for purposes of heavy foundation and general building. So far as the writer was able to judge, from the short time he was on the ground, the rock is of excellent quality, but needs to be selected with care, as certain portions, those in proximity to the ore veins, are abundantly charged with pyrite, which oxidizes readily on exposure.

New Hampshire.—Those of the New Hampshire granites that are best known as building materials belong, according to Prof. Hitchcock,* to what is called the Montalban or White Mountain series of the Eozoic formations, a series extending,

---

* Geology of Northern New England, p. 10.

though not continuously, over fully two-thirds of the central and eastern part of the State. These granites are, as a rule, of a light gray, nearly white, color, fine grain, and are quarried in Concord, Fitzwilliam, Milford, Farmington, Hooksett, Pelham, Salem, Marlboro, Troy, Sunapee, Allentown, Hanover, Rumsey, Mason, and elsewhere. By far the most important of these, and indeed one of the most important granites of the United States, is the muscovite-biotite granite of West Concord in Merrimack county.

This stone consists, according to Dr. Hawes,* of clear, glassy quartz, penetrated in every direction by minute, dark, rutile-like needles, snow-white twin orthoclase crystals, finely banded oligoclase, both white and black mica, and an occasional microscopic apatite crystal. In texture it is as fine as many marbles, though at times slightly porphyritic. Its remarkable feature, aside from color, texture and freedom from flaws, pyrite or other injurious constituent, is the wonderful ease with which it can be worked. Owing to its well developed rift and grain, blocks can be split out with a hammer with almost the ease of blocks of wood, though at the same time neither of these qualities are sufficiently prominent to prevent its being worked readily with the tool in any direction. It can, therefore, be used in statuary work, and is also used for general building and monumental work in the eastern cities. The quarries, of which there are several, are situated upon the eastern slope of Rattlesnake Hill, and means of transportation are furnished by the Concord and Claremont Railroad, which skirts its base. The quarry openings are as a rule, situated in the hillside, allowing thus natural drainage and abundant room for quarry dump, aside from ready facilities for quarrying and loading the material upon teams to be hauled to the rail-

---

* Mineralogy and Lithology of New Hampshire, p. 194.

road. The rock as shown at the openings is quite massive, and separated by two sets of irregular horizontal and vertical joints into natural blocks of varying sizes. Blemishes as seen at the quarries are surprisingly rare, and confined to a slight discoloration at the joints, and an occasional vein of fine grained granitic material.

That the stone is eminentely durable is shown by the State-house and old State's-prison buildings, at Concord ; the former having been erected in 1816–19, and the latter in 1812. Although the stone in both of these cases was a result of mere surface quarrying and presumably scarcely better than that which is thrown into the dump to-day, both buildings are in an admirable state of preservation, and evidently, so far as the stone is concerned, good for centuries to come. This same stone has been used in the new post-office buildings at Concord and Manchester, and is the one selected for the new Congressional Library building in Washington, D. C.

The gneisses of the State are less extensively quarried, and their uses are more local. A fine light gray stone of good quality comes from Peterborough, and a light pinkish stone, flecked with black and greenish, from Lebanon.

New Jersey.—The Archæan area, within which are comprised all the granitic and gneissiod rocks of New Jersey, crosses the State in a northeasterly and southwesterly direction in the form of a belt less than twenty miles in width at its greatest extension, and less than half that amount at its southeastern extremity. The belt enters the State from New York at a point comprised between the Ramapo River, in Bergen County, and the so-called Drowned Land, bordering along the Pennsylvania railroad in Sussex County. The southern limit lies in Warren, with a slight extension into the northern part of Hunterdon County.

But few quarries are worked throughout the area above

roughly outlined, though in a number of localities the gneissic rocks are so situated as to be worked at a comparatively small expense. Quarries at Dover, in Morris County, have furnished a large amount of stone for railroad construction. The stone is of medium texture and of a greenish gray color.

A large quarry was opened a few years ago near Franklin, on the mountain east of the village; but the place, though promising, was soon abandoned. The stone was adapted for heavy work. The transportation appeared to be too expensive for it to compete with stone coming by water routes.*

Granites of the hornblende-biotite type, of fine grain and even texture, occur in the Vernon valley, along the eastern foot of Pochuck Mountain. The stone is regarded as of good quality, but little that is definite can as yet be said, owing to insufficient development.†

New York.—This State, although rich in marbles, limestones, and sandstones, produces little of general interest in the way of granite rock, though according to Smock‡ "granites, syenites, gneisses, and mica schists occur in the counties of Rockland, Orange, Westchester, Putnam, and Dutchess, and on New York island. For constructive material quarries have been opened at many points, generally near railway lines on the Hudson river." The Breakneck and Storm King Mountain granite quarries were opened many years ago, and produce a gray, coarsely crystalline material, little of which finds its way outside of the State. The more important of the true granites of the State, for monumental work, would seem to be the red variety produced at the various quarries on Grindstone Island (Jefferson County), in the St. Lawrence River. The stone,

---

* Annual Report of State Geologist of New Jersey, 1886, pp. 41–42.
† Annual Report of State Geologist of New Jersey, 1889.
‡ Bull, New York State Museum, No. 3, March, 1888, p. 11.

as represented in the National collection, is deep red and coarsely crystalline, taking a high lustrous polish, and may well take rank as one of our most beautiful granites. The stone is designated by the writer in the tenth census report * as a hornblende granite, carrying in addition to quartz, red orthoclase and hornblende, a copper red mica, a few small apatite and zircon crystals, together with scattering pyrites and a little secondary calcite. The last two substances, if prevalent throughout the quarry, must prove detrimental for exposed work. As shown by the two finely polished columns in the Senate Chamber of the new capitol building at Albany, New York, it is, however, a magnificent stone. There are said to be many outcrops of the stone on the island, especially on the western side, and small quarries have been opened at more than twenty different points. Prof. Smock states that the stone is shown by the outcrops to be very durable, and that in the larger quarries blocks twenty feet in length by six feet square are obtainable, The greater part of the product goes to Western cities, as Chicago, Cincinnati and Toledo, and to Canada. Much of the output is used for paving blocks, and the waste for granulitic pavements in Montreal. The price is stated to range from $1.00 to $2.00 per cubic foot for blocks in sizes under twenty cubic feet.

North Carolina.—About 6 miles N. by E. of Concord, in Cabarrus County, there occurs a fine-grained, homogeneous deep pink granitic rock, almost wholly lacking in mica, which works readily and is admirably adapted for rock-faced work. The stone combines the warm and pleasing colors characteristic of many free stones, with the strength and general enduring qualities of granite, and with proper treatment leaves little to be desired, particularly for suburban residences.

---

* Vol. x. Building Stone and Quarry Industry, p. 22.

Some nine miles south of Salisbury, in Rowan County, occurs another granite eminently suited for rock-faced work. This is also of a pink cast, though very much lighter than that of Cabarrus County, and of a coarser texture. The stone is stated to occur in unlimited quantities, and blocks 60x40x30 feet are said to be obtainable.

It weathers well and has been quarried for local use since 1878. A better stone could scarcely be desired for massive buildings where the ordinary gray granite is objectionable owing to its cold and gloomy aspect.

Other pink granites, though of a dull and less desirable shade, are found at Cedar Creek, some 9 miles S. E. of Louis-burg, in Franklin County, and near Hillsboro, in Orange County. A peculiar dull red and buff-mottled gneissic stone is found some three-quarters of a mile west of Mooresville, in Iredell County, the character of the mottling corresponding to that of the so-called " raindrop " sandstone from L'Anse and Marquette, Michigan. The stone is stated to weather and work well, and occurs in such outcrops as to give a quarry face of from 40 to 50 feet.

A coarse red granite, stated to be well adapted for general building, as well as ornamental work, occurs in bold outcrops at the crossing of Contentnea Creek and the Wheeling and Weldon R. R., in Nelson County. The stone has been used mainly for railroad work. A similar stone occurs near Wilson, in Wilson County.

A dark-gray or sometimes reddish granite rendered porphyritic by large pink crystals of feldspar, and which recalls, in a general way, the well-known Shap granite of Cumberland, England, occurs near Rockingham, in Richmond County, on the line of the North Carolina Central R. R. Some two or three miles west of Rockingham is a somewhat similar stone. but with a peculiar olive tinge. The porphyritic structure of the stone is less striking than that of the Shap granite above noted, and the weathering qualities perhaps doubtful. Some 5 miles S. E. of Davidson College, in Mecklenburg County, there occurs a coarse gray granite made up of white feldspars and opalescent quartz thickly studded with large deep greenish-black spots, caused by segregations of black mica or hornblende. The stone is as yet used only for foundations. The exposures are stated to cover an area of half an acre.

Some four miles south of Salisbury are other occurrences of medium grained homogeneous gray granites outcropping in huge ledges forming the so-called Dunn's Mountain. The stone has been used in the post-office building at Raleigh.

Gray granite closely simulating the ordinary types from the coast of Maine occur about four miles south of Winston, in Forsyth County, and some ten miles southwest of Greensborough, Guilford County. The first mentioned is stated to weather well, to be procurable in any quantity, and in blocks of any desirable size. The Greensborough quarry is in close juxtaposition to the railroad, and is reported as producing a fair quality of stone, though of somewhat variable character.

Other gray granites worthy of notice occur some $2\frac{1}{2}$ miles north of Toisnot, in Edgecombe County ; near Gastonia, in Gaston County, and at Mount Airy, in Surry County. The first mentioned is used for general building and bridge work, and a railroad runs to the quarry. The principal market is Wilmington.

Still other granites and gneisses at present of local importance only occur in various parts of Buncombe, Stokes, Wake, Vance, McDowell, and Cleveland Counties.

A very peculiar variety of granite, and one which may prove of value for ornamental purposes, occurs at Coolomee, in Davie County. The stone is composed of radiating green

augites in rounded masses an inch or more in diameter, imbedded in a white or pinkish ground mass of quartz and feldspar.   On a polished surface the effect is quite unique.

Pennsylvania.—Although ranking as second in importance
in the list of stone-producing States, Pennsylvania furnishes very
little in the way of granitic rock, and absolutely nothing in this
line of more thân local interest.   " The southern gneisses district, described in the geological reports of Pennsylvania as
ranging from the Delaware River at Trenton to the Susquehanna, south of the State line and lying south of the limestone
valley of Montgomery, is the district in which are located
nearly all the quarries of gneiss in the State, and those furnishing most of the material are in the vicinity of Philadelphia."
The rock, which is for the most part a dark-gray hornblende
gneiss, is quarried at Rittenhousetown, Twenty-first ward, and
Germantown, Twenty-second ward, and Jenkinstown, in
Montgomery County, and is used principally for the rough
work of foundations in the near vicinity.   In Chester, Delaware County, the gneiss bears mica in place of hornblende and
is, as a rule, lighter in color.   The quarries are in close proximity to the Delaware River, which affords an easy method of
transportation to Philadelphia, the principal market.   This
stone is also used almost wholly for foundations, though in
some cases it has been used as rock-faced work in the fronts of
private dwellings, with rather a pleasing effect.

Rhode Island.—The granites of this State are nearly all fine-
grained light gray or pink biotite granites, the principal quarries of which are situated some 2 miles east from Westerly, in
Washington County.   The rock is of fine and even texture and
of excellent quality, and is much used for monumental work
and general building.   Other quarries of biotite granite occur
at Smithfield, West Greenwich, Newport, and Niantic.   A
greenish, fine gray, hornblende gneiss is quarried at Diamond

Hill, in Providence County. Aside from the Westerly rock the most of this material is for local market only.

South Carolina.—Although no granites from this State are to be found in our principal markets, it by no means follows that there is any deficiency in the supply. The collection in the National Museum shows, on the contrary, that excellent stones of this class occur in various localities.

Near Winnsborough, in Fairfield County, quarries have recently been opened which furnish fine-grained gray biotite granite fully equal to any in the market. The quarries, as we are informed by the owner, Mr. W. Woodward, cover some 70 acres of bowlders and two large ledges, one 11 acres in extent and the other 6. The stone works readily and acquires an excellent polish. A pinkish granite also occurs in this same county. Other granites in this State, of which I have seen specimens, but concerning which I have but little accurate information, occur near Columbia, Richland County ; and in Newberry, Lexington, Edgefield, and Aiken Counties. The Columbia stone is of a light-gray color, apparently of excellent quality. It was used in the construction of the State House in that city, and is stated to be very durable.

Tennessee.—At the present time scarcely anything in the line of granitic rock is quarried in this State, and owing to the limited areas occupied by granite ledges it is more than doubtful if the granite quarrying ever assumes any great importance. Small outcrops of granite, gneiss, or mica schist occur in the extreme eastern and southern parts of Polk, Monroe, Cocke, Washington, Carter, and Johnson Counties, in the eastern part of the State, but even these are not in all cases suitable for any but the roughest work. The National collections contain an extremely coarse greenish epidotic granite, with large red porphyritic crystals of orthoclase, from Bench Mountain, in

Cocke County, which might perhaps be worked if there were a market.

Texas.—Red granites, both coarse and fine, occur in Burnet County, in this State, though at present neither are quarried to any extent. Both varieties carry biotite as the chief accessory mineral. The coarser variety corresponds closely with the coarse red granite from Platte Cañon, Colorado. Their colors are dull and they seem better adapted for rough building than for monumental work, though the weathering qualities of either are, to say the least, doubtful. Red and gray granites also occur in Gillespie County.

Utah Territory.—A coarse, light gray granite occurs in inexhaustible quantities in Little Cottonwood Cañon, not far from Salt Lake City. So far the stone has been quarried only from bowlders that have been rolled down the cañon, and the parent ledge remains untouched. This stone has been used in the construction of the new Mormon temple at Salt Lake City. It is apparently of excellent quality.

Vermont.—This State furnishes but little for the general market in the way of granitic rocks, from the fact that few of her quarries produce material not found elsewhere in New England, where there are better and cheaper facilities for transportation. Except in the north-eastern portion, embracing nearly the whole of Essex County, granite is met with only in isolated outcrops, either in the form of mountain uplifts, as Black Mountain in Dummerston, or in narrow belts traversing the calcareous mica schist formation, as at Marshfield and Barre. In the gneiss formation, extending through Reading, Cavendish, Chester, and Grafton, on the western limit of the calcareous mica schist formation, the gneiss passes by insensible gradations into granite, and in many places there are afforded excellent opportunities for quarrying both stones equally well. The granite found in connection with the gneiss in these cases, is said to be, as a rule light colored, and of fine texture, but generally harder to work than those of the isolated outcrops, like that of Barre. This last mentioned stone is a fine grained biotite granite of excellent quality, and is found in inexhaustible quantities. The stone occurs in sheets varying in thickness from a few inches to several feet.*

Other granites deserving of especial mention are found in Brunswick, Essex County; Morgan, Orleans County ; Ryegate, and St. Johnsbury, Caledonia County, and Woodbury in Washington County. A very light, almost white, muscovite-bearing rock is also quarried at Bethel, in Windsor County. These granites, or at least the eruptive varieties, are regarded by Prof. Hitchcock as of Silurian or possibly Devonian age. The gneisses extending in a continuous belt from the Massachusetts line through the central portion of the State to Canada, furnish much valuable material for local building, curbing and flagging.

Virginia.—The Archæan area of Virginia, as mapped by Rogers,† comprises the tract lying east of the Blue Ridge Mountains, and a line extending from a point near Alexandria in Fairfax County southerly through Spottsylvania, Henrico, Chesterfield, Dinwiddie, Sussex, and Southampton Counties into North Carolina. But a small part of this area furnishes outcrops of quarriable material, and the principal works thus far developed are in Chesterfield and Dinwiddie Counties, on the James River, and in the immediate vicinity of Richmond.

The quarries on the Richmond and Alleghany Railroad, near Richmond, produce a massive gray granite used for general building purposes, paving stone, and monumental work, and which is shipped more or less to all the States and cities

---

*Geology of Vermont, vol. II. 1860, p. 737.
†Geology of the Virginias, 1884.

south of New England and as far west as Nebraska. Much of the material is dressed at the quarry, polishing works being located on the ground. Other quarries in Chesterfield County produce a very similar stone, the principal markets of which are in Richmond, Washington, Norfolk, Lynchburgh, and Philadelphia. Important quarries are also located at Manchester in this same county. Other important quarries are in the Tuckahoe district, Henrico County, and Namozine district, Dinwiddie County. Stone from the last named locality was used in the construction of the post-office and custom house at Petersburgh, Virginia. The most important building yet constructed of the Virginia granites is the State, War, and Navy building in Washington. This is probably the most elaborate granite structure in the country. Near Fredericksburgh is found a fine light gray muscovite-biotite granite closely resembling those of Hallowell, Maine., and Concord, New Hampshire, but it is not at present quarried to any extent. The granites of this State are, as a rule, fine-grained, biotite-bearing rocks, and of a light-gray color, and correspond in a remarkable degree with those of New England.

In Amherst and Campbell Counties, near Lynchburg, a fine blue-gray biotite gneiss is quarried for general building purposes in the towns of the near vicinity.

At Milan's Gap, in Madison County, is found a coarse somewhat porphyritic granite of rather unique type, and which might be used with good effect in certain forms of ornamental work. The rock consists of quartz, a dull red feldspar, and compact aggregates of dull green epidote. The effect in either rock-faced or polished work, is quite pleasing. The same rock is stated to occur in the Unaka Mountains, of North Carolina and East Tennessee, and is hence known as *Unakyte.**

---

* Dana, Manual of Mineralogy and Lithology.

Wisconsin.—The extensive outcrops of granitic rock in this State have been scarcely at all worked up to the present time, owing to the lack of transportation facilities. At the present writing the most important quarries are at Montello, Marquette County, and Wausau, Marathon County. The Montello rock is very fine grained, compact, and of a dull pink color. Quarries were first opened here to furnish paving stones for the Chicago market, but the stone has since been used to a considerable extent for general building and monumental work.

According to Prof. T. C. Chamberlain* the great Laurentian area of the northern part of the State is occupied largely by granite and gneiss, among which are some of exceptional excellence. Granitic rocks of greater or less excellence crop out along the upper reaches and tributaries of the Menominee, the Peshtigo, the Oconto, the Wolf, the Wisconsin, the Yellow, the Black, the Chippewa, the Flambeau, the Bad, and the Montreal Rivers. These are now being brought within the reach of cheap transportation, and should be utilized to the mutual benefit of those who work and those who use.

Wyoming.—" The only building stone which is quarried in Wyoming is at Sherman, the highest point of the Northern Pacific Railroad. At this point—the summit of the Black Hills—the road cuts through a heavy body of red granite similar to the Scotch, but with much larger crystals." This stone has been used to some extent in San Francisco and Sacramento, but is hard to work, owing to its coarseness and lack of tenacity.†

---

* Geology of Wisconsin, vol. I. p. 66.
† Report of Tenth Census, vol. X. p. 278.

(6) FOREIGN GRANITIC ROCKS.

Egypt.—Granite of Syene. The now well-known red granite formerly called syenite, from near Syene, Egypt, and from which was constructed the numerous obelisks of the Egyptians, is stated to have been brought from Upper Egypt, where it occupies large tracts between the first cataract of the Nile and the town of Assonan, the ancient Syene. It was quarried by the Egyptians as far back as one thousand three hundred years before the Christian era, and has been fashioned into obelisks, sarcophagi, and colossal statues innumerable.* The rock, which is very coarse, is of a general reddish color and is composed of large crystals of red and whitish feldspars intermixed with clear, glassy quartz, and coal-black mica and hornblende. Some of the red feldspars are very large, exceeding an inch in length. This rock, though having proved very durable under Egyptian skies, possesses in itself no evident powers of resistance over thousands of other granites that might be mentioned.

BRITISH PROVINCES OF NORTH AMERICA.

British Columbia.—Gray granite of good quality is said to have been obtained in considerable quantity from the large drift bowlders in the vicinity of Victoria. Granite occurs on Nelson Island in the Jarvis Inlet, and has been quarried to some extent. The Vancouver market is said to be supplied with an excellent variety of gray granite from the North Arm of Burrard Inlet.†

Canada.—Inexhaustible quantities of light gray granite are

---

* See Hull, *op. cit.*, p. 51; also Gorringe's "The Egyptian Obelisk," N. Y.; 1882, or Journal Geological Society of London, vol. VII, 1850–'51, p. 9.

† Annual Report Geological Survey of Canada, 1887–'88.

stated * to occur in the township of Stanstead, just north of the Vermont line in the Province of Quebec. Other quite similar granites occur in the townships traversed by the Grand Trunk Railway, as at Barnston, Barford and Hereford, and many localities around the lakes at the heads of the St. Francis and Megantic rivers. Great Megantic Mountain is a mass of granite covering an area of twelve miles in the townships of Marston, Hampden and Ditton. A beautiful red hornblendic granite occurs in the townships of Greenville, Chatham and Wentworth. Hornblende granite is also found on Barrow and other islands in the St. Lawrence. These contain less hornblende and more quartz than do those of Grenville and are said to resemble the red Scotch granite from Aberdeen.

Quarries of red granite are also worked by Canadian companies at Kingston at the outlet of Lake Ontario in Ontario Province. It is stated that blocks of large size can be obtained free from all blemishes and flaws, and that the quantity is inexhaustible.

New Brunswick.—In the vicinity of St. George, Kings County, occurs an inexhaustible supply of a red hornblendic intrusive granite, which is beginning to be extensively worked, and which has been introduced into the markets of the United States, where it is known as " Bay of Fundy granite." In texture the rock is medium coarse, very like that of Calais and Jonesborough, Maine, from which, however, it differs in depth of color and in bearing hornblende in place of mica. It is tough and compact, takes a brilliant polish, and is apparently durable. The quarries now worked are situated about $2\frac{1}{2}$ miles from the town of St. George, where the rock occurs in rugged hills, and of varying shades of color from deep red to cream color or gray, the latter colors occurring in occasional large patches, 20 to 40

---

* Geology of Canada, 1863, p. 810.

feet across, and of indefinite length. The quarries are opened along the hillside, where the rock is very conveniently jointed for getting out large blocks.*

Nova Scotia.—Gray mica-bearing granites of apparently excellent quality, and varying in texture from medium fine and homogeneous to coarsely porphyritic are quarried at Shelburne, and at Purcell's Cove, in Halifax County. These are exported to some extent into the United States.

ENGLAND AND SCOTLAND.

The granites brought into this country from Scotland are the coarse red from Peterhead, and the gray from Aberdeen. Both are excellent stones and are used very largely for monumental work, door-posts, and pillars in all our cities and towns. In point of beauty they are inferior to many of our native granites, but their well-established reputation will probably cause their being used for many years to come. The Peterhead granite is stated † to weigh 165.9 pounds per cubic foot, and to be composed of quartz, orthoclase, albite, and black mica. The Aberdeen granite has the same composition, except-ing that its triclinic feldspar is oligoclase in place of albite, and there is sometimes present a little white mica. It is of this latter stone that the city of Aberdeen is largely built. A coarse gray granite with large, well-defined porphyritic crystals of pink orthoclase is also imported from Shap, in northern England. None of these stones have any exact counterpart among the granites of this country, so far as now known.‡

---

* Report of G. F. Mathew, Geological Survey of Canada, 1876-'77, pp. 345–349.

† Building Construction, p. 20.

‡ See Harris' Granites and our Granite Industries (London, Crosby, Lockwood & Co.,) for detailed accounts of the English, Irish and Scotch granites.

THE PORPHYRIES, OR PORPHYRITIC FELSITES.

(1) COMPOSITION AND ORIGIN.

The term porphyry, as properly used, refers simply to the structural features of the rock, and does not in itself alone indicate any particular kind of stone. It denotes that throughout a mass of rock of quite even texture are distributed numerous crystals of a mineral which having been the first to assume crystalline form, on the cooling of a molten magma, are larger and of a more perfect outline than those which formed subsequently. This structure is very common in many granites, but is not particularly noticeable, owing to the coarse crystallization of the stone and the nearly uniform color of most of the constituents. Occasionally, as in the well known Shap granite from Cumberland in northern England, the large porphyritic feldspars are of a flesh-red color, while the main mass of the stone is but gray, or pinkish, and the contrast is therefore very striking.

There is, however, a class of rocks, in which the mass of the rock, the *groundmass*, as it is technically called, is so dense and compact as to seem practically amorphous or non-crystalline, and in which are imbedded large, scattering, quite perfectly formed crystals, usually of quartz or feldspar. These large crystals being of a different color from the groundmass in which they lie, stand out in marked and often very beautiful contrast. It is to rocks of this nature that the name porphyry has in times past, been chiefly applied. According to Hull * the name was originally applied to certain kinds of igneous rocks of reddish or purple tints, such as the red porphyry of Egypt. Be this as it may, the term is now used

---

* Building and Ornamental Stones, p. 63

mainly in its adjective sense, since any kind of rock may, under certain conditions attending crystallization, assume this structure. We thus have porphyritic granites, diabases, diorites, felsites and even limestones. Nevertheless there is a group of igneous rocks closely related to the granites in chemical composition, in which this structure is so characteristically developed, that the names *quartz* or *feldspar porphyry*, or *porphyritic felsite*, are often applied to the entire group.

(2) VARIETIES OF PORPHYRY.

Accordingly as these porphyries vary in mineral composition they are divided into two principal varieties: (1) Quartz porphyry, which consists of the fine-grained groundmass in which quartz alone or quartz and orthoclase are porphyritically developed, and (2) quartz-free or orthoclase porphyry, in which orthoclase alone prevails, no quartz appearing either porphyritically or in the groundmass. This last variety, it will be seen, bears the same relation to the quartz porphyries as does syenite to the granites. Through an entire disappearance of the porphyritic crystals, the rock passes into felsite. The porphyries bear the same accessory minerals (hornblende, mica, etc.), as do the granites, but these are usually in such small particles as to be invisible to the naked eye.

Porphyries, like granites, are of a variety of colors; red, purple, gray, green, brown and black of a variety of shades are not uncommon, and when, as is so often the case, the porphyritic minerals contrast in color in a marked degree with the groundmass, the effect on a polished surface is very beautiful.

(3) USE OF PORPHYRY.

The porphyries are as a rule intensely hard, tough and without rift or grain. As a consequence they are scarcely at all used in this country, although among the most beautiful and indestructible of our rocks. The celebrated porphyries of Elfdalen, Sweden, are wrought into a variety of objects of art, and with exceedingly beautiful effects. Visitors at the Centennial Exposition in Philadelphia will recall the beautiful large column and inlaid table of this stone that were there displayed.

(4) PORPHYRIES OF THE VARIOUS STATES AND TERRITORIES.

Inexhaustible quantities of porphyries of a variety of colors and great beauty occur at Saugus, Malden, Lynn and Marblehead, and other localities in eastern Massachusetts, but which have never been utilized to any extent owing to the cost of working. Many of these are of exceptional beauty, presenting colors red as jasper, through all shades of pink, gray and even black, often beautifully variegated and brecciated in a variety of colors. Flow structures caused by the onward flowing of the rock while in a partially cooled condition often gives rise to a beautiful banding and interweaving of colors impossible to decribe, and which must be seen to be appreciated. The striking beauty of this flow structure is sometimes heightened by the presence of angular fragments of variously colored portions of the rock, which, becoming broken from the parent mass, have been imbedded in a matrix of quite different color, as at Hingham, where the writer has found bright red fragments imbedded in a yellowish paste. The rock acquires a beautiful polish, and the fact that it has not ere this come into more general use is a sad comment upon the taste of our wealthier citizens. Nearly as indestructible as glass, and as beautiful as an agate, it is yet almost wholly ignored except for purposes of rough construction.

A large variety of porphyries, varying in color from black to red, occurs also in New Hampshire, particularly near Waterville, some of which would make fine ornamental stones. At Franconia, in the White Mountains, there occurs a porphyry conglomerate formed of fragments of jasper-red porphyry closely cemented into a compact rock, which is particularly beautiful.

Porphyries are abundant in many other States, but are scarcely at all used. Maine, Pennsylvania, Missouri, Minnesota, and Wisconsin all contain good material, though, as little or no search has been made for the highly ornamental varieties, it is impossible to say what they can produce.

At Green Lake, in the last named State, there occurs a beautiful stone of this class, almost black in color, with white porphyritic feldspars. It has been quarried to some extent near the town of Uttny, and polished columns of it may be seen in the German-American Bank Building and Union Depot at Saint Paul, Minnesota. It is greatly to be regretted that no economic method of working so beautiful and durable material has as yet been discovered.

Near Charlotte, in Mecklenburgh County, N. C., there occurs a very light colored, almost white, quartz porphyry, which is penetrated by long parallel streaks or pencils of a dead black color. These are so arranged that, when cut across, the surface appears studded thickly with roundish and very irregular black points of all sizes up to half an inch in diameter. Cut parallel with the direction of the pencils, the surface is streaked with black lines, which sometimes assume beautiful fern-like or dendritic forms.

The rock is intensely hard, tough and without definite rift. It can therefore be worked only at great cost, and is not regularly quarried. It has been used only locally for rough purposes, as for curbing, steps and sills. An analysis of this rock is given in the tables.

A deep reddish quartz porphyry, somewhat resembling the Egyptian red porphyry, has been reported by the United States geologists as occurring near the Great Bend of the Carson River in Nevada.

(5) FOREIGN QUARTZ PORPHYRIES.

Russia.—From the Isle of Hoghland, in the Gulf of Finland, the National Museum has received a variety of quartz porphyries. These have mostly a dull red, very compact base, and carry large, nearly white, pinkish or reddish feldspars and glassy quartz in great profusion. The rocks acquire a good surface and polish, but are intensely hard. Other porphyritic and compact rocks, variously called diorites, keratites and porphyries, were received from the district of Katharinenburg, in the Urals, as noted in the published catalogue of the collections.

THE LIPARITES.

(1) ADAPTABILITY FOR CONSTRUCTIVE PURPOSES.

Tertiary and post-Tertiary rocks of any kind are at present very little used for constructive purposes in the United States, owing, in the case of fragmental rocks, to their state of imperfect consolidation and consequent feeble tenacity, and in the case of eruptives to their almost entire absence in those portions of the country that have become permanently settled, and where as a consequence there has arisen a demand for a more durable building material than wood. Of the eruptive rocks of this class only the liparites, andesites, and basalts have been at all utilized, and these to but a small extent. Their textures are, as a rule, such as to fit them only for the rougher kinds of construction, since, with the exception of the glassy varieties, they will not polish, and their rough appearance unfits them for any kind of interior decorative work.

(2) MINERAL AND CHEMICAL COMPOSITION OF LIPARITE.

Under the head of liparites are classed those acid eruptive rocks or lavas consisting chiefly of quartz and sanidin (the glassy variety of orthoclase) which are not older than Tertiary and which may be regarded as the younger effusive equivalents of the granites, quartz porphyries, and felsite pitchstones.

In texture they vary from coarsely granitoid rocks, entirely crystalline throughout, through all intermediate felsitic stages to clear glassy forms. Structurally they vary from fine, compact, even-grained to coarsely porphyritic, vesicular, and spherulitic forms; well marked fluidal structure is common. The prevailing colors are chalky white to dark gray; more rarely greenish, brownish, yellowish, and reddish varieties occur.

The average chemical composition of liparite (quartz-trachyte) as given by Zirkel is silica, 76.36; alumina, 11.97; iron oxides, 2.01; lime, 1.09; magnesia, 0.56; potash, 3.70; soda, 4.53. Specific gravity, 2.55.

(3) VARIETIES OF LIPARITE.

According as they are crystalline throughout, felsitic and porphyritic or entirely glassy, liparites are classed as (1) granitic liparites or *nevadites,* (2) *rhyolites,* and (3) glassy liparites as *obsidian, pumice, pearlite,* and *pitchstone.* Of these only the felsitic and porphyritic variety *rhyolite* is as yet quarried.

(4) LIPARITES OF THE VARIOUS STATES AND TERRITORIES.

Near the Mokelumne Hills, in Calaveras County, California, rhyolite occurs in several different colors, and has been quarried to some extent for use in the immediate vicinity. The rock is also abundant in Colorado, New Mexico, Nevada, Utah, Montana, and other of the Western States and Territories.

The glassy variety of rhyolite called obsidian is very abundant in certain parts of the West, and though as yet no attempt has been made to utilize the material there would seem no good reason for its not being used in small pieces for the finer kinds of decorative work. The rock, which is a natural glass formed by the rapid cooling of a molten magma, is of various colors, black, red, and greenish, and often beautifully spotted and streaked.

The National collections show from the Yellowstone National Park, Glass Butte, Oregon, and other sources specimens of red obsidian spotted and streaked with black wavy lines in a way that is highly ornamental. The stone occurs naturally in a badly jointed condition, and could be obtained only in pieces of small size. Owing to its glassy fracture also it could be worked only with plain flat or rounded surfaces; but, as it takes a high glass-like polish, it would be very desirable for tops of small stands, paper weights, and inlaid work.

THE SYENITES, TRACHYTES, AND PHONOLITES.

(1) DEFINITION OF SYENITE.

Under the name of Syenites are here included those rocks consisting essentially of orthoclase with or without one or more of the accessory minerals, mica, hornblende, or augite.

They differ from granites only in the absence of quartz, and otherwise present a precisely parallel series. Thus we may have mica syenite (minette), hornblende syenite, augite syenite, etc.*

(2) LOCALITIES OF SYENITE.

At the present time syenites are but little quarried in this country, though there would seem to be no lack of material and of good quality.

In and about Portland, Maine, there occur in the glacial drift many bowlders of a beautiful syenite, the exact source of which is not known to the author, but which can not be far to the northward. The rock consists mainly of bright lustrous gray orthoclase and coal-black hornblende, with occasionally a little black mica. In texture it is not too coarse, and the contrast of colors such that one can scarcely imagine a more beautiful stone for rock-faced work. It is very tough, and, to judge from the bowlders, is also very durable, and not at all liable to discoloration on exposure.

Hawes † describes augite syenites as occurring in Jackson, Columbia, and on Little Ascuntney Mountain, in New Hamshire; also hornblende syenites as occurring at Red Hill and Moultonborough, Columbia, Sandwich, Stark, and Albany, in

---

* Formerly it was customary to call by the name syenite a rock consisting of quartz, hornblende, and orthoclase, or what is now called a hornblende granite. The name takes its origin from Syene, Egypt, where a rock supposed to answer this description was originally quarried. Investigation has, however, shown that the Syene rock contains more mica than hornblende, and hence at best can not be classed as a true syenite even according to the old definition. According to recent lithologists the Syene rock is a hornblende mica granite, while true syenite, as above stated, is a quartzless rock.

† Geology of New Hampshire, vol. III. part IV

the same State.   Dr. Wadsworth* also mentions a syenite as occurring in eastern Massachusetts, where it occupies a large proportion of the coast line between Salem and Manchester. None of these are as yet quarried.

Near Hot springs, in Arkansas, there is quarried under the name of granite a tough gray rock of variable texture, consisting mainly of hornblende and elæolite, and which would therefore be classed as an elæolite syenite.   Some portions of the rock, as shown by the large block in the National collection, are fine-grained and homogeneous, while in others the elæolite crystals reach some 2 or 3 inches in length.   The appearance of the stone is excellent, but portions of it contain a large amount of pyrite and it needs to be selected with care if designed for exterior or highly ornamental work.

According to Professor Branner† these syenites occur in the vicinity of Little Rock where they form the Fourche Mountains, to the south-west of that city in Saline County, and at Magnet Cove on the Hot Springs Railroad in Hot Springs County.   In the Little Rock district are found both blue-gray and light-gray, as well as several intermediate varieties.

Both varieties have been used more or less, but it is only within the last two years that they can be said to have been put upon the market.   The syenites of both the Little Rock and and Magnet Cove regions are intrusive, having penetrated rocks of Lower Carboniferous age ; whether those in Saline County are contemporaneous with the others is not as yet known but it seems probable that they are.   The blue beds of the Fourche Mountains are all, so far as they have been uncovered, more or less jointed so that the rock comes out in angular masses of all sizes, many of them being much too large to be

* Geological Magazine, May, 1885, p. 207.
† Stone, Oct., 1889.

handled. These masses, however, are perfectly solid and homogeneous. The blue-gray variety is now extensively used for street paving as well as for architectural purposes. It is one of the best and handsomest of building stones, its colors making a pleasing contrast with other stones and bricks. The county Court-house and the fronts of most of the new business blocks in Little Rock are built of this stone. The light-gray variety usually occurs in extensive massive beds from which blocks of any desired size can be quarried. These rocks cover an area of many square miles, and there is no possibility of the beds ever becoming exhausted. They are moreover convenient to railway transportation, being cut by the Iron Mountain Railway near Little Rock, while the Diamond Jo quarry in the Magnet Cove area is within a thousand feet of the Hot Springs Railway.

The cathedral in Little Rock is of the light-gray variety, which has also been employed in many minor structures.

A syenitic rock bearing abundant elæolite and frequently cancrinite and sodalite, and which must, therefore, also be classed as an elæolite syenite occurs abundantly in the vicinity of Litchfield, Maine, and specimens of the rock have found their way into the building-stone collections of the National Museum. An examination of the rock does not, however, impress one particularly in its favor. Its durability is, to say the least, doubtful, and its varying texture and colors rather against it.

(3) THE TRACHYTES AND PHONOLITES.

Under the name of trachytes are comprehended by Rosenbusch those massive Tertiary and post-Tertiary volcanic rocks consisting essentially of sanidin and hornblende, augite or black mica, and which may be regarded as the younger equivalents of the syenites, and quartz free porphyries.

The average chemical composition is silica, 63.55% ; alumma, 18.0% ; iron oxide, 6.15% ; lime, 1.96% ; magnesia, 0.88%. Specific gravity, 2.65.

In structure trachytes are rarely granular, but usually possess a fine scaly or micro-felsitic groundmass, rendered porphyritic by the development of scattering crystals of sanidin, hornblende, augite, or black mica. The texture is porous and possesses a characteristic roughness to the touch ; hence its name from the Greek word τραχυς rough. The prevailing colors are gray, yellowish or reddish. They may be divided into hornblende, biotite, or augite trachytes, according as either of these accessory minerals predominates.

Phonolites differ from trachytes in carrying one or both of the minerals nepheline or leucite in addition to the other constituents named. They bear the same relations then to the trachytes as do the elæolite syenites to the syenites proper.

Neither trachytes nor phonolites are, so far as now known, common rocks in the United States. Zirkel* describes numerous trachytes from the areas covered by the Fortieth Parallel survey, and Caswell † describes both trachytes and phonolites from the Black Hills, Dakota. Recent investigations by Wadsworth‡ and Messrs. Hague and Iddings § show, however, that the supposed trachytes of Zirkel were in large part if not altogether andesites, and it is very probable that similar tests applied to many other cases heretofore described would be productive of similar results. However this may be, the utility of the rocks in America is purely prospective.

Their colors and textures are such that they can never be

---

* Microscopic Petrography of the Fortieth Parallel.

† Geology of the Black Hills of Dakota.

‡ Proceedings Boston Society Natural History, vol. XXI. 1881, p. 243, and vol. XXII. 1883, p. 412.

§ American Journal Science, vol. XXVI. 1884, p. 453.

used for other purposes than rough construction, as is the case with the majority of the younger eruptives.

AUGITE (ENSTATITE, HYPERSTHENE) PLAGIOCLASE ROCKS.

(1) DIABASE.

Diabase, from the Greek word διάβασις to pass over ; so called because the rock passes by imperceptible gradations into diorite.

The diabases are crystalline granular rocks, composed essentially of plagioclase feldspar and augite, or a rhombic pyroxene, with nearly always magnetite and frequently olivine. Geologically they are pre-Tertiary eruptive rocks, basic in composition, occurring in dikes, intruded sheets and bosses. In structure they are as a rule massive, but schistose varieties occur and more rarely spherulitic forms. The texture is as a rule fine, compact, and homogeneous, though sometimes porphyritic or amygdaloidal. The colors are somber, varying from greenish through dark gray to nearly black, or sometimes black when freshly quarried, but becoming greenish on drying.*

According to Zirkel, the average chemical composition of diabase is as follows :

	Per cent.
Silica	49.54
Alumina	14.05
Iron protoxide	14.27
Lime	8.20
Magnesia	5.28
Potash	1.16
Soda	3.88
Water	2.29

---

* Mr. J. P. Iddings suggests that the change in color from dark blue black, to greenish, as noticed in diabase of New Jersey, is due to the drying of the serpentine or chlorite, which results from the alteration of the included olivine. (American Journal of Science, May, 1886, p. 330.

Average specific gravity, 2.8, which is equal to a weight of 175 pounds per cubic foot. In classification two principal varieties of diabase are recognized, the distinction being founded upon the presence or absence of the mineral olivine. We thus have (1) olivine diabase, or diabase with olivine, and (2) diabase proper, or diabase without olivine. Owing to its lack of definite rift, compact texture, and hardness, diabase can, as a rule, be worked only with difficulty and usually at a cost considerably greater than that of granite. It is therefore not extensively quarried, though of late years it has come into more general use for paving purposes, and still more recently for building and monumental work. The green *antique porphyry* or *Marmor Lacedæmonium viride*, formerly much used for pavements and general inlaid decorative work in Greece and Rome, is according to Delesse, a diabase consisting of large greenish crystals of labradorite embedded in a fine compact groundmass of the same feldspar, together with augite and titaniferous iron. The quarries from which the stone was taken are stated by Hull to be situated between Sparta and Marathon, in Greece. A stone of a similar character and closely resembling it in color and structure is abundant among the drift bowlders of eastern Massachusetts, but its exact derivation is unknown.

In the eastern United States the dikes and sheets of diabase are frequently associated with deposits of red or brown Triassic sandstone, which are also extensively quarried, as will be noticed further on. Concerning these dikes Professor Dana writes :*

"It is remarkable that these fractures (through which the diabase was forced to the surface) should have taken place in

---

* Manual of Geology, third edition, p. 417.

great numbers just where the Triassic beds exist, and only sparingly east or west of them ; and also that the igneous rock should be essentially the same throughout the thousands of miles from Nova Scotia to North Carolina. The igneous and aqueous rocks (sandstone) are so associated that they necessarily come into the same history. Mount Tom and Mount Holyoke, of Massachusetts, are examples of these trap ridges ; also East Rock and West Rock, near New Haven, and the Hanging Hills, near Meriden, in Connecticut ; the Palisades along the Hudson River, in New York ; Bergen Hill and other elevations in New Jersey.

" In Nova Scotia trap ridges skirt the whole red sandstone region and face directly the Bay of Fundy ; Cape Blomidon, noted for its zeolitic minerals, lies at its northern extremity on the Bay of Mines.

" In Connecticut the ridges and dikes are extremely numerous, showing a vast amount of igneous action. . . . They commence near Long Island Sound, at New Haven, where they form some bold eminences, and extend through the State and nearly to the northern boundary of Massachusetts. Mounts Holyoke and Tom are in the system. The general course is parallel to that of the Green Mountains.

" Although the greater part of the dikes is confined to the sandstone regions, there are a few outside, intersecting the crystalline rocks and following the same direction, and part, at least, of the same system.

" Even the little Southbury Triassic region, lying isolated in western Connecticut, has a large number of trap ridges, and such a group of them as occurs nowhere else in New England outside of the Triassic. Their direction and positions in overlapping series are the same as in the Connecticut valley.

" The trap usually forms hills with a bold columnar front and sloping back. When nearly north and south in direction the bold front is to the westward in the Connecticut Valley, and to the eastward in New Jersey. It has come up through fissures in the sandstone, which varied from a few inches to 300 feet or more in breadth. In many cases it has made its way out by opening the layers of sandstone, and in such cases it stands with a bold front, facing in the direction toward which it thus ascended."

Connecticut.—The extensive diabase outcrops noted above as occurring at East and West Rocks, north of New Haven in this State, are quarried for foundation walls and for. paving purposes in the near vicinity. The rock is too dull in color for ornamental work.

Maine.—Diabase is quarried at three localities in this State, Addison, Vinalhaven, and Tenant's Harbor. At Addison the rock occurs in extensive outcrops close by the water's edge. Single blocks 66 by 10 by 20 feet have been moved in the quarries, and natural blocks 90 by 10 by 15 feet occur. The chief defects in the stone are said to be the so-called "knots," which consist of irregular patches of coarse feldspar and dark crystals of hornblende. There are also occasional seams, causing the rock to split unfavorably. The rock is moderately fine-grained, very dark gray, sometimes almost black or spotted black and white on a polished surface and of a fine appearance. It has been used in the walls inclosing the Capitol grounds at Washington, in the construction of a bank at Montreal, and is quite generally used for monuments in Boston, New York, Brooklyn, Washington, Montreal, and Quebec. The Vinalhaven diabase is less extensively worked on account of its hardness. It is of finer grain than the Addison stone and uniformly dark-gray, nearly black in color. It is used to some extent for building material and also in cemetery work. The Tenant's Harbor (St. George, Knox County) stone closely resembles that of Addison, and is used for similar purposes.

These are all most excellent stones, and it is a matter for con-
gratulation that they are being so extensively introduced, and,
to some extent, replacing the marbles in monumental work.
The cost of working is, owing to their compact structure,
somewhat greater than that of granite, but the results fully
justify the increased outlay.   All the above, it should be noted
are known commercially as black granite.*

Massachusetts.—Diabase is quarried for foundations walls,
general constructive purposes, and monumental work, at Med-
ford and Somerville in this State.   The stone from these localities is coarser, lighter in color, and much inferior in point of
beauty to that just described.

Missouri.—Intrusive masses of diabase occur at various
points in the southeastern part of this State, particularly in
Madison County.   Attempts have been made to quarry the
material from outcrops near Mine La Motte Station at Skrain-
ka, but the works are no longer in operation.   The rock is
stated to be covered with from ten to thirty feet of stripping
and to have been so violently contorted and broken that it is
impossible to quarry dimension stone from it.   It is fine grained dark gray to almost black in color, splits and dresses easily,
and takes an excellent polish, but cannot be utilized for monumental purposes for reasons above noted.   Up to date it has
been used mainly in the manufacture of paving blocks.†

New Jersey.—The extensive outcrops of diabase, or "trap

---

* It should be remarked that all of these diabases differ radically in structure
and composition from any others here mentioned, and deserve a more thorough
and careful study than they have yet received.   All contain a rhombic pyroxene
pleochroic in red, green, and brown colors, and which is evidently hypersthene,
while certain sections of the Addison rock show a pyroxenic constituent carrying an abundance of the rhombic inclosures so characteristic of entstatite.
Prof. Rosenbusch in his recent work includes this rock with the gabbros.

† Bulletin No. 1 Missouri Geological Survey, 1890, p. 42.

rock," known as the Palisades of the Hudson River, in north-eastern New Jersey, furnish an inexhaustible supply of this material, and which is at present quite extensively quarried about Guttenberg, Weehawken, west New York, and southward along the Palisades as far as Montgomery Avenue in Jersey City. The rock is used chiefly for paving, and the quarries are small affairs worked by gangs of from two to five men. Two sizes of blocks are prepared. The larger, which are known as specification blocks, are 4 by 8 or 10 inches on the head and 7 to 8 inches deep. The second size, which are called square blocks, are 5 to 6 inches square and 6 to 7 inches deep. The specification blocks bring about $30 per thousand in the market, and the square only about $20 per thousand. It is estimated that some 4,000,000 of the specification and 1,000,000 of the square blocks were quarried in 1887, valued at $140,000.

There are three principal grades of the rock quarried. A fine-grained variety at Mount Pleasant, a rocky hill north of the Pennsylvania Railroad ; a light-gray variety at Bergen Cut, south of the railroad ; and a dark, almost black, variety at Weehawken and West New York. Other quarries of this rock are worked at Orange Mountain ; Snake Hill, Hudson County, and at Morris Hill in Paterson. In the western part of the State the outcrops are not so extensive, but quarries are worked at Rocky Hill, near Titusville, Smith's Hill, and near Lambertville. At Rock Church, 4 miles from Lambertville, the rock is quarried and used for monumental work as well as for general building purposes, being put upon the market under the name of black granite. The rock from the Palisade quarries has also been quite extensively used in and about Jersey City for building purposes. St. Patrick's Cathedral, and the Hudson County Court-house, as well as many private buildings, are of this stone, but the effect as a whole is

not pleasing, owing to the sombre colors of the material. Employed in connection with brick or lighter stone, to give variety and contrast, the effect is admirable.

The finely broken stone is also used very extensively for railroad ballast and road-making. Several of the quarries near Orange Mountain have machines for breaking up the stone for this purpose.*

Pennsylvania.—The principal quarries of diabase in this State are at Collins Station, Lancaster County, and near York Haven, York County. At the latter place the face of the quarries is about 70 feet in height. The rock lies in huge natural blocks sometimes weighing hundreds of tons and having curved outlines giving them a sort of oval shape. Stone from this quarry is used only by the Northern Central Railroad in the construction of bridges and culverts.

At Collins Station diabase is more extensively quarried than at any other locality in the State. The stone is used for all manner of building purposes and monumental work. The foundation of the new Harrisburg Post-office and the Soldiers' Monument in this city are from this material.

In the vicinity of Gettysburg diabase is quite extensively quarried, and has been used for head-stones in the national cemetery at this place. It is also used for general building being put on the market under the name of Gettysburg granite.

Virginia.—As in the States to the east and north, the Triassic beds of Virginia are cut by large dikes of " trap " or diabase, and which in some cases are capable of affording excellent material for paving blocks and general building and ornamental work. So far as the author is aware quarries have been opened upon these dikes in but two localities, at Cedar

---

* See Annual Report State Geologist of New Jersey, 1881, pp. 60–63.

Run, near Catlett's Station on the Virginia Midland Railroad, and near Goose Creek, about three miles east of Leesburgh, in Loudoun County. Specimens of these rocks which the writer has examined represent the coarser varieties of our Mesozoic diabase, are of a dark gray color, very strong, and apparently durable. That from Goose Creek has been found to stand a pressure of 23,000 pounds per square inch, and, as the author has observed, undergoes no change on an exposure of twenty-five years other than a slight and in no way objectionable darkening of color. Neither stone has been used as yet for other than paving purposes and bridge abutments, though they are apparently well adapted to all kinds of work for which their color and hardness qualify them.

(2) GABBRO AND NORITE.

The rock gabbro differs from diabase mainly in containing the foliated pyroxene diallage in place of augite. It is not at present quarried to any extent in this country, though for no apparent reason other than that it is difficult to work.

Very extensive outcrops of a dark gray, almost black gabbro of medium fineness of texture occur in the immediate vicinity of Baltimore, Maryland, but which have been quarried only for purposes of rough construction close at hand. The rock is popularly known as "niggerhead" owing to its hardness, dark color, and its occurrence in rounded bowlders on the surface.*

At Rice's Point, near Duluth, Minnesota, there occurs an inexhaustible supply of a coarse gabbro, which has been stud-

---

* This is the rock the interesting petrographical features of which have lately been made known by Dr. Williams, of Johns Hopkins University. See Bull. U. S. Geological Survey, no. 28.

ied and described by Professor Winchell.* The feldspar of the rock, which is labradorite, according to the authority quoted, sometimes prevails as at Beaver Bay, in crystals one-half to three-fourths of an inch across, and to the almost entire exclusion of other constituents. In this form the rock varies from lavender blue or bluish gray to light green, and acquires a beautiful surface and polish, and is considered as constituting a valuable material for ornamental slabs and columns. The typical gabbro of the region is of a dark blue-gray color, and "has been employed in a few buildings at Duluth, both in cut trimmings and for rough walls." It has also been used for monuments and for bases, to which it is especially adapted, being cut under the chisel and polished more easily than any of the crystalline rocks that contain quartz. The stone is known popularly as Duluth granite. The same kind of rock occurs at Taylor's Falls, but is little used, though favorably situated for quarrying and transporting.

A rock closely allied to the gabbros and diabases is the so-called norite, which consists essentially of the minerals hypersthene and a plagioclase feldspar. Rocks of this type are now quarried on the north and west slopes of Prospect Hill, near Keeseville, Essex County, New York and at Vergennes, Vermont. The stone of the first named locality is known commercially as Au Sable granite, and the second as Labradorite granite. Both are coarse-grained, dark-gray rocks, much resembling the darker varieties of the Quincy granites, from which, however, they differ radically in mineral composition. They take a high lustrous polish, frequently show a beautiful bright bluish chatoyant play of colors and are seemingly admirably adapted for polished columns, pilasters, and other decorative work.

---

* Geology of Minnesota, vol. I, pp. 148–9.

The lasting power of the norites, when polished, is yet to be ascertained. After an exposure of untold years in the quarry bed the surface has turned white. No data are obtainable for calculating their lasting qualities in the finished structure. As seen by the writer the Keeseville rock in the quarry bed is cut by innumerable clean sharp joints at intervals of every few feet, and in some cases of even fractions of an inch.

In the freshly quarried stone these are quite invisible and appear on a polished surface as faint parallel lines, as fine, straight and sharp cut as though made with a diamond. As a measure of precaution such jointed blocks had best be avoided for purposes of fine monumental work, since it seems extremely probable that the joints will open on exposure for prolonged periods. Professor Egleston who tested this stone for the company, reports that on exposure to the heat of a furnace at temperatures varying from 800 to 1,850 Fahr. samples turned light chocolate-brown, but did not seriously disintegrate. Its crushing strength as given by the same authority is 29,000 pounds per square inch.*

A dark greenish black norite or hypersthene gabbro with accessory hornblende and black mica is found in Anson County, North Carolina on the line of the Carolina Central Railway. The stone has been worked for the Raleigh market, and so far as may be judged from small pieces compares very favorably with other of our so-called black granites. It corresponds more nearly with the Addison [Maine] gabbro than with either of the above mentioned rocks. A fine grained dark gray rock of this nature showing abundant small flecks of dark mica and carrying in microscopic proportions abundant hypersthene occurs at Clifton, Maine. The rock though not now quarried is admirably adapted for rock-faced work, and so

---

* See Smock's Building-stone in New York, p. 232.

far as may be judged from appearances would be found to work readily.

The rock compares in general appearances with the mica diorite of Croton Landing, New York, but is of finer grain. A coarser, more granitic variety of the same rock is found in Calais in Washington County, and has, as I am informed, been worked experimentally by the Red Beach Granite Company.

(3) MELAPHYR.

The melaphyrs, as defined by Prof. Rosenbusch, are massive eruptive rocks, consisting of plagioclase, augite, and olivine, with free iron oxides and an amorphous or "porphyry" base. They are thus of the same mineral composition as the basalts and olivine diabases, but differ structurally, and belong in great part to the Carboniferous and older Permian formations. Although very abundant in many parts of the United States, they are scarcely at all quarried owing to their dull colors and poor working qualities.

In the Brighton district of Boston, but a few miles out of the city proper, and in other localities in the vicinity, there occur small outcrops of a greenish or sometimes purplish melaphyr, or "amygdaloid," the lithological nature of which was, I believe, first correctly stated by E. R. Benton* The prevailing color of the rock is greenish, often amygdaloidal, the amygdules being composed often of epidote, thus spotting the surface with greenish-yellow blotches. The rock is greatly altered, only the feldspars of the original constituents remaining now recognizable, while chlorite, quartz, calcite, epidote, and several other minerals occur as secondary products. The rock is neverthe-

---

* Proceedings Boston Society, vol. XX, p. 416.

less very firm, compact, and durable, and is being quarried to some extent for rough work. It would seem fitted for a yet wider architectural application.

(4) BASALT.

This rock differs from diabase only in point of geological age, being a product of post-Tertiary eruptions. It is, as a rule, less perfectly crystalline, still retaining portions of its glassy magma. Owing in great part to the fact that basalts occur in this country only in the western and more recently settled portions, as do also the andesites and rhyolites, they have been heretofore but little utilized. There would seem, however, no reason for excluding the rock from the list of available building materials in those regions where it occurs in such form as to be accessible. At Petaluma, Bridgeport, and other places around the bay of San Francisco there lie immense sheets of this rock, but which are worked now only for paving materials. Like the andesites and rhyolites the basalts will not polish, and their colors are such as to exclude them from all forms of interior decorative work.

AMPHIBOLE PLAGIOCLASE ROCKS (TRAP AND GREEN STONE, IN PART).

(1) DIORITES AND KERSANTITES.

The name diorite from the Greek word $\delta\iota o\rho\iota\sigma\epsilon\acute{\iota}\nu$, to distinguish, is used to designate a group of pre-Tertiary eruptive rocks consisting essentially of the minerals hornblende and plagioclase, and occurring in the form of dikes, bosses and intrusive sheets. The individual crystals composing the rock are sometimes grouped in globular aggregations forming the so-called orbicular diorite or kugel diorite. The texture is as a rule compact, fine and homogeneous, though sometimes porphyritic. The common colors are dark gray or green. According to Zirkel the average composition is:

	Per Cent.
Silica	48.50 to 60.88
Alumina	15.72 to 22.12
Protoxide of iron	6.26 to 11.92
Lime	5.47 to 7.99
Magnesia	0.54 to 9.70
Potash	1.05 to 3.79
Soda	2.20 to 5.21
Water	0.60 to 1.90

In classification two principal varities are recognized, mica diorite or diorite in which black mica is present in excess of the hornblende, and hornblende diorite or diorite proper. The presence of quartz gives rise to the variety quartz diorite. The name *tonalite* was given by Vom Rath to a quartz diorite containing the feldspar andesite and very rich in black mica and which occurs in the southern Alps, and the name *kersantite* has been applied to a dioritic rock carrying black mica as its chief accessory and differing from the ordinary mica diorite chiefly in structure. The diorites together with the diabases and melaphyrs have in times past, owing to a lack of definite knowledge of their mineral nature, been commonly known as *traps* or *greenstones.*

The rocks of this group are as a rule exceeding compact and strong, but are scarcely at all used for building purposes owing to their lack of rift and poor working qualities in general. Their sombre colors are also a draw-back to any form of architectural display.

In England diorites are stated by Hauenschild to be largely used for road materials. The kugel diorite or napoleonite mentioned above is but a peculiar structural variety of diorite proper. The chief constituents—hornblende and feldspar— are frequently grouped in radially concentric masses of an inch or more in diameter, and which show up on a polished surface as oval or circular areas of alternating green and white zones encircling a granular nucleus and interspersed irregularly throughout a greenish granular groundmass. The rock has been used to some extent for ornamental purposes. The source is the island of Corsica.

Porphyritic diorites, or porphyrites, may be said to bear the same relation to true diorites as do the quartz porphyries to granites. That is, they consist of a compact felsitic base in which hornblende or feldspar is porphyritically developed. The celebrated red Egyptian porphyry or *Rosso Antico* is a porphyrite as shown by Delesse. The source of this rock is stated by this authority to be the Dokhan Mountains, about twenty-five miles from the Red Sea and eighty-five miles from ancient Captos (now called Kypt). Rocks of this class, though in no way comparable from the standpoint of beauty, have been described by Hawes * as occurring in New Hampshire at Campton Falls, North Lisbon, Dixville, and Dixville Notch : a mica diorite is also described as occurring at Stewarttown. None of these are put to any practical use.

A dark gray granitic-appearing diorite of variable texture occurs near Reading, Berks County, Pennsylvania, which may answer for rough construction. It is not a handsome stone, and is moreover, hard to work.

The National collections contain a cube of a compact light greenish gray diorite, carrying quite an amount of greenish mica, and plentifully besprinkled with white porphyritic feld- spar, from near El Paso, Texas. This cuts to a sharp edge,

---

* Geology of New Hampshire, vol. III, part IV, p. 160.

and acquires a good surface and polish.   It appears like a good stone for ordinary purposes of construction.

A somewhat similar stone is found near Monarch, Chaffee County, Colorado.

A quartz diorite of a coarse granitic structure is found and quarried at Rocklin, Placer County, California.   The stone resembles granite in general appearances, and works with equal facility.

The rock kersantite has, so far as is now known, a rather limited distribution in the United States.   Some years ago B. K. Emerson described a dike of kersantite cutting the zinc ores of Franklin Furnace, New Jersey, but the outcrops are too small to be of value.   Prof. Newberry* has more recently described outcroppings of this rock near Croton Landing, on the Hudson River, in New York State, and which he regards as of value for architectural purposes.

The stone is described by this authority as having the aspect of a dark gray granite, and varying in texture from fine and compact to coarsely crystalline varieties, in which the white feldspars and brown biotite are an inch or more in length.   In the outcrop the stone is more or less jointed, but without distinct bedding, and is found to work with equal facility in any direction.

Its strength is stated to be equal to 20,250 pounds to the square inch, and weight 178¼ pounds to the cubic foot.   The stone takes a fine polish and is regarded as very durable.†

Kersantite is regarded by Chateau ‡ as one of the best of rocks for constructive purposes, though unfortunately rare and difficult to obtain in blocks of large size.

---

* School of Mines Quarterly, vol. XIV, no. 4, July, 1887, pp. 330–332.

† Subsequent studies have shown this rock to be more closely related to the mica diorites than to the true kersantites.

‡ Technologie du Batiment, vol. I, p. 377.

The rock takes its name from Kersanton in Brittany, where it has been quarried and utilized in architectural work for many years.

(2) THE ANDESITES.

Under the name of andesite is included a group of volcanic rocks (lavas) of Tertiary and post-Tertiary age, and consisting essentially of a triclinic feldspar and hornblende, augite, or black mica.

In structure the andesites are rarely entirely crystalline, but usually present a fine densely microlitic or partly glassy groundmass. According as they vary in composition four principal varieties are recognized: (1) Quartz andesite (dacite) or andesite in which quartz is a prominent ingredient; (2) hornblende andesite; (3) augite andesite; and (4) mica andesite, each taking its name according as hornblende, augite, or mica is the principal accessory mineral. Hypersthene andesite, or andesite in which the mineral hypersthene is a leading constituent, is also common in many of the Western States and Territories.

The andesites are as yet but little used for structural purposes, and this largely for the same reasons as were given in the chapter on liparites. Like the rhyolites, they will not polish, and are in no way suited for decorative work. Although very abundant throughout many of the Western States and Territories, they have been quarried only in a few instances, and in an itinerant way. Near Virginia City, Storey County, Nevada, occur coarse, dark blue, gray, and reddish brown porphyritic andesites, which have been used in the near vicinity for structural purposes. At Reno, in Washoe County, is also quarried a light gray andesite, which has been used for foundation walls, in the construction of the prison and a few stores in

Reno.   In Virginia City, Madison County, Montana, the writer has also observed shop fronts built of andesite quarried from some of the numerous outcrops in the near vicinity.

SCHISTOSE, OR FOLIATED ROCKS.

(1) THE GNEISSES.

The gneisses, as already noted, have essentially the same composition as do the granites, from which they differ mainly in their foliated or schistose structure.   On account of this schistosity the rocks split in such a way as to give parallel flat surfaces, which render the stone serviceable in the construction of rough walls and for street curbing.   This structure, which is caused mainly by the arrangement of the mica and other minerals in parallel layers, is, however, a drawback to the uniform working of the stones, and hence they are more limited in their application than are the granites.   These rocks are frequently called by quarrymen *stratified* or *bastard* granites. The name *gneiss*, it should be stated, is of German origin, and should be pronounced as though spelled *nice*, never as *nees*. For reasons already given, the gneisses have been included under the chapter on granites in the present work.

(2) THE SCHISTS.

The general name of schists is applied to a widely varying group of rocks having a more or less pronounced schistose structure as a common characteristic.   Quartz may be considered as the only essential constituent, and is accompanied, as a rule, by one or more minerals of the mica or hornblende groups as principal accessory.   Accordingly as one or another of these prevails, we have therefore *mica, hornblende, talcose,* or *chloritic* schists. They differ from the gneisses, it will be' observed, only in the lack of feldspar as an essential constituent. In company with these latter rocks the schists were once supposed to be, in all cases, metamorphosed sediments, to which fact they owed their marked foliated or stratified structures. Modern investigation has, however, shown that these same structures may be produced in massive eruptive rocks by dynamic and incident chemical agencies. While they are therefore undoubtedly *metamorphic* rocks, we must not fall into the error of regarding them in all cases as metamorphosed sediments. But whatever their origin, this schistose structure is from our present standpoint the most important consideration. The rocks split with great readiness, and frequently with very smooth and even surfaces parallel with this schistosity, but break with considerable difficulty, and often very ragged edges at right angles to it. These peculiarities of the schists are not such as to render them favorites for purposes of fine construction. They are, however, in most instances broken out from the ledges with comparative ease, and for rough construction, such as foundations and bridges, as well as for flagging, they are extensively employed.

FRAGMENTAL ROCKS.

(1) SANDSTONES, BRECCIAS, AND CONGLOMERATES.

(a) COMPOSITION AND ORIGIN.

Sandstones are composed of rounded and angular grains of sand so cemented and compacted as to form a solid rock. The cementing material may be either silica, carbonate of lime, an iron oxide, or clayey matter. Upon the character of this cementing material, more perhaps than upon the character of the grains themselves; is dependent the color of the rock and its adaptability for architectural purposes. If silica alone is present the rock is light-colored, and frequently so intensely hard that it can be worked only with great difficulty. Such are among the most durable of all rocks, but their light colors and poor working qualities are something of a drawback to their extensive use. The cutting of such stones often subjects the workmen to serious inconvenience on account of the very fine and sharp dust or powder made by the tools, and which is so light as to remain suspended for some time in the air. The hard Potsdam sandstones of New York State have been the subject of complaint on this score. If the cement is composed largely of iron oxides the stone is red or brownish in color, and usually not too hard to work readily.* When the cementing material is carbonate of lime the stone is light colored or gray, soft, and easy to work. As a rule such stones do not weather so well as those with either the siliceous or ferruginous cement; owing to the ready solubility of the lime in the water of slightly acidulated rains the siliceous grains become loosened, and the rock disintegrates. The clayey cement is more objectionable than any yet mentioned, since it readily absorbs water and renders the stone more liable to injury by frost. Many sandstones contain little if any cement, but owe their tenacity simply to the pressure to which they were subjected at the time of their consolidation. Such stones are generally of a grayish hue, easy to work, and,

---

* Julien states that in the Tertiary sandstones of the Appalachian border the ferruginous cement is largely turgite ; in the Triassic and Carboniferous sandstones it is largely limonite, and in the Potsdam sandstones of Lake Champlain and the southern shore of Lake Superior it is largely hematite. (Proceedings of the American Association for the Advancement of Science, vol. xxviii. 1879, p. 408.)

if the amount of cohesion be sufficiently great, are very durable. The finer varieties of these stones, such as the Euclid "bluestone" and "Berea grits," are utilized in the manufacture of grindstones and whetstones. Since they contain little cementing material they do not become polished when exposed to wear, but crumble slowly away, presenting always fresh, sharp surfaces to be acted upon. In certain of our Potsdam sandstones the siliceous cement is found to have so arranged itself with relation to the grains of sand as to practically convert it into a crystalline rock or quartzite. This has already been referred to in the chapter on microscopic structure.

Sandstones are not in all cases composed wholly of quartz grains, but frequently contain a variety of minerals. The brown Triassic sandstones of Connecticut, New Jersey, and Pennsylvania are found, on miscroscopic and chemical examination, to contain one or more kinds of feldspar and also mica (see Fig. 6, Plate II), having, in fact, nearly the same composition as a granite or gneiss, from which they were doubtless originally derived. According to Dr. P. Schweitzer,* a fine-grained sandstone from the so-called Palisade range in New Jersey contains from 30 to 60 per cent of the feldspar albite. That quarried at Newark, in the same State, contains, according to his analysis, albite, 50.46 per cent; quartz, 45.49 per cent; soluble silica, .30 per cent; bases soluble in hydrochloric acid, 2.19 per cent, and water, 1.14 per cent.

Sandstones are of a great variety of colors; light gray (almost white), gray, buff, drab or blue, light brown, brown, pink, and red are common varieties, and, as already stated, the color is largely due to the iron contained by them. Accord-

* American Chemist, July, 1871, p. 23.

ing to Mr. G. Maw * the red and brownish-red colors are due to the presence of iron in the anhydrous sesquioxide state, the yellow color to iron in the hydrous sesquioxide state, and the blue and gray tints to protoxide carbonates of iron. It is also stated that the blue color is sometimes caused by finely-disseminated iron pyrites, and rarely by an iron phosphate.† (See page 40.)

In texture sandstones vary from almost impalpably fine-grained stones to those in which the individual grains are several inches in diameter. These coarser stones are called *conglomerates*, or, if the grains are angular instead of rounded, *breccias*.

All sandstones, when freshly quarried, are found to contain a variable amount of water, which renders them soft and more easily worked, but at the same time peculiarly liable to injury by freezing. So pronounced is this character that many quarries in the northern regions can be worked only in the summer months, as during the cold season the freshly quarried material would freeze, burst, and become entirely ruined. It is customary also for dealers to refuse to assume any risks of injury from freezing to which such stone may be liable after shipment. After the evaporation of this "quarry water," as it is called, the stone is found to be considerably harder, and hence more difficult to work. This hardening process is explained by Newberry and others by the theory that the quarry water holds in solution certain of the cementing materials, as noted elsewhere.

(b) VARIETIES OF SANDSTONES.

Many varieties of sandstones are popularly recognized, the distinctions being founded upon their composition, structure,

---

* Quarterly Journal of the Geological Society of London, No. XXIV. p. 355.
† Notes on Building Construction, part III. p. 35.

the character of the cementing material, or their working qualities. *Arkose* is a sandstone composed of disintegrated granite. *Ferruginous, siliceous,* and *calcareous* sandstones are those in which these substances form the cementing material. *Argillaceous* sandstones contain clay, which can easily be recognized by its odor when breathed upon. *Flagstone* is a sandstone that splits readily into thin sheets suitable for flagging ; the same term is applied to other rocks, as the schists and slates, which serve a similar purpose. *Freestones* are so called because they work freely in any direction, their bedding or grain not being strongly enough marked to in any way interfere with this property. *Graywacke* is a compact sandstone, composed of rounded grains or fragments of quartz, feldspar, slate, and other minerals, cemented by an argillaceous, calcareous, or feldspathic paste. This term is no longer in general use. *Quartzites* result from the induration of sandstones, a result brought about either by pressure or, more commonly, by the deposition of silica between the granules.

Sandstones occur among rocks of all ages, from the Archæan down to the most recent ; none are, however, at present used to any great extent for building purposes in this country that are of later origin than Cretaceous. In the list of natural building materials of the United States sandstone ranks third in importance.

(*c*) SANDSTONES OF THE VARIOUS STATES AND TERRITORIES.

Alabama.— On the line of the Alabama Great Southern Railway, some 60 or 100 miles from Chattanooga, Tennessee, there occurs a yellow sandstone that is sufficiently soft when first quarried to be cut with an ax, and which hardens sufficiently on exposure to be very durable in that climate.

Arizona.—There is at present little demand for building

stone in this Territory, and consequently but little is known regarding its available material.

Near Flagstaff in Yavapai County, on the line of the Atlantic and Pacific railroad, there occurs a fine-grained light pink, brownish and red sandstone, evidently of Triassic age, which on account of its warm and pleasing colors and easy working qualities would offer great temptations to the Eastern architect and builder were it more accessible. It is quarried to some extent for the California market, but unfortunately as shown by analysis (see table p. 420) contains so large a percentage of free calcite that its enduring powers are to say the least very doubtful.

Arkansas.—Brown massive " freestone " that will make a good building stone is stated by Owen* to occur in Van Buren County. The northern part of the State is said† to contain a great quantity of cream colored calciferous sandstone which, on account of its color, firmness and massiveness, is a desirable stone for architectural purposes. Gray sandstones are common throughout the coal regions of the State, but thus far have been used only to a slight extent. In the Boston Mountains and its spurs is a beautiful, massive, snuff-colored sandstone which is one of the handsomest building stones of the State. The beds in which this stone occurs are tolerably widespread, though they have been quarried at but one or two places along the St. Louis and San Francisco railroad in the northwestern part of the State. This stone has been used in a few buildings in Fort Smith.

At Batesville in Independence County, and through the country west of that point and north of the Boston Mountain range are beds of cream-colored sandstone which are extensively used in those portions of the State for building and street pav-

---

* Geology of Arkansas, 1858, p. 75.   † J. C. Branner, *Stone*, Oct. 1889.

ing.   It is easily quarried and splits in blocks of any desired thickness.   The business part of Batesville is built of this stone.

California.—Around the Bay of San Francisco there occur sandstones of a considerable variety of colors, which are beginning to come into use to some extent.   The prevailing hues here are brownish and gray.   On Angel Island, in Marin County, there occurs a fine sandstone of a bluish or greenish-gray color, which has been used in the Bank of California building, and others of a lighter shade are found in various parts of Alameda County.   A few miles south of San José, Santa Clara County, there are also inexhaustible supplies of light gray and buff stone, but which are at present worked only in a small way.

Other beds more or less worked are found near Almaden in this same county; in the Santa Susanna Mountains in Los Angeles County and near Henley in Siskiyou County ; near Redwood City in San Mateo County and near Arroyo Grande, San Luis Obispo County.

According to Prof. Jackson * the Angel Island stone consists of grayish white quartz and feldspar, black mica scales, and angular fragments of black clay slate varying in sizes from 15 m m. or more in diameter, to minute black particles that are thickly disseminated through the stone.   These granules and fragments are held in a dull, earthy, scarcely perceptible cement, hardened somewhat by carbonate of lime.   Submitted to the fumes of strong acid the stone lost its bluish tint and turned to a light gray, discolored by streaks and patches of yellow iron oxide.   The loss in weight during the exposure amounted to 2.13 per cent.   Heated in a muffle furnace to bright redness and allowed to cool to just below red heat the

---

* Annual Report State Mineralogist of California, 1888, p. 886.

cube was found to be cracked completely through in several directions, and on then being plunged into cold water became friable and fell to fragments on handling. As shown in the bank building above mentioned the stone weathers unfavorably. Although erected only in 1864 disintegration has already gone so far that recourse has been had to a coating of paraffine in hope of arresting further decay.

The San José stone is described by the above authority as of rather a coarse and uneven texture, friable in small pieces, and containing carbonate of lime in its cement. On exposure to acid fumes the color was leached out of a zone an inch in depth all over the fragment experimented upon, and concentrated in streaks on the surface. Fissure joints were developed, not visible on the fresh specimen, and fragments could easily be separated by the hand in places; the loss by disintegration was 1.94 per cent. The stone stood the test of heat and subsequent immersion without serious disintegration.

The Alameda County stone is described as light grayish, yellow and fine grained, though somewhat variable in texture, and quite friable. Samples when exposed to the strong acid fumes became still more friable and lost by disintegration 3.43 per cent in weight. The color was also leached out of a superficial zone and concentrated on the surface in dark yellowish-brown streaks. On exposure to bright red heat the stone changed in color to a light reddish brown, and underwent no further change on plunging it while still hot into cold water. The crushing strength and ratios of absorption of these stones are given in the tables (p. 413). Near Sespe in Ventura County are also several outcrops of a fine-grained, brown sandstone, which are now supplying material for the San Francisco market. Like the other mentioned it carries a considerable amount of calcareous matter, but it is nevertheless regarded by Prof. Jackson as a valuable stone. Exposed to the acid fumes, samples bleached somewhat and lost by disintegration 2.37 per cent.

In the Santa Susanna Mountains, about eight miles from San Fernando Station in Los Angeles County and on the Southern Pacific railroad occur inexhaustible deposits of coarse and fine yellowish sandstone and which are now being worked from bowlders by a Los Angeles company. Prof. Jackson reports * the coarse variety, when treated as above, as absorbing 5.33 per cent of water, and losing on treatment with acid fumes 7.3 per cent of its weight by disintegration, besides becoming discolored. Highly heated the stone changed to a beautiful brownish red, but did not crack or scale when dropped into cold water. The finer-grained variety from this source is described as a beautiful evenly fine-grained stone, of nearly uniform light grayish yellow color, minutely specked with black and silver-white mica scales. This variety absorbed 6.19 per cent of water and in the acid fumes lost by disintegration 16.9 per cent of its weight besides staining yellowish in spots. In the heat test it behaved as did the coarser variety. The Henley sandstone is described as a moderately fine grained light bluish gray stone, showing to the unaided eye, dark gray and whitish quartz granules with numerous black and few white mica scales, held together by an argillaceous and calcareous cement. The absorption of water was 4.07 per cent. In the acid fumes it lost by disintegration 5.55 per cent, and changed to a bright yellow color. In the muffle samples at full red heat turned to a brownish red color, cracked and scaled somewhat, but underwent no further change when dropped in cold water. The stone is stated to work readily, and as shown by the specimens is free from flaws. The beds as above noted are quarried near Henley, at a point within one mile of Hornbroke Station on

---

* Seventh Annual Report State Mineralogist of California 1887, p. 209.

the California and Oregon Railroad. The supply is inexhaustible.

Near Cordelia, Solano County, there occurs a coarse, dark-gray volcanic tuff, that can, perhaps, be utilized for rough construction should occasion demand.

Colorado.—This State contains a variety of sandstones, of good quality, but which owing to lack of transportation facilities and the thinly settled condition of a large portion of the country, are as yet in little demand.

According to Mr. George H. Eldridge the strata of the Lower Trias—the "Red Beds" of the West—yield at various points in Colorado building stones of great variety of shades, texture and strength. As a rule those east of the main range of the mountains occur within 500 feet of the top of the series: a zone generally of much finer material than is met with at points lower down in the formation. Within this distance three particularly distinguishable varieties of stone occur each well adapted to its own special use: the first a handsome light red, used frequently in superstructures; the second a hard, banded, rather thin bedded variety employed as flagging and in foundations on account of its great compressive strength; the third a white siliceous quartzite, the homologue of the creamy sandstones employed extensively west of the Mississippi for curbing, flagging and paving.

The first of the above varieties, known as Manitou stone from the locality from which the chief supply is derived, is of a warm, light red color and of a soft texture, but varying considerably in compressive strength from point to point along its outcrop. The latter rarely falls below the degree required for private residences, but in its selection for heavy business blocks a careful choice of the quarries furnishing it should be made.

The composition of this stone is chiefly an aggregate of fine, well rounded quartz grains, a little feldspar, and an occasional

grain of magnetite, the whole being impregnated with the sesquioxide of iron. The rock is heavily bedded, from 5 to 15
feet, the beds being sometimes separated by narrow seams of
clay or shaly sandstone. Weathering has extended usually
but a slight distance beneath the surface, the stripping being
consequently reduced to a minimum. At Manitou the beds
stand at an angle of 80° or 90° with the horizon, dipping
usually toward the east, the strike being toward the north.
The end joints are sufficiently far apart to permit the quarrying of blocks of any practical size.

At the quarries now in operation the natural rift of the
rock is not often utilized, the beds standing so nearly vertical,
and being frequently of so great thickness that channeling is
employed almost exclusively.

The Manitou stone works with great ease and is well adapted for a variety of architectural uses as displayed in numerous
private and public buildings in Denver. The geological position of the stone is about 400 feet below the top of the Lower
Trias.

The second variety of stone, that used for flagging and
foundations occurs at approximately the same horizon as the
Manitou stone and also from this up to the summit of the Red
Beds proper where it locally passes gradually into the third
variety, the Creamy sandstones, which are used for the same
purposes as the second and for paving purposes as well.

Quarries have been opened in the above described beds at
Bellevue, Stout, and Arkins in Larimer County, Lyons in
Boulder County, and at other points in the vicinity.

The first named are situated about 9 miles west of Fort
Collins. The stone is here heavy bedded, harder and with a
compressive strength considerably in excess of that of the
other strictly building stones east of the range. Blocks 5 or 6
feet in thickness and of any desired length are readily obtained.

The color is a deep and rather sombre red. The stone is regarded by Mr. Eldridge as admirably adapted for use in the lower courses of superstructures and in other portions of buildings requiring especial strength.

At the quarries the stone is of nearly uniform texture throughout, consisting mainly of fine quartz grains with an occasional accessory mineral, the whole colored by iron oxides. The beds lie at an angle of about 30° with the horizon, and the rocks form a bold outcrop 100 feet in height to the west, the quarry opening being on the backs of the strata, on the eastern side of the ridge.

But from 3 to 6 feet of stripping is necessary to reach stone of good quality.

The quarries at Stout and in its vicinity are limited to foundation and paving stones. The stone here is practically a quartzite, and it is stated has shown a crushing strength of 30,000 pounds per square inch. It is thin bedded and shows a well marked grain, whereby quarrying is rendered fairly easy, but the stone is too hard for general building. The prevailing color is white, though sometimes tinted a faint red or locally dotted with small spots of hydrated oxide of iron. The stone from both the Bellevue and Stout quarries has long been designated as Fort Collins stone owing to the fact that the town of this name is the leading one of the region.

The Arkins stone is stated to be similar to that of Stout. The Lyons quarries are located about the town of this name, which lies about 12 miles west of Longmont at the terminus of the Denver, Longmont and Lyons branch of the Burlington R. R. system. The product of these quarries closely resembles that of Bellevue and it is used exclusively for flagging, curbing, and sills. The stone is regarded as very durable.

Along the low bluffs of Cretaceous sandstone forming the

north bank of St. Vrains Creek, about 3 miles east of Longmont, Boulder County, have been opened numerous quarries
which furnish fine yellow and blue gray stone of good quality
for general building. The upper layers only are yellow, owing
to an increased amount of iron oxides. Both yellow and gray
varieties are stated by the authority quoted to be rather
porous, and their durability remains yet to be tested.

At Glencoe, above Golden, in Jefferson County, there occurs a deep salmon-red Triassic stone of a beautiful warm and
lively hue. It is said to work with considerable difficulty, but
is much sought on account of its color. Its principal market is
now Chicago, but it is a matter of regret that it cannot be introduced into our Eastern markets. Near Morrison, in the same
county, there occur extensive beds of red and nearly white
sandstone. The white is not considered desirable, but the red
is much sought for trimming purposes. It is stated to absorb
water readily, and hence to be peculiarly liable to damage from
frost.

At Coal Creek, in Fremont County, is a fine grayish or buff
stone of Laramie age, and which closely resembles the sub-
Carboniferous stone of Berea, Ohio. As seen by the writer in
the stone-yards of Denver, this is a most excellent material,
being free from flaws, of good color, and cutting to a sharp
edge. It is stated that it occurs in exhaustible quantities and
is obtainable in blocks of large size.

The light-colored stone used in the construction of the
court-house at Denver was obtained from these beds near
Canon City. Trinidad, Las Animas County, also furnishes a
good sandstone, which is used in Denver ; another important
stone of good quality is brought from Amargo, in Rio Arribo
County, across the line in New Mexico.

Connecticut.—As already noted (*ante*, p. 6) the first quarries of sandstone to be systematically worked in this country

were those located in the now well-known Triassic beds at Portland and Middletown, in this State. The area of the Triassic deposit in New England as given by Dana * extends from New Haven on Long Island Sound to northern Massachusetts, having a length of 110 miles and an average width of 20 miles. The stone is at present quarried at Portland, Middletown, and Middlesex County, East Haven, New Haven County, and Manchester, Hartford County; though small quarries have been worked from time to time to furnish stone for local consumption at East Windsor, Hayden's Station, Suffield, Newington, Farmington, and Forrestville in this same county. The Manchester stone is a beautiful fine-grained reddish variety, and that from East Haven is represented as excellent for rock-faced work. The Portland quarries are, however, by far the most important of any of these, and it is estimated that from their combined areas not less than 4,300,000 cubic feet of material have been taken.

As now worked at this place the quarries descend with nearly perpendicular walls on three sides for a depth in some cases of upwards of 150 feet, the fourth side being sloping to allow passage for teams or workmen. The stone is of medium fineness of texture, of a uniform reddish-brown color, and lies in nearly horizontal beds varying from a few inches to 20 feet in thickness. Natural blocks 100 by 50 by 20 feet occur, and hence blocks of any desired size can be obtained. In quarrying, channeling machines are used to some extent, though in

---

* Manual of Geology, p. 404. The entire area of the Triassic sandstones in the United States as given by this authority is divided into three parts : (1) the Connecticut area as given above ; (2) the Palisade area, commencing along the west side of the Hudson River in the south-east corner of New York, near Piermont, and stretching southwestward, through Pennsylvania, as far as Orange County, Virginia, about 350 miles long ; and [3] the North Carolina area, commencing near the Virginia line and extending through North Carolina over the Deep River region, 120 miles long.

PLATE VII.

To face page 258.

SANDSTONE QUARRY AT PORTLAND, CONNECTICUT.

many cases large blocks are first loosened by means of deep
drill holes and heavy charges of powder, and these then split
up by wedges. (See plate VII.) The blocks are roughly trimmed down with picks at the quarry and shipped thus to New
York and other large cities to be worked up as occasion
demands. Until lately but little of the material ˑhas been
dressed at the quarries. The stone has been used in all our
leading cities, particularly in New York, and has even been
shipped to San Francisco via Cape Horn. But little quarrying
is done in cold weather, as care must be taken against freezing
while the stone is full of quarry water, a temperature of 22° F.
being sufficient to freeze and burst fine blocks of freshly quarried material. About a week or ten days of good drying
weather is considered sufficient to so season a stone as to place
it beyond danger from frost.

Great outcry has from time to time been raised against the
Portland stone on account of its disposition to scale or flake off
when laid in exposed places. While it is undoubtedly true
that much of it is unfit for carved work in exposed situations,
still the author can but feel that the architect and builder are
largely responsible for the many ruined fronts caused by this
scaling, to be seen in New York and elsewhere. It is the
almost invariable custom in building to split the stone with the
grain into slabs but a few inches thick and to veneer the walls
of buildings with these slabs placed on edge. Let thicker
blocks be used and the stone laid on its bed, as nature laid it
down in the quarry, and this defect will prove less serious, if it
be not entirely remedied. But no stone that is capable of
absorbing so large a percentage of water, as is much of the
Connecticut and other of our Triassic stones, can be more than
very moderately durable in the very trying climate of our
Northern States.

There is, however, a vast difference in material from the

same quarry. I have seen tombstones perfectly sound and legible after an exposure of nearly two hundred years, while others begin to scale in less than ten. The remarks made in the chapter on selection of stone are especially applicable here.

Georgia.—No sandstones are at present quarried in this State, but it is stated that "the Chattooga Mountains contain a considerable variety and of various shades of color, among which are white, gray, buff, brown, and red. Some of these exist in massive compact beds, while others have a jointed structure that make them easily quarried. The thickness of the entire sandstone series is about 800 feet. Building stone of this character may be had also on Lookout and Sand Mountains, in the Cohutta range."* The writer has as yet seen none of the above.

Idaho.—The National collection contains samples of a rather coarse, very light-colored sandstone of fair quality from Boisé City, in this State, but the writer has no information regarding their availability or the extent of the deposits.

Illinois.—Carboniferous sandstones of light and dark-brown color and good quality are found near Carbondale, in this State. The stone is of medium texture, works readily, and closely resembles some of the Triassic brownstones of Connecticut. The beds are about 14 feet thick and are capable of furnishing blocks of large dimensions. A very fine grained light bluish-gray laminated stone is quarried in a small way near Xenia, and other sandstones of fair quality occur at Suka, Marion County, Chester, Randolph County, and various points in Perry and Greene Counties.

Indiana.—The better class of sandstones of Indiana are stated by Prof. Collett† to come from the conglomerate sand-

* Commonwealth of Georgia, p. 136.
† Twelfth Annual Report State Geologist, 1882, p. 20.

rock beds forming the base of the coal-measures, and occurring in a broad belt extending from the Illinois line, in Warren County, south and south-east through the counties of Fountain, Vermillion, Montgomery, Parke, Putnam, Clay, Owen, Green, Martin, Pike, Dubois, Orange, Perry, Crawford, and Harrison to the Ohio River. The beds in various parts of this area, though irregular in color and physical characteristics, present a very great quantity of excellent building material. In these beds in Warren, Orange, Lawrence, Crawford, and Harrison Counties are found also extensive beds of gritstone of great utility for grind and whetstones, including the well-known Hindostan stone, favorably known in our own and foreign markets. The sandstones of the Coal-measures proper, while not fully equal to the above, are yet used extensively for foundations, piers, and other purposes of rough construction.

Iowa.—This State produces but little of value as building material in the way of sandstones. Coarse, dark-brown stones of Carboniferous and Cretaceous ages occur in Muscatine and Cass Counties, and have been quarried to some extent, but their qualities are not such as to cause them to be used for other than rough work in the near vicinity.

Kansas.—Good sandstones are stated by Professor Broadhead to occur in several of the counties in the southwestern part of this State, though so far as we have observed, few if any of these are of such a quality as to acquire other than a local market. A fine, deep blue-gray, laminated stone is found at Parsons, and a brownish one at Oswego, in Labette County, also a brownstone at Pawnee, Crawford County, and others of various hues in Bourbon, Neosho, Montgomery, Wilson, Woodson, Greene, and Elk Counties.

Kentucky.—The sandstones of this State, so far as shown by the National collections, are all of a light color, fine-grained and rather soft. Light buff and pinkish colors are found in

Simpson, Grayson, Todd, Johnson, and Breckenridge Counties, some of which are of a beautiful mellow tint. Light gray stones of apparent good quality, and closely resembling the Berea of Ohio, occur at Blue Lick Mountain, Livingston, in Rockcastle County, and in Pineville, Bell County. The writer is unable to give further information regarding them.

Maine.—Maine is preëminently a granite State, producing little of more than local importance in the way of other building stones. No sandstone quarries are now worked within the State limits. Good freestone are said to exist among the beds of Devonian sandstone in Washington County, and quarries were at one time worked near Perry. The stone is said to have been of good quality, and to resemble the brownstone of Portland, Connecticut. The red sandstones near Machiasport are also regarded as promising.*

Maryland.—Sandstone of such a nature as to be in demand for other than local uses is quarried in but a single localty in this State. In Montgomery County, near the mouth of Seneca Creek, about 30 miles north-west from the city of Washington, there occurs a considerable bed of Triassic sandstone, which for many years has been quarried, more or less, to furnish material for the Washington market. The stone is as a rule light reddish-brown in color, of fine and even texture, and well adapted for all manner of building and ornamental work. The writer has examined this stone, both in the quarry and in various buildings, and does not hesitate to pronounce it one of the best of our Triassic stones. Clay holes abound in some portions of the rock, but can be avoided by careful selection. The stone is not at all shaly and shows little, if any, disposition to scale when exposed to the weather. The Smithsonian Institution building, erected in 1848-'54 from this stone, shows few defects

---

* Natural History and Geology of Maine, C. H. Hitchcock, 1861.

from weathering alone, and these only in those cases where they might have been avoided by judicious selection. On blocks of the stone in the aqueduct of the Chesapeake and Ohio Canal which have been constantly permeated by water every season for fifty years, the tool-marks are still fresh and no signs of scaling are visible other than are produced by too close contact at the joints.

Massachusetts.—The beds of Triassic sandstone, which furnish in Connecticut the well-known " Portland brownstone," are continued up the valley of the Connecticut River to the northern boundary of Massachusetts and furnish in several places valuable deposits of building material. At East Long Meadow, in Hampton County, quarries are worked in this formation which produce a rather finer-grained stone than that of Portland and of a bright brick-red color. Like all the Triassic stones it is soft and works readily, and on account of its warmth of color can be used with very pleasing effects in a variety of combinations.

The extensive formation of Primordial conglomerate in Dorchester, Roxbury, Brookline, and other towns south and west of Boston furnishes an inexhaustible supply of durable building material for rough work, but which, owing to its coarseness, is unsuited for ornamental work of any kind. The stone is quite variable in different localities, but may, as a whole, be said to consist of a greenish-gray groundmass or paste in which are embedded rounded pebbles of all sizes up to several inches in diameter of quartz, granite, melaphyre, felsite, and a variety of rock. This composition renders the smooth dressing of the stone a practical impossibility, and it is used only in the rough state, advantage being taken of the numerous joint faces, which in building are placed outward, thus forming a comparatively smooth wall. The stone thus forms a very durable building material, and has been used with good effect in several churches and other buildings in and around Boston.

Michigan.—According to Professor Conover * the beds of Potsdam sandstone occurring with frequent outcrops in the northern part of the Upper Peninsula in this State are likely to furnish the largest quantity and the best quality of building material found within the State limits. The stone quarried from this formation at Marquette is of medium fineness of texture, of a light brownish-red color, often curiously spotted or mottled with gray. These gray spots are generally rounded and vary in size, according to Mr. Batchen, from that of a pea to 12 or 18 inches in diameter. These blotched portions are usually rejected in building, although when used they give striking and not unpleasant effects. The spots are stated by the above-mentioned authority to be equally durable with the rest or colored portion. This stone is known locally as rain-drop stone, its mottled character giving it the appearance of having been spattered with rain-drops when in a condition to receive their impressions. Similar stone is quarried at L'Anse, in Baraga County. Their chief defects are flint pebbles, which fly out in process of dressing, and clay holes. Both defects can be avoided by proper selection of the stone. In color the Marquette and L'Anse stone are both richer than the Connecticut or New Jersey brownstones, and apparently would prove more durable, although as yet they have been too little used to establish this point to a certainty. Besides the localities mentioned, these stones occur at various places along the lake shore west of Keweenaw Point, and also near the eastern end of the coast of Lake Superior, along the valley of the Laughing Whitefish River and around it. At this latter locality the stone is very hard, compact, heavily bedded, split-

---

* Report Tenth Census, vol. x., 1880, p. 227.

ting readily into slabs of any required thickness, and is especially suited for heavy masonry.

At Portage entry at the end of the peninsula which separates Portage River and Keweenaw Bay, there is also quarried a red sandstone, uniform in color and of excellent texture. The rock is horizontally bedded and covered with 16 to 24 feet of soil and worthless rock. This stone has been used in the new Mining School building at Houghton, Michigan. An analysis of the stone is given in the tables, p. 420.

There are also deposits of sandstone in the Coal-measures of Southern Michigan which are of very fair quality for building purposes. The best quarries are in Jackson and in Eaton Counties, as in Parma and Ionia townships.*

Minnesota.—According to Professor Winchell† the red sandstones of Fond du Lac are the most valuable of their kind that the State possesses. They are of the same formation as the New Ulm quartzite described below, but were less hardened at the time of their upheaval. The stone is of medium texture and of a brown or reddish color, closely resembling the Connecticut brownstone, but much harder and firmer. A similar rock comes from Isle Royal and Sault Ste. Marie at the eastern end of Lake Superior. At this latter place it is often mottled with gray or greenish. The stone consists almost wholly of quartz cemented with silica and iron oxides. Its crushing strength is said to vary between 4,000 and 5,000 pounds per square inch.

At New Ulm and in other places in Cottonwood, Watonwan, Rock, and Pipestone Counties, there occurs a very hard, compact, red quartzite, which has been used to some extent for building purposes, though its intense hardness is a great

---

* Annual Report Commissioner of Mineral Statistics, 1888, p. 104.

† Geology of Minnesota, vol. 1.

drawback, but it is practically indestructible and hence valuable. In Pipestone County the rock occurs associated with the beautiful and interesting red pipestone or catlinite, famous on account of its being used by the Indians for pipes and ornaments. At this point the rock is jasper red in color and very hard, but is beginning to be used for ashler work, producing very striking effects. I am informed by the quarry owners that the entire bed at Pipestone is some 75 feet in thickness and the stone is quarried entirely by means of bars and wedges, no explosives being necessary. A polished slab of the stone of great beauty was exhibited at the Chicago Exposition in 1886.

In Courtland Township, Nicollett County, the same quartzite occurs of a beautiful deep red, almost purple, color. Samples cut at the National Museum were found to work with great difficulty, but were very beautiful. The same stone, but of lighter color, occurs at Sioux Falls, South Dakota. At Dresbach, in Winona County, there occurs a fine-grained, rather soft, light gray stone which bears a close resemblance to the Berea stone of Ohio. It is quarried to some extent and is regarded by Professor Winchell as promising of future usefulness. A fine light-pink sandstone occurs in Pine County, where it is stated to occur in heavy beds and to be easy to quarry. It is regarded by Professor Winchell as fully equal to the Cleveland, Ohio, freestone. The sandstone occurring at Jordan, Scott County, is of a light color, and while suitable for general building purposes is not regarded as fitted for first-class structures.

Mississippi.—Sandstones of gray and light buff color occur in Jefferson, Rankin, and Tishomingo Counties, in this State. Samples of these were on exhibition at the exposition at New Orleans in the winter of 1884–'85, and from thence were transferred to the National collection at Washington. As shown by these specimens the stones are fine-grained, but rather soft and friable, and in no way remarkable for their beauty. Their durability would depend apparently altogether on climatic influences. The writer has no information regarding the uses to which the stones have been put, if, indeed, they have as yet been used at all.

Missouri.—The best available sandstones of this State belong according to Prof. Broadhead* to the Potsdam formations in Madison, Saint François, and Iron Counties in the southeastern part of the State ; to the sub-Carboniferous of Saint Genevieve, Newton, Cedar, Pettis, Howard and Cooper Counties, and to the Carboniferous of the south-west, chiefly in Barton, Vernon, Cedar, Saint Clair, Henry, Johnson and Carroll Counties. The so-called Second sandstone (Lower Silurian) occurring along the Osage River and on the hills of the southwestern part of the State is also stated to furnish a good building stone.

One of the best of the above is the fine light-buff or yellowish sub-Carboniferous stone occurring about four miles from the town of Saint Genevieve. Some twenty-five feet of good quality of rock in beds of from eighteen inches to five feet in thickness is here exposed, and which will afford blocks of any desired size and shape within these limits. The stone has shown good weathering qualities in the climate of St. Louis, but is stated to be discolored badly by smoke. Near Miami Station, in Carroll County, and Warrensburgh in Johnson County, the Carboniferous beds furnish fine gray sandstone which when well selected, is said to be good and durable. That at Miami frequently carries concretionary masses which weather out on exposure.

The Johnson County sandstone is stated to be of good

---

* Report Tenth Census vol. x. p. 270 : also Building Trades Journal, Aug. 1888.

quality in certain situations. It has been used in several important structures in the State, and stands the test of time
without scaling, only becoming stained and darkened with age.
It is quite light, weighing only 140 pounds per cubic foot when
seasoned, or 145 to 150 pounds when freshly quarried.

Montana.—A fine light-gray Cretaceous sandstone somewhat resembling the well-known stone of Berea, Ohio, occurs
in considerable abundance in Rocky Cañon, Gallatin County,
and is coming into general use in Boseman. The writer is informed* that it can be obtained in blocks of large dimensions,
and that it works readily when first quarried, but hardens on
exposure, though, like the Ohio stone, it stains with reddish
streaks from oxidation of pyrite. A compact red quartzite
from near Salesville, west of the west Gallatin, is also coming
into use to some extent. A fine, very light stone of uncertain
age is also quarried near Dillon for use in Butte, Deer Lodge
County. So recently has the State become settled that there
has as yet arisen but little demand for other materials than
wood for building. The great scarcity of this article in the
most thickly settled portions of the State, together with the
abundance of easy-working, but in so dry a climate, durable
sandstone, will doubtless bring about a radical change within
a very few years.

Nebraska.—An intensely hard Cretaceous quartzite furnishing stone for heavy foundations and general building, is stated
by Aughey† to occur in Dakota County, this State. Fine
grained micaceous sandstone suitable for both flagging and
building is also found in Nemaha County.

Nevada.—A coarse, gray, friable stone is quarried at Carson,
in this State, but it is unfit for any sort of fine work or foundation, owing to its softness and porosity.

---

* By Dr. A. C. Peale, United States Geological Survey.
† Physical Geography and Geology of Nebraska.

New Jersey.—The largest and most extensively worked quarries of stone of any kind in this State are in the Triassic belt of red or brown sandstone which extends from the New York line in a general southwesterly direction across the State to the Delaware River. The principal quarries are in various towns in Passaic, Essex, Hunterdon, and Mercer Counties. The stone, like that of Connecticut and other Triassic areas described, is a granitic sandstone, cemented by iron oxides, silica, and carbonate of lime ; the colors varying from light brownish-gray to reddish-brown. As shown in the National collections, the stone is as a rule of finer texture than that of Connecticut, and less distinctly laminated, consequently scaling less readily when exposed to atmospheric agencies. According to Professor Cook,* this stone has been used from an early date in Bergen, Passaic, and Essex Counties for building purposes and for monuments and gravestones, where it has shown good proof of its durability. It has also been very extensively used in New York and neighboring cities. At the quarries, as is usually the case, the surface stone is found more or less broken up and blocks of small size only can be obtained, but the beds become more solid as they are followed downward. At some of the Belleville quarries blocks containing 1,000 cubic feet have been broken out. In one of these quarries over 2 acres have been excavated to an average depth of 60 feet. Some of the quarries, as at Passaic, produce stone of several varieties of color, as light brown, dark brown, and light gray ; the fine-grained dark brown is usually considered the best and is the most sought. In several of the quarries trap rock (diabase) also occurs.

New Mexico.—In the vicinity of Las Vegas Hot Springs and Albuquerque occur beds of light gray, brown, and pink

---

* Annual Report State Geologists, 1881, p. 43.

sandstone, of fine texture and apparently excellent quality. They are not as yet much used, owing simply to lack of demand for stone of any kind. A soft, very light gray volcanic tuff occurs at Santa Fé, which may prove of value for building purposes in a dry climate, or one where the temperature does not often fall below the freezing point.

New York.—The principal sandstones now quarried in this State may be divided into three groups, belonging to three distinct geological horizons, each group possessing characteristics peculiar to itself and so pronounced as to be readily recognized thereby.

The first of these belong to the Hamilton period of the Devonian formations, and are fine-grained, compact, dark bluegray stones, very strong and durable.* They give a pronounced clayey odor when breathed upon, and have been designated *greywackes* by Professor Julien, though popularly known as " bluestones " on account of their color. The second group belongs to the Medina period of the Upper Silurian formations. These stones are largely siliceous, of coarser, more distinctly granular texture than the last, and are of a gray or red color. The third and last group belongs to the Potsdam period of the Cambrian formations. Like the Medina stone, they are largely siliceous, and contain a much larger proportion of siliceous cementing material. These are usually light red or nearly white, and intensely hard and refractory.

---

* Microscopic examination has shown the Devonian sandstones of New York to consist chiefly of " angular to subangular grains of quartz and feldspar, with their interstices occupied by smaller grains of magnetite, scales of chlorite, and particularly short fibres of hornblende interlacing the grains of the other constituents. The result is an 'argillaceous sandstone,' flagstone, or greywacke, peculiarly compact and impermeable, which has retained its fresh condition to an extent which could not otherwise have been expected from an aggregate so liable to ready decomposition." A. A. Julien in Proc. A. A. A. S., vol. XXVIII, 1879, p. 372.

Discussing each group more in detail, it may be said that the " bluestone " district is confined to comparatively narrow limits west of the Hudson River, and mainly to Albany, Green, and Ulster Counties. It begins in Schoharie County, passes to the south-east and enters Albany County near Berne, and from there passes around to the south and south-west across Green, Ulster, and Sullivan Counties, and across the west end of Orange County to the Delaware River and into Pike County, Pennsylvania.*

The typical bluestone belongs to the Hamilton period, and is a fine-grained, compact, tough, and eminently durable rock of a deep, dark blue-gray color. Owing to the fact that it occurs usually in thin beds and splits out readily in slabs but a few inches thick, it has been used very extensively for flagging, curbs, sills, caps, steps, etc. Its sombre color is something of a drawback to its use for general building purposes. As a rule the quarries are shallow affairs, and the work carried on by the crudest possible methods. At Quarryville, Ulster County, the quarries have been worked for upwards of forty years, and vast quantities of the material removed. The quarries lie in lines along three parallel ledges, which have a general north-east and south-west direction, the beds of sandstone overlying each other from west to east, with strata of slate and hard sandstone between them. The quarries in the easternmost ledge extend about a mile in length, 175 feet in width, and have been worked to an average depth of about 12 feet. In the middle ledge the line of quarries extends over an area about 1½ miles in length, 150 to 500 feet in width, and have been quarried to a depth of from 12 to 20 feet. Quite heavy beds occur in some of the quarries, and the joints allow blocks of very large size to be obtained. In the western ledge the quarries are in a line some

---

* Report of the Tenth Census, vol. x, 1880, p. 130.

1,000 feet long by 150 wide, and are worked to an average depth of about 12 feet. The total thickness of the layers in this region is from 4 to 20 feet, and the stripping from 6 to 17 feet in depth. In working the quarries but little capital is required beyond the value of the necessary tools, they being commonly leased and royalty paid at the rate of one-half cent per square foot of stone quarried. The larger size of blocks have dimensions of about 15 by 8 feet, though some 20 by 15 feet have been taken out. At the time of taking the census in 1880 there were upwards of one hundred and fifty quarries within the bluestone district as given above. All, however, agree so closely with those of Quarryville, that further description seems unnecessary.

The quarry district in the Medina sandstone extends from Brockport, Monroe County, to Lockport, Niagara County. The stone is, as a rule, moderately fine-grained in texture, hard, and of a gray or red color, the red variety being most used for building purposes, while the gray is used in street paving. The red variety has a bright and pleasing appearance; both red and gray are sometimes used together, with good effect. Most of the stone buildings in Lockport and Buffalo are of the Medina stone. The most important feature of the stone is, however, its adaptability for street-paving, in place of the usual granite or trap blocks. It is said that the sandstone blocks have the advantage of not wearing smooth, as do the granites and traps, while at the same time they are nearly if not quite as durable.

The stratum of quarry rock is put at about 30 feet in thickness, the different layers of which vary in thickness from 18 to 30 inches.

Three miles south of the town of Potsdam, in Saint Lawrence County, the Raquette River cuts across the Potsdam formation, and quarries are worked along the banks of the stream. The outcrops at this point are some 2 miles in width from north to south. In the quarry the strata dip to the south at an angle of about 45°, the beds increasing in thickness somewhat from the top downward, until at a depth of 40 feet they are some 2 or 3 feet in thickness. In color the stone is light reddish or reddish-brown, and though, when first quarried, soft enough to work economically, becomes most intensely hard on seasoning.

I consider this, from the standpoint of durability, almost an ideal stone. Composed wholly of quartz grains, it has, by deposition of interstitial silica, become converted into a compact quartzite, impregnated with just enough iron oxide to give it a reddish or brownish-red color. (See Fig. 5, Plate II.) It is therefore practically non-absorptive, and its surface affords no foothold for growing organism. Strong as the strongest granite and not liable to chemical disintegration from atmospheric agencies, the stone deserves even a wider recognition than it has yet received. Stone from these quarries has been used in many churches and private residences in Potsdam, in the buildings of Columbia College in New York City, All Saints Cathedral in Albany, and in the Dominion Houses of Parliament in Ottawa, Canada.

At Fort Ann, in the same county, the quartzite is much lighter in color and composed of almost pure silica, there being an almost entire absence of iron oxides in the cementing material. The stone is, as a consequence, extremely hard, but equally tough and durable with that above described.

At Port Henry, in Essex County, the Potsdam quartzite crops out at the side of the railroad and in the hillsides west of the town. The rock is here light gray in color and rather brittle. In the quarry bed the rock is divided by irregular vertical joints with smooth surfaces, so that quarrying can be carried on wholly by wedging and without the use of powder.

The stone is used mainly in the immediate vicinity. A similar stone occurs at Keeseville and at Ausable Chasm. It is thin bedded and can be quarried to supply the local demand merely by the use of bars. It is used largely for flagging, and shows frequently very perfect ripple-marking and cross-bedding.

North Carolina.—The narrow belt of Triassic sandstone already mentioned as passing through this State furnishes fine, compact, light and dark reddish-brown stone of a quality not at all inferior to any of that in the more northern and eastern States.

At Wadesborough, in Anson County, the stone lies in beds from 2 to 10 feet in thickness, which are inclined at an angle of about 25° from the horizontal. It is of fine, even grain, quite massive, and of dark brown and reddish colors. Heretofore it has been used chiefly for railroad work and for steps and general trimming purposes in Charlotte and Wilmington, but is worthy of a wider application. Within the past four years steps have been taken to introduce it into the markets of Washington and other of our eastern cities. The chemical composition and crushing strength are given in the tables.

At Sanford the stone is of a brown color and is said to lie in the quarries in nearly horizontal strata from 1 to 5 feet in thickness. The stone from near Egypt is quite similar in appearance. Near Durham it becomes in part of a gray color, but otherwise is little different. This stone has been used in Raleigh for upwards of thirty years, and shows itself to be strong and durable.

Ohio.—According to Professor Orton, * those rocks of the sub-Carboniferous period, called by the Ohio Geological Survey the Waverly group, are the most important as to production of building stone in the geological scale of this State.

* Report of the Geological Survey of Ohio, vol. v, p. 578.

The following section shows the arrangement of this formation :

1.	Maxville limestones, in patches.	4.	Berea shale.
2.	Logan group.	5.	Berea grit.
3.	Cuyahoga shale.	6.	Bedford shale.

Of these, number 1 occurs but seldom. Number 2 consists of fine-grained sandstones overlying and alternating with massive conglomerate in the central and southern part of the State. In thickness about 100 feet. The Waverly conglomerate is a member of this group. Number 3, about 300 feet in thickness, is a blue argillaceous shale in many parts of the State, but in many places contains scattered courses of sandstone of great value. Number 4 is from 10 to 30 feet thick, and number 5 is the Berea grit, the great quarry rock of northern Ohio. This formation is from 10 to 75 feet in thickness, and extends in a belt from Williamsfield, in the southeastern corner of Ashtabula County, westward into Erie County, and thence nearly directly southward in Adams County to the Ohio River. The stratum of sandstone where it is best developed consists of heavy sheets, with often a course at the top of thin, broken layers, called *shell rock*, and of no value for building stone. Number 6 is from 10 to 100 feet in thickness, and furnishes no building stone, excepting in Cuyahoga County, where it yields the well-known " Euclid bluestone."

The Berea grit, as quarried for building purposes, may be described as a fine-grained homogeneous sandstone, of a very light buff, gray or blue-gray color, and very evenly bedded, the individual sheets varying from a few inches to 10 or more feet in thickness. In many places this evenness of bedding is especially remarkable, as in some of the quarries of Trumbull County, where blocks of stone 10 feet square and only 1½ inches thick have been extracted, and with surfaces so smooth

and straight that a straight-edge laid upon them would touch
at every point. Slabs but 1 or 2 inches in thickness are said
to have such strength that they go into general use without
question. In one case a strip 150 feet long, 5 feet wide, and
but 3 inches thick was reported as raised intact from the
quarry bed. The various layers, although closely compacted,
are, however, perfectly distinct, adhering to one another
" scarcely more than sawn planks in a pile."

Like many of the sandstones of this horizon, the Berea grits
contain but little cementing material, the various particles
being held together mainly by cohesion induced by the pressure to which they were subjected at the time of their consolidation. They are, therefore, soft, working readily in any direction, and are particularly sought for carving.

This property also renders the stone of especial value for
the manufacture of grindstones, since the presence of a cement
will nearly always cause a stone to glaze and its cutting power
be thereby nearly if not quite destroyed. Unfortunately the
Berea stone nearly always contains more or less sulphide of
iron (pyrite) and needs to be selected with care. The best
varieties will usually become yellowish on long exposure, but
this is not in all cases injurious. Indeed, this property of
" mellowing with age " is now claimed as one of the good qualities of the stone. When, however, the pyrite occurs in such
quantities as to produce by its oxidation unsightly blotches its
presence is, of course, objectionable.

The principal quarries of the stone at present writing are
situated in the towns of Amherst, Berea, East Cleveland, Ilyria,
and Independence in Lorain and Cuyahoga Counties.

At Amherst the quarries are located in a series of ledges
which were once the shore cliffs of Lake Erie. The elevated
position of the stones is a great advantage, since the light and
uniform color seems due to the fact that this elevation pro-

duces a free drainage, and the stones have been traversed by atmospheric waters to such a degree that all processes of oxidation which are possible have been very nearly completed. The stone here as elsewhere varies considerably in character and solidity within limited distances. The following section of one of the Amherst quarries is given by Professor Orton :

	Feet.		Feet.
Drift material	1 to 3	Grindstone	2
Worthless shell-rock	6 to 10	Building and grindstone	10
Soft rock for grindstones only.	12	Building stone	4 to 7
Building stone	3	Building stone or grindstone.	12
Bridge stone	2		

Nearly all of the quarries exhibit this diversity of material, although the order of arrangement is not always the same. The colors are light buff and bluish gray, the buff stone occurring above the line of perfect drainage and extending down as far as the 2 feet of bridge stone, forming a total thickness of 27 feet. In most of the Amherst quarries the relative amount of buff stone is greater. Difference in color and texture has given rise to various local names which may be mentioned here. The colors are denominated simply by " blue " and " buff." The regularly and evenly stratified stone is called " Split rock ;" that in which the stratification is irregular and marked by fine transverse and wavy lines is called " Spider web," and the homogeneous stone showing little or no stratification is called " Liver rock."

As regards composition the stone contains usually about 95 per cent of silica with small amounts of lime, magnesia, iron oxides, alumina, and alkalies. Analysis has shown them to contain from 5.83 to 7.75 per cent of water when first taken from the quarry, and from 3.39 to 4.28 per cent when dry. The quarries can be operated only about eight months of the year owing to the injury caused by freezing when the stone is full of its quarry water.

In the town of Berea nearly 40 acres of territory have been quarried over to an average depth of 40 feet. The stratum is 65 to 75 feet in thickness, the individual sheets varying from 2 inches to 10 feet. The stone is as a rule a little darker than the Amherst bluestone. It is used mostly for building purposes, though grindstones and whetstones are also manufactured quite extensively.

The well known " Euclid bluestone " is obtained from the Bedford shale formation in Newburgh and Euclid, Cuyahoga County. The stone differs from the Berea in being of finer and more compact texture, and of a deep blue-gray color. Like the Berea stone, however, it unfortunately contains considerable quantities of pyrite, and, as a general thing, is not a safe stone for other than bridge-work and foundations or flagging, for which last purpose it is eminently suited. Even when free from pyrite it does not weather in uniform colors, and needs always to be selected with great caution.

In the vicinity of Marietta and Constitution, in Washington County, a fine-grained buff and blue-gray sandstone, belonging to the Upper Coal-measures series, is quite extensively quarried for grindstones and building purposes. Different portions of the stratum furnish stone of all varieties of texture for wet grinding, and the grind stones are shipped to all manufacturing points in the United States. The principal market for the building-stone is in Marietta and various towns along the Ohio River.

At Piketown there is quarried a very pretty, fine-grained brown-stone, soft and easy to work, and apparently fairly durable. It has been used in some of the finest stone fronts in Columbus, in this State.

According to Professor Orton, however, this stone is brown only on the outcrop, and a few feet from the surface it assumes a dark blue-gray color, and loses its value as an ornamental stone, since it contains a large amount of soluble iron protoxide, which produces bad discoloration on exposure. An analysis of this stone is given in the tables.

Oregon.—Two miles south of Oakland, Douglas County, in this State, there occurs an extensive deposit of a fine, dark blue-gray sandstone, which changes to a drab color on exposure. It occurs in layers of 17 to 36 inches in thickness, parted by shaly seams, and is readily quarried by means of wedges. Quarries were opened in 1879, but have not been extensively worked as yet. A fine-grained sandstone, said to be suitable for either building or ornamental work, also occurs about 14 miles from Portland, in Clackamas County. It has been quarried since 1866, and used in some prominent structures in Portland.

Pennsylvania.—The belt of Triassic sandstones passing through southeastern Pennsylvania is described as beginning at the west bank of the Hudson River and extending in a broad belt from the Bay of New York to the base of the first ledges of the Highlands, being bounded on the north-west by this chain and its continuation. To the southwestward it traverses New Jersey, Pennsylvania, Maryland, and, in a somewhat interrupted manner, Virginia and part of North Carolina, its total length being not less than 500 miles, and of a width varying from 10 to 50 miles. The principal quarry in this formation in Pennsylvania is situated on the south side of a hill in Hummelstown, Dauphin County, the stone dipping to the north at an angle of about 40° and the ledge being about 85 feet in thickness. The rock is evenly bedded, the courses varying from 3 to 10 feet in thickness, the joints regular and from 4 to 40 feet apart, so that blocks of any practicable size can, it is said, be obtained. The texture is about medium fineness, and the color a deep bluish brown, slightly purple. The topmost layers are, however, of a reddish brown color, closely resembling the Portland stone. The stone compares very favorably with any of the Triassic stones, its chief defect, so far as the author has observed, being occasional clay holes, which sometimes have an unpleasant way of making their presence known in unexpected and undesirable places. The Hummelstown stone is now in very general use in all our principal eastern cities.

According to D'Invilliers,* the main bulk of good stone from this formation in the Lebanon Valley seems to be confined to that portion of the territory lying south of Hummelstown and Swatara, though there is little doubt but a larger field could be secured on more active search. At any one place, however, the good stone seems to be fairly limited, not so much on the line of dip as along the strike, and it is presumably not possible to locate an indefinite number of quarries on any one bed. It is, moreover, pretty well assured that beds of good stone are to be found in different parts of the formation, the two large quarries immediately south of Hummelstown being certainly worked on beds separated by several hundred feet of measure and both dipping conformably northward toward the valley. At the Hummelstown brownstone quarry the following section is given by the above-named authority:

(1) Shale and thin sandstone; stripping ....
(2) Sandstone..20 feet.
(3) Shale and slate..1 foot.
(4) Sandstone..15 feet.
(5) Shale...10 feet to 1 to 6.
(6) Sandstone..22 feet.
(7) Shale and slate...............................0 to 6 feet.
(8) Sandstone, red and massive.........................15 feet.

Such a section will not, however, hold good over any extent of territory, and even in any one quarry there is likely to

---

* Annual Report Pennsylvania Geological Survey, 1886, part IV.

be considerable variation. At the quarries of Francis Painter & Co. the following section is given :

(1) Loose soil and sandstone in blocks............. 6 feet.
(2) Red shale, poor and worthless................. 8 "
(3) Thin bedded sandstone and shale............... 12 "
(4) Massive sandstone, top layer................... 4 "
(5) Red slate seam, thin.......................... 1 "
(6) Sandstone, bottom layer...................... 3 "
(7) Slate .... 0 " 6 in.
(8) Massive sandstone bed; best stone.............. 15 "
(9) Sandstone, lower bed, good................... 4 " 6 in.

Stone from the same formation as the above and differing, if at all, only in slight color and textural peculiarities is quarried more or less in other towns along the belt, particularly Goldsborough, Reading, Bridgeport, and several towns in Bucks County.

The Carboniferous sandstones of Pennsylvania are little quarried excepting for local use, although occasionally of good quality. Near Pittsburgh and Allegheny, and other towns in Allegheny County, there are many quarries which produce gray stone of medium texture and of apparently good quality. They are said, however, to weather unevenly, owing to the presence of calcareous matter, and to be very sensitive to frost when first quarried. In several places in Westmoreland County the stones of this age are of a gray, reddish, or brownish color, fine grained and of good quality. They are used to some extent for building and also for flagging and paving.

The sub-Carboniferous formations, so valuable in Ohio for the building stone they supply, are in this State of little value, or at least up to date have been but little quarried for purposes of construction. At Venango, in Franklin County, a fine-grained, evenly-bedded buff stone, somewhat resembling the buff varieties of the Berea grit, is quarried for sidewalks and buildings in the near vicinity. Other quarries are located at Titusville, and also at Uniontown, Altoona, and Scranton.

Aside from the Triassic stones, the most important sandstones at present quarried in the State are from the Devonian formations. In several towns in Pike, Carbon, Luzerne, Wyoming, Susquehanna, and other counties, stones belonging to this formation, of a fine, compact texture and dark blue-gray color, are quite extensively quarried. So far as can be judged from the material examined, this is one of the most valuable stones in the State for building as well as for flagging purposes. The Wyoming County stone is known to the trade as " Wyoming Valley stone," and is in considerable demand. It agrees very closely in general appearance with much of the New York bluestone already described.

South Dakota.—The pink and red quartzite from Sioux Falls in this State is one of the most promising stones of the West. Chemically the stone is almost pure silica, with only enough iron oxide to impart color to it. It is so close grained as to be practically impervious to moisture, so strong as to endure a pressure of 25,000 pounds to the square inch, and will take a polish almost like glass, with which it may favorably compare in durability. In color the stone varies from light pink to jasper red, and it is one of the few stones at present quarried in the United States which is equally well adapted for rough building and for ornamental work, both interior and exterior. Professor Winchell, in reporting upon this stone, states that it bears a heat up to that of redness without cracking or scaling. The stone has been introduced into the Eastern markets for tiling, decorative work, and general building purposes. Its chief drawback, as may readily be imagined, is its great hardness, which is fully equal to that of pure quartz, or 7 of the scale as given on page 20. It however possesses a remarkably perfect rift and grain, and by especially designed apparatus the company expect to be able to put it upon the market at such prices as shall insure its adoption, and at the same time return a fair profit.

The stone has been used in the construction of the Queen Bee flouring mill at Sioux Falls, a structure 100 feet long, 80 feet wide, and 106 feet high, the walls being 5 feet thick at the base and averaging 2 feet 9 inches throughout. It has also been used in the construction'of several private residences, and the Dakota penitentiary in this same city, and in the buildings of the deaf mute school at Keokuk, and those of the Grinnell College at Grinnell, Iowa. It has also been used in polished columns and pilasters in the German-American Bank and Union Depot Buildings at Saint Paul, Minnesota.

Tennessee.—Fine grained light pink and coarse buff sandstones occur at Sewanee, in this State, and coarse gray at Parksville. The writer is in possession of no information regarding the extent to which these are used or their weathering properties.

Texas.—So far as is yet known this State produces but little of value in the way of sandstones. In Burnet County there are coarse dark-brown and red Lower Silurian (?) sandstones that may do for purposes of rough construction in the near vicinity. A fine, light buff Carboniferous stone, closely resembling the light-colored Ohio sandstone, occurs also at Mormon Mills, on Hamilton Creek, in this same county. A very light gray distinctly laminated stone occurs at Riverside, in Walker County, but to judge from the sample in the Museum collection it is of very poor quality. A fine-grained light buff stone, studded with fine black points, is found at Ranger, in Eastland County, and several varieties of apparent good quality, ranging in color from light buff to deep ferruginous red, in Parker County. So far as the writer can learn none of these are quarried to any great extent.

Carboniferous sandstones of a gray color and good quality are represented as occurring on the line of the Texas and Pacific Railroad near the Brazos River. Material from these beds has been used in the construction of the United States court-house at Dallas and in several private buildings both in Dallas and Fort Worth.*

Utah.—No sandstones of any kind are now regularly quarried in this Territory, though there is no lack of material. At Red Butte, near Salt Lake City, there occur inexhaustible supplies of Triassic sandstone of various shades of red or pink color. These have been used to some extent in Salt Lake City.

Virginia.—The belt of Triassic sandstone upon which the quarries of Seneca Creek, in Maryland, are situated extends across the Potomac River in a southwesterly direction as far as the Rapidan River, in Virginia. So far as the writer is aware, but few attempts have been made to quarry this material. On the line of the Manassas and Virginia Midland Railroad, at a point not far from Manassas, quarries were opened about 1868, and up to the time of the taking of the tenth census some 400,000 cubic feet of material had been moved. As represented in the National collections the stone is fine-grained, light reddish brown in color, closely resembling the lighter varieties from Seneca Creek, from which, however, it differs in being softer and a trifle more absorbent. The quarries are represented as being situated near the top of a low eminence, the strata being nearly horizontal, with but a slight dip toward the south. The surface only of the ledge has been quarried, and this to a depth of about 20 feet. The beds vary from 1 to 6 feet in thickness and are separated by a greenish shale.

---

* First Report Geological and Mineralogical Survey of Texas, 1888, p. 50.

No other sandstones of any importance are at present quarried within the State limits, although formerly the beds of light gray or buff Juro-Cretaceous stone in the vicinity of Aquia Creek were worked to a considerable extent to furnish material for the public buildings in Washington City. It required but a few years, however, to demonstrate the entire unfitness of this material for any sort of exposed work, and the quarrying has therefore been discontinued.

Washington.—On Chuckanut Bay, adjoining Bellingham Bay, in this State, is a very large deposit of a blue-gray Carboniferous sandstone that has been quarried to furnish material for the United States custom-house at Portland, Oregon, and for use in other towns on Puget Sound. The quarry is situated on a bluff which is represented as from 50 to 150 feet in height and about a mile in length. The supply of workable material is inexhaustible and it is said blocks 30 feet in length can be obtained without a flaw. The quarries are so situated that vessels of large size can be brought directly to the pier for loading.

West Virginia.—According to Professor Orton this State abounds in building stone, of which, however, but a small percentage is strictly first-class material. With the exception of one or two points on the Baltimore and Ohio Railroad, none is quarried for the general market. Near Rowlesburgh, on the banks of the Cheat River, there occurs a deposit of fine deep blue-gray Devonian sandstone that has been quarried to the depth of 40 feet, over an area of perhaps one-fourth of an acre. The quarry lies at the very foot of the mountains, and the amount of stripping is accordingly very great and continually increasing. The stone resembles very closely the Devonian bluestone of New York, especially that quarried in Chenango County and the lighter varieties of Ulster County. It is said to be highly esteemed and very durable.

According to the same authority the Kanawha River and its tributaries throughout the whole region about Charleston are walled with rock, and quarries are possible everywhere, but not all of the stone is equally good. The engineers employed in the erection of the Government building at Charleston, after thoroughly testing all the prevailing varieties, finally decided upon that from a comparatively thin bed, 6 to 10 feet in thickness, that forms the cap to the Mahoning sandstone formation near Charleston. This rock is light gray, siliceous, somewhat conglomeritic, but strong and eminently durable. Frost seemed to have no effect upon it, and no efflorescence is perceptible upon exposed blocks. Continual vigilance must, however, be exercised in selecting stone, as much of it contains shaly pockets and pyritiferous seams. The bluestone from this same region, which has been largely used in the Government works of improving the Kanawha River, is a strong stone, experiments having shown it to have a crushing strength of about 14,000 pounds per square inch of surface, but much of it is pyritiferous, and great care must be used in selection. This stone has been used in one or two important buildings, and with very bad results, it beginning to discolor and exfoliate within two or three years.

At Grafton, in Taylor County, a light gray sandstone belonging to this same formation (Carboniferous) has been extensively quarried for railroad work. The quality of the stone is said to be good, and it is strong enough for the heaviest work. The thickness of the stratum here is from 150 to 200 feet, and the amount of stone available is beyond computation, there being literally mountains of it. There are several other localities in this region where sandstone is quarried for local purposes, but which can not be noticed here.

Wisconsin.—The sandstones of this State, so far as the writer has had opportunity of observing, are mostly of a very

light color and uninteresting appearance, such as are not likely
to ever be in demand for other than local uses. Near Darlington, La Fayette County, there is stated by Professor Conover
to occur a large outcrop of Silurian sandstone, of a brown and
brick-red color passing into grayish-pink. This is regarded by
the above-named authority as the best-appearing stone in that
part of the State, though little quarried, owing to the large
amount of worthless stone associated with it and the cost of
transportation. The Potsdam formations in the region of Lake
Superior are regarded as capable of furnishing desirable sandstones, yellowish to deep brown in color. The chief defect in
these is the presence of numerous and large clay holes, necessitating great care in selecting the material. Many exposures,
as at Douglas and Bayfield Counties and on the Apostle Island,
are so situated that the quarried material could be shipped
directly upon vessels, with but little carting.

(*d*) FOREIGN SANDSTONES.

(1) *British Provinces of North America.*

Ontario.—On Vert Island, Nipigon Bay, in the northern
part of Lake Superior, there occurs an extensive deposit of
sandstone of Potsdam age, in which quarries have been opened
within a few years, and the product of which has already found
its way into the principal markets of Canada and the Lake
cities of the United States. The stone is of fine and even
grain, not distinctly laminated, hard, and of a bright reddish-
brown color. It is said to occur in inexhaustible quantities,
and that blocks as large as can be handled can be readily
obtained.

An 18-inch cube from this locality in the collections of the
National Museum shows it to be one of the most attractive
appearing of our red sandstones. It cuts to a sharp and firm

edge, and every appearance would indicate it to be very durable, though possibly liable to fade slightly on exposure. I am informed that its hardness is such that it can not be sawn with sand in the usual manner, but must be cut either with diamond-toothed circular saws or by means of chilled iron globules.

A thin section of the stone submitted to microscopic examination shows it to consist of closely compacted grains of quartz and feldspar, and an occasional shred of mica interspersed with iron oxides, which serve as a cement and give color to the stone. The feldspars are often kaolinized, and there is an occasional grain of calcite.

Quebec.—The greenish-gray sandstones of the Sillery (Lower Silurian) formation, both above Quebec and at Point Lévis, produce a very durable stone which has been used at the points mentioned.*

New Brunswick and Nova Scotia.—Sandstones, varying in color from red to yellow and light gray with an olive-green tint, are very abundant among the Lower Carboniferous rocks of Albert and Westmoreland Counties in the province of New Brunswick. They are, as a rule, soft enough to be readily cut when first quarried, but harden on exposure.† So far as the author is aware the only one of these varieties extensively used in the United States is the olive-green from Dorchester, Hopewell, and neighboring localities near Shepody Bay, at the head of the Bay of Fundy. The stone is of fine and even grain, works readily, and has been used both in carved and plain work with excellent effect in New York and neighboring cities. The author has had no opportunity of investigating personally the weathering properties of the stone. By some it is claimed as very durable, while by others it is regarded as unfit for

---

* Annual Report Geological Survey of Canada, 1887–88, vol. III. part II. p. 114 k.

† Dawson, Acadian Geology, p. 248.

finely-carved work exposed to the atmosphere. It is probable that sufficient time has not elapsed since its introduction to fully show its qualities, either good or bad. Sandstones of quite similar appearance and of the same geological age are quarried in various parts of Nova Scotia, particularly at Saw Mill Brook, near the head of Pictou Harbor. These are exported to some extent to this country.

Owing to the fact that the Nova Scotia stone was the earliest introduced into our market, it has become confounded with that of New Brunswick, which it closely resembles, and it is customary to speak of all stone from this region as Nova Scotia stone. It is stated, however, that fully 95 per cent of the imported material is, in reality, from Westmoreland and Albert Counties, New Brunswick.

British Columbia.—Cretaceous sandstones from Nanaimo and vicinity have been used in Victoria. Brownish-gray stone from Newcastle Island was used in the construction of the Mint in San Francisco.*

(2) *Scotland.*

So far as I am aware, the only Scotch sandstones regularly brought to the United States are those of Corsehill, near Annan, in Dumfriesshire ; those of Ballochmile Forfarshire, and a third variety from Gatelaw Bridge, about 30 miles from Ballochmile, in Dumfriesshire.

Of these the Corsehill stone is of greatest importance. Samples in the National collections are of a fine and even grain, distinctly laminated, and of a bright red color. The stone is stated by the agents to have been first introduced into this country about 1879, since which it has been quite extensively

---

* Annual Report of Geological Survey of Canada, 1887–88.

used for trimmings and general building.   It is regarded as a durable stone and well adapted for ashlar work, for carving, and for columns.   The strength and chemical composition of this stone are given in the tables.

The other varieties mentioned are of the same general appearance as the Corsehill stone, and are used for the same purposes.

As these stones are brought chiefly as ballast by vessels sailing from Carlisle, England, they are known commercially as Carlisle stone, regardless of their true source.

There are in the National collections samples of other Scotch sandstones from quarries in Morayshire, Nairn, Caithness, Sutherland, and Ross.   These are all of a light color and seemingly possess no qualities to warrant their use in preference to materials obtainable nearer home.

(2) VOLCANIC FRAGMENTAL ROCKS.   TUFFS

(*a*) Definition, Origin, and Composition.

Under the general name of tuff it is customary to include those fine-grained fragmental rocks formed by the consolidation of volcanic detritus, such as ashes, sand, and lapilli, or by the breaking down and reconsolidation of volcanic rocks of various kinds.   This consolidation, may have taken place either under water or on dry land ; in either case they are as a rule distinctly stratified.   Those of the tuffs which are formed from Tertiary or post-Tertiary erupted materials are   naturally but slightly consolidated, soft and easy to work.   It follows, almost as a matter of course, that they will absorb a proportionally large amount of water, and hence be less durable in the exceeding trying climate of the Eastern and Northern States.

The older tuffs are often so firmly compacted that recourse to the microscope must be had to determine their fragmental nature.

(*b*) VARIETIES OF TUFFS.

According to the nature of the lava, from the disintegration of which the tuffs are formed, they are designated by special names. *Rhyolite* tuff is composed of disintegrated rhyolite ; *trachyte* tuff of disintegrated trachyte, etc.

(*c*) LOCALITIES AND USES.

These rocks are very abundant throughout our Western States and Territories, but are scarcely at all used for building purposes, owing in part to the newly settled condition of the country in which they occur and in part to their state of incomplete consolidation. They are, however, soft, and easy though rather unsafe working stones, owing to lack of definite rift and grain, often plucky fracture, and the presence of numerous dry seams and clay holes. They are, moreover, light, frequently weighing only from 75 to 100 pounds per cubic foot, though moderately strong. When not exposed to too wide variations of climate they must prove very durable. Although no systematic experiments have as yet been made, appearances indicate that they would prove extremely refractory in case of fire.* They present a great variety of colors ; white, gray, pink, red, lavender, salmon, green, and even black, are common.

With these qualities there seems no reason for their not proving a valuable material in dry climates for all kinds of

---

* Newberry states that the tuffs found near Challis, Idaho, are of "considerable importance as they are extensively used in place of fire-brick for lining lead-smelting furnaces," being very refractory and easily dressed into shape with an old ax—Transcript from the New York Academy of Science, Dec. 1881.

structural purposes where only the rougher kinds of finish are employed, their textures being almost invariably such that they will not polish.

The light gray and pink rhyolite tuff occuring in Douglass County, Colorado, has been used in the construction of the Union Depot, Windsor Hotel, and other buildings in Denver.

This may rank as a fairly durable material, but it contains clay holes and other imperfections that unfit it for fine work of any kind. The National collections contain other samples of tuffs of various kinds from California, New Mexico, Idaho, and Utah, but they are not at all used at present, and their fitness or unfitness for any sort of building purposes is a problem for the future to decide. Near Phœnix, Arizona, occurs a tuff consisting only of the firmly compacted shreds of volcanic glass or pumice, and which is stated to have been used locally to some extent.

Although so little used in this country, tuffs are very generally employed for building purposes in many foreign localities. They are found abundantly in the volcanic districts of central France, and in the Haute-Loire, where they have been used in the construction of churches and dwelling-houses. The so-called " peperino " of the campagna of Rome and Naples, is a tuff formed by the consolidation of volcanic ashes, and has been used in some of the buildings of these cities. It was also used in the construction of the houses of Herculaneum and Pompeii. *

Rhyolite tuffs are, as I am informed by Signor Aguileria, very largely used for general building in certain parts of Mexico, the climate being such as to render almost any material very durable. There is now a large collection of these stones in the National Museum at Washington.

* Hull, Building and Ornamental Stones, p. 283.

3. ARGILLACEOUS FRAGMENTAL ROCKS. THE SLATES.

(a) COMPOSITION AND ORIGIN.

Ordinary clay or roofing slate is but an indurated and more or less metamorphosed siliceous clay. It is therefore classed here with the fragmental rocks although microscopic examination has shown that it frequently contains crystalline matter, and that the rocks pass by insensible gradations into what are called argillitic mica schists. Microscopic examination of slates from Littleton, New Hampshire by Hawes[*] showed them to consist of a mixture of quartz and feldspar in fragments as fine as dust. There was also noted a considerable quantity of some amorphous coaly matters; and many little needles of a brightly polarizing substance assumed to be mica. The clay slate of Hanover in the same State was found by this same authority to contain many minute crystals of garnet and staurolite. An examination of some clay slates from the Huronian region of Lake Superior, by Wichman[†] showed them to consist of a "colorless isotropic groundmass in which the other constitutents are apparently imbedded, whilst throughout are found dust-like particles of a deep gray color, which represent the chief constituent, and consist probably of clay substances, the greater part of them probably kaolin." Besides these constitutents there were also noticed a few quartz and feldspar particles, scales of hydrated oxide of iron, flakes of coaly matter, minute tourmaline and mica fragments. The Maine slates as observed by the author contain quite large flakes of greenish mica, and many quartz and carbonaceous particles. As a rule the dark color of slate seems to be due to these carbonaceous particles, they occurring abundantly in the black and blue-black slates of Maine and Pennsylvania, and being almost

---

[*] Geology of New Hampshire, vol. III. p. 237.
[†] Quarterly Journal Geological Society of London, vol. XXXV. 1879, p. 158.

entirely lacking in the green and red varieties from Vermont and northeastern New York. The red slates of the last-named State are made up of a groundmass of impalpable red dust in which are imbedded innumerable quartz and feldspar particles, all arranged with their longer axes parallel with the cleavage direction of the slate. Below is given an analysis of (I) a clay slate from Llangynog, North Wales, and (II) for comparison that of a fire clay from Illinois.

	I.	II.
Silica	60.15	60.97
Alumina	24.20	26.38
Iron Oxide	7.75	1.46
Lime, Magnesia and Alkalies	4.29	1.90
Water	3.72	8.93

The above, taken in connection with Fig. 3, drawn from a thin slice of slate cut across the direction of cleavage, will suffice to convey some idea of the composition and structure of this class of rocks. There remains, however, for our consideration, a very important matter, that relating to the origin of the slates and the cause of their eminent cleavage, or fissility.

As above noted the slates are essentially indurated clays.

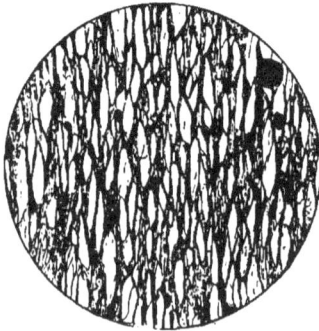

FIG. 3.

They originated as deposits of fine silt on ancient sea-bottoms. Such deposits, gradually accumulating through long periods of time, would be thrown down in parallel and approximately horizontal layers, but individual layers would naturally vary somewhat in texture and perhaps color according as the tributaries by which the silt was brought from the land down to the sea periodically varied in the rapidity of their currents, a swift turbulent stream carrying down more and less finely assorted material than one flowing more gently and with lesser volume. In the course of the ages following the beds thus laid down and subsequently covered by thousands of feet of other materials, became converted into stone. They owe their present accessibility to their having been raised above the ocean level and carried even to mountainous altitudes through the incalculably slow and yet almost never ceasing folding and faulting of the earth's crust. Formed in this way it would be but natural to suppose that the very decided tendency to cleave into thin smooth sheets would be developed always parallel to the ancient bedding, i.e., parallel to the plane in which they were first laid down. Such, however, is far from being the case. Indeed, as a rule, the fissile structure is developed at very considerable, though ever varying angles with the bedding, and is in no way connected with it genetically.

To what then is this fissility due, and how is it to be accounted for? The fact that a mass of stone will split up indefinitely into sheets of sometimes less than one-eighth of an inch in thickness, and into plates of large size, with smooth parallel surfaces, and this too directly across or at a sharp angle with the bedding or grain, is indeed a remarkable feature and one worthy of careful study.

A common feature of many slates, particularly those of Pennsylvania, is the presence of bands of varying width and darker color running across the cleaved surface. These, which occur at varying intervals, from less than an inch to a few feet (see Fig. 4) are technically called ribbons and represent the original lines of bedding, are due in fact to the dissimilarity of the materials brought down and deposited during the various stages of the slate-making process. But as above noted and as shown in the figure, the slate cleaves with great readiness at varying angles with the ribbons, while it breaks only with the greatest difficulty and with ragged and wavy lines in a direction parallel to them or to the original bedding, which is the same thing. This is explained as follows: In Fig. 4 we will suppose the horizontal lines to represent the fine clay sediment as it was first laid down on the bottom, the broken and disconnected lines illustrating the trifling difference in consistency of the various layers. Now as has been shown by the experi

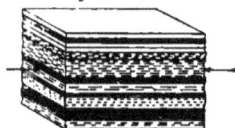   

FIG. 4.   FIG. 5.

ments of Sorby, * Daubree † and others, if while the clay was still more or less plastic, a gradual but very powerful pressure was brought to bear from the direction indicated by the arrows, there would be produced (1st) a very considerable shortening in this direction, and (2nd) a decided fissile structure in a direction at right angles with the direction of pressure or in a vertical direction in this case as shown in Fig. 5. A fold might or might not be produced at the same time.

This last condition of affairs actually exists in many of the Pennsylvania slate quarries as will be noted later (see Pl. VIII).

This property of assuming a platy structure when pressed, rolled or pounded, is by no means confined to clays, but is manifested to a greater or less extent in almost all substances, as is illustrated by the flaking of pastry when rolled, or the exfoliation of rails subjected to the continuous hammering of car and engine wheels. The effect of the lateral pressure upon the internal structure of the stone is beautifully shown by cutting a thin section from the slate parallel to the front face shown in Fig. 5, i.e., across the cleavage, and submitting it to examination under a microscope of high power, when it will be seen that all the minute quartz, feldspar and other mineral particles,

* Edinburgh Philosophical Journal, vol. IV. 1853, p. 137.
† Geologie Experimentale, p. 391.

originally laid with their longer axes horizontal, have been made to reverse their positions, as in the experiments of Sorby and Daubree already alluded to, and now lie with their shorter axes in the direction of pressure as is shown in Fig. 3. It has not infrequently happened, however, as is beautifully shown in many of the Pennsylvania quarries, that certain layers of the slaty material were not of such a nature as to readily assume a platy or fissile structure, but bent or broke under the pressure. Such portions gave rise to the peculiar crimped or puckered forms of ribbons which are known to the quarriers as "curly slates." Frequently a layer of material of considerable thickness will occur of such a nature as to completely resist all attempts on the part of Dame Nature to produce the desired fissility, but will bend or break repeatedly or sometimes remains a hard dense homogeneous mass, in the midst of a quarry, the slates on both sides assuming their ordinary character. Since in preparing the quarried material for the market for roofing and other purposes, all such non-fissile, crimped and curly portions must be rejected, the processes of slate manufacture are enormously wasteful, and the entire country in the older quarry regions is often covered by huge piles of debris on the extreme outer edges of which are precariously pitched at every conceivable angle, the long lines of splitters' shanties.*

---

* The proportion of slate waste is sometimes enormous. Davies (Slates and Slate Quarrying) states that in the Welsh quarries 16 or 20 tons of waste to one of merchantable material is a frequent occurrence, and good paying quarries have been worked where 100 tons of rock must be removed to obtain 3½ tons of good slate.

Within a few years there has been made in Pennsylvania an attempt to utilize this slate waste for brick making, but as yet the demand for the material for this purpose has not been sufficient to make appreciable inroads on the supply. The slate is finely pulverized, mixed into clay, moulded and baked like an ordinary brick. The result is a trifle more porous in texture and of a duller color than a clay brick, but is stated to be good and durable.

(b) USES OF SLATE.

Besides for roofing purposes, slates are used for billiard-tables, mantels, floor-tiles, steps, flagging, and in the manufacture of school-slates. For the last-named purpose a soft, even-grained stone is required, and almost the entire supply is at present brought from Pennsylvania and Vermont. Of late years the business of marbleizing slates for mantels and fire-places has become an important industry. All kinds of stones can be imitated by this process, but that most commonly seen is the green verd-antique marble and the variegated marbles of Tennessee. Like many counterfeits, however, the work is too perfect in execution, and need deceive none but the most inexperienced.

The following table gives the various sizes of slate made for roofing, and the number that are necessary for a " square," i.e., a space 10 feet square, or containing an area of 100 square feet.*

SIZE.—INCHES.	No. of slates to a square.	SIZE.—INCHES.	No. of slates to a square.	SIZE.—INCHES.	No. of slates to a square.
24 by 14	98	18 by 9	213	10 by 7	588
24 13	105	18 8	230	10 6	686
24 12	114	16 10	222	10 5	823
24 11	124	16 9	246	10 4	1,039
24 10	138	16 8	247	9 8	600
22 13	116	16 7	316	9 7	686
22 12	126	14 9	300	9 6	800
22 11	138	14 8	327	9 5	960
22 10	151	14 7	374	9 4	1,200
20 12	141	14 6	436	8 6	960
20 11	154	12 8	400	8 5	1,152
20 10	169	12 7	457	8 4	1,440
20 9	188	12 6	570	7 5	1,440
18 11	174	12 5	640	7 4	1,800
18 10	192	10 8	514	7 3	2,400

* From Report D 3, vol. 1, p. 142, Second Geological Survey Pennsylvania.

(*c*) SLATES OF THE VARIOUS STATES AND TERRITORIES.

Arkansas.—A bed of purple slate suitable for mantel and slab work is stated* to occur near Little Rock in this State, and also another some nine miles west of Hot Springs.

California.—Slate of excellent quality and color is said † to occur in El Dorado County, near Placerville, where it has been quarried to some extent ; the color is blue-black.

Colorado.—A slate of good quality is stated to occur on the road between Colorado Springs and Cañon City.

Dakota.—Good roofing slate is said to occur on Pennington and Slate Creeks, in South Dakota.

Georgia.—Slates sufficiently cleavable to be applicable for roofing purposes are stated ‡ to exist in great quantities along or near the line of contact between the Silurian and Metamorphic Groups, near the Cohutta, Silicoa, Pine Log, and Dug Down Mountains in this State. The most noted locality for roofing slates is on the eastern side of Polk County. The outcrops are in steep hills and are apparently of great thickness. They have been worked quite extensively at Rock Mart, though in a crude and itinerant manner, since as early as 1859, the material being shipped chiefly to Atlanta and neighboring towns. Other dark-colored slates are found in Bartow, Gordon, Murray, and Fannin Counties, while buff and light green varieties are found in large quantities in the northwestern portion of Bartow County. None of the above are to be found in the general market, and that from Rock Mart is the only one samples of which the writer has had opportunity of examining.

---

* Mineral Resources of the United States, 1887, p. 525.
† Eighth Annual Report State Mineralogist of California, 1888, p. 199.
‡ Commonwealth of Georgia, p. 137.

This is of deep blue-black color, of fine and even texture, and splits readily with an even surface into slabs of moderate thinness. It is apparently less fissile than the slates from the Pennsylvania regions, but is more like those of Vermont. The cleavage is apparently parallel with the original bedding of the stone.

Maine.—The clay slates of Maine are regarded by Prof. Hitchcock as of Cambrian and Silurian age. According to this authority * two large and three smaller areas of the stone are to be found within the State limits. The first and more northern of these in the form of an irregular band from 10 to 25 miles in width extends from a point near the State line in the northern part of Franklin County northeastward through Somerset and the north-west corner of Piscataquis into Aroostook County, and thence northward to New Brunswick, occupying the whole width of the St. John and St. Francis boundary line. The second large belt extends from near the western boundary of Somerset County (near Lexington) in the form of a belt of about equal width in a more nearly easterly direction to near Houlton also in Aroostook County, crossing thus Somerset, Piscataquis, and Penobscot Counties. Of the three smaller areas one is on the Kennebec River, south of Skowhegan, and the two others in Washington County, about Baskahegan Lake and near Princeton. So far as the author is aware portions of the two large areas only furnish material sufficiently fissile for roofing purposes. At various times quarries have been opened at different points in these localities, but the principal ones at this time worked are in the towns of Monson, Blanchard, and Brownville, Piscataquis County. The slates here produced are all of a blue-black color, and are reported by Mr. J. E. Wolff as of most excellent quality, being hard, yet splitting readily

---

* Geology of Northern New England, p. 2.

into thin sheets with a fine cleavage surface, not subject to dis-coloration and giving forth a clear ringing sound when struck. Although seemingly susceptible of being used for all purposes to which slates are usually applied, they are at present utilized mainly for roofing.

Maryland.—The principal quarries of slate in this State are in Harford County, adjoining Pennsylvania. The ridge upon which the quarries are situated extends across the State line into York County, where several other quarries are worked within a radius of about 1 mile. As the Harford and York County stones are practically identical we will reserve a complete description of their qualities until we come to speak of the latter. Other quarries were formerly worked in the town of Ijamsville, in Frederick County. The stone here is of a blue-black color and is represented to be of good quality, but for some reason unknown to the writer the quarries are no longer worked.

Massachusetts.—Although, as already noted, slate was one of the stones to be earliest quarried in eastern Massachusetts, the material was of such a nature as to be of little value except for rough construction, and hence the industry has always remained of slight importance. The only quarries now worked from which slate suitable for roofing or other fine work can be obtained are at Lancaster, in Worcester County. This quarry is stated by Marvin* to have been opened by a Mr. Flagg over a century ago, and the slates were in use as early as 1750 or 1753 (*ante*, p. 9). Owing to lack of favorable transportation facilities the work was discontinued more than fifty years since, and it was not till 1877 that it was recommenced. The slate though porous is said to hold its color well and to be durable. Another outcrop of slate of good quality is said to occur about

---

* History of Lancaster.

1 mile north of Clinton, in this same county. It is not, however, as yet quarried.

The clay slates occurring in the vicinity of Boston and
Cambridge have long been used for road materials, but for
purposes of construction only to a slight extent. They are
not sufficiently fissile for roofing purposes. The stone is
regarded by Professor Shaler as of great value for rough building, as it is durable, easily quarried, and very effective when
placed in a wall. The Shepherd Memorial Church in Cambridge is the only building of importance yet constructed of
this material.

Michigan.—An extensive deposit of Huronian slates occurs
in the northwestern portion of the northern peninsula of this
State, principally in the towns of Houghton, Marquette, and
Menominee. But a small portion of the entire formation will
furnish material sufficiently fissile, homogeneous, and durable
for roofing purposes; nevertheless the supply of good material
is so abundant as to be practically inexhaustible. At L'Anse
the beds extend down to the lake shore, but are badly shattered,
not homogeneous, nor of sufficient durability in this immediate
vicinity to be of value. Good roofing slate is, however, found
about 15 miles from L'Anse, on the northwestern side of the
Huron mountain range, and about 3 miles from Huron Bay,
where extensive quarries have been opened. The stone here
is susceptible of being split into large, even slabs of any desired
thickness, with a fine silky, homogeneous grain, and combines
durability and toughness with smoothness. Its color is an
agreeable black and very uniform. Several companies have
located their quarries along the creek which runs parallel with
the strike of the slate, and a tramway about 3½ miles in length
has been built down to the bay, where a dock has been erected
for the unloading of vessels and for the convenient shipment
of the material.*

* Geology of Michigan, vol. III. part I. p. 161.

Minnesota.—At Thompson, Carlton County, where the Saint Paul and Duluth Railroad crosses the Saint Louis River, there occurs, according to Professor N. H. Winchell* an inexhaustible supply of hard, black, and apparently eminently durable slate suitable for roofing, school-slates, tables, mantels, and all other purposes to which slate is usually applied. Quarries were opened here by the railroad company in 1880, but for some unknown reason were discontinued before any of the stone had been put upon the market.

New Hampshire.—Professor Hitchcock† states that the only formation in this State likely to furnish good roofing slates is the Cambrian range along the Connecticut River. There have been quarries upon this belt in the towns of Littleton, Hanover, and Lebanon, but they have not now been worked for several years. The stone is stated to be not quite equal to that of Maine and Vermont, but certain portions of it might be utilized locally to good advantage, as for tables, platforms, curbs, and flag-stones. In Littleton the band of rocks suitable for working is nearly an eighth of a mile wide, and has been opened at two localities. The strata are vertical and the outcrops on a hill where good drainage can be had to a depth of a hundred feet. The stone is soft, apparently durable, and of a dark blue color, but does not cleave so thin as the slate from Maine. At East Lebanon the valuable part of the slate bed is 30 feet in width. The stone does not split sufficiently thin for roofing, but can be utilized to good advantage for chimney-pieces, table-tops, and shelves ; also for sinks, cisterns, flooring-tiles, etc. The waste material was formerly ground and bolted into slate flour.

New Jersey.—The belt of Silurian slates and shales extend-

---

* Preliminary Report on the Building Stones, etc., of Minnesota, 1880, p. 17.
† Geology of New Hampshire, vol. III. p. 81.

ing in a northeasterly and southwesterly direction entirely
across the northern part of this State includes several quarriable areas, but which have up to the present time been utilized
only to a limited extent. Quarries have been worked at La
Fayette and Newton, in Sussex County, and also at the Delaware Water Gap in Warren County. The product of these is
represented by Professor Cook* as of good quality and suitable
not only for roofing material, but also for school slates, tiles,
and mantels.

New York.—The roofing slates of this State occur in two
geologically distinct belts, ranging in a general northeasterly
and southwesterly direction through the counties of Orange,
Dutchess, Columbia, Rensselaer, and Washington, and thence
onward into Vermont, one of them furnishing by its continuation the well-known roofing slates of the last-named State.
The irregular outlines and intimate associations of the two
beds can be well understood only by reference to maps such as
it has been found inexpedient to reproduce here.† Throughout both areas the beds dip at high angles to the south and
east, the cleavage being coincident, or varying at a very slight
angle with the bedding. In this respect these stand in strong
contrast with the slates of eastern Pennsylvania, yet to be
noted. In none of the New York quarries, so far as observed,
do the slates possess the eminently fissile character of those
of the above-named State, the split slates being thicker and
with more uneven surfaces.

Of the two formations mentioned, the lower, or Cambrian
bed extends in the form of a broad though interrupted belt
through the central part of Rensselaer County and the western

---

* Annual Report State Geologist of New Jersey, 1881, p. 66.

† See Walcott's "The Taconic System of Emmons," American Journal of
Science, May, 1888.

part of Washington, crossing the State line into Vermont some five miles north-west of Bennington, Vermont. At its greatest development it is not above ten miles wide in an east and west direction, and it thins out rapidly north of Fairhaven, becoming a mere wedge and ultimately disappear- • ing a few miles north-west of Middlebury, Vermont, to appear once more in the northern part of Chittenden County as a narrow belt running in the same general direction across the State into Canada. The rock is interstratified with shales and limestones, and but a small part of the area furnishes quarriable material, the productive quarries in both belts being, according to Professor Smock,* all in Washington County, and limited to a narrow belt running from Salem northeast through the towns of Hebron, Granville, Hampton, and Whitehall. The output from this, the Cambrian belt, varies from purplish to green in color, is of excellent quality, and is used for all purposes to which slates are usually applied ; it is extensively marbleized.

The upper, or Hudson River bed of slate, occurs in the form of very irregular and often interrupted areas following the same general trend as the Cambrian slates, but thinning out rapidly north of Granville, though continuing in the form of an irregular interrupted belt through Vermont into Canada. It appears on the Vermont side of the line west of the Cambrian slates, only in detached areas in Bennington and Rutland Counties; east of the Cambrian it appears as a long, narrow, though not continuous belt, in Addison, Chittenden, and Franklin Counties.

The slates of this formation are of a brick-red and green color, both varieties occurring often in the same quarry, and indeed the split slate in slabs not above $\frac{3}{10}$ of an inch in thickness are often found to be red on one side and green on the

---

* Bulletin No. 3, New York State. Museum.

other. The red variety is the more highly valued, bringing about three times the price of the ordinary varieties. It is used mainly for roofing and tiling. As shown at Granville, this red slate belt, which runs nearly parallel with the Vermont line, is very narrow, in places not over 30 rods wide, and outcrops in numerous low, glaciated knobs or ledges. The quality of the red slates is stated by Professor Smock to improve as the quarries are worked to a greater depth.

Although the beds of this formation pass over into Vermont, the brick-red slates are confined mainly to the areas on the New York side of the line, and the quarries of the towne above noted furnish the entire supply for the United States.

Pennsylvania.—The narrow slate-belt already noted as occurring in Harford County, Maryland, crosses the State line into the extreme eastern portion of York County, in Pennsylvania, and thence sweeps around in a gradually narrowing curve to the Susquehanna River, appearing again on its eastern bank, in Fulton Township, Lancaster County, where it finally disappears. It is from this narrow belt, at its greatest dimensions less than a mile wide and scarcely more than six miles long, that has been quarried for many years the justly celebrated blue-black " Peach Bottom Slate." The stone is stated to rank very high for strength and durability. It is tough, fine, and moderately smooth in texture, and is stated not to fade on exposure, buildings on which it has been exposed for upwards of seventy-five years still showing it fresh and unchanged.

The stone is less fissile than the majority of those from Pennsylvania, New York, Vermont, or Maine, yielding as a rule but four slabs to the inch, while the Monson and Slatington slates readily yield twice or even three times that number. A microscopic examination shows the stone to have undergone a greater amount of metamorphism than have those from the other regions described, being in fact no longer a fragmental rock, but rather a highly carbonaceous, crystalline schist. This fact, while not perhaps accounting for its lack of fissility, does in part at least account for the increased strength and elasticity of the stone as well as its great durability.

An analysis of this slate is given in the tables. The principal quarries now worked are at Bangor and West Bangor, York County, in Pennsylvania, and at adjacent points just across the line in Maryland.

Persifor Frazer * regards these slates as of Huronian age, and but local modifications of the interbedded chloritic schists. According to this authority the bands of merchantable slate are rarely more than a few yards in width, and the strata so capricious that the greatest perseverance and ingenuity on the part of the quarrymen are indispensable to avoid sustaining loss, and even the spoiling of the quarry by injudicious mining.

On account of the narrowness of the belt and the steepness of the dip, which is sometimes nearly vertical, the quarries are very deep in proportion to their surface areas. To the cost of working these deep quarries is added that of the enormous amount of waste material—estimated as in some cases equal to 88 per cent—and as a consequence the works have not in all cases proven very profitable.

The Utica and Hudson River slate formation, in which lie the largest and most important quarries of slate at present worked in the State, extends in a belt of from 7 to 12 miles in width throughout the entire northern parts of Northampton and Lehigh Counties, and thence in a gradually though unevenly narrowing band in a general southwesterly direction through Berks, Lebanon, Dauphin, Cumberland, and Franklin Counties, whence it passes into Maryland.

---

* Thèses Présentées a la Faculté des Sciences de Lille, Université de France, 1883. Also Report CCC. Second Geological Survey of Pennsylvania, 1880.

The geological character of the beds and the details regarding the quarries have been described with considerable detail by Mr. R. H. Sanders, * and it seems unnecessary to repeat them here in full.

According to this authority the structure of the slate belt throughout the region, is in general a series of anticlines and synclines, which are closely folded and mostly overturned (Plate VIII.) So abundant indeed, are the folds, that in several of the quarries of Washington township the opening is directly across the axis of the fold. In this respect, the slates of the Pennsylvania regions stand in marked contrast with those of New York and Vermont (yet to be described). The cleavage property is due wholly to pressure which acted in a direction practically at right angles with these folds, and the quarries therefore not infrequently produce, at different depths, slates cleaving parallel, directly across, and at all intermediate angles with the bedding of the stone. This feature gives rise to "ribbon" and "curly" slates and causes large amounts of waste in the preparation of material for roofing purposes, inasmuch as the ribbons, which represent the original lines of bedding as described on p. 295, must be rejected. Only those portions of uniform texture and composition lying between the ribbons are suitable for roofing. For tiling, mantels, billiard tables etc., the ribbons are not however objectionable. It is the presence of these that gives rise to the dark bands, an inch more in width, such as may so frequently be seen running across the large slabs.

The slates throughout the entire region now worked are or a quite uniform dark blue or blue-black color and are used for roofing, school slates and all purposes to which the material is commonly applied. The waste slate is in some cases utilized in the manufacture of brick.

---

* Second Geological Survey of Pennsylvania, Report D. 3, vol. 1. p. 83-148.

PLATE VIII.

SLATE QUARRY AND SURROUNDINGS AT BANGOR, PENNSYLVANIA.

To face page 308.

In the manufacture of school-slates a softer and finer grade of material is requisite than for most other purposes. These are split from the block in the same manner as roofing-slates, their edges trimmed with a saw, and the faces smoothed by a drawing-knife, after which they are rubbed down with a cloth and fine slate dust till the surface is smooth and even. They are then mounted in wooden frames and packed for shipment.

But a very small part of the above roughly outlined area is of such a nature as to furnish stone for economic purposes. The quarries at present worked, beginning with the eastern-most, are situated in the various townships in the northern part of Northampton County, and in Washington, Heidelburgh and Lynn townships in Lehigh County. The quarry industry as here pursued has given rise to a number of small villages bearing such suggestive names as Slateford, Slatedale, and Slatington, or Bangor and Penargyl, after their Welsh proto-types. No quarries are as yet worked on any of the beds east of the Schuylkill river, though there is no reason for supposing good material may not here be found. The red slate outcrops occurring through the western part of Berks County, and which continue on toward the centre of Cumberland County, are thought by the State geologists to be worthy of investigation, and may yet furnish valuable material.

South Carolina.—Clay slates are stated* to occur in this State in a broad band extending along the edge of the Tertiary formations from Edgefield County, on the south-west, to Ches-terfield, on the north-east. The present writer has seen none of this material nor has he any knowledge regarding its adapt-ability for any form of architectural work.

Tennessee.—A large bed of slate is stated† to have been dis-

---

* South Carolina, Resources, Population, etc., 1883, p. 133.
† Mineral Resources of the United States, 1886, p. 553.

covered on Abrams Creek, some one and a half miles from the Little Tennessee river in Blount County.

Texas.—Bluish-black slates of a jointed and thinly stratified structure, resembling the surface slates of New Hampshire and Vermont, and promising of great utility, are stated to occur in Llano and Presidio Counties.* The writer has seen none of these.

Vermont.—The roofing slates of Vermont are stated by Professor Hitchcock † to exist in three distinct and nearly parallel belts, occupying the eastern, middle, and western portions of the State. The eastern belt extends from Guilford, one of the most southern towns in the State, to Waterford, and probably as far north as Burke, in Caledonia County, where it is cut off by an immense outcrop of granite. The slate of this belt differs from that of the other divisions in presenting a more laminated appearance, resembling closely a mica schist, the cleavage corresponding closely with the lamination, which varies, if at all, but a trifle from the planes of stratification. The stone is represented as of good color, tough, and durable. Besides for roofing purposes it was used largely for tombstones prior to 1830, when marble began to be used in its place. The first quarry opened in this belt is stated by the above authority to have been that of the New England Slate Company, who commenced operations in 1812. At the present time, so far as the author is aware, no quarries whatever are worked in this belt.

The middle range of slate extends from Lake Memphremagog in a southerly course as far as Barnard. The slate found in this differs from that of the eastern belt in that it splits more readily into thin sheets, is not so distinctly laminated,

---

* Second Annual Report Geology of Texas, 1876, p. 26.
† Geology of Vermont, vol. II, 1861, p 791.

and is more uniform in color, "being nearly black and apparently free from the traces of iron oxides." A single quarry is now in operation in this belt, that of the Adams Slate Company, in Northfield, Washington County.

The western and most important of the slate belts of the State extends from a point near the town of Cornwall, on the north, southward through Castleton, Fairhaven, Poultney, Wells, and Pawlet, and passes into the State of New York at Granville, as already noted. In this slate it is stated " there is a marked difference between the stratification and cleavage planes, the dip of the latter being greater than the former." In color the slates of this region are said to closely resemble those of Wales, being of dark purple, with blotches of green, while some of the strata are green throughout. In some portions of the formation a red slate occurs, similar to that found across the line in New York State. This variety is not, however, now quarried. Though a deep reddish-brown variety is produced at Fairhaven, and some of those from Castleton and Pawlet are of a more reddish than purplish tinge.

This western area furnishes. the most fissile and valuable slates of the State, and is very extensively worked. The slate is soft and uniform in texture, and can be readily planed or sawn with a steel circular saw, such as is used in sawing lumber. It is well adapted and extensively used, not only for roofing purposes, but for school slates, slate-pencils, blackboards, table-tops, mantels, etc. It is very extensively marbleized. It is stated by Prof. Hitchcock that the first quarry opened in this region was that of Hon. Alanson Allan, who began the manufacture of school slates at Fairhaven in 1845. The beds are of Cambrian age.

Virginia.—On Hunt Creek, a tributary of Slate River, in Buckingham County, in this State, there occur extensive deposits of blue-black slate of a quality suitable for a variety of uses, although they are now worked mainly for roofing material. The principal quarries are at or near the towns of Buckingham, New Canton, and Ore Banks. The beds extend up the creek for several miles, the trend being practically paralled with Slate River.

Another belt of slate of the same geological age (Archæan) as that just mentioned is stated to occur near the southeast base of the Blue Ridge, in Amherst and Bedford Counties.

(d) FOREIGN STATES.

Canada.—Slates of excellent quality, smooth, homogeneous, and strong, and of green, red, purple, and blue-black colors, occur in Richmond County, in the Province of Quebec. These are now being quarried and are to be found in the principal markets of the United States. The leading quarries, as given by Newberry,* are those of the New Rockland Slate Company, the Melbourne Slate Company, the Rankin Hill Slate Company, and the Danville School Slate Company.†

Slate of good quality is stated ‡ also to occur in New Canaan and on the Middle River of Pictou, in Nova Scotia.

Great Britian.—The finest roofing slates of Great Britain are stated by Hull § to be derived from the Cambrian and Lower Silurian formations of North Wales. The Cambrian slates are stated to be generally of a green and purple color, while those of the Silurian formations vary from pale gray to nearly black. The stone splits with wonderful facility into very thin sheets, and the quarries are especially favorably

---

* Report of Judges, p. 164.

† Further details regarding the slate areas of Canada are given in Geology of Canada, 1863, pp. 830, 831.

‡ Dawson, Acadian Geology, p. 593.

§ *Op. cit.* p. 292.

situated both for working and for shipment. Material from these sources has been sent to every quarter of the globe, and has been more extensively used for roofing than any other slate now quarried.*

---

* For a detailed account of the Welsh slates and the methods of quarrying see Davies Slate Quarrying, Crosby, Lockwood & Co.

PART III.

METHODS OF QUARRYING AND DRESSING STONE.

(I) GENERAL CONSIDERATIONS.

There are certain structural features common to rocks, features due in part to method of formation and in part to subsequent events, that are worthy of a somewhat extended notice inasmuch as they have an important bearing upon quarry methods and quarry resources.

In the chapter on processes of rock formation, the rocks it will be remembered were divided into three groups. 1st. Sedimentary, 2nd. Eruptive and 3rd. Metamorphic, the last comprising members of the first two, but which had been so changed by the processes of metamorphism that their original nature was not in all cases evident. Certain of the structural features referred to are common to all classes, others are confined to a single one.

In all sedimentary rocks there is a more or less evident bedding, due to the fact that the sediments were laid down in approximately parallel layers. The different layers or beds in such cases often vary greatly in texture and color, and it may be are separated from one another by thin beds of fine shaly material as shown in plates VII and IX.

This bedded structure is of the greatest importance from

314

an economic standpoint, since upon the thickness of the beds and their homogeneity is dependent the size and quality of blocks obtainable. If however the beds are too thick and massive the expense of quarrying is greatly increased, in that it necessitates splitting out the rock with wedges into convenient sizes for handling, as shown in plate IX. The varying character of the layers in these bedded rocks is often a source of trouble to the quarriers. One of the finest of the Triassic sandstones of the Eastern United States is no longer worked, for the reason that the thick beds of desirable stone are separated by from one to several feet of thin shaly material, quite worthless, and which involves so considerable an outlay for its removal as to destroy all profit.

Naturally a stone splits most readily along the line of bedding, or stratification, which is the same thing. The same feature is common to many metamorphic rocks, as the marbles and gneisses, and in certain cases is due to the same causes. This direction of splitting most readily, is called the rift as already noted (p. 39).

The position occupied by the beds of stratified rocks is of very great importance. If as at Portland, Connecticut, and in the Berea regions they lie nearly horizontal the process of quarrying is greatly simplified and consists practically in cutting a vertical hole down into the earth, thus passing through one layer or bed after another. This arrangement has at least one disadvantage in that in a new region the quarrier has nothing to guide him and no means of ascertaining what the next bed is going to be like. If on the other hand the beds are turned up at a considerable angle, it is possible to tell from surface indications what quality of stone each bed is likely to produce and perhaps several varieties of stone may be produced at the same time as in the Vermont marble quarries, where the beds are comparatively thin and vary greatly.

Obviously where the beds are steeply inclined or curved as at Rutland the openings take the form of mines rather than quarries (see Plate V.) and the expense of quarrying is somewhat increased. Another disadvantage lies in the fact that, whatever the character of the material for which they have orders, all the beds must be worked down alike unless the opening is restricted to a single layer, which would be scarcely profitable.

Among the eruptive rocks no such bedding exists and in very massive rocks it is always necessary to split the stone into suitable blocks by means of under cutting or gadding. It is fortunate for the quarrier that however massive a stone may be, and whether eruptive or sedimentary, Nature has in most instances herself broken it into blocks of varying sizes by means of sharp seams or fractures called joints.

These vary greatly, according to the nature of the rock in which they occur, sometimes being so fine as to be almost imperceptible, or again perfectly distinct and capable of being traced for many yards, or even miles. In stratified rocks (limestones, sandstones, schists, etc.), according to Professor Geikie, the joints, " as a rule," run perpendicular, or approximately so, to the planes of bedding, and descend vertically at not very unequal distances, so that the portions of the rock between them, when seen from a distance, appear like so many wall-like masses. An important feature of these joints, as mentioned by this authority, is the direction in which they intersect each other. In general they have two dominant trends, one coincident on the whole with the direction in which the strata are inclined from the horizon, and the other running transversely at a right angle or nearly so. The first are called " dip joints" or " end joints" by the quarrymen, since they run with the dip or inclination of the rock, while the last are called " strike joints," since they conform in direction to the strike of the rock. These last are also called "back joints."

In massive rocks like granite and diabase, joints, though prevalent, have not the same regularity of arrangement as in the stratified formations; nevertheless, most rocks of this class are traversed by two intersecting sets, whereby the rock is divided into long, quadrangular, rhomboidal, or even polygonal masses. Frequently, also, there exists a third series of joints running in an approximately horizontal direction, or corresponding more nearly with the bedding in stratified rocks. These are called by quarrymen "bottom joints," since they form the bottom or floor of the quarry.

These joints owing to atmospheric action are usually more conspicuous at and near the surface, and indeed often seem to wholly disappear when the quarry is opened to a sufficient depth. It is only in appearance however, since from their very method of formation they must extend far below any practical depth. Their apparent absence is due to the fact that the faces of the stone having been held resting against one another with all the force of their immense weight for untold years, are often more closely united than would be possible by any artificial means. Indeed the blocks are often actually cemented together by the deposition of an exceeding thin film of calcite, silica or iron oxide. The writer has in mind a quarry of beautiful deep gray coarsely crystalline granitic rock, which when first opened was found so full of joints that blocks of only small size and very irregular shape could be obtained. So abundant were these joints that on the surface for short distances the stone would often separate into slabs of but from one to two or three inches in thickness. At a distance of not above 25 feet from the surface the joints disappeared entirely, and large, handsome and apparently sound blocks were being taken out. Knowing, however, from the surface indications that the joints must be there nevertheless, I looked for them with care, and on the polished shaft of a finished monument was able to point out three, running perpendicularly, each as fine, sharp, and straight as though made with a glazier's diamond. They were simply so small as to be overlooked by others than an expert. Being there they are bound in time to open under the persuasive action of heat and frost. How long a time may elapse before they will open sufficiently to become conspicuous, can be determined only by actual experiment. The only safe way, however, is to avoid them wholly.

It is the preponderance of joints of one kind or another that gives rise to what are known technically as block and sheet quarries. In the one case, as at Quincy, Massachusetts, or Red Beach, Maine, the joints divide the rock into approximately rectangular blocks but a few feet in diameter, and which are especially adapted for the finer grades of monumental work. The quarriers early learn to recognize this fact, and in making contracts govern themselves accordingly. In other quarries, as those of Hallowell, Maine (Plate VI.), the rock by a series of nearly horizontal joints is divided up into inbricated layers varying from the fraction of one to six or more feet in thickness and so slightly adhering to one another as to need almost no artificial means to free them from the bed. These layers, as shown in the plate, are thin at the edges and gradually thicken toward the centre. Such are called sheet quarries, in distinction from the block quarries just mentioned, and within the limits of the sheet's thickness blocks of almost any desired size may be obtained. At Vinalhaven blocks not over 10 feet in thickness and nearly 300 feet in length have been loosened from the quarry bed intact. In still other quarries the bottom joints are so numerous and persistent that sheets above 10 or 15 inches thick are rarely obtainable, and in the face of such a quarry the stone may be seen lying one sheet above another, each receding a foot or more from the one below like a flight of stairs. Such quarries are best adapted for furnishing material for street curbs and paving blocks.

In the basic eruptive rocks such as the basalts and diabases another form of jointing, due apparently to the cooling of the molten mass, is not infrequent. This gives rise to a series of more or less regular five or six sided columns such as are shown in figures of the Giant's Causeway and Fingal's Cave. Such jointing practically ruins the stone for quarrying dimensions material, and fortunately is found to any extent only in stones which on account of their color and hardness are little desired for architectural work.

The cause of joints, it may be stated, has never been fully and satisfactorily explained. By some they are supposed to be due to contraction caused by cooling or drying, and by others it is supposed that they are fractures produced by earthquakes.* Obviously, the matter can not be discussed here, and the reader is referred to the various text-books on geology. But whatever may have been their origin, their presence is a matter of great importance to quarrymen, and, indeed, the art of quarrying has been well stated to consist in taking advantage of these natural planes of division. By their aid large quadrangular blocks can be wedged off which would be shattered if exposed to the risk of blasting.†

---

* W. O. Crosby, Proceedings Boston Society Natural History, xxiii., 1885.

† A good illustration of the utility of jointed structure as an aid to quarrying sedimentary rocks is offered in the Primordial conglomerates about Boston. These consist of a greenish gray groundmass, in which are embraced a great variety of pebbles of granite, quartzite, melaphyr, and felsite of all shapes and sizes. The beds are traversed by two series of vertical joints which cut the rock and its included pebbles, granite, quartz, melaphyr, and felsite alike, with almost as sharp and clear a cut as could be made by the lapidary's wheel. The

(2) GRANITE QUARRYING.

The methods of quarrying naturally vary with the kind and quality of the material to be extracted. In all, the object aimed at is to obtain large and well shaped blocks with the least outlay of time and money, and this, too, so far as possible, without the aid of explosives of any kind, since the sudden jar thus produced is extremely liable to develop incipient fractures and so shatter as to ruin valuable material.

In quarrying granite there is less to fear from the use of explosives than in either sandstone or marble, while, at the same time, the greater hardness of the stone renders the quarrying of it by other means a matter of considerable difficulty and expense.

In the leading quarries of Maine and Massachusetts no machinery is used other than the steam drill and hoisting apparatus. By means of the drills a lewis* hole or a series of lewis holes is put down at proper intervals to a depth dependent upon the thickness of the sheets. These are then charged, not too heavily, and fired simultaneously. In the Hallowell quarries, where the sheets of granite are entirely free from one another, this is all that is necessary to loosen the blocks from the quarry, and they are then broken up with wedges. In many quarries, however, where the sheets are thicker or the bottom joints less distinct, it is necessary to drill a series of horizontal holes along the line where it is wished to break the rock from the bed and then complete the process with wedges.

joints are very abundant, and in many cases quarrying would be a practical impossibility without them. Whenever smooth walls are required the stone is laid on its bed with the joint face outward.

* I find the word also spelled *louis*. For description see Glossary.

(3) MARBLE QUARRYING.

In quarrying marble and other soft rocks, channelling machines are now largely used. These, as shown in the illustration, run on narrow tracks, back and forth over the quarry
bed, cutting as they
go, vertical channels
some 2 inches in
width and from 4 to
6 feet in depth. After
the channels are com-
pleted a series of
holes from 8 inches
to 2 feet apart are
drilled along the bot-
tom of the block,
which is then split
from its bed by means
of wedges. This under
drilling is called by
quarrymen "gadd-
ing," and special ma-
chines, which are
known as "gadding
machines," have been
designed for the pur-
pose. (See figures on

FIG. 6.—WARDWELL CHANNELLING MACHINE.

pages 340 to 343). At the Vermont marble quarries both the
Sullivan diamond pointed drill and the Ingersoll impact drill
are used for gadding. The bottom holes are usually drilled
to a depth equalling about one-half the width of the block
to be extracted, though this depth, as well as the frequency

of the holes, must necessarily vary with the character of the rift of the rock.

(4) SANDSTONE QUARRYING.

In the quarrying of the Triassic sandstones at Portland, Connecticut, the channelling machine is also used to some extent, but the prevailing method of loosening large blocks is by deep drill holes charged with heavy blasts of powder. These holes are made by a crude machine driven by cranks, like an ordinary derrick, and are 10 inches in diameter and about 20 feet deep. Into these are put from 25 to 75 pounds of powder, contained in a flattened or oval tin cannister, with the edges unsoldered and closed at the ends by paper or cloth. This is placed in the hole in such a position that a plane pass-ing through its edges is in line with the desired break, and fired. In this way large blocks are freed from the quarry, and these are then broken to any required size, as follows : The workmen first cut with a pick a sharp groove some 4 to 8 inches deep along the full length of the line where it is desired the stone shall break. Into this groove are placed, at intervals of a few inches, large iron wedges, which are then in turn struck repeated blows by heavy sledge-hammers in the hands of the quarrymen until the rock falls apart. This process will be made plain by reference to Plate IX. In some of the quarries of softer sandstone no machines at all are used, the channelling being done entirely by hand-chisels or with picks, and the stone forced out by means of iron bars alone, or split out with plug and feather. To allow of this, however, the stone must be evenly and thinly bedded, and the different sheets adhere to one another with but slight tenacity, as is the case with certain of the New York " bluestones " and Berea grits of Ohio. In the New York quarries the vertical joints are said to be so

PLATE IX.

SPLITTING OUT STONE WITH WEDGES, PORTLAND, CONNECTICUT.

To face page 350.

numerous as to practically do away with the necessity of channelling.

Powder is still largely used in most of the smaller quarries, and in all those of granitic rock for throwing off large masses. If properly used with these harder varieties, it is doubtful if any serious harm results, but in the quarrying of marble and other soft stones, its use can not be too strongly condemned. It has been suggested that the rapid disintegration of the Carrara marble is caused in part by the incipient fractures induced through the crude methods of quarrying employed. Excepting when, as in the case of granite, no other means can be employed, explosives of all kinds are to be avoided. When necessary, they should be used in a lewis hole, whereby direction may be given to the force of the discharge and the shock distributed over large surfaces.

(5) CUTTING AND DRESSING STONE.

In cutting and dressing stone the same slow hand processes that were in vogue hundreds of years ago are still largely employed. There have been, it is true, many machines invented for this purpose, but the majority of them are far from satisfactory in their working qualities, or the cost of running them is so great that they can be used only by the larger and wealthier firms. After a large mass has been split from the quarry bed it is broken into blocks of the required size and shape by means of wedges. A series of holes, three-fourths of an inch in diameter and a few inches deep, is drilled along the line where it is desired the stone shall break, and into each of these two thin half round pieces of soft iron called "feathers" are placed, and a small steel wedge or "plug" placed between. The quarryman then moves along this line striking with his hammer each wedge in its turn till the desired strain is produced and the stone falls apart.

There is a chance for a greater display of skill in this work than may at first appear. Nearly every stone, however compact, has a distinct grain and rift, along which it can be relied

FIG. 7.—DRILLING HOLES FOR SPLITTING STONE WITH PLUG AND FEATHERS.

on to split with comparative ease and safety. To know the rift and be able to take proper advantage of it is an important item, and it is astonishing how readily an experienced workman will cause a stone to take the desired shape through a knowledge of this property.

This process of splitting stone with wedges is said * to have been first brought into general use in this country by a poor mechanic named Tarbox, of Danvers, Massachusetts. Through the influence of Governor Robbins, who stumbled upon samples of his work by the merest accident, this man was induced in 1798 to go to Quincy and teach his art to the quarrymen of that place. So much did the adoption of this simple method facilitate granite-working that the price of the cut material dropped within the space of a few months over 60 per cent. Prior to this time the stone after being blasted from the quarry in irregular blocks was squarred down to the proper size by cutting a groove along a straight line with a sharp-edged tool called an axhammer, and then striking with a heavy hammer repeated blows on both sides of the groove until the rock was broken asunder.†

---

* Proceedings American Academy, vol. IV. 1859, p. 353.

† In Pattee's History of Old Braintree and Quincy occurs this passage : " On Sunday, 1803, the first experiment in splitting stone with wedges was made by Josiah Bemis, George Stearns, and Michael Wilde. It proved successful, and so elated were these gentlemen on this memorable Sunday that they adjourned to Newcomb's hotel, where they partook of a sumptuous feast. The wedges used in this experiment were flat, and differed somewhat from those now in use. "

As to who can justly claim to be the first to bring this method of splitting into general use the author has no means of ascertaining. That none of the above can justly claim to have *invented* the process is evident from the following :

" I told thee that I had been informed that the grindstones and millstones were split with wooden pegs drove in, but I did not say that those rocks about this house could be split after that manner, but that I could split them, and had been used to split rocks to make steps, door-sills, and large window cases all of stone, and pig-troughs and water-troughs. I have split rocks 17 feet long and built four houses of hewn stone, split out of the rocks with my own hands. My method is to bore the rock about 6 inches deep, having drawn a line from one end to the other, in which I bore holes about a foot asunder, more or less, according to the freeness of the rock ; if it be 3 or 4 or 5 feet thick, 10, 12, or

This method is said to have been introduced into Quincy
somewhere about 1725-'50, by German emigrants, and, crude

16 inches deep. The hole should be an inch and a quarter diameter if the rock
be 2 feet thick, but if it be 5 or 6 feet thick the holes should be an inch and
three-quarters diameter. There must be provided twice as many iron wedges
as holes, and one-half of them must ·be fully as long as the hole is deep and
made round at one end, just fit to drop into the hole, and the other half may be
made a little longer, and thicker one way, and blunt pointed. All the holes must
have their wedges drove together, one after another, gently, that they may
strain all alike. You may hear by their ringing when they strain well. Then
with the sharp edge of the sledge strike hard on the rock in the line between
every wedge, which will crack the rock ; then drive the wedges again. It generally opens in a few minutes after the wedges are drove tight. Then, with an
iron bar or long levers, raise them up and lay the two pieces flat and bore and
split them in what shape and dimensions you please. If the rock is anything
free you may split them as true almost as sawn timber, and by this method you
may split almost any rock, for you may add almost any power you please by
boring the holes deeper and closer together."

(From letter of John Bartram to Jared Elliot, dated January 24, 1757. See
Darlington's Memorandum of Bartram and Marshall, p. 375.) The precise date
at which these four stone houses were built is not stated, but the work above
quoted contains an illustration of John Bartram's house, near Darby, Delaware
County, Pa. This house, which is of stone, was erected about 1730. Hence
we must conclude that the art of splitting stone in this manner was known to
some at least as early as this date.

It is stated (Grueber, Die Baumaterialien-Lehre, pp. 60, 61) that in Finland,
even at the present day, granite is split from the quarry-bed through the expansive force of ice. A series of holes, from a foot to 15 inches apart and from 2
to 3 feet deep, according to the size of the block to be loosened, is driven along
the line of desired rift after the usual custom. These holes are then filled with
water and tightly plugged. The operation is put off until late in the season and
until the approach of a frost. The water in the holes then freezes, and by its
expansion fractures the rock in the direction of the line of holes. Blocks of 400
tons weight are stated to be broken out in this way. A more ancient method
consisted in simply plugging the holes with dry wooden wedges and then
thoroughly saturating them with water, the swelling wood acting in the same
way as the freezing water. Another ancient and well-known method consisted
in building a fire around the stone, and when it was thoroughly heated striking
it with heavy hammers or throwing cold water upon it. In splitting stone the

as it may seem, was a vast improvement over that used in pre-pairing stone for the construction of King's Chapel, erected in 1749-'54, on the corner of School and Tremont streets, Boston. Here we are told the stone was first heated by building a fire around it, and then broken by means of heavy iron balls let fall from a considerable height. With such difficulties as these to contend with it is not surprising that the building should have been considered a wonder when completed, and that people coming to Boston from a distance made it a point to see and admire the structure. The wonder, however, was not that the granite could be broken into shape by such methods, but "that stone enough could be found in the vicinity of Boston fit for the hammer to construct such an entire building. But it seemed to be universally conceded that enough more like it could not be found to build such another."

After a block is broken from the quarry bed it is trimmed to the desired size and shape by means of a variety of imple-ments, according to the hardness of the stone and the charac-ter of the desired finish.

In dressing granite and other hard stone the tools ordinarily

ancient Romans are said to have sprinkled the hot stone with vinegar, though whether they thereby accelerated the splitting or caused the stone to break along definite lines is not known. Quartz rocks, it is stated, can be made to split in definite directions by wetting them while hot, or laying a wet cord along the line it is desired they shall cleave. The wet line gives rise to a small crack, and the operation is completed by striking heavy blows with wooden mallets. According to M. Raimondi, the ancient Peruvians split up the stone in the quar-ry by first heating it with burning straw and then throwing cold water upon it. To carve the stone and obtain a bas-relief, this writer contends that the work-men covered with ashes the lines of the designs which they intended to have in relief, and then heated the whole surface. The parts of the stone which were submitted immediately to the action of fire became decomposed to a greater or less depth, while the designs, protected by ashes, remained intact. To com-plete the work the sculptor had but to carve out the decomposed rock with his copper chisel.

used are the set or pitching chisel, the spalling hammer, pean hammer, bush hammer, hand hammer, chisel, and point. With the set the rough block is trimmed down to a line. Then the irregular surface is worked down by the point, which is driven by the hand hammer. After pointing, are used the pean and the patent or bush hammers in turn, beginning with the 4-cut, and thence working down with the 6-cut, 8-cut, 10-cut, and 12-cut, or until the desired surface is obtained. The condition of the hammered surface at the completion of one of the hammerings should be such that each cut in the hammer traces a line its full length on the stone at each blow.

The single cut or pean hammer should leave no unevenness exceeding one-eighth of an inch, and each finer cut reduces the unevenness left by the preceding. The 12-cut should leave no irregularities upon the surface of the stone other than the indentations made by the impinging of the plates in the hammer. The lines of the cut are made so as to be vertical in exposed vertical faces when the block is in position. On horizontal and unexposed faces they are cut straight across in any convenient direction. With sawn surfaces of course much of the preliminary work is done away with, as the surface is already sufficiently smooth. It is at present customary to saw only such stone as are designed for polishing or some kind of smooth finish.

In preparing a stone for polishing, the surface is first made smooth as possible by sawing or by the means above designated. It is then further reduced by means of wet sand and emery of varing degrees of fineness. Small blocks are now usually ground on a revolving iron bed, on which the abrading material is shovelled and kept wet by a stream of water from overhead. With larger blocks a slab of stone is drawn by the workmen back and forth across the surface on which the wet sand has already been placed. On the finer grades of white marble emery is not used, as it stains; fortunately, owing to the softness of these stones, it is readily dispensed with. After being ground, the surface is rubbed by a sharp, evenly gritted sandstone called a hone, and then with pumice-stone.

On granites it is often customary to give a " skin coat " by rubbing the block, after the final emerying, on the smooth, wet grinding bed, without any abrading material, until a perfectly smooth surface and dull polish is obtained. When this point is reached—and the surface must be quite free from scratches and blemishes, or a good polish is impossible—the polish is produced by means of polishing putty (oxide of tin) rubbed on with wet felt. In cheap work it is customary to use oxalic acid in connection with or entirely in place of the polishing putty. This enables the production of a polish with less labor, but it is also less durable.

A high grade of polish can only be produced by skilled workmen, and each one has his own peculiar methods, varying in trifling particulars from that given above. In many of the larger works where steam power is used, it is said to be customary to mix a quantity of very finely ground metallic lead with the putty. By this means a higher gloss is produced, and also one that is very durable. All the larger works now use machinery in both grinding and polishing. Descriptions of these will be given in the following chapter.

Sundry attempts have been made to utilize the sand-blast process, so extensively used in glasswork, for carving on stone; but so far, with few exceptions, these attempts have met with but poor success. In 1875-'76, Messrs. Sheldon & Slason, of West Rutland, having a large Government contract in preparing head-stones for soldiers' graves in National cemeteries, introduced the system with considerable success. The process consisted in covering those parts of the stone to be left uncut with an iron shield, while letters and figures of chilled iron were placed upon those portions which were to stand out in relief. The blast then being directed against the stone cuts away very quickly the unprotected parts. By this means the name, company, regiment, and rank of soldiers, could be cut on a stone in less than five minutes, and two hundred and fifty four thousand stones thus lettered and having dimensions of 3 feet in length, 10 inches in width, and 4 inches in thickness, were placed in the national cemeteries at a cost of but $864,000. The sandblast process has also been used with good results on the hard red quartzite of Sioux Falls, as will be noted later.

(6) QUARRYING AND SPLITTING SLATE.

In quarrying slate the methods vary greatly according to the disposition of the beds, and no attempt will be made here at a detailed description. Ordinary blasting powder is employed in loosening the blocks, and great skill and sagacity is shown by experienced quarry-men in so manipulating the blast as to produce the desired effects of freeing the rock from the quarry-bed without shattering the stone. After a block is removed from the quarry it is subject to special treatment according to the purpose to which the stone is to be put. If for roofing-slate, the block is taken from the quarry to the splitters' shanty, where it is taken in charge by a splitter and his two assistants. The first assistant takes the block and reduces it to pieces about 2 inches in thickness, and of a length and breadth a little greater than those of the slates to be made. This is done by a process called "sculping," which is as follows : A notch is cut in one end of the block with the sculping chisel, and the edge of this notch is trimmed out with a gouge to a smooth groove extending across the end of the block and perpendicular to the upper and lower surfaces ; the sculping chisel is then set into this groove and driven with a mallet until a cleft starts, which by careful manipulation is guided directly across the block. The upper surface of the block is kept wet with water so that the crack may be more readily seen. If the slate is perfectly uniform in shape and texture, and the blows upon the sculping chisel are directed straight with the grain, the crack follows the grain in a straight

Fig. 8.

line across the block. Almost invariably, however, the crack deviates to the right or left, when it must be brought back by directing the blow on the sculp in the direction in which it is desired to turn the break, or by striking with a heavy mallet on that side of the block toward which it is desired the crack shall turn. Some slates can be sculped across the grain, but nearly all must be broken in this direction. From the first assistant or "sculper," the block goes to the splitter who by means of a mallet and broad thin chisel splits it through the middle, continuing to thus divide each piece into halves until the desired thinness is obtained. It is necessary to keep the edges of the blocks moist from the time they are removed from the quarry until they are split. From the splitter the thin but irregularly shaped pieces pass to the second assistant who trims them into definite sizes and rectangular shapes. This is done either by hand or by machine. To trim by hand a straight edged strip of iron or steel is fastened horizontally upon one of the upper edges of a rectangular block of wood some 2 to 4 feet in length. The trimmer then lays the sheet of slate upon the block allowing the edge to be trimmed to project over this strip, and then by means of a long heavy knife with a bent handle cuts off the overlying edge, thus reducing it to the required size and shape. Two kinds of machines for doing this work are now in use. In general they may be said to consist of an iron frame-work some $2\frac{1}{2}$ feet high, with a horizontal knife-edge upon its upper edge. Against this knife is made to work by means of a treadle another knife, curved in out-line, which is thrown upward again by means of a spring, after being brought down by the treadle-movement. At right angles to this knife-edge, on one side of the machine, an iron arm projects toward the workman; this arm has notches cut into it for the different sizes of the slate. The difference between the two kinds of machines is said to consist chiefly in the arrangement of the cutting-knife, one working as stated above, while the other revolves on an axle something in the manner of an ordinary corn cutter. See Fig. 8.

Slates are sawn by means of an ordinary circular saw, such as is used in sawing lumber, and are planed by machines such as are used in planing metals, as are other soft stone. Some of the hard slates used for tiling have to be cut by means of circular saws with teeth of black diamond.*

In trimming out school slates at the Pennsylvania quarries

---

* Detailed and very closely resembling accounts of the methods of working slate are given by F. W. Sperr, in Report Tenth Census, vol. x, pp. 38–42, and E. Prime, Jr., Report D 3, vol. i, pp. 138-143, 2d Geology Survey, Pennsylvania. To these the reader is respectfully referred.

PLATE X.

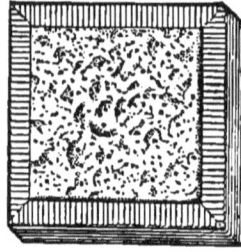

1

2

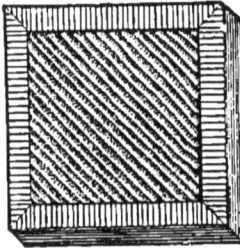
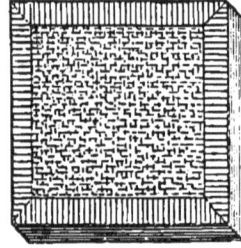

3

4

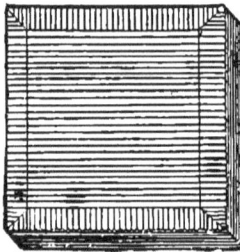
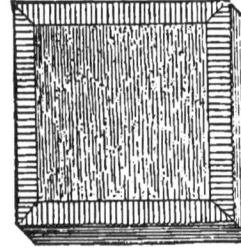

5

6

KINDS OF FINISH.

Fig. 1. Rockface.   Fig. 4. Toothed chiseled.
Fig. 2 and 3. Pointed face   Fig. 5. Square drove.
              Fig. 6. Patent hammered.

To face page 333.

there is used a square saw of chilled iron some ten or twelve inches in diameter and with one long projecting tooth at each of its four corners. This revolves with great rapidity and clips off the thin edges as quickly and neatly as could be desired.

(7) KINDS OF FINISH.

The more common kinds of finish applied to stone are described below; the figures on Plate x. being drawn from samples in the National collections at Washington.

(1) *Rock face.*—This is the natural face of the rock as broken from the quarry, or but slightly trimmed down by the pitching tool. As in this and all the figures given, it is frequently surrounded by a margin of drove work.

(2) *Pointed face.*—In this finish the natural face of the rock has been trimmed down by means of the sharp-pointed tool called a point. It is used principally for exterior work, as in the walls of a building. Two common styles of pointing are shown.

(3) *Ax-hammered face.*—This finish is produced by striking upon the surface repeated blows with a sharp-faced implement called an ax or pean hammer. It closely resembles the next, but is coarser. Used in steps, house trimmings, and other exterior work.

(4) *Patent hammered.*—This finish is produced by striking repeated blows upon the smooth surface of the rock with the rough-faced implement called a patent hammer. Five grades of fineness are commonly recognized, the 4-cut, 6-cut, 8-cut, 10-cut, and 12-cut surfaces, made by hammers composed of four, six, eight, ten, and twelve plates, respectively. A very common finish for the finer kinds of exterior work.

(5) *Bush hammered.*—This finish resembles closely the tooth

chiseled or very fine pointing. It is used mostly on soft stone. (See descriptions of bush and patent hammers on p. 348).

(6) *Square drove.*—The square drove surface is made with a wide steel chisel with a smooth edge, called a drove. It is quite common to use this style of finish as a border to the rock-face or pointed surfaces in many kinds of exterior work.

(7) *Tooth chiselled.*—This finish is produced by means of a wide steel chisel with an edge toothed like that of a saw. This and the square drove are used principally upon limestones, marbles, and sandstones, the granites being too hard to cut in this manner.

(8) *Sawed face.*—This is the surface of the rock as left by the saw ; the saw used for the purpose being a thin, smooth blade of soft iron, fed with sharp sand or chilled iron. This and the following styles, although possessing distinctive characteristics easily recognizable by the eye, are of such a nature that their likenesses cannot be well reproduced on paper. Hence no attempt at illustration has been made.

(9) *Fine sand finish.*—To produce this finish the chiselled or sawn surface is rubbed smooth by means of a block of stone and fine wet sand, or on the machines yet to be described.

(10) *Pumice finish.*—This is a very smooth but unpolished surface produced by smooth rubbing with pumice or Scotch hone.

(11) *Polished surface.*—Two kinds of polished surfaces are made—the acid gloss and the putty gloss. For either the surface of the stone is made as smooth as possible by means of sand, or emery, and pumice, or hone, after which it is rubbed with moist woollen cloth and oxalic acid, or polishing putty. The latter produces the best and most lasting gloss, but re-

quires more labor. Frequently the two methods are combined. especially in tombstone work.

MACHINES AND IMPLEMENTS USED IN STONE-WORKING.

(I) DRILLS AND DRILLING MACHINES.

Of the many machines that have from time to time been in-vented for working stone we can here mention only the principal ones that are to-day in actual use.

Drills. — The old time method of drilling by means of a flat pointed drill called a jumper,* which is held by one workman while others strike upon it alternate blows with heavy hammers, al-though still in use at many quarries, has been largely superseded by steam-drills of various kinds. A simple form of the steam-drill, and one now in very general use, is that shown in the accom-panying figure. The drill

FIG. 9.—ECLIPSE ROCK DRILL.

proper is fastened directly to the piston, which can be inclined

---

* In English quarries the name jumper is given to a hand drill some four and a half to five and a half feet long and with an iron ball welded to the middle of the rod. In using it the workman places one hand under the ball or the knob, and with the other grasps the rod about half way between the knob and

at any angle, thus fitting it for ordinary quarrying or for tun-
nelling. It is driven either by steam or by compressed air. A
different adaptation of the same principle is employed in the
channelling and gadding machines used in getting out dimension stone. Figures of these are also here given. The drill
and cylinder are attached to the horizontal bar by means of a
clamp, which can be loosened or tightened at will. By this
means a dozen or more holes can be cut by simply sliding the
drill along the bar and without moving the entire machine.

(2) CHANNELLING MACHINES.

The channelling machine shown on page 321 was invented
by George J. Wardwell of
Rutland, Vermont. The first
successful machine being
built by him in 1863.

As may be seen, the
channeller is essentially a
locomotive machine driven
by power, usually steam,
moving over a steel-rail track
which is placed on the quarry
bed. It carries a single gang-
drill on one side, or two
such drills—one on each

FIG. 10.—IMPROVED QUARRY BAR.

side. These are raised and dropped by a lever and crank ar-

the upper end. Then standing upright on the block of stone he lifts the jumper
allowing it to fall again of its own weight repeatedly upon the spot where the
hole is to be made. It is mainly used in drilling small holes for plug and
feather splitting. (Harris' Granite and our Granite Industries, p. 117.)

rangement. The gang of cutters forming the drill is composed of five steel bars, 7 to 14 feet in length, sharpened at the end and securely clamped together. Of the five cutters, two have diagonal edges; the other three their edges transverse. The centre of the middle largest extends lowest, so that the five form something like a stepped arrangement, away from the centre. The drill, lifted, drops with great force and rapidly creases a channel into the rock. The single gang machine is operated by two men, the double by three. As it runs backward and forward over the rock the machine is reversed without stopping, and as it goes the cutters deliver their strokes, it is claimed, at the rate of one hundred and fifty per minute. The machine feeds forward on the track half an inch at each stroke, cutting half an inch or more every time of passing. The single machine will cut from 40 to 80 square feet of channel per day in marble or limestone and at a cost of from 5 to 20 cents per square foot.

FIG. II.—SAUNDERS CHANNELLING MACHINE WITH BOILER ATTACHED.

The double machine will do twice the amount of work. A good workman by the old hand process would formerly cut from 5 to 10 feet; that is, a groove one foot deep and from 5 to 10 feet long per day. For this he would receive from 25 to 30 cents per foot.*

Another machine for doing the same work as that just described is the Saunders channelling machine shown in the illustration (Figs. 11 and 12), and which has recently come into use in the Vermont quarries. This differs from the Wardwell in several important particulars, prominent among which are these : (1) The cutting tool is attached rigidly to the piston, so that the blow is dealt directly by the steam pressure in the cylinder and without the intervention of any cranks, levers, or springs. (2) The cutting tools are made adjustable at any angle—to the right, left, forward, or backward. The machine is thus capable of making transverse and sidehill cuts, and does what is known as "cutting out the corners" in quarrying: and (3) it can be used in chambers where the distance between the floor and roof is but six feet and can be used in tunnels and headings.

FIG. 12.—SAUNDERS CHANNELLING MACHINE MAKING SIDEHILL CUTS—BOILERS DETACHED.

The machine carries five drills in the gang, with three

---

*The Marble Border of Western New England, p. 44.

straight points and two diagonal ones.   These are arranged as seen in the accompanying cut :

' The average capacity of the machine, as claimed by the company's circular, is as follows :

In marble, 80 to 100 square feet of channel in ten hours.

In sandstone, 150 to 200 square feet of channel in ten hours.

In limestone, 120 to 150 square feet of channel in ten hours.

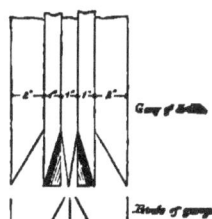

FIG. 13.

The diamond channelling machine is shown in the figure on page 340.   According to the company's circular this machine employs $1\frac{3}{4}$ inch drill-bits, which are attached to drill-rods of varying lengths, adapted to any required depth of channel up to $9\frac{1}{2}$ feet.   The channel may be made open or partly closed, the latter by leaving slight spaces between the holes, to be afterward chipped out.   But the whole operation of a clear cut is made simultaneously with the boring by means of an intercutting guide, which answers this purpose very well.   The drill can be made to vary in direction from perpendicular to 50 degrees slant for putting down the tunnel and angle cuts.   If necessary the boiler can be left at a distance from the machine, the steam being conveyed by hose.

(3) GADDING AND GADDING MACHINES.

The diamond gadder is shown on page 341. According to the company's circular the machine takes its name from the class of work for which it was especially designed and which is known among quarriers as gadding. When the requisite channel cuts are made about a block of marble to be removed, it is necessary to undercut the block in order to release it. This is usually accomplished by drilling a series of holes beneath it, and then, by wedges, the block is split from its bed.

FIG. 14.—DIAMOND CHANNELLING MACHINE.

The machine is placed upon a platform on trucks arranged to run upon a track. When adjusted for work it may be braced by the pointed legs shown. The boring apparatus is attached by a swivel to a perpendicular guide - bar. This guide-bar is secured to the boiler behind it, which forms the main support of the machine. Upon the guide-bar the boring apparatus may be raised or lowered at pleasure, for the purpose of boring a series of holes in a perpendicular line if desired. Upon the swivel the boring apparatus may be turned, so as to bore in any direction within the plane of the swivel-plate.

The illustration shows the drill-rod or spindle placed near the base of the machine, and so as to bore horizontally. At one end of the spindle is the drill - head, armed with carbons, and supplied with small apertures or outlets for water. At the other end of the spindle is attached a hose for supplying water to the drill-head. A rapid revolving movement is communicated to the drill-spindle by the gears shown. The speed and feed movement may be regulated by the operator with reference to the hardness or softness,

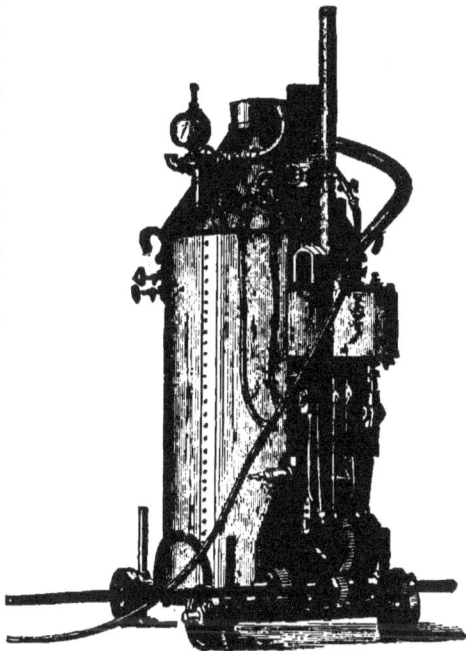

FIG. 15.—DIAMOND GADDER.

coarseness or fineness, of the material to be bored ; and the feed movement may be instantly reversed at pleasure. The machine is so constructed that the drill-spindle may be removed and another inserted in the same holder, adjusted to bore in the opposite direction, the boring apparatus being

driven by a double-cylinder engine. A continuation of one
of the piston-rods through the cylinder forms the plunger to

FIG. 16.—INGERSOL STANDARD GADDER
AT WORK.

a small pump placed above
the cylinder, which supplies
water to the boiler and also
forces it through the drill-
spindle and head. These jets
of water wash out all the
borings made, and keep the
drill-head from heating. The
usual feed of this drill in
marble is from 4 to 5 inches
per minute.

Still another style of gad-
ding-machine is used in the
Vermont quarries, and which
is but an especial adaptation
of the eclipse-drill shown on
page 335. It is claimed that
this machine will "put in
holes close to the bottom of
the quarry, in a horizontal position along the bench, into the
roof, or perpendicularly into the floor, as desired."

(4) GRINDING AND POLISHING MACHINES.

In the larger works the grinding and polishing already
described is now done by steam power. For flat surfaces a
circular horizontally revolving iron plate or grating, attached
to the lower end of a vertical shaft, with elbow joint, is used,
the workman guiding it to any portion of the surface he may
desire by means of the handle; the abrading substance being

sand or emery, as before. With felt attached to the plate the same form of machine is also used for polishing. Blocks of such size as can be handled by the workmen are usually ground upon horizontally revolving iron beds some 8 or 10 feet in diameter.

In making straight or only slightly-curved moldings the form is first carved out with the chisel, and then a plate of cast iron, fitted as accurately as possible, is made by means of a long arm, to travel back and forth over the stone with sand or emery, or putty powder and felt, as the case may be. These are called pendulum ma-chines. The actual labor is

FIG. 17.—PLAIN QUARRY FRAME IN POSITION FOR UNDERCUTTING OR GADDING.

thus greatly reduced, and a higher and more lasting polish obtained than is possible by the old hand methods.

(5) LATHES AND PLANERS.

For turning posts and pillars lathes are now very generally used for granite as well as for softer stone. In easy working varieties, as sandstone, limestone, or serpentine, the cutting tool is a simple chisel, much like that used in turning metals, and held in a clamp in the same manner. With the harder rocks, like the granites, however, this method is ineffectual, and the cutting tool is in the form of a thin steel disk some 6 or 8 inches in diameter, which is so arranged as to revolve with the stone in the lathe when pressed against it at a sharp angle. By this means large and beautiful columns can be made at far less cost than by the old hand-processes. A monster machine of this character, seen by the writer in the Vinalhaven quarries in 1880, is capable of taking a block 25 feet in length and 5 feet in diameter and turning it down to a perfect column.

With the softer varieties of stone a plain surface, sufficiently smooth for flagging, is produced by means of planing machines similar to those in use for planing metals. For doing the same work on hard material like granite a planer, with revolving cutting disks of chilled iron, similar to those used in the lathes, has been devised. This machine is shown in the accompanying figure, page 346.

(6) MACHINES FOR SAWING.

In sawing marble and other soft stones the same method, with some modifications, is employed as was in use, according to Professor Seely,* three hundred years before the Christian era.

The principle consists simply of a smooth flat blade of soft iron, set in a frame and fed with sharp sand and water. The saws are now frequently set in gangs of a dozen or more in a single frame, and several gangs are tended by one man, who shovels on the wet sand as it is needed, while fine streams of water from overhead wash it beneath the blade as it swings backward and forward in its slowly deepening groove. Some attempts at automatic feeders have been made, but they are not as yet in general use.

This method has been found inapplicable to cutting granite, owing to the greater hardness of the material. Recently a

---

* The Marble Border of Western New England. Proceedings Middlebury Historical Society, vol. I. part II. p. 28.

sand composed of globules of chilled iron has been used to good advantage, and still more recently crushed steel. The great drawback to the use of these materials, so far as the author has observed, is the care necessary to avoid staining the stone by rust from the wet metal during the time the machine is not running. This is done by wetting down the stone in the saw frame with a thick solution of lime-water (whitewash) prior to leaving the saws for the night. Circular saws, with diamond teeth, have been used to some extent, but have been found too expensive for ordinary work. In sawing slate circular saws are used, such as are employed in sawing lumber. Philo Tomlinson, who was engaged in marble sawing at Marbledale, Connecticut, near the date 1800, is stated by Professor Seely* to have been one of the first to successfully apply the gang-saw system in this country.

For sawing circular apertures in the tops of wash-stands or getting out tops for small tables a saw made of plates of soft iron bent in the form of a cylinder and revolved by a vertical shaft is used. Sand, emery, or globules of chilled iron form the cutting material, as in the saws just mentioned.

A recent European invention for sawing stone consists of a twisted cord of steel made to run around pulleys like a band-saw. The cord is composed of three steel wires, loosely twisted together, but stretched tightly over the pulleys, and is made to run at a high rate of speed. The swift successive blows from the ridges of the cord, delivered along the narrow line, disintegrates the stone much more rapidly, it is claimed, than the iron blades fed with sand, the usual rate of cutting in blocks of soft limestone being about 24 inches an hour, and in Carrara marble a little more than 9 inches an hour. Brittany granite is cut at the rate of nearly

---

* *Op. cit.* p. 29.

1¼ inches an hour, and even porphyry can be worked at the rate of eight-tenths of an inch an hour. In certain Belgian marble quarries the saw is said to have been used to advantage in cutting the rock from the quarry bed. In thus utilizing it the floor is first cleared as for channelling machines, and then, by means of large cylindrical drills, fed with metallic sand, a shaft 27 inches in diameter is cut to the desired depth, the cores being removed entire, as in the common tubular diamond drills. Two of these holes are sunk at proper distances apart and guides set up in them, on which move frames carrying pulleys of a diameter somewhat less than that of the holes; over these pulleys the cord saw is stretched; motion is then imparted to the pulleys by a simple system of transmission, and the saws cut without interruption until the bottom of the drill-pit or shaft is reached. A great saving of time and material is claimed for this invention, but although it seems to promise well it is not at present

FIG. 18.—McDONALD STONE CUTTING MACHINE.

in use in this country, nor has the author ever had opportunity for examining it.*

(7) THE·SAND BLAST.

As already noted, the sand blast has been utilized to some
extent in the work of lettering head-stones, and for producing
delicate tracings on the Sioux Falls quartzite. That the process is still so little used is due, as I am informed, to the oppo-
sition of trades-unions, and not to any deficiency of adaptability in the process itself.

(8) HAND IMPLEMENTS.

Face Hammer.—This is a heavy square-faced hammer,
weighing from 15 to 25 pounds, and used for roughly shaping
the blocks as they come from the quarry. It is sometimes
made with both faces alike or again with one face flat and the
other drawn out into a cutting edge (Fig. 10, Pl. XI.) The cavil
differs only in having one face drawn out into a pyramidal
point.

Ax or pean hammer.—A hammer made with two opposite
cutting edges, as seen in Fig. 13, Pl. XI. The edges are sometimes toothed roughly, when it is called the toothed ax.

Patent or bush hammer.—A hammer made of four, six,
eight, ten, or more thin blades of steel, bolted together so as to
form a single piece, the striking faces of which are deeply and
sharply grooved. This hammer is said to have been invented
by Mr. Joseph Richards, of Quincy, Massachusetts, about

---

* This apparatus was figured and described in the Scientific American for
March 6, 1886, p. 147. A more detailed description, fully illustrated, has since
appeared in Stone (Indianapolis, Indiana), Sept., 1889.

1831–'40. As first constructed the head was composed ot a single piece, instead of several, as now (see Fig. 12, Pl. XI). In some works this is called the bush hammer.

Crandall.—This consists of a bar of malleable iron, about 2 feet in length, and slightly flattened at one end, through which is a slot three-eighths of an inch wide and 3 inches long. Through this slot are passed ten double-headed points of one-fourth inch square steel, 9 inches long, which are held in place by a key. The writer has never seen this instrument in use.

Hand hammer.—A smooth-faced hammer, with two striking faces, weighing from 2 to 5 pounds. It is used for hand-drilling, pointing, and chiselling in the harder kinds of rocks (see Fig. 16, Pl. XI). The usual form has both faces alike.

Mallet.—This is a wooden implement, with a cylindrical head, used in place of the hammer in cutting the softer stones, as marbles and sandstones (Fig. 15, Pl. XI).

Sledge or striking hammer.—A heavy, smooth-faced hammer, weighing from 10 to 25 pounds, used in striking the drills in hand-drilling or in driving large wedges for splitting stone, Fig. 11, Pl. XI.

Pick.—An instrument resembling the ordinary pickax used in digging, but somewhat shorter and stouter. It is used on the softer varieties of stones, for rough dressing or for channelling prior to wedging.

Pitching chisel.—A steel chisel, the cutting face of which is rectangular in outline and with sharp angles or corners. It is used for trimming down the edges to a straight line. See Fig. 7, Pl. XI. The chipper (Fig. 6) is used for very similar purposes.

Chisel or drove.—This is a steel chisel, the cutting edge of which is drawn out wide and thin as shown in Fig. 2, Pl. XI. It

PLATE XI.

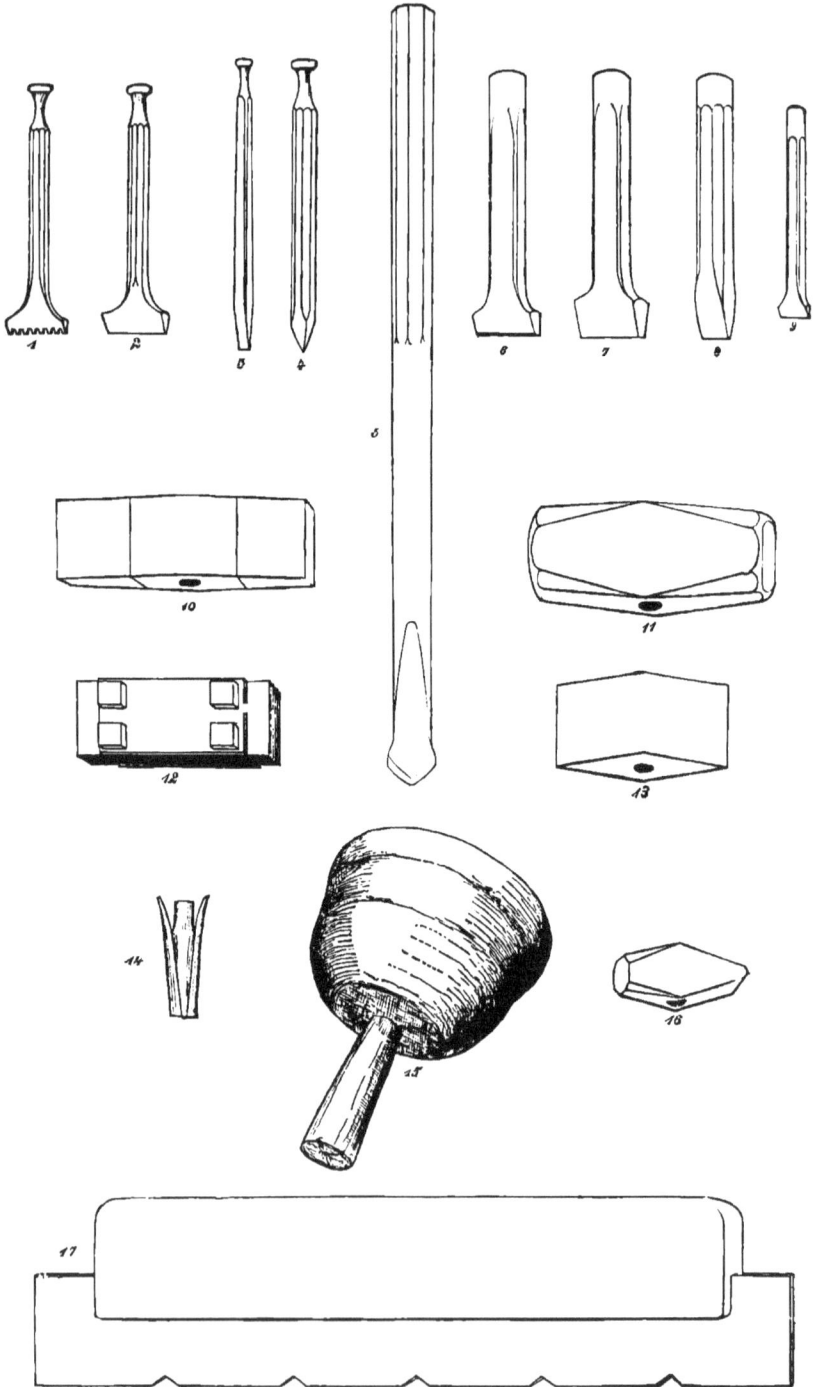

HAND IMPLEMENTS USED IN STONE WORKING.

is used principally on the softer varieties of rock in producing the so-called " drove-work."

Splitting chisel.—A steel chisel, made as shown in Fig. 8, Pl. XI, and used for splitting and general cutting on hard stone like granite. Other forms of chisels, used only on soft stone and driven with the wooden mallet, are shown in Figs. 3 and 9.

Tooth chisel.—A chisel like the drove chisel, but with the edge toothed like a saw (see Fig. 1, Pl. XI), used only on soft stones like marble and sandstones.

Point.—A steel implement, with the cutting end in the form of a pyramidal point (see Fig. 4, Pl. XI), used in the production of the finish known as point work and also in the smoothing down of rough surfaces prior to using the ax or some other tool for fine work. Points for use on hard stone and driven by the hammer have the upper end finished as shown in Figs. 6 and 7.

Wedge or plug.—Steel wedges vary greatly in size. Those used in the process of splitting, called plug and feather (Fig. 14, Pl. XI), are but two or 3 inches in length, while those used in quarrying for splitting off large blocks are often a foot or more long and correspondingly large.

Hand drill.—A small steel drill from 8 to 15 inches in length, held in one hand and driven by the hand-hammer (Fig. 5), used in making holes for " plug and feather " splitting and other light work.

Grub saw.—A saw for cutting stone by hand. It consists of a plate of soft iron from one-twentieth to one-tenth of an inch in thickness and from 6 inches to 4 feet in length ; the blade is notched on the lower edge and fitted with a wooden back for convenience in handling and to prevent bending. Sand or emery is the cutting material, as with the steam saws (Fig. 17, Pl. XI).

THE WEATHERING OF BUILDING STONE.

That all stone are not equally well adapted for the various kinds of structural purposes must be apparent to the most casual observer. Not merely is there a wide difference in durability among stones of various kinds, but materials well adapted for some situations may, owing to an inherent weakness prove quite unfit for use where climatic or other conditions are such as to render injuriously conspicuous defects wholly unapparent under more favorable circumstances. Stones, as a whole, do not possess the firm and unchangeable characteristics commonly attributed to them by the popular mind. There is perhaps as wide a variation in lasting qualities as among woods, mortars and cements.

It is true that the various detrimental changes which may take place are often the product of years of exposure, but this is no excuse for the ignoring of such a possibility. He who designs or constructs a house builds not for himself alone, but for the entire community and for future as well as present generations.

Whatever he may do with the interior is to a certain extent his own affair, but not so with the exterior. The construction of a dwelling, business block, public building or monument, is a matter in which each individual citizen has a perfect right to have an active interest, since the structure once erected becomes for a time a fixed feature of the landscape and an object by which not merely the taste and abilities of the architect and builder are to be judged, but that of the community as well.

The external features of the structure are constantly before the public and must exercise some influence either beneficial or derogatory upon public taste. It behooves the builder therefore, quite aside from all economic considerations, to select for his purpose such material as shall be most harmonious in the finished structure, and possess as well such qualities as shall be enabled to withstand the ravages of time without serious injury.

There are few things more conspicuously unsightly than a rich and elaborate building constructed from materials which under the ordinary chemical and physical agencies of the atmosphere have become discolored or disintegrated. Yet our cities and towns are replete with illustrations of such lack of forethought or of ignorance on the part of builders.

One of America's greatest architects has designed a structure of more than ordinary merit, but in which the walls are of massive granite, while the window stools, caps, cornices and projections in general, which of all parts of the structure are most liable to injury from disintegration, are of a soft and friable sandstone. The items of color and cost alone were apparently here considered. The Executive Mansion and portions of the Patent Office and Capitol buildings in Washington are of a sandstone so poor in enduring qualities that it has been found necessary to paint them periodically in order to keep them in a condition anyway presentable.

The gigantic pile designed as a monument to the Father of his Country and which stands upon the banks of the Potomac in this same city is, so far as quality of material is concerned, not merely wrong side out, but wrong end up, as well. The best and most enduring material in the entire structure lies in the inner courses of the upper portion. The poorest and weakest is comprised in the outer portion of the first 150 feet measured from the ground up, where it has to bear the weight of the entire superincumbent 300 feet, and receives as well the wash from all the rain which falls upon the portion above.

The cracked and scaling fronts of brownstone in New York and other of our older cities furnish again abundant illustrations of lack of care and judgment in the selection of materials, while the House of Parliament in London, which is said to have so badly scaled and disintegrated in certain portions as to necessitate repairing before the structure was actually finished, shows that such a failing is by no means confined to America.

Within the last fifty years many more or less complex series of tests of durability have been inaugurated when the erection of public buildings have been under consideration, but the subject has as yet by no means received the attention it deserves. It is for the purpose of emphasizing the necessity of care in the selection of such materials that the chapter herewith presented has been written.

The term weathering, as applied to stone, includes the series of physical changes induced by alternations of heat and cold, or by friction, as well as the more complex series of chemical changes, such as may be comprised under the heads of oxidation, deoxidation, hydration, and solution.   Since a stone exposed in the walls of a building may be subjected to the influence of any one or the combined influences of several of these agencies, whereby serious consequences, as of discoloration or disintegration may result, it is important to consider in more or less detail, their comparative energies under varying conditions and upon the various kinds of stone commonly employed for structural purposes.

(1) PHYSICAL AGENCIES.

Heat and cold.—It is safe to say that none of the conditions under which a stone is commonly placed are more trying than those presented by the ordinary changes of temperature in a climate like that of our Northern and Eastern States. Stones, as a rule, possess but a low conducting power and slight elasticity. They are aggregates of minerals, more or less closely cohering, each of which possesses degrees of expansion and contraction of its own. In the crystalline rocks these dissimilar elements are practically in actual contact ; in the sandstones they are removed from one another by a slight space occupied wholly or in a part by a ferruginous, calcareous or siliceous cement. As temperatures rise, each and every constituent expands more or less, crowding with resistless force against its neighbor : as the temperatures decrease a corresponding contraction takes place. Since with us the temperatures are ever changing, and within a space of even twenty-four hours may vary as much as forty degrees, so within the mass of the stone there is continual movement among its particles. Slight as these movements may be they can but be conducive of one result, a slow and gradual weakening and disintegration.

This constant expansion and contraction is often sufficient in amount to be appreciable in stone structures of considerable size. Thus Bunker Hill Monument, a hollow granite obelisk, 221 feet high by 30 feet square at the base, swings from side to side with the progress of the sun during a sunny day, so that a pendulum suspended from the centre of the top describes an irregular ellipse nearly half an inch in greatest diameter.*

Under such circumstances as these it is not at all strange

---

* Dana, Manual of Geology, p. 720.

that many stones show a decided weakening and tendency to disintegration after long exposure, and particularly on those sides of buildings exposed longest to the sun, and which are, therefore, subject to the full range of temperature variations. Professor Julien has called attention to the marked decay thus produced on the western face of the tombstones in Trinity church-yard and elsewhere. It is stated further that the ashlar base of the steeple of the church at Thirty-seventh Street and Fifth avenue, New York City, is beginning to exfoliate from this cause on the south side (where the sun shines the longest) but not on the north and east. Other examples are seen on the stone stoops of the east and west streets, where the western face of the dark-brown sandstone is badly disintegrated and exfoliated, while the eastern face remains much longer in a perfect condition. The author has observed similar effects, but in a less marked degree, on the Smithsonian building, at Washington, D. C. The south and west sides frequently show exfoliation, while the north and east, upon which the sunshines but a small portion of the day, are almost untouched.

This same expansion and contraction of stone sometimes produces disastrous effects other than those of disintegration within its own mass.

The difficulty of obtaining permanently tight joints even with the strongest cements led Colonel Totten to institute a series of experiments with a view to ascertain the actual expansion and contraction of granite, sandstone and marble when subjected to ordinary temperatures. Upwards of thirty experiments on each of these varieties of stone showed the rate of expansion and contraction, which seemed to be uniform throughout the range of temperatures employed, to be for granite .000004825 inch per foot each degree Fahrenheit : for marble .0000005668 inch, and for sandstone, .000009532 inch.*

Supposing, then, two coping stones each five feet long be laid in midsummer at a temperature of 96° Fahr. In winter the temperature falls to zero, a change of 96°. If the stones contract toward their centres, the whole length of stone put in motion will be five feet. In the case of granite, then, the shrinkage amounts to .027792 inch, in marble .03264 inch, and in sandstone to .054914 inch. This shrinkage, small as it seems, from necessity gives rise to cracks at the joints, which admit the passage of water ; continual shrinkage and expansion must in time crumble the cement and leave the joint permanently open.†

The effects of moderate temperatures upon stone of ordinary dryness are, however, slight when compared with the destructive energies of freezing temperatures upon stones saturated with moisture. At a temperature of 30° Fahr. the pressure exerted by water passing from a liquid to a solid state amounts to not less than 138 tons to the square foot, or as Professor Geikie has strikingly put it, is equal to the weight of a column of ice a mile high. It is therefore not surprising that a porous sandstone exposed in a house-front to be saturated by a winter's rain and then subjected to temperatures perhaps several degrees below the freezing point shows signs of weakness and exfoliation after a single season's exposure. Indeed the injurious effects produced by the freezing of stone, and particularly sandstone, when freshly quarried and saturated with water, have long been recognized by quarriers, who refuse

---

* Adie found the rate of expansion for granite to be .00000438 inch, and for white marble, .00000613 in.—Transactions Royal Society of Edinburgh, XIII. p. 366.

† W. H. C. Bartlett on Contraction and Expansion of Building Stone, American Journal of Science, vol. XXII. 1832, p. 136.

to assume any risk from such free*z*ing after the stone is delivered for shipment.   In the northern and New England States
quarrying, as a rule, ceases on the approach of the cold season,
owing in part to the liability to injury of the freshly quarried
material, and when expedient it is often customary to flood
the quarries with water ; if left unprotected there is always a
considerable loss of surface stone due to its having frozen and
burst, or at least become shaky.   (See remarks on time of
quarrying, p. 383.)

The injurious effects of artificial heat, such as is produced by
a burning building, are, of course, greater in proportion as the
temperature is higher.   Unfortunately sufficient and reliable
data are not at hand for estimating accurately the comparative
enduring powers of various stones under these trying circumstances.   It seems, however, to be well proven that of all stones
granite is the least fire-proof, while the fact that certain of the
fine-grained siliceous sandstones are used for furnace backings
would seem to show that if not absolutely fire-proof, they are
very nearly so.*

---

* Cutting's experiments ("Weekly Underwriter") showed that up to the point
at which they are converted into quicklime, limestones are less injured by heat
than either granite or sandstones (a result not fully borne out by the experiments of Winchell, Geology of Minnesota, vol. 1, p. 197–201).   According to
this authority the heat resisting capacity of building-stones, when water is not
applied, stands somewhat in the following order :—1, Marble ; 2, Limestone ;
3, Sandstone ; 4, Granite ; 5, Conglomerate.   In Dr. Cutting's own words,
"The limestones and marbles seldom crack from heat or water, but when heat
from the outside is excessive, they slightly crumble on the outside, if water is
thrown on them.   When they are cooled without the application of water, the
injury is much less."

" The specimens tested stood fire well, as a whole, up to the temperature of
heat necessary to convert them into quicklime, and at such a heat, if long continued, they are changed so as to slake off and crumble down.   In most cases
this heat is greater than 900 degrees (Fahrenheit), and in some cases beyond
1,000 degrees."

It must be remembered, however, that the sudden cooling of the surface of a heated stone, caused by repeated dashes of cold water, has often more to do with its disintegration than heat alone.

Effects of friction.—The amount of actual wear to which stones in the walls of a building are subjected is naturally but slight in comparison with those in the sills, steps, and walks, which are subject to the friction of feet and other agencies. Nevertheless it is sufficient in many cases to become appreciable after the lapse of several years. The striking effect produced by wind-blown sands in the Western States and Territories has often been alluded to* and even in the Eastern States, as at Cape Cod, Massachusetts, there may frequently be seen window-panes so abraded by blowing sand as to be no longer transparent. †

This same abrading process is going on in all city streets, where the wind blows dust and sand sharply against the faces of the buildings; not with sufficient force, it may be, to perceptibly wear away the fresh stone, but yet forcibly enough to crumble away the small particles already loosened by atmospheric decomposition and thus expose new surfaces to be acted upon. Professor Egleston ‡ states that in many of the churchyards of New York City the effects of this abrasive action can be seen where the stones face in the direction of the prevailing winds. In such cases the stones are sometimes

---

* On the Grooving and Polishing of Hard Rocks and Minerals by Dry Sand. W. P. Blake. Proceedings American Association for the Advancement of Science. Providence meeting.

† There is on exhibition in the National Museum a plate of glass formerly a window in the light-house at Nauset Beach, Massachusetts, that was so abraded by wind-blown sand during a storm of not above forty-eight hours' duration as to be no longer serviceable. The grinding is as complete over the entire surface as though done by artificial means..

‡ American Architect, September 5, 1885, p. 13.

worn very nearly smooth and are quite illegible from this cause alone.

Effects of growing organisms.—It is in such exposed situations as those above mentioned that a stone is often protected from serious loss by a coating of lichens or mosses, which by growing over its surface shield it from the abrasive action. The full effect of growing organisms upon the surface of stones is still, however, a matter of dispute. By some authorities* it is thought that they give rise to small amounts of organic acids which exercise a corrosive influence. By others they are considered as beneficial, since they protect the stone from the sun's rays and the rain and wind. It seems probable that they may exert either a harmful or beneficial action according to the kind of stone on which they grow and its environment. More observations are necessary before anything definite can be said.†

---

* See Winchell, Geology of Minnesota, vol. I. p. 188.

† The vegetation of microscopic lichens takes place upon the surface of the stone, when, from any cause, that surface becomes roughened so as to afford a lodgment for the seeds or spores of these plants. These growing, still further hasten the disintegration of the stone, and accumulating about them the fine dust floated by the atmosphere becomes points for the absorption of more water, which, on freezing, still further roughens the surface, and the patch of lichen gradually extends. These lichens often gain attachment upon the surface of a finely dressed stone, from some little inequality of texture, or from softer material that more readily becomes decomposed or more readily accommodates the growth of the plant. Such stones in time become partially or entirely covered by lichens, and present an unsightly aspect. The amount and degree of this growth varies with position in reference to the sun and with a more or less elevated situation.

It should not be forgotten, however, that any stone giving root to lichens is not one of those which most easily disintegrates, for in these the destruction goes on so rapidly that the surface does not allow the growth of such plants. The lichen-covered rocks in nature are usually those of great strength and durability. None of the softer or rapidly decaying rocks produce this vegetation. (Report on Building Stones by James Hall, 1868, pp. 54 and 55.)

(2) CHEMICAL AGENCIES.

Composition of the atmosphere.—The atmosphere in its normal state consists of a mechanical admixture of nitrogen and oxygen in about the proportions of four volumes of the former to one of the latter, together with minute quantities of carbonic acid, ammonia, and vapor of water. In the vicinity of large manufacturing cities, however, it carries in addition to increased proportions of carbonic acid,* appreciable quantities of sulphurous, sulphuric, nitric, and hydrochloric acids.† These, when brought by rains into contact with the walls of buildings, are capable, throughout many years of time, of producing marked effects, especially when aided by the extreme diurnal ranges of temperature common in the eastern and northern United States.

---

* Twenty-one tests of the air in various parts of Boston during the spring of 1870 yielded Mr. Pearson 385 parts of carbonic acid in 1,000,000. Eleven tests of the winter air at Cambridge yielded Mr. Hill 337 parts of the acid in 1,000,000 (Second Annual Report Massachusetts State Board of Health, 1871, p. 52). Dr. Kidder found the outdoor air of Washington to contain from 387 to 448 parts in 1,000,000. Mr. Agnus Smith (Air and Rain, p. 52), after an elaborate series of experiments, reports the air of Manchester (England) to contain on an average 442 parts of the acid in 1,000,000.

† Dr. Smith (*op. cit.*) found the proportions of these acids in London, Liverpool and Manchester to be as follows:

Localities.	Sulphuric.		Hydrochloric.		Nitric.	
	Grains per gallon.	Parts per million.	Grains per gallon.	Parts per million.	Grains per gallon.	Parts per million.
London..............	1.4345	20.49	.0872	1.250	....	.840
Liverpool	2.7714	39.56	.7110	10.16	....	.582
Manchester............	2.9163	41.66	.4055	5.79	....	.886

He also found the *total* acids for Manchester to average for 1870 3.7648 grains per gallon. It should be noted, however, that these acids were not considered

Chemical action of the atmosphere.—The series of changes induced by these agencies are, as above indicated, chemical in their nature and may all, as first suggested, be conveniently grouped under the heads of oxidation, deoxidation, hydration, and solution.   These may as well be considered in the order given.

Oxidation.—The process of oxidation is commonly confined to those stones which carry some form of iron as one of their constituent parts.   If the iron exists as a sulphide (pyrite or marcasite), it very probably combines with the oxygen of the air on exposure, forming the various oxides and carbonates of iron such as are popularly known as "rust."   If the sulphide occurs scattered in small particles throughout a sandstone the oxide is disseminated more evenly through the mass of the rock, and aside from a sight yellowing or mellowing of the color, as in certain of the Ohio sandstones, it does no harm.   Indeed as suggested by Professor Winchell,* it may result in positive good, by supplying a cement to the individual grains, and thus increasing the tenacity of the stone.   In all other than sandstones, however, the presence of a readily oxidizable sulphide is a serious defect, since crystalline rocks require no such cement, and the change in color can in very few cases be

---

as existing in the atmosphere entirely in an uncombined state, but were probably in large part combined with other substances to form chlorides, sulphates, etc.   L. P. Gratacap (School of Mines Quarterly, May, 1885, p. 335), from a series of tests at Staten Island, New York, computed the entire amount of chlorine brought down by the rains during 1884 to have been some 46.23 pounds for each acre of ground.   This is regarded as in large part combined with sodium to form sodium chloride (common salt).   Egleston (" Cause and decay of Building Stone," p. 5) estimates that the 4,500,000 tons of coal annually burnt in New York City discharge into the air 78,750 tons of sulphuric acid.   In 65 cubic centimeters of rain-water caught during an exposure of forty-one days, this same authority found 4½ milligrams of sulphuric acid.

* Geology of Minnesota vol. i. p. 189.

considered other than a blemish. This is well illustrated in some of the lower courses of granite in the new capitol building at Albany, New York, to which reference has already been made. More than this, the pyrite, in decomposing in contact with the gaseous atmosphere of cities, may give rise to small quantities of sulphurous and sulphuric acids, which by their corrosive action upon the various mineral constituents of the stone may give rise to efflorescent magnesian salts, besides rendering it porous and more liable to the destructive effects of frost. (See p. 31.) The conversion by oxidation of a sulphide into a sulphate is moreover attended with an increase in volume ; there is thus brought to bear a mechanical agency to aid in the work of disintegration.

Iron in the form of ferrous carbonate is a common constituent of many calcareous rocks, and in the form of this and other readily decomposable protoxide compounds occurs not infrequently in the cementing material of fragmental rocks lying below the water level. All these compounds are susceptible to oxidation on exposure to atmospheric influences, and to these, more than to the presence of sulphides, is presumably due the mellowing commonly observed in white marble or the light gray sub-Carboniferous sandstones.

Iron, in the form of magnetite—a mixture of the ferrous and ferric oxides—is liable to hydration and still further oxidation, becoming converted wholly into the hydrous or anhydrous ferric oxide. Thus, if abundant, the rock assumes a rusty hue, and perhaps gradually falls away to a coarse sand, as is the case with certain of our diabases.*

---

* "In one part of the dikes that form the Hanging Hills at Meriden, Connecticut, the rock (diabase) is quite black, and the amount of iron (nearly 14 per cent of magnetite) has been the cause of rapid disintegration."—Hawes, American Journal of Science, vol. IX. 3d, 1875, p. 188.

Black mica, hornblende, augite, and other silicate minerals rich in iron are also liable on long exposure to change through the further oxidation of this ingredient, but when a stone is placed high and dry, as in the walls of a building, this change must necessarily be so slow as to be of little moment, though of the greatest importance from a geological standpoint. Mr. Wolff, however, states * that tombstones of diabase in cemeteries about Boston have in some cases turned a rust-brown color, the change apparently occurring in the hornblende and augite. The feldspars of the granites used in this same city were also observed in many cases to have become liver-brown, rusty-red, or yellow owing to the higher oxidation of the iron contained by them.

Deoxidation.—The process of deoxidation, whereby a ferric is changed to a ferrous oxide, is possible generally only in presence of organic acids and continual moisture. It is likely, therefore, to affect only those stones used for foundations, and need not be further considered here. The same may be said in regard to hydration, whereby an anhydrous is changed to a hydrous oxide. The blotching and variegation of beds of sandstone, as those of Marquette, Michigan, is due presumably to the deoxidation and hydration of the iron oxides forming their cement, together with a partial removal of the same by the aid of organic acids. Such changes are possible only in the quarry bed or in moist foundations and bridge abutments.

Solution.—The subject of solution can not, however, be passed over so lightly. Pure water alone is practically without effect on all stones used for building purposes. Rain-water, however, as already noted, may contain appreciable quantities of various acids which greatly add to its solvent power, as the rapid destruction of certain classes of rocks only too well at-

---

* Report, Tenth Census, vol. x.

tests. Carbonate of lime, the material of ordinary marbles and limestones, is particularly susceptible to the solvent action of these acids even when they are present in extremely minute quantities, and to this agent is largely due the rapid deface- ment of the marble tombstones in church-yards, and the mar- ble-faced buildings in cities.

It is to the ready solubility of calcium carbonate that is also due in large part the poor weathering qualities of sandstones with calcareous cements. The cement is slowly removed by solution ; the silicious grains thus become loosened, and, falling away under the influence of wind and rain, expose fresh sur- faces to be acted upon. Certain of the ferruginous cements are likewise susceptible to the influence of the acidulated rains, though the anhydrous oxides occurring in the Potsdam stones are naturally less soluble than are the hydrated forms occur- ring in those of Triassic age. The feldspars of granites and other rocks are also susceptible to the same influence, though in a much less degree. The acidulated rains aided by the dis- integration produced by temperature changes may in time par- tially remove, in the form of carbonates, the alkalies—potash and soda—and the rock slowly disintegrates into sand and clay. The feldspars of the gneiss, used so extensively in years past in and about Philadelphia, are said to have proved peculiarly liable to this change, and it has been found necessary in many instances to paint some of the older structures formed from it to avoid serious disintegration.

(3) INDURATION OF STONE ON EXPOSURE.

The changes produced by weathering are not in all cases those of decomposition. All stones, and especially the lime- stones and sandstones, undergo at first a process of hardening on being removed from the quarry or when exposed in the quarry bed, as will be noted further on. This hardening is explained by Newberry and others on the supposition that the water with which the stones are permeated, holds in solution, or at least in suspension, a small amount of siliceous, calcareous, ferruginous or clayey matter. On exposure to the atmosphere this *quarry water*, as it is technically called, is drawn by capillarity to the surface of the block and evaporated. The dissolved or suspended material is then deposited, and serves as an additional cementing constituent to bind the grains more closely together. It is obvious that the amount of induration must in most cases be quite small, and limited to but a thin outer crust on each block; also that when this crust has once formed it can, if removed, never be replaced since the stone in the walls of a building is cut off from further supply of quarry water, and as a matter of course, after whatever quantity contained within its own mass has come to the surface and evaporated, no further hardening by this means can take place.*

It is on this account that the practice of setting rough stone in a wall, and leaving them to be carved when the structure is completed, is strongly condemned by some,† as in so doing the hard outer crust that began to form as soon as the stone was exposed to evaporation is entirely removed, and the delicate carving disintegrates much more rapidly than otherwise would have been the case. The carving, it is argued,

---

* This induration sometimes takes place in a peculiarly rapid and interesting manner. Dr. Wadsworth, in writing on some Potsdam and St. Peter's sandstones near Mazo Manie, Wisconsin, states that those portions of the stone which are exposed to atmospheric influences have become by induration converted into compact quartzites, while the protected portions still retain their porous and friable nature. So rapidly does this change take place that an exposure of but a few months is sufficient to produce very marked results on a freshly broken surface.—Proceedings Boston Society of Natural History, voL XXII. 1883, p. 202.

† Le Duc, "Story of a House," p. 143.

should be done at once, while the quarry water is still present: the crust then forms upon its surface, and it is thus better able to resist atmospheric action. The rescouring and honing of buildings and works of art is strongly objected to on similar grounds.*

(4) WEATHERING PROPERTIES OF STONES OF VARIOUS KINDS.

Let us now consider the effects of the various agencies just enumerated upon the different classes of rocks in common use for building materials.

Granites are liable to disintegration chiefly from the constant expansion and contraction caused by natural temperatures. The chemical changes to which they are subject, such as the kaolinization of the feldspars or rusting of the micas, being as a rule scarcely noticeable in the walls of a building, while they are so compact as to be practically non-absorbent and hence not liable to injury by freezing alone. The same may be said respecting the diabases, melaphyrs, and basalts when not particularly rich in magnetite or secondary calcite. Dr. Hague, in describing the decay of the granite obelisk in Central Park, New York, says: "In my opinion the process of disintegration has been an extremely slow one, caused by a constant expansion and contraction of the constituent minerals near the surface, due to diurnal variations of temperature. In a climate like that of New York, where these diurnal changes are frequently excessive at all times of the year, the tension between the minerals would naturally tend to a mechanical disintegration of the rock. Granite being a poor conductor of heat, the effect of these changes would be felt only at short distances below the surface, causing in time minute fractures

---

* See Chateau, under " Inconvénience du grattage à vif," p. 353.

and fissures along lines of weakness. Into these openings percolating waters, upon freezing, would rapidly complete the work of destruction." *

Helmerson explains the rapid disintegration of the Alexander column in St. Petersburg, Russia, on the grounds that it contains many large crystals of a triclinic feldspar, which when subjected to the extreme temperatures of Russian climate expand and contract unequally in the direction of their three crystallographic axes and hence cause the crumbling.† This view seems plausible, but we believe it yet remains to be shown that rocks rich in triclinic feldspars in reality disintegrate more rapidly than others.

Granite was for a long time popularly believed to be a nearly fireproof material. The great fires of Portland, Boston, and Chicago not merely exposed this delusion but proved the direct opposite—that instead of being the most fire-proof it was the least so, ranking below either sand- or limestone. The peculiar susceptibility of the stone to the effect of heat may be ascribed to its compact and complex structure, each of its constituent minerals possessing different degrees of expansibility.‡

---

* Science, December 11, 1885, p. 511.

† See Science, January 22, 1886, p. 75.

‡ The co-efficient of cubical expansion for several of the more common rock-forming minerals has been determined as follows :

Quartz	.000036	Tourmaline	.000022
Orthoclase	.000017	Garnet	.000025
Adularia (feldspar)	.0000179	Calcite	.00002
Hornblende	.0000284	Dolomite	.000035
Beryl	.000001		

The quartz, it will be noticed, has a co-efficient of expansion double that of the orthoclase, and nearly a third greater than hornblende. The matter is further complicated by the fact that each individual mineral expands unequally along the direction of its various axes. Thus quartz gives a co-efficient of

It has also been suggested by certain authors that the minute water-filled cavities in the quartz of these rock may be an important factor, since, when highly heated, the water is. converted into steam and an explosion results, causing the quartz to fly into fragments. After microscopic examination of a very large number of our granites the writer can but feel that the results thus produced are too small to merit serious consideration.

The relative durability of sandstone and granite under fire is stated to have been well shown not long since at the burning of St. Peter's Church at Lamerton, England. The church itself, which was built in great part of granite, was completely ruined, while the tower, built of a local freestone, around which the heat of the fire was so great as to melt six of the bells as they hung in the belfry, was left intact, although the granite window-jams and sills were destroyed.*

Limestones and dolomites, both marbles and the common varieties, are perhaps less affected than granite by the purely mechanical agencies, but make up for this in their susceptibility to the solvent action of gaseous atmospheres. Limestones are in this respect less durable than dolomites, so that, the tenacity being the same, a dolomite might, under the same circumstances, be considered as promising greater durability than a limestone (see p. 381). A thoroughly crystalline or non-crystalline compact and homogeneous limestone or dolomite is scarcely, if any, more absorbent than a granite, and hence it is as little liable to injury from freezing. Professor Geikie, in

---

.00000769 parallel to the major axis, and of .00001385 perpendicular to this axis; adularia gives .0000156, .0000000659, and .00000294 for its three axes; and hornblende for the same axes gives .0000081, .00000084, and .0000095. (See Clarke's "Constants of Nature," Smithsonian Miscellaneous Collection, vol. XIV.)

* American Architect, vol. IV. 1878, p. 80.

studying rock-weathering, as displayed by the marble tombstones in Scottish cemeteries, observed that the process presented three distinct phases, all of which were at times observable on the same slab. These were (1) *superficial solution,*
caused by the carbonic and sulphuric acids of the atmosphere;
(2) *internal disintegration,* accompanied or preceded by the
formation of an exterior coat or film of sulphate of lime; and
(3) *curvature and fracture.* The first phase manifested itself
in loss of polish and gradual roughening of the surface, followed by the formation of minute rifts and final rapid disintegration. One case is mentioned in which a stone erected in
1785 became so far decayed as to require restoration in 1803,
and at the time of writing (1880) was and had been for some
years so corroded as to be entirely illegible.

The second phase, that of internal disintegration, manifested itself in a peculiar manner. In a number of cases examined it was found that the sulphuric acid brought in contact
with the stone by rains had reacted upon the calcium carbonate, producing a superficial coating, varying in thickness from
that of a sheet of paper to a millimeter, of sulphate of lime.
This, so long as it remained intact, seemed to protect the stone
from other atmospheric influences. On the breaking of the
crust, however, it was found that the cohesion of the crystalline granules beneath had been destroyed and the stone crum-
bled rapidly to sand, the cause of which is attributed largely
to mechanical agencies.

The third phase, that of curvature and fracture, was observed only on thin slabs of marble which had been placed in
a horizontal or vertical position and confined by a frame of
sandstone. It manifested itself in the bulging outward of the
slab like the bellying of a well-filled sail. In one case examined, that of a slab of marble 30¼ inches long, 22⅜ inches wide,
by three-fourths of an inch thick, which had been thus secured

against a wall, the slab was found to have escaped from its fastenings at the sides, though still held at the top and bottom, and to have bulged outward sufficiently to allow the insertion of the hand and arm between it and the wall at the widest point. It had also expanded laterally so as to be one-half an inch wider in the center than at the ends. The outer surface of the slab where the greatest strain was produced by the bending was filled with minute cracks or rifts, the largest of which were some one-tenth inch in diameter. The cause of the bulging is believed by Professor Geikie to be due to expansion caused by the freezing of water absorbed from rains. The conclusions arrived at from the examination of a large number of cases, were to the effect that in all but exceptionally favorable and sheltered localities slabs of marble exposed to the weather in such a climate as that of Edinburgh lost their polish after an exposure of but a year or two and became entirely destroyed in less than a century; hence that the stone was quite unfitted for outdoor work in that vicinity.*

These results are greatly in exaggeration of what takes place in our own cemeteries. Professor Julien states that in the city cemeteries about New York the polish on marble tombstones often survives for ten years, and, in protected places, as near the ground in suburban cemeteries, for half a century. He further states that while of the tombstones in St. Paul's churchyard in New York City, about one-tenth of the inscriptions dating back to the latter part of the eighteenth century are illegible, he has never seen the same effect produced in suburban cemeteries in the same length of time. The author's own observations on the subject are to the effect that in the cemeteries of the smaller towns and cities of New England marble tombstones will retain their polish for a period of ten or fifteen years,

---

* Geological Sketches, pp. 170-172.

and up to thirty or thirty-five present no sign of disintegration of a very serious nature. Beyond this time, however, the surface becomes rough and granular, and the edges of the stone may be found filled with fine rifts into which particles of dirt become lodged or lichens take root, giving it a dirty and unkempt appearance.* Such stone are frequently taken down, rehoned and polished, and again set up to do duty for another term of years.

A closely crystalline or non-crystalline, compact and homogeneous limestone is probably as little affected by frost as are the granites. Very many of the limestones and dolomites used for ordinary building are, however, by no means sufficiently non-absorbent to protect them from injury by freezing, nor are they sufficiently uniform in texture to weather evenly, the disintegration going on more rapidly in some layers than others, thus producing rough and unsightly walls. Professor Winchell, writing on the weathering of the Trenton limestone used at St. Paul and Minneapolis says : † " The stone itself has an attractive and substantial aspect when dressed under the hammer, the variegations due to the alternating shaly and limy parts giving the face a clouded appearance, as of gray marble, without being susceptible of a uniform polish. Where protected from the weather the shale will endure and act as a strong filling for the framework of calcareous matter for a long time; but under the vicissitudes of moisture and dryness, and of freezing and thawing, it begins to crumble out in a few years. This result is visible in some of the older buildings, both in St. Paul and Minneapolis." Professor Hall, writing on rock weathering,‡ says : " In the gray or bluish-gray sub-

---

* The fine-grained saccharoidal marbles, used for statuary are even less durable, and in extreme cases have shown serious disintegration at the end of three or four years' exposure.

† Preliminary Report on Building-stones, etc., 1880, p. 13.

‡ Report on Building-stones, p. 36.

crystalline limestones the argillaceous matter, instead of being distributed throughout the mass, is usually present in the form of seams which are parallel to the lines of bedding or distributed in short, interrupted láminæ. These seams, whether continuous or otherwise, are fatal to the integrity of the stone, and there is scarcely a limestone structure in the country, of twenty-five years standing which is not more or less dilapidated or unsightly, from the effects of absorption of water by the clay seams, and the alternate freezing and thawing. When laid in the position of the original beds, which is the usual mode, the separation by the clay seam is slower; but when used as posts or pillars, with the lines of bedding vertical, the change goes on more rapidly."

Sandstones, on account of their widely varying textures and degrees of compactness, together with an equal variation in composition and character of cementing materials, are influenced, to a greater or less extent, by all the atmospheric influences enumerated. In the order of its apparent importance may be mentioned first the effects of freezing. As will be noticed by reference to the tables in the appendix, sandstones will absorb from about one-fiftieth to one-eighth of their weight in water in twenty-four hours, or from 2 per cent to $12\frac{1}{2}$ per cent. The approximate amount which a stone may absorb with impunity cannot, of course, he stated, since much depends on its position in a building and the strength and structure of the stone itself. It is not too much to say, however, that any stone which will absorb 10 per cent of its weight of water during twenty-four hours should be looked upon with suspicion until, by actual experiment, it had shown itself capable. of withstanding, without harm, freezing when in this condition. Half of this amount may be considered as too large when the stone contains any appreciable amount of calcareous or clayey matter. (See p. 387, also foot-note on p. 379.)

It is to their great absorptive power that is due the large amount of disintegration and exfoliation seen in the softer sandstones, as the Triassic of the eastern United States and the sub-Carboniferous of Ohio. When a stratified rock, and especially one that is distinctly laminated, is placed on edge the water filters into it from above, and, there freezing, from necessity produces the scaling so often noted in the Connecticut brownstones. If placed on the bed the effect is not nearly as disastrous, but with a porous stone the effect of continual freezing and thawing can but be injurious. It was with an apparent entire disregard of the probable effect of these agencies that was selected the soft and porous Juro-Cretaceous sandstone from Acquia Creek, Virginia, for the construction of the White House, central part of the Capitol, and other public and private buildings in Washington, a stone so susceptible to these influences, that it is only by a most prodigal use of paint and putty that the buildings are kept in a condition at all presentable.*

Acid gases are naturally without effect upon the silicious particles of a sandstone, and can be productive of injury only in dissolving out the ferruginous and calcareous cements. This is actually accomplished in many cases, and much disintegration results as a consequence. Indeed, Egleston * seems

---

* Other reasons than that of lack of durability can be given against the use of a too porous stone in a house wall. "A red sandstone house may be a very handsome building, but then it may be holding tons of water, and such a wall, if exposed to the north-west, in an open country, in our neighborhood, in a rainy winter, would, no doubt, get saturated. This means expending more fuel to convert part of this water into vapor. The difficulty is surmounted to a great extent by building hollow walls, the inner wall being of brick. Woe unto the man who has not taken this precaution." (T. Mellard Reade, in Proceedings Liverpool Geological Society, p. 445 and 446, 1883-'84.)

† Cause and Prevention of Decay in Building-stone.—Transactions American Society Civil Engineers, xv. 1886.

to regard the serious decay into which the stone of Trinity Church, New York, has fallen, to be due chiefly to this cause, supplemented by the action of frost after the cement had been removed and the stone thus rendered porous. The relative solubility of the various ferruginous cements has been always alluded to (*ante*, p. 363). Oxidation is likely to play a more noticeable part in sandstones than in most other rocks, owing to their porous nature, which allows ready access of water and air. The effects of oxidizing pyrite and ferrous carbonates in producing the mellowing and other color changes in stones of this class is sufficiently dwelt upon elsewhere, as is also the effect of heat, both natural and artificial.

On account of their porosity and natural roughness of surface sandstones are of all stones most likely to afford foothold for the growth of algæ, lichens, and mosses. While it is yet to be proved that these are actually injurious, they are at least suggestive of an unhealthy dampness. A stone once covered by these organisms will absorb more water and give it up more slowly to evaporation than one whose surfaces are not thus protected.

Serpentines when free from bad veins are as a rule non-absorptive and not affected by gaseous atmospheres, hence are durable if free from bad joints. The Pennsylvania serpentines sometimes fade or turn whitish on exposure, but so far as observed do not disintegrate.

Soapstone, although too soft and possibly too slippery for general building, is nevertheless one of the most durable stones, being not only proof against atmospheric and chemical agencies, but when well seasoned fire-proof as well.

Gypsum is too soft and too soluble in ordinary terrestrial waters to be of great value.

ON THE SELECTION AND TESTING OF BUILDING STONE.

(1) GENERAL CONSIDERATIONS.

From what has gone before it must be evident that there are many more factors which go to determine the value of stone for structural purposes than are ordinarily taken into consideration. It may therefore not be out of place here to mention a few general principles to be observed in selecting stone for any purpose in which durability, or stability of color are matters of importance. It should be stated at the outset that the problem of ascertaining by laboratory or other tests the actual qualities, good or bad, of any stone, is peculiarly complicated and difficult.* In the present state of our knowledge nothing like definite rules of procedure with any probability of accurate and reliable results can be given. That the difficulties may be better appreciated it may be well to note here the main points to be considered. In the order of their apparent importance they are :

(1) Resistance to changes in temperature.

(2) Resistance to chemical action of the atmosphere.

(3) Crushing strength and elasticity.

(4) Resistance to abrasive action of feet and wind-blown sand.

The order as above given may be subject to modification to suit individual cases. In many instances the actual strength of a stone is a matter of little importance, and in protected situations the quality mentioned under (4) may be left wholly out of consideration. In still other cases, as in bridge abutments,

---

* See article " On the Testing of Building-stone," by the writer, in American Architect for February 16, 1889.

strength and elasticity are matters of greatest import, while that of change of color can have no essential value. In the arrangement given above, especial regard has been had to stone exposed in the exterior walls of a building, and in a varied climate like that of the northern and eastern United States.

The first item for consideration is then the matter of climate. This, together with the location in which a structure is to be erected, with especial reference to proximity to large cities and manufacturing establishments, and even the directions of the prevailing winds and storms, are of primary importance and need consideration as well as do the physical and chemical properties of the stone itself.*

Our Northern and Eastern States, with an annual precipitation of some thirty-nine or forty inches and a variation in temperature amounting in some cases to not less than 120°, are necessarily more trying than those where the precipitation is less or the temperature more uniform. There is many a porous sand- or limestone which could endure an exposure of hundreds of years in a climate like that of Florida or New Mexico,

---

* " As an instance of the difference in degree of durability in the same material subject to the effects of atmosphere in town and country we may notice the several frustra of columns and other blocks of stone that were quarried at the time of the erection of St. Paul's Cathedral in London, and which are now lying in the island of Portland, near the quarries from where they were obtained. These blocks are invariably found to be covered with lichens, and although they have been exposed to the vicissitudes of a marine atmosphere for more than one hundred and fifty years they still exhibit beneath the lichens their original forms, even to the marks of the chisel employed upon them, whilst the stone which was taken from the same quarries and placed in the cathedral itself is in those parts which are exposed to the south and south-east winds found in some instances to be fast moldering away." (Gwylt's Encyclopædia, of Architecture p. 458.)

It is stated that in England the northern part of a building is always in a better state of preservation than the southern, owing to the more uniform amount of moisture and less heat from the sun.

but which would probably be found in a sad state of disintegration at the end of a single season in some more northern State. We are accustomed to hear a great deal regarding the wisdom of the ancients, and especially the Egyptians, as shown in the selection of enduring materials for their obelisks and monuments,* a wisdom or prudence which modern builders " admire more than they imitate," and we are referred to the still legible inscriptions and sharp sculptures on the surfaces of these obelisks, even after thousands of years of exposure, as proof of this marvellous foresight on the part of a semi-barbarous people. It must be borne in mind, however, that nature herself had vastly more to do in this matter than Egyptian foresight, and it is more than probable that at that time materials were selected with as little knowledge of their lasting qualities as they are to-day. The Syene granite, so durable under Egyptian skies, is no better than those in common use in this country, as the transported obelisks in New York and London have plainly shown. It is a matter of climate more than of material, and this fact should never for a moment be ignored. Were the climate of the United States like that of Egypt, southern Italy, or Mexico there would have arisen no occasion for the compilation of this chapter.†

---

* *Vide* " Matériaux de Construction," par L. Malécot, p. 30.

† " From the manner in which the buildings and monuments of Italy, formed of calcareous materials, have retained to a wonderful degree the sharpness of their original sculpturing, unless disfigured by the hand of man, it is clear that a dry and smokeless atmosphere is the essential element of durability. In this respect, therefore, the humid sky and gaseous atmosphere of British towns must always place the buildings of this country at a comparative disadvantage as regards durability." (Hull, p. 282.)

" La Grèce, la Basse-Italie, et notamment la Sicile, dit il, ont cet étrange privilége que tout s'y conserve intact, presque sans se détériorer, pendant des siècles consécutifs. Aussi les monuments, les statues, les marbres blancs eux-

(2) PRECAUTIONS TO BE OBSERVED.

The precautions which should be observed in selecting a stone for building purposes may here be briefly noted. In those portions of the northern and eastern United States that have been subjected to glacial action,* and where the great mass of rotten rock that had accumulated during previous geologic ages has been entirely removed, if the surface of the rock as displayed in the quarry or natural outcrops presents a fresh and undecomposed appearance, this may be construed as a strong argument in its favor, though it can not in all cases be accepted as conclusive.† A purely calcareous rock may

---

mêmes, qui, chez nous (en France), deviennent noirs en deux ans, rougés en dix ans, ruinés en cinquante, chez eux sont à peine noircis au bout de trois ou quatre siècles d'exposition en plein air. Sous terre ou dans un appartement ils gardent intactes leur forme et jusqu'à leur blancheur, à perpétuité pour ainsi dire.

" J'ai vu retirer de terre à Pouzzoles, près de Naples, des marbres enfouis depuis plus de deux mille ans, qui avaient l'air de sortir des mains du sculpteur.

" A Palerme, les statues et les marbres en plein air sont, il est vrai, assez noirs; mais ils n'ont jamais été touchés, m'a-t-on dit, depuis leur mise en place, et il y a là des statues qui datent de dix siècles." (E. Carrey, as quoted in Malécot's Matériaux de Construction, p. 31.)

* This includes all of New England and those portions of other States lying north of a line running irregularly from a point near the western end of Long Island across New Jersey ; thence northwesterly across Pennsylvania into New York State south of Buffalo ; thence southwesterly to near central Ohio ; thence due south nearly to the Ohio River ; westerly along the river to a point north of Louisville, Kentucky ; thence northerly again nearly to Indianapolis, Indiana ; thence southwesterly so as to include nearly all of Illinois ; thence northwesterly to a point near St. Louis ; westerly toward Jefferson City, Missouri ; thence along the Osage River and northwesterly through Kansas near Topeka ; through the eastern half of Nebraska, through Dakota west of Bismark, and thence onward into Montana.

† " No artificial structure or position will ever subject the stone to the same degree of weathering influence to which it is exposed in its natural position. . . . The rock which has withstood these influences is quite equal to withstand

weather rapidly and yet leave no debris, since its constituents are soluble and may all be carried away by running water, leaving no traces to tell of the havoc going steadily on. Impure limestones and all silicious rocks, however, leave more or less debris as mark of their decay.

But in regions south of the glaciated area the rock is still covered by the decomposed mass, and hence no clew can thus be obtained. In such cases one can only have recourse to structures that have already been erected from the stone in question and there observe its weathering qualities, or, if these are lacking, observe the stone in those parts of the quarry that have not recently been worked. In opening a new quarry, blocks should always be tested by allowing them to lie and season for at least a year before using. At the end of this time the presence of any readily oxidizable sulphide or carbonate will have made its presence known, and the amount of disintegration, or induration, as the case may be, will furnish a slight clew regarding its future behavior. Indeed, this seasoning of stone prior to its introduction into a building should always be insisted upon, whatever its character. A good building stone, whatever its kind, should possess a moderately fine and even texture, with the grains well compacted, should give out a clear ringing sound when struck with a hammer * and show always a clean, fresh fracture. It should also be capable of absorbing only a proportionally small amount of water.†

---

the exposure of a few centuries in an artificial structure." (Hall, Report on Building Stone, p. 24.)

 * In a report on some experiments on the transverse strength and elasticity of building stone, Mr. T. H. Johnson states "the resonance of each piece tested was proportional to the modulus of elasticity as found by the test." (Report State Geologist of Indiana, 1881, p. 3S.)

 † En un mot, les qualités essentielles des pierres tant dures que tendres sont d'avoir le grain fin et homogène, la texture uniforme et compacte ; de résister

The porosity of any stone is usually characteristically shown by its manner of drying after a rain ; some will dry quickly, while others that have absorbed a larger quantity of water will remain moist for a long time. In the case of a sandstone it may be said that the grains should be closely compacted, so that the proportion of cement necessary to entirely fill the interspaces is comparatively small. Of all cementing materials the argillaceous and calcareous are the least durable, and the purely silicious the most so, the ferruginous cements standing intermediate in the series. Indeed a purely silicious sandstone cemented closely by a silicious cement may be classed as one of the most durable of stones, although unfortunately on account of their hardness and poor colors such can be utilized only at a considerable expense and not always with good effect. Professor Geikie* mentions an instance in which a fine silicious sandstone erected as a tombstone in Greyfriars church-yard about 1646, and defaced by order of the Government in 1662, still showed the marks of the defacing chisel upon its polished surface after a lapse of over two hundred years.

(3) COMPARATIVE DURABILITY OF STONES OF VARIOUS KINDS.

In this connection the following table upon the "life" of various kinds of building stone in New York City is of interest ; by the term *life* being understood the number of years

à l'humidité a la gelée, et de ne pas élater au feu en cas d'incendie. (Chateau, Vol. I. p. 272.)

"Any sandstone weighing less than 130 pounds per cubic foot, absorbing more than 5 per cent of its weight of water in twenty-four hours, and effervescing anything but feebly with acids, is liable to prove a second-class stone as regards durability where there is frost or much acid in the air." (Notes on Building Construction, p. 36.)

* Geological Sketches, p. 175.

that the stones have been found to last without discoloration or disintegration to the extent of necessitating repairs.*

Life in years.

Coarse brown-stone...	5 to 15	/ ²
Fine laminated brown-stone	20	50	*8*
Compact brown-stone....................................	100	200	*3*
Blue-stone (sandstone), untried, probably centuries.		
Nova Scotia sandstone, untried, perhaps.................	50	200	*5*
Ohio sandstone (best silicious variety), perhaps from one to			
many centuries.			*1.*
Coarse fossiliferous limestone...........................	20	40	*10*
Fine oolitic (French) limestone	30	40	*9*
Marble, coarse dolomitic		40	*11*
Marble, fine dolomitic	60	80	7
Marble, fine	50	100	*6*
Granite....	75	200	*4*
Gneiss, 50 years to many centuries.			*2*

The fact that certain quarries have furnished good material in the past is no guarantee of the future output of the entire quarry. This is especially true regarding rocks of sedimentary origin, as the sand and limestones, different beds of which will often vary widely in color, texture, composition, and durability, though lying closely adjacent. In many quarries of calcareous rocks in Ohio, Iowa, and neighboring States, the product is found to vary at different depths all the way from a pure lime-stone to magnesian limestone and dolomite. The cause of this remarkable variation is little understood and can not here be touched upon, but the fact that such occurs is of importance, since in many and perhaps the majority of cases an equal varia-tion exists in point of durability. By English as well as many other authorities a dolomite is, other things being equal, con-sidered more durable than a limestone, and beyond doubt this is the case in localities where the atmosphere is at all acidic,

* Report Tenth Census, 1880, vol. x. p. 391.

since dolomite, as already noted, is but little affected by these agencies. Aside from this it would seem yet to be proven that, in the United States, a pure limestone was less durable than one that contained the necessary magnesia to constitute a true dolomite. * Indeed, Professor Hall considers the magnesian limestones, as a whole, " more friable, more porous, and less firm " (and consequently less durable) than the pure limestones. †

Stones which are mixtures of limestone (or calcite) and dolomite are liable to weather unevenly, the calcite crystals becoming eaten out, while the dolomite particles are left to project and impart a rough and lusterless surface.

Coarsely fossiliferous stones are usually to be avoided for exposed work, as they weather unevenly, owing to the unequal hardness of the fossils and the matrix in which they are embedded. ‡ Thus the coarse gray Niagara limestone from Lockport, New York, used in the construction of the Lenox Library building in New York City, began to show signs of decay even

---

* " The nearer a magnesian limestone approaches a dolomite in composition the more durable it is likely to be." " In the formation of dolomite some peculiar combination takes place between the molecules of each substance ; they possess some inherent power by which the invisible or minutest particles intermix and unite with one another so intimately as to be inseparable by mechanical means. On examining with a high magnifying power a specimen of genuine magnesian limestone . . . it will be found not composed of two sorts of crystals, some formed of carbonate of lime and others of carbonate of magnesia, but the entire mass of stone is made up of rhomboids, each of which contains both earths homogeneously crystallized together. When this is the case we know by practical observation that the stone is extremely durable." (Smith's Lithology, Building Construction, p. 40.)

† Report on Building-stone, p. 40.

‡ The limestone of which was constructed the State capitol building at Nashville, Tennessee, has proved so inferior, owing to the weathering out of the numerous fossil orthocera, that the quarries have been discontinued on this account alone.

before the structure was completed. It should be remarked, however, that this extreme rate was due in part to the fact that the stone was laid on edge and not on the natural bed. Mr. Wolff * mentions the case of a monument of shell marble in a Boston cemetery, in which, after seventy years' exposure, the fossil shells stand out in bold relief; the stone is also covered with fine cracks and is otherwise decomposed.

Veined stones are also subject to unequal weathering when exposed; this being due to the unequal hardness of the vein matter and the mass of the rock. This is true of all stones, but is especially noticeable in the so-called verdantique marbles, where the white veins of calcite or dolomite lose their polish and crumble away more rapidly than the serpentine composing the bulk of the rock. Good examples of this are to be seen in the bases of the two statues in front of the City Hall in Boston. Stones which, like many marbles, contain seams of mica, talc, or other minerals, are objectionable for like reasons. Thus the marble column supporting the statue of Lincoln in front of the City Hall at Washington, though having been in place but some twenty years, is to-day cracked from top to bottom, owing to the opening of one of these seams of talc. It may be stated further that in the majority of marbles and such other stones as are used chiefly for decorative work, those variously colored lines and veins or structural features which give the stone its chief beauty are in reality flaws and lines of weakness. There is many a beautiful imported marble which when sawn into a thin slab will scarcely bear its own weight, but must be backed by cheaper and stronger material.

It may be said here that the essential qualities of a marble, aside from color, which may vary almost indefinitely, are that it shall possess a texture sufficiently compact and hard to take

---

* Report Tenth Census, vol. x. p. 290.

a smooth surface and acquire a high polish. The chief defect in nearly all American marbles, and one that does not as yet seem to be fully realized, is that they are too coarsely crystalline. This not only renders the production of a perfect surface difficult, but the cleavage facets frequently reflect the light from below the surface in such a way as to destroy its uniformity. However good the color may be, a stone of this nature must always rank lower than one that is so fine grained as to appear non-crystalline or amorphous. It is this fact, and this alone, that renders the American marbles now in the market inferior to such as are imported from Belgium, the French Pyrenees, Italy, or northern Africa. Those who are seeking new sources of material will do well to bear this in mind.*

Time of quarrying.—The season of year during which a stone was quarried may also, in certain cases, be worthy of note. It is well known that many stones can be quarried with safety only during the summer season, but Grüber goes a step further and states† that while the best time for quarrying is during the summer, the freshly quarried material should not be allowed to lie in the sun and dry too quickly, as it is liable thereby to become shaky. This he regards as particularly likely to happen to sandstone. Stone quarried in winter, or during very wet seasons, is liable, according to this authority, to have but slight tenacity when dried, and to remain always particularly susceptible to the effects of moisture. Finally, he states, a stone is liable to disintegration if built immediately into a wall without seasoning. Stones for carved work are to be quarried in the spring, since such longest retain their quarry water, and this, if once lost, no subsequent wetting can restore.

---

* Stone, Indianapolis, Indiana, February, 1889.
† Die Baumaterialien-Lehre, p. 61.

(4) THE TESTING OF BUILDING STONE.

The present methods of testing building stone are at best extremely unsatisfactory and the results obtained very unreliable. In the majority of the cases, indeed, no attempt is made to ascertain the resistance of the material to the action of fire, frost, or the general effects of weathering. This is due in part (1) to a lack of knowledge of methods by which such tests can be made, (2) to a lack of appreciation of the necessity of such tests, (3) to a desire on the part of quarriers to get the stone immediately upon the market without the delay necessitated by a long series of experiments, (4) to the expenses attendent upon such experiments, and (5) in altogether too many cases to a desire on the part of interested parties to sell the stone regardless of its qualities. Even the tests that are now applied are in many cases practically valueless, owing to a lack of definiteness in stating results, or our inability with our present knowledge to interpret them properly. Take for instance the chemical analysis of a sandstone as ordinarily given. This shows the presence of certain percentages of iron oxides, alumina, lime, and silica, but we have no means of knowing in just what conditions these substances exist ; whether the iron occurs as a hydrous or anhydrous oxide, is confined wholly to the cementing material, or is a constituent of the various minerals composing the stone itself. The same may be said regarding at least a part of the silica, alumina, and lime. These difficulties may be in part avoided if the analysis is supplemented by a microscopic examination, whereby is ascertained the mineralogical nature of the stone, its structure, and the freedom from decomposition of its constituent parts. And indeed as a rule it may be said that while the analysis of any stone is of interest in a general way, it fails completely to give more than an approximate idea of its value for constructive purposes. Any analysis should always be preceded by a microscopic examination, and if the results of such examination should show it to be essential this should be followed by pulverization and mechanical separation of the mineral constituents, which may in their turn be in part or wholly subjected to analysis.

Strength and ratio of absorption.—The test of compressive strength is at the present time the principal test to which a stone is put to ascertain its adaptability to any particular kind of structural application. The value of the results are, it seems to the author, greatly overestimated. It is a rule among builders to never place a stone where it will be subject to more than one-tenth the pressure it has shown itself by actual experiment capable of bearing. Even under these circumstances there is scarcely a stone in the market that would not be found when freshly quarried strong enough for all ordinary purposes of construction. The problem is not what will a selected and carefully prepared sample of the stone bear to-day, but what will it bear after many seasons' exposure to heat and frost. For all ordinary purposes of construction the excess of strength of any stone over 15,000 pounds per square inch is of little value excepting so far as it denotes density, and hence greater resistance to atmospheric influences.

The size of the cubes tested and the methods used in their preparation are matters that need consideration in making comparisons of results in any series of experiments. General Gillmore found* that within certain limits " the compressive resistance of cubes per square inch of surface under pressure increases in the ratio of the cube roots of the sides of the

---

* Report on compressive strength, etc., of building stone, Annual Report Chief of Engineers, 1875.

respective cubes, expressed in inches." Thus a series of cubes varying in size from one-fourth inch to 4 inches square were found to give results varying from 4,992 pounds to 11,720 pounds per square inch of surface. It naturally follows that ambitious dealers desiring any stone to show great power of resistance would select the larger sized cubes to be experimented upon.* That the method of preparing a cube to be experimented upon is of moment will become apparent when we consider that in the process of dressing a small sample by hammer and chisel it becomes filled to a greater or less extent with small fractures and hence will break under less strain than if carefully sawn out and ground down to a smooth and even surface.

Since, as every quarryman knows, no stone, however strong, can endure the enormous strain to which it would be subject if frozen solid when holding any considerable amount of water confined within its pores, it is but natural to conclude, as a matter of course, that other things being equal those stones are most durable which will absorb and retain the least moisture.†

This rule is not to be accepted, however, without a considerable grain of allowance, since a coarsely porous stone, though capable of taking up a large amount of moisture will also part with it readily, or if frozen while saturated will permit a considerable proportion of the expansive force of the solidifying

---

* See further, Gillmore's remarks under " Compressive Resistance of Various-sized Cubes," on pp. 20–29 of his Notes on the Compressive Resistance of Free-stone, Brick Piers, Hydraulic Cements, Mortars and Concretes. (Wiley & Sons, 1888). The law as above given does not appear to hold good for blocks of large size, such as are used in actual building.

† " Other things being equal, it may probably be said that the value of a stone for building purposes is inversely as its porosity or absorbing power." (Hunt, " Chemical and Geological Essays," p. 164.)

water to be expended otherwise than in pushing apart the grains composing it. Otherwise expressed, the water will freeze out of a coarsely porous stone, while in one that is compact it may create sad havoc. This is well illustrated by the common occurrence of water freezing in straight cylindrical or widely-expanding vessels, and in narrow-necked pitchers and bottles. In the first instance the open space above is sufficient to allow all the expansion to take place vertically. The narrow-necked vessel, on the other hand, is almost invariably broken.

To ascertain the porosity or ratio of absorption of any stone is nevertheless an important test: To ascertain the ratio of absorption and resistance to freezing while saturated is a most important, and for a single test the most conclusive of any one test yet suggested. Nevertheless it is one which is at present almost wholly ignored. I will refer to methods which have been employed to some extent in times past.

Obviously the best method of ascertaining the power of a stone to withstand the effects of frost is to actually expose prepared blocks to such a temperature, when saturated with water, as to freeze them solid and then note the amount of disintegration, or loss in strength. Unfortunately this can not at all times of the year and in all places be done, and artificial methods must be resorted to. Brard's process, as modified by M. Héricart and Thury, consisted in boiling the cube to be experimented upon for half an hour in a saturated solution of sulphate of soda (Glauber salt) and then allowing it to dry, when the salt taken into the pores crystallized and expanded in a manner supposedly somewhat similar to that of water when freezing.*

This process is not now in general use, as experiment has shown that the salt exercised a chemical as well as mechanical

---

* Chateau, Technologie Du Batiment, vol. I. p. 262.

action, and produces results somewhat at variance with that of freezing water. The most important series of experiments ever performed with the process in this country were those of Mr. C. G. Page, made with reference to the selection of material for the Smithsonian Institution building at Washington. The results are given in the following table : *

MATERIALS.	Specific gravity.	Loss in grains.
Marble, close-grained, Maryland........................	2.834	0.19
Marble, coarse "alum stone," Baltimore County, Maryland.	2.857	0.50
Marble, blue, Maryland...............	2.613	0.34
Sandstone, coarse, Portland, Connecticut................	....	14.36
Sandstone, fine, Portland, Connecticut...	2.583	24.93
Sandstone, red, Seneca Creek, Maryland.... ·	2.672	0.70
Sandstone, dove-colored, Seneca Creek, Maryland........	2.486	1.78
Sandstone, Little Falls, New Jersey.....................	....	1.58
Sandstone, Little Falls, New Jersey....................	2.482	0.62
Sandstone, coarse, Nova Scotia....	2.518	2.16
Sandstone, dark, coarse, Seneca Aqueduct, Peters's quarry	....	5.60
Sandstone, Acquia Creek, Virginia.....................	2.230	18.60
Sandstone, 4 miles above Peters's quarry, Maryland......	....	1.58
Sandstone, Beaver Dam quarry, Maryland...............	....	1.72
Granite, Port Deposit, Maryland......................	2.609	5.05
Marble, close-grained, Montgomery County, Pennsylvania.	2.727	0.35
Limestone, blue, Montgomery Coun ty, Pennsylvania.....	2.699	0.28
Granite, Great Falls of the Potomac River, Maryland.....	....	0.35
Soft brick...·...............	2.211	16.46
Hard brick........	2.294	1.07
Marble, coarse dolomite, Mount Pleasant, New York......	2.860	0.91

The specimens operated upon, it should be stated, were cut in the form of inch cubes. Each was immersed for half an hour in the boiling solution of sulphate of soda, and then hung up to dry, this performance being repeated daily throughout the four weeks which the experiment lasted.

Although as above noted this process is practically abandoned, the series of tests given was productive of certain

---

* From Hints on Public Architecture, by Robert Dale Owen, p. 119.

results which are well worth a moment's consideration. Thus the red sandstone from Seneca Creek, Maryland, with a specific gravity of 2.672, or a weight per cubic foot of 167 pounds, lost by disintegration but 0.70 grains. This was the stone ultimately selected for the Smithsonian Institution building, and the structure as a whole is to-day probably in as good a state of preservation as any of its age in the United States. The second stone, from Acquia Creek, Virginia, with a specific gravity of 2.23, or a weight per cubic foot, of but 139.37 pounds, and which lost 18.6 grains is the one used in the construction of the White House, and the old portions of the the Capitol, Interior Department and Treasury buildings. This stone has proven so poor and disintegrates so badly that the buildings are kept in a condition anywise presentable only by repeated applications of paint and putty. The results obtained with hard and soft brick are also very striking: the one weighing at the rate of 138 pounds per cubic foot losing 16.46 grains, while the harder brick, weighing at the rate of 143 pounds, lost but 1.07 grains. If anything can be learned from the series, it is, that with substances having the same composition, those which are the most dense—which are the heaviest, bulk for bulk—will prove the more durable. The results obtained on coarse and fine varieties of Portland sandstone, suggest at least, that water would freeze out of the coarser stone, and therefore create less havoc than in that of finer grain, a probability to which I have already referred. That, however, the ratio, of absorption cannot in all cases be considered the controlling item is shown in the case of the coarse "alum marble" from Baltimore County. This stone is actually so poor as to be no longer in general use, yet in the test it lost but 0.50 grains, less than did the durable Seneca stone. It is probable that the difference in durability here lies in the solubility of the marble in the water of rainfalls, together with a mechanical disintegration produced by temperature changes on a rock so coarsely crystalline. These agencies have been referred to elsewhere.

The specific gravity or density of stone having been considered by many as sufficiently indicative of their strength to be authoritative, the series of tests given below were made by Dr. Böhme. The results obtained seem to show that while with limestones this might be true, with sandstones such tests could not be relied upon. A moment's reflection will be sufficient to show us the cause of this, since the strength of any stone, which is but an aggregate of minerals, is necessarily dependent not upon the hardness, density, or toughness of the individual minerals themselves, but upon the tenacity with which the adhere to one another. (See *ante*, p. 38.)

(a) *Limestone with a specific gravity of* 2.68.

	Five wet samples.	Five dry samples.
Lowest strength	7,154.16	7,267.95
Highest strength	9,984.54	10,581.91

(b) *Limestone with a specific gravity of* 2.70.

	Eleven wet samples.	Eleven dry samples.
Lowest strength.......................	8,050.22	8,050.22
Highest strength...................	10,738.36	12,515.80

(c) *Limestone with a specific gravity of* 2.71.

	Six wet samples.	Six dry samples.
Lowest strength ....,........	7,196.83	7,879.54
Highest strength....................................	12,316.72	13,668.60

(a) *Limestone with a specific gravity of 2.72.*

	Five wet samples.	Five dry samples.
Lowest strength	9,073.27	9,600.50
Highest strength..................................	15,033.71	14,934.15

(e) *Sandstone with a specific gravity of 2.54.*

	Wet samples.	Dry samples.
No. 1	12,487.40	13,668.60
No. 2	15,488.80	14,607.02

(f) *Sandstone with a specific gravity of 2.56.*

	Wet samples.	Dry samples.
No. 1	10,169.44	9,700.10
No. 2	18,518.24	18,902.37

(g) *Sandstone with a specific gravity of 2.59.*

	Wet samples.	Dry samples.
No. 1	8,932.04	9,700.10
No. 2	11,051.27	11,349.56
No. 3	17,224.45	16,754.40

See American Architect, November 4, 1882.

By the term *modulus of elasticity* is understood the amount of force in pounds requisite to stretch a bar of any material 1 inch square to twice its original length, provided the rate of stretch could continue uniform throughout the trial without the breaking of the material. The *modulus of rupture* is the force requisite to break a similar bar 1 inch square resting upon supports 1 inch apart, the load being applied in the middle.

So far as the writer has been able to learn, but few tests of this nature have been made upon stone. The following are from the report of Mr. T. H. Johnson.*

It will be noticed that there is a strong discrepancy in favor of sawn over tool-dressed stone.

Kind of stone.	Modulus of rupture.	Modulus of elasticity.	Crushing strength.
Oolite limestones, Indiana, tool dressed*..	1,477	2,679,475	7,857
Oolite limestones, Indiana, sawn†	2,338	4,889,480	12,675
Granite, Hallowell, Maine, tool dressed ‡ ..	1,754½	2,511,800	....
Sandstones, Ohio, sawn §.............. ...	479	398,234	... .
Compact limestones, Indiana, sawn ‖......	2,825	6,300,000	16,312

* Average of twelve determinations.   § Average of five determinations.
† Average of four determinations.   ‖ Average of four determinations.
‡ Average of two determinations.

As to the method of testing :

Assume first that the stone is designed for use in the exterior walls of a building, subjected to all the vicissitudes of our northern climate, and to only such conditions of pressure and strain as may exist in any large buildings.

All things considered, it seems best that the tests be made on two-inch cubes. These should be prepared by sawing and grinding, never by hammer and chisel. After drying at a temperature not exceeding that of boiling water, the ratio of absorption should be determined by complete immersion for a period of not less than twenty-four hours. The cubes should then be repeatedly frozen and thawed while in this saturated condition, and the amount of disintegration ascertained by careful weighings. If the stone is a fragmental one (sandstone), and it is found to suffer appreciable disintegration

---

* Report State Geologist of Indiana, 1881, p. 45.

by freezing, it may be well to ascertain the loss in strength also. This can be done by crushing these same cubes after the freezing tests, and also freshly prepared cubes of the same material not otherwise tested. The freezing can be brought about by means of such apparatus as is used in the manufacture of artificial ice or as Chauvenet has done, by placing the saturated cubes in the centre of a large box which is then placed in a mixture of pounded ice and salt.*

The question of durability of color and resistance to atmospheric action, can, in the laboratory, be settled only by chemical and microscopic tests. The condition of the iron, whether in the form of sulphide or protoxide carbonates is the main question to be considered. A little may perhaps be learned by submitting the stone to the action of artificial atmospheres, samples being suspended for a period of several weeks under bell-glasses charged with acid fumes. The resistance to the action of carbonic acid, can perhaps be best determined as Professor Winchell has done † by placing the samples in a basin of water through which carbonic acid gas is kept constantly bubbling. This test is scarcely necessary, except upon calcareous rocks, or fragmental rocks with ferruginous or calcareous cements. The determination of the modulus of elasticity as made by processes now in vogue, is apparently sufficiently accurate. When as sometimes happens, it is desirous to ascertain the relative powers of resistance to wear, as in pavements, or from wind-blown sand, this can readily be done by means of a carefully regulated sand-blast, such as is used in the Tilghman process of stone-carving. This property might almost equally well be learned by observing the manner

---

* Second Biennial Report Board of Capitol Managers to the General Assembly of Colorado, 1886.
† Geology of Minnesota. Final Report, vol. I.

in which the stone works under the chisel. Pressure tests when necessary at all, may be made on the two inch cubes prepared as above, and crushed between steel plates, as in any of the leading testing machines.

After all that has been said and written, there are no tests or series of tests equal to an examination of the stone in its natural outcrops, or in structures of long-standing. However careful, elaborate and apparently exhaustive may be a series of tests in the laboratory, they should always be supplemented, when possible by such field examinations. Indeed if the writer were called upon to-day to decide a question of this kind, upon any but the purely calcareous rocks, and was restricted to either field examinations or laboratory tests, he unhesitatingly declares that, with good natural outcrops, or quarry openings of long standing, he would choose the field examination, no matter how elaborate the other tests might be.

A very essential item in this connection, is that all the tests be made under the direct supervision of one thoroughly acquainted with the mineral and chemical character of the rocks, their structure, origin, mode of occurrence, and characteristic manner of weathering. A purely theoretical knowledge is worse than valueless, and only one who has devoted much time to the work, both in the laboratory and in the field, can hope to deal with the matter successfully. One great difficulty with all such work, is that we are prone to expect too much, to obtain immediately results which, in the ordinary course of events, can be brought about only by months and perhaps years of careful observation, experiment and study.

METHODS OF PROTECTION AND PRESERVATION.

(I) PRECAUTIONARY METHODS.

Position in wall.—All authorities agree that stratified stone should be placed in the walls with the bedding horizontal, or at right angles to the direction of greatest pressure. Not only are they as a rule strongest in this position, but as they will absorb less water they are correspondingly less liable to suffer from the effects of frost. This fact has already been sufficiently dwelt upon. The denser and harder stones should as a rule be used in the lower courses; the lighter ones in the superstructure. The non-absorbent stones should be used in the ground and in plinths, sills, strings, courses, and weather beds of cornices, etc.; the softer and more absorbent ones may be used for plain walling.*

The necessity of laying non-absorbent stones in the ground becomes apparent when we consider that in this position they are in contact with more or less moisture, which, when absorbed, is liable to cause discoloration, and damp, unhealthy walls. If from necessity porous stone are used, a coating of water-proof material, as asphalt, should be interposed between those courses that are in contact with the ground and those of the superstructure.†

In laying the lower courses of Lee dolomite in the walls of

---

* Cyclopedia of Arts and Sciences, vol. VII. p. 839.

† T. Egleston, American Architect, Sept. 5, 1885. This authority states further, that in the exterior walls of Trinity Church, New York, the stone for the first 60 or 70 feet in height is more decomposed than above this point. This is in part accounted for on the supposition that the atmosphere near the ground contains a larger proportion of acid gases than at higher altitudes.

the Capitol at Washington, the stone was observed to show a brownish discoloration, due to the absorption of unclean water from the mortar. This difficulty was finally remedied by coating the lower surfaces of the stones where they came in contact with the mortar with a thin layer of asphalt which prevented such absorption.*

No one who has given the subject any attention can have failed to remark how, in town and city houses constructed of the Connecticut or New Jersey brown sandstones, the blocks in the lower courses—those in close proximity to the sidewalks —almost invariably scale after an exposure of but a few years, while those in the courses above remain intact for a much longer period. This is due to the fact that these lower courses are kept almost constantly wet, receiving not only the water that falls as rain upon the walls above, but also that which splashes from the walk or is absorbed from the ground. As noted by Chateau,† it is not those portions of a wall that receive the water from rains direct that are most and earliest liable to decomposition, but the under and partially protected portions, as those under the cornices, the entablatures and the tablettes of balustrades upon which the water drips or runs more slowly. It is for this reason that architects advocate the under-throating of window sills and other projections in order that the water may be thrown off from the building and not allowed to run down over the face of the stone beneath. The disastrous effects from neglect of this proceeding have been dwelt upon by Julien in reference to buildings in New York City. The author has in mind the costly residence of a former Cabinet minister in Washington in which the middle portion of the brownstone entablatures are almost continually wet

---

* Silliman's Journal, XXII. 1856, p. 36.

† Op. cit., p. 11.

throughout the winter months by the soaking through of water from above. The stone steps in the same house are constantly wet and show a whitish efflorescence. Both these defects are liable to appear in so porous a material, but might in large part have been averted by exercising proper care in building.

It may not be out of place here to comment on the folly of placing iron railing on steps, platforms, etc., of finely finished granite, since in spite of paint and other means of protection the iron invariably rusts, staining and badly defacing the entire surface beyond possibility of repair.

The method of dressing a stone has an important bearing upon its durability. As a rule it may be set down that the less jar from heavy pounding the surface is subjected to the better; this for the reason that the constant impact of the blows tend to destroy the adhesive or cohesive power of the grains, and thus renders the stone more susceptible to atmospheric influences. It is stated by Mr. Batchen that some of the dolomites used in Chicago, although apparently perfectly sound when quarried, shortly showed a tendency to scale on exposure. On examination it appears that, in dressing, these surfaces were both ax- and bush-hammered, the implements used weighing from 8 to 12 pounds, and capable of striking blows of not less than 150 or 200 pounds. The effect of these heavy blows was to "stun"* the surfaces for the depth of from one-sixteenth to one-eighth, or even one-fourth, of an inch, and on exposure scaling resulted, leaving them ragged and unsightly. Sawn surfaces of the same stone, on the contrary, do not usually show the slightest tendency to scale.

Results such as these are what one is naturally led to expect, but further experiments are necessary before it will answer to speak too positively regarding the merits or demerits

---

* *I.e.,* to break the grains and produce minute fissures.

of various kinds of finish. With compact crystalline rocks like the granites and diabases it would seem probable that rock-faced work, untouched by chisel or hammer, would prove most durable, since the crystalline facets thus exposed are best fitted to shed moisture and the natural adhesion of the grains has not been disturbed.*

With the softer and more absorbent stones on the other hand, the rock surface from its irregularity and roughness is more susceptible to the attacks of moisture and atmospheric acids, and hence would probably be found less durable, although from its roughness at the start any disintegration is less noticeable than on finely-finished work. With such stones a smoothly-sawn or polished surface seems best adapted to our variable climate. †

---

* The single experiment of Pfaff, in which a polished granite was found to weather more rapidly than one unpolished, seems too anomalous to be accepted until further proof is offered. A polished surface must naturally shed water more readily than a sawn or tool-dressed one, and hence it would seem that it should be more durable. It is of course possible that, owing to the manner in which the smooth surface necessary for polishing was produced, the surface minerals were badly shattered, and hence succumbed the more readily on exposure.

† " Professor Hall, writing on the methods of dressing certain argillaceous limestones (Report on Building Stones, p. 36, 37),says : " In the dressing of limestone the tool crushes the stone to a certain depth, and leaves the surface with an interrupted layer of a lighter color, in which the cohesion of the particles has been partially or entirely destroyed ; and in this condition the argillaceous seams are so covered and obscured as to be scarcely or at all visible, but the weathering of one or two years usually shows their presence.

" The usual process of dressing limestone rather exaggerates the cause of dilapidation from the shaly seams in the material. The clay being softer than the adjacent stone the blow of the hammer or other tool breaks the limestone at the margin of the seam and drives forward in the space little wedge-shaped bits of the harder stone. A careful examination of dressed surfaces will often show the limestone along the seam to be fractured with numerous thin wedge-shaped slivers of the stone which have been broken off and are more or less driven forward into the softer parts. In looking at similar surfaces which

(2) PROTECTION BY MEANS OF SOLUTIONS.

Many methods have been devised for checking or altogether preventing the unfavorable action of the weather upon building stone of various kinds, but none of them can be considered as really satisfactory. The problem, as may be readily under-stood, consists in finding some fluidal substance into which the stone may be dipped or which may be applied with a brush to its outer surface in such a manner as to fill its pores and thus prevent all access of moisture. Whatever the substance, it must be of such a nature as in no way to discolor or disfigure the stone.

Paint.—This is one of the substances most generally used, and which has been employed on the porous sandstone of the Capitol, White House, Patent Office, and other public buildings in Washington. It is found necessary to renew the coating every two or three years, and even then the results are unsatisfactory.

Oil.—This always discolors a light-colored stone, while it renders a dark-colored one still darker. The oil is applied as follows: The surface of the stone is washed clean, and after drying is painted with one or more coats of boiled linseed oil, and finally with a weak solution of ammonia in warm water. This renders the tint more uniform. This method has been

have been a long time exposed to the weather, it will be seen that the stone adjacent to the seam presents an interrupted fractured margin, the small fragments having dropped out in the process of weathering. Limestones of this character are much better adapted to rough dressing, when the blows are directed away from the surface instead of against it, and when the entire surface shall be left of the natural fresh fracture. By this process the clay seams have not been crushed, nor the limestone margining them broken, and the stone withstands the weather much longer than otherwise. The attempt at fine hammer-dressing is injurious to any stone, for the cohesion of the particles is necessarily destroyed, and a portion of the surface left in a condition to be much more readily acted upon by the weather."

tried on several houses in New York City, and the water-proof coating thus produced found to last some four or five years, when it must be renewed.

Paraffine.—This, dissolved in coal-tar naphtha, is spoken of, * but is not recommended. A better method consists in brushing over the surface of the building with melted paraffine and then heating it gently until it has been nearly all absorbed into the pores of the stone. This produces little or no discoloration, but it is thought doubtful by some if the heating of the stone is not more injurious than the paraffine is beneficial. The preparation used in coating the Egyptian obelisk in Central Park, New York, is said by Mr. Caffal † to have consisted of paraffine containing creosote dissolved in turpentine, the creosote being considered efficacious in preventing organic growth upon the stone. The melting point of the compound is about 140° Fahrenheit. In applying, the surface to be coated is first heated by means of especially designed lamps and charcoal stoves, and the melted compound applied with a brush. On cooling it is absorbed to a depth dependent upon the degree of penetration of the heat. In the case of the obelisk, Mr. Caffal states that, in his belief, it was absorbed to the depth of half an inch. Some 67¾ pounds of the material was used in going over the 220 square yards of surface. An equal surface of brown sandstone is stated to require ordinarily about 40 or 50 pounds. The cost of treating an ordinary 25-foot brownstone front, with a porch, is given by this authority at from $200 to $300. This process, like the last, has been objected to by some on the ground that the heating was liable to injure the stone. Just how much injury is likely to result from a temperature lower than that of boiling water, it is per-

---

* Notes on Building Construction.
† Transactions New York Academy of Science, November, 1885, p. 66.

haps yet too early to say. It seems scarcely possible that a good quality of sandstone laid on its bed could be at all unfavorably affected; neither, it is safe to say, would brick.

Soft soap and alum solution; Sylvester's process.—This consists of three fourths of a pound of soft soap to one gallon of boiling water and one half a pound of alum in 4 gallons of water. It is said to answer well in exposed situations in England, but to require frequent renewal. It is stated,* however, that this solution was applied in 1863 to the stone-walls forming the back bays of the gate-houses of the Croton reservoir in New York for the purpose of rendering them impervious to water, and that up to 1870—the date of the report—it had served the purpose intended.

Ransome's process.—This consists in saturating the stone as far as practicable with a solution of silicate of soda or potash (water glass) and afterwards applying a solution of chloride of calcium. This last coming in contact with the silicate produces by double decomposition an insoluble silicate of lime, cementing the grains of which the stone is composed firmly together.†

"The solution of silicate is first applied in a dilute form so as to be absorbed readily into the pores of the stone. Several coats are applied with an ordinary whitewash brush and when thoroughly dry the surface is washed with rain water, again allowed to dry, and the calcium solution applied in the same manner. The precautions to be used are: (1) the stone must be clean and dry before applying the solution; (2) the silicate must be applied until the stone is fully saturated, but no excess must be allowed to remain on the surface; the calcium must

---

* Transactions American Society Civil Engineers, vol. I. p. 203.
† Dobson, Masonry and Stone-Cutting, p. 141. See also American Archi tect and Builder, 1877, II. p. 21, 38, and Notes on Building Construction, p. 79.

not be applied until after the silicate is dry ; a clear day or so should intervene if possible ; (4) care must be taken that either solution is not splashed upon the windows or upon painted work, as it cannot be removed therefrom ; (5) upon no account should the same brush be used for both solutions. Under ordinary circumstances about 4 gallons of each solution will be required for every 100 yards of surface."

Szerelmey's stone liquid is stated to be a combination of Kuhlman's process with a temporary wash of some bituminous substance. The wall being made perfectly dry and clean, the liquid is applied in two or three coats with a painter's brush, until a slight glaze appears on the surface. This composition was used with some success in arresting for a time the decay of the stone in the House of Parliament.*

Kuhlman's process consists in simply coating the surface of the stone with a silicate of soda or potash solution. It is open to the objection that the potash absorbs carbonic acid from the air and produces a disagreeable efflorescence, which, however, disappears in time.

M. Lewin's process consists in coating the surface of the stone with solutions of an alkaline silicate (silicate of potash) and alumina, the latter in the form of sulphate. It is stated that this wash will give so close a surface to sandstone that it can be polished.(?) Either of the solutions can be colored if desired.†

Various other solutions, including those of beeswax, rosin, and coal-tar, have been tried, both in this country and in Europe; but in nearly every case with indifferent success. The problem of devising a perfectly satisfactory preservative yet remains to be solved.

---

* Notes on Building Construction, p. 79.
† Journal Franklin Institute, 3rd, LXIX, 1875, p. 338.

PART IV.

. ———

APPENDIX I.

THE QUALITIES OF BUILDING STONE AS SHOWN BY THEIR CRUSHING STRENGTH, WEIGHT, RATIO OF ABSORPTION, AND CHEMICAL COMPOSITION.

TABLE SHOWING THE SPECIFIC GRAVITY, STRENGTH PER SQUARE INCH, WEIGHT PER CUBIC FOOT, AND RATIO OF ABSORPTION OF STONES OF VARIOUS KINDS.

Kind of stone.	Locality.	Size of cube. (Inches)	Position.	Strength per square inch. (Pounds)	Specific gravity.	Weight per cubic foot. (Pounds)	Ratio of absorption.	Remarks.
Granite	Penryn, Cali.	2.03×1.04	Bed	6,117	2.77	173.45	.032	Burst suddenly; pores supposed filled with red pigment.
Do.	Rocklin, Cali.	2.02×2.07	Bed	5,239	2.68	167.25	.054	Burst suddenly
Do.	Mt. Raymond, Cali.	2.03×2.04	Bed	5,970				
Do.	Grape Creek, Colo.	2.03×2.04	Bed	14,492	2.603	162.375	.018	
			Edge	17,332				
Granite	Grape Creek, Colo	2.05×2.07	Edge	14,492	2.603	162.375	.048	
			Edge	17,352				
	Brownsville, Colo.	2.02×2.03	Bed	15,244	2.700	168.426	.004	
		2.02×2.03	Edge	20,731				
	....do	2.07×2.08	Bed	15,625	2.713	169.236	.004	
		2.08×2.09	Edge	20,694				
Biotite granite	Lawson, Colo.	2.00×2.07	Bed	17,512	2.629	163.997	.006	
		1.97×2.06	Edge	18,226				
Do.	Platte Cañon, Colo.	2.04×2.08	Bed	14,585	2.625	163.747	.006	
		1.97×2.00	Edge	14,634				
	Cotopaxi, Colo.	1.99×1.98	Bed	18,654	2.667	166.367	.003	
		1.99×1.98	Edge	23,358				
Diorite (?)	Monarch, Colo.	2.08×2.03	Bed	15,170	2.760	172.168	.012	
		2.00×2.02	Edge	15,698				
Gran??	Gunnison, Colo.	2.01×2.06	Bed	12,976	2.713	169.361	.006	
		2.02×2.04	Edge	15,504				
Biotite granite (?)	Niantic, Conn.	2	Bed	9,550	2.600	162.5	7/8	Burst suddenly; pores supposed filled with red pigment.
Do.	....do	2	Bed	9,450	2.580	161.2	7/8	Burst suddenly
Gneiss	Sachemshead, Conn.	2	Bed, Edge	15,937	2.620	161.7	7/8	
Hornblende biotite gneiss	Greenwich, Conn	2	Bed	14,000 / 11,500	2.835	177.2		Average of two determinations; broke suddenly without cracking.
Biotite granite	New London, Conn	2	Edge	12,500	2.660	166.25		Broke suddenly without cracking.
Do.	....do	2	Edge	14,175	2.660	166.25		....do
Do.	Millstone Point, Conn.	2	Edge	17,468	2.706	168.7		Average of two determinations; broke suddenly without cracking.
Do.	Mystic River, Conn.	2	Bed	18,125	2.620	164.4		....do
Do.	....do	2	Edge	22,250	2.630	164.4		
Do.	Stony Crook, Conn.	2	Bed	15,000	2.645	165.4	7/8	Burst suddenly
Do.	....do	2	Bed	16,750	2.645	165.4	7/8	
Granite	Milford, Conn	5.93×5.93, 5.97, 5.95×5.91		22,610				
Do.	....do			22,600				

Kind of stone	Locality	Position	No.	Crushing strength	Specific gravity	Weight per cubic foot	Absorption	Remarks
Biotite granite	Vinalhaven, Me		51	13,381	2.660	166.3		Average of two determinations; broke suddenly without cracking.
Do	do	Bed	2	14,950	2.720	170		Average of two determinations
Do	do	Bed	2	16,031	2.630	164.4		Finely marked; bluish
Do	do	Bed	2	18,000	2.630	164.4		Finely marked
Do	do	Bed	■	15,098	2.608	163		Average of six determinations; boldly marked; resembling fine breccia.
Do	Fox Island (Vinalhaven), Me		2	14,875	2.631	164.1		Burst suddenly
Do	Dyer's Island, Me	Bed	2	18,000	2.620	163.7		Average of two determinations; boldly marked; resembling fine breccia.
Do	City Point, Me	Bed	2	15,046	2.650	165.6		do
Do	Dix Island, Me	Bed	2	15,000	2.635	166.5		Burst suddenly
Do	Jonesboro, Me		2	13,164				Average of two determinations; broke suddenly without cracking.
Do	Sprucehead, Me			15,500	2.750	171.9		do
Do	Hewitt's Island, Me	Bed	2	14,718	2.634	161.6		do
Do	Hurricane Island, Me	Edge	2	14,425	2.670	166.9		Burst suddenly
Dx	do	Bed	2	14,937	2.670	166.0		Split off considerably before bursting
Do	Huron Island, Mich	Bed	2	14,000	2.670	161.4		do
Do	do	Edge	2	18,125	2.630	166.2	2/100	do
Granite	East Saint Cloud, Minn	Bed	2	20,650	2.66	163.7	3/1000	Soaked a week for absorption
Do		Edge		14,425	2.62		3/100	
		{ Bed / Edge }		28,000 / 28,250	2.602	168.2	Trace.	
Do	Saint Cloud, Minn	{ Bed / Edge }	2	16,000 / 18,500	2.69	168.2	1/10	
Do	East Saint Cloud, Minn	{ Bed / Edge }	2	28,000 / 26,250	2.609	163.1	2/10	
Do		{ Bed / Edge }	2	26,250 / 25,750	2.609	163.1	1/100	
Do	Watab, Minn	{ Bed / Edge }	2	23,000 / 23,750	2.639	168.4	1/100	
Do	do	{ Bed / Edge }	2	21,500 / 25,000	2.606	162.8	1/10	
Do	Sank Rapids, Minn	{ Bed / Edge }	2	26,500 / 25,750	2.683	167.7	1/10	
Do	Beaver Bay, Minn	{ Bed / Edge }	2	19,750 / 13,100	2.603	162.7	1/10	
Biotite granite	Port Deposit, Md	{ Bed / Edge }	2	15,750 / 12,423	2.720	170		Coarse; strongly dashed with black
Do	do	Bed	2	10,500	2.720	170		Average of two determinations
Hornblende granite	Cape Ann, Mass	do	2	16,300				Broke suddenly without cracking
Do	do	Bed	2					do
Do	Rockport, Mass	Bed	2	19,750	2.610	163.2	1/10	
Do	Quincy, Mass	Edge	2	17,750	2.660	166.2		Cracked before bursting

(3) TABLE SHOWING THE SPECIFIC GRAVITY, STRENGTH PER SQUARE INCH, ETC.—Continued.

Kind of stone	Locality	Size of cube (Inches)	Position	Strength per square inch (Pounds)	Specific gravity	Weight per cubic foot (Pounds)	Ratio of absorption	Remarks
Do.	...do...	2	Bed	14,750	2.695	168.7		...do...
Biotite granite	Fall River, Mass	2	Bed / Edge	15,937 / 9,250	2.635	165		Burst suddenly, first split vertically.
Granite	Monson, Mass	7.6 × 7.4 / 6.1 × 7¼	Bed	15,390				
Do.	...do...	2	Edge	12,720				
Biotite granite	Keene, N.H	2	Bed	10,375	2.656	166		Used in inside of new capitol, Albany, N.Y.
Do.	...do...	2	Bed	12,875	2.656	166		Cracked before bursting
Biotite gneiss	Tarrytown, N.Y	2	Bed	18,250	2.635	162.2		Broke suddenly without cracking
Do.	Morrisania, N.Y	2	Bed	15,600	2.720	170		Cracked before bursting
Biotite granite?	Staten Island, N.Y	2	Bed / Edge	22,250 / 13,370	2.861	178.8		
Granite?	North River, N.Y	2	Bed	12,500	2.580	161.3		
Gneiss	Madison avenue, N.Y	2	Edge	11,250	2.920	182.5		
Do.	...do...	2	Bed	18,770	2.920	182.5		Soaked a week for absorption
Granite	Chaumont Bay, N.Y	2	Bed	14,687	2.65	165.4		Broke suddenly without cracking
Biotite granite	Westerly, R.I	2	Bed	17,184	2.670	166.9		Broke suddenly without cracking
Do.	...do...	2	Edge	14,937	2.670	166.9		Average of two determinations
Do.	...do...	2	Bed	17,500	2.646	165.6		Broke suddenly without cracking
Biotite granite	Westerly, R.I	2	Bed	14,100 / 13,873	2.630	164.4		Average of three determinations; broke suddenly without cracking
Do.	Richmond, Va	2	Bed	19,104	2.727	170.5		Average of two determinations
Do.	...do...	2	Bed	11,916	2.600	162.5		
Hornblende granite	Bay of Fundy, New Brunswick	2	Bed	7,750 / 9,500	2.600	162.5		
Diabase	New Haven, Conn	2	Edge / Bed	17,187 / 17,631	2.800	175		
Gabbro	Duluth, Minn	2	Bed	27,250 / 26,250	2.802	175.1		
Do.	...do...	2	Bed	26,250 / 26,250				
Gabbro?	...do...	2	Edge		3.000	187.5		{Waxy looking, having a resinous lustor; burst suddenly.}
Diabase	Taylor's Falls, Minn	2	Bed	20,750 / 20,750	2.704	169		Average of four determinations
Labradorite (massive)	Beaver Bay, Minn	2	Edge					

Kind	Locality	No.	Bedding	Load (lbs.)	Sp. gr.	Wt.	Ref.	Remarks
Diabase	Near Duluth, Minn		{ Red / Edge / Bed	28,250 / 26,250 / 21,500	3.005	187.8	33e	Very dark color; average of two determinations.
Do	Jersey City Heights, N. J.	2	Bed		3.03	189.5		Average of three tests, taken from near the surface.
Do	Pompton, N. J.	2	Bed	24,040				
Do	Goose Creek, Loudoun County, Va.	1		23,000				
Limestone (marble)	Colton, Cali.	1.42×1.41 / 1.43×1.42 / 1.46×1.42 / 1.51	{ Bed / Edge	17,783 / 17,095	2.75	172.06	4	
Limestone [marble]	Canaan, Conn		Bed			160		Average of three trials; burst without cracking.
Dolomite	Joliet, Ill	2	Bed	5,812 / 14,775	2.56	160		Crushed with loud explosion.
Limestone ?	Quincy, Ill	2	Bed	9,087	2.570	160.6		do.
Do	Lemont, Ill	2	Edge	9,787	2.510	136.9		Burst without cracking.
Dolomite	do	2	Bed	12,000	2.645	165.3		do.
Limestone	Putnamville, Ind	2	Edge	14,000	2.645	166.36		
Do	Greensburgh, Ind			16,875		169.98		
Do	Near Saint Paul, Ind			16,000		168.09		
Do	Harrison County, Ind			10,250		149.50		
Do	Mount Vernon, Ind			15,750		165.43		
Do	Bloomington, Ind			13,750		137.24		
Limestone (oolitic)	Spencer, Ind			7,500		140		
Do	do			8,750		145.16		
Do	Ellotsville, Ind			13,500		142.23		
Do	Bedford, Ind			12,628		152.39		
Do	do			6,500		147.03		
Do	do			10,125		152.39		
Do	Salem, Ind			6,750		140.3		
Do	Bardstown, Ky			8,625		144.28		
Limestone ?	do	2	Bed	16,250	2.67	166.9		Used for Louisville and Portland Canal.
Do	do		Edge	15,000		166.9		do
Dolomite. [Marble]	Lee, Mass	5.91× / 5.92 / 5.92 / 5.91 / 5.91 / 5.90	{ Edge / End	22,860	2.67			Sustained maximum load of testing-machine without apparent injury.
Do	do		Bed	22,900				Flaked off along one edge.

TABLE SHOWING THE SPECIFIC GRAVITY, STRENGTH PER SQUARE INCH, Etc.—(Continued.)

Kind of stone.	Locality.	Size of cube.	Position.	Strength per square inch.	Specific gravity.	Weight per cubic foot.	Ratio of absorption.	Remarks.
		Inches.		*Pounds.*		*Pounds.*		
Do	do	5.89, 6.00, 5.00, 5.9, 5.91, 5.90½, 5.93, 5.93, 5.93, 5.92, 5.92, 5.01	Bed	21,700				Crushed suddenly with report
Dolomite	do		End	20,504				Burst into fragments suddenly
Do	do		Bed	22,370				Effect of loading, slight flaking of one face of block; did not break
Dolomite. [Marble]	do		End	22,820				Sustained maximum load of testing-machine without perceptible injury
Limestone?	Marquette, Mich	2	Edge	7,850	2.34	146.3		Average of two trials
Do	do	2	Bed	7,285	2.34	146.3		Burst without cracking
Do	Lime Island, Mich	2	Bed	19,475	2.54	150		Average of three trials; burst without cracking
Dolomite	Frontenac, Minn	2	Bed / Edge	11,250 / 12,500	2.421	151.3		
Do	Stillwater, Minn	2	Bed / Edge	25,000 / 16,250	2.762	172.6		
Do	Winona, Minn	2	Bed / Edge	16,250 / 23,000	2.450	153.1		
Dolomitic limestone	Red Wing, Minn	2	Edge / Bed	23,250 / 10,750	2.595	162.2		
Do	Stillwater, Minn	2	Edge / Bed	12,750 / 18,500	2.567	160.4		
Do	Kasota, Minn	2	Edge / Bed	16,750 / 9,500	2.519	157.4		
Do	Mantorville, Minn	2	Bed / Edge	10,000	2.310	144.3		
Limestone?	Billingsville, Mo	2	Bed	6,650	2.32	145		Burst without cracking
Do	do	2	Edge	7,250	2.32	145		do
Do	Canton, Mo	2	Bed	7,500	2.31	148		Average of four trials
Magnesian limestone	Glen's Falls, N.Y	2	Bed	11,475	2.700	168.8		Burst without cracking
Do	do	2	Edge	10,750	2.700	168.8		do
Do	Lake Champlain, N.Y	2	Bed	25,000	2.75	171.9		do
Do	do	2	Bed	21,500	2.75	171.8		do
Do	Canajoharie, N.Y	2	Bed	20,700	2.685	169.8		do
Do	do	2	Edge	19,250	2.685	169.8		do

Material	Locality	Bearing	Dimensions	Crushing weight	Sp. gr.	Weight per cub. ft.		Remarks
Limestone?	Kingston, N.Y.	Bed	2	13,900	2.69	168.2		do
Do.	do	Edge	2	11,050	2.69	165.?		do
Do.	Garrison's Station, N.Y.	Bed	2	18,590	2.635	161.7		do
Do.	do	Edge	2	18,275	2.635	161.7		do
Do.	Williamsville, N.Y.	Bed	2	18,092	2.61	163.6		Average of three trials.
Do.	do	Bed	2	12,550	2.64	165		Burst without cracking.
Do.	Tuckahoe, N.Y.	Edge	2	12,375	2.64	165		do
Dolomite. [Marble]	do	Bed	2	13,070	2.837	177.6		Average of four trials; burst without cracking.
Do.	Pleasantville, N.Y.	Bed	2	22,383				
Bituminous dolomite.	Marblehead, Ohio.	Bed	2	11,517	2.42	152	3i	Average of three trials.
Limestone. [Marble]	Montgomery County, Pa.	Bed	6.55× / 6.05× / 6.02	13,700				{ Probable reduction in strength from uneven bearing.
Do.	do	End	6.50× / 6.03 / 6.05× / 6.01×	10,120				
Do.	do	End	6.00× / 6.01 / 6.60× / 6.01×	9,590				{ Failed immediately after first signs of rapid yielding.
Do.	do	Bed	6.4× / 6.33× / 6.02 / 6.40× / 6.02	10,940				No signs of failure till block burst.
Do.	do	Bed	5.94× / 5.90× / 5.02	11,470				Block split up along stratification.
Do.	do	End	5.02× / 5.85× / 5.92	10,420				{ Failed immediately after first signs of weakness.
Limestone	Conshohocken, Pa.	End	5.50× / 6.01× / 6.01	14,090				
Do.	do	Bed	2	16,340				
Limestone. [Marble]	Vermont	Bed	2	13,400				
Do.	Dorset, Vermont.	Edge	2	8,670	2.683	167.8		Crushed with slight explosion.
Do.	do	Bed	2	7,812	2.635	164.7	⅟₁₆	do.
Limestone?	Door County, Wis.	Bed	2	20,025	2.800	175		Crushed with quiet explosion.
Do.	do	Edge	2	13,700	5.600	175		Crushed with slight explosion; sand cracks.
Do.	Big Sturgeon Bay, Wis.	Bed	2	21,500	2.78	173.8		A remarkably solid, stable stone.
Do.	do	Edge	2	16,087	2.75	171.9		Burst without cracking.
Limestone (Tertiary).	Caen, France	Bd.	2	3,550	1.900	118.8		Average of two trials; burst without cracking.
Limestone. [Marble]	Italy	Bed	2	12,156	2.690	168.2		Burst without cracking.

TABLE SHOWING THE SPECIFIC GRAVITY, STRENGTH PER SQUARE INCH, Etc.—Continued.

Kind of stone.	Locality.	Size of cube. (Inches.)	Position.	Strength per square inch. (Pounds.)	Specific gravity.	Weight per cubic foot. (Pounds.)	Ratio of absorption.	Remarks.
Sandstone	Buckhorn, Larimer Co., Colorado	2.06×2.07 / 2.04×2.06	Bed / Edge	18,573 / 17,261	2.379	168.402	.040	Broke into wedges and sand. / Broke suddenly.
Do.	Thistle, Utah	2.06×2.06 / 2.02×2.04	Bed / Edge	8,254 / 9,405	2.407	150.211	.063	Crushed into large wedge, not suddenly. / do.
Do.	Trinidad, Las Animos County, Colorado	2.01×2.03 / 1.94×2.00	Bed / Edge	10,110 / 9,665	2.380	145.906	.009	Crushed into sand and large wedges. / Crushed into parallel pieces and wedges.
Do.	Manitou, El Paso Co., Colo	2.01×2.05 / 2.06×2.07	Bed / Edge	13,046 / 11,442	2.207	137.672	.094	Broke suddenly into thin pieces. / Broke suddenly into wedge-shaped pieces and sand.
Do.	Ralston, Colorado	2.04×2.04 / 1.99×2.02	Bed / Edge	11,118 / 9,701	2.245	140.013	.090	Broke suddenly into fine fragments and sand.
Do.	Left Hand, Colorado	1.98×2.00 / 2.03×2.03	Bed / Edge	11,278 / 13,653	2.340	139.731	.042	Broke into wedge-like pieces. Broke into large irregular pieces. Broke into fine fragments.
Do.	Saint Vairns, Colorado	2.00×2.01 / 2.00×2.04	Bed / Edge	11,505 / 17,187	2.399	149.275	.061	Broke suddenly into wedge-like pieces.
Do. Rhyolite tuff	Douglas County, Colo	2.04×2.01 / 2.02×2.02	Bed / Edge	3,544 / 3,492	2.101	136.674	.184	Broke suddenly into finer pieces. / Crushed into irregular pieces and sand.
Do.	Fort Collins, Larimer County, Colorado	2.03×2.05 / 2.00×2.04	Bed / Edge	11,707 / 10,784	2.252	40.679	.072	Broke into irregular fragments and sand.
Do.	Fort Collins, Larimer County, Colorado	2.00×2.01 / 1.99×1.99	Bed / Edge	12,740 / 17,487	2.432	151.648	.051	do.
Do.	Stout, Larimer County	2.07×2.07 / 2.08×2.10	Bed / Edge	10,514 / 12,585	2.363	141.165	.066	do.
Do.	Coal Creek, Fremont County, Colorado	2.02×2.02 / 1.96×2.01	Bed / Edge	2,879 / 2,411	2.033	120.818	.167	Crushed without noise into sand and irregular fragments.
Do.	Oak Creek, Fremont Co.	2.03×2.04 / 2.02×2.03	Bed / Edge	2,657 / 2,475	1.953	121.828	.193	do.
Do.	Coal Creek, Fremont County, Colorado	2.05×2.05 / 2.08×2.04	Bed / Edge	3,570 / 3,381	2.067	128.939	.158	do.
Do.	Gunnison, Gunnison Co.	2.02×2.02 / 2.00×2.02	Bed / Edge	6,127 / 5,524	2.066	128.877	.146	Broke suddenly into irregular pieces.
Do.	Cañon City, Colorado	1.99×2.00 / 1.97×2.00	Bed / Edge	5,716 / 3,820	2.301	143.536	.100	Broke into small irregular pieces.
Do.	Manitou, El Paso Co., Colorado	1.95×1.91 / 2.01×1.96	Bed / Edge	6,224 / 10,152	2.333	139.291	.120	Broke suddenly into small fragments.

Kind	Locality	Size	Position	Load				Remarks
Do.	Gunnison, Gunnison Co., Colorado	1.98×2.02 / 2.02×1.96	Bed / Edge	5,250 / 5,492	2.204	137.485	.090	Crushed suddenly into fine pieces and sand.
Do.	La Porte, Larimer Co., Colorado	2.03×2.04 / 2.03×2.00	Bed / Edge	10,567 / 8,620	2.235	145.033	.079	Broke into irregular shaped pieces.
Do.	Brandford, Fremont County, Colorado	2.01×2.02 / 2.02×2.01	Bed / Edge	3,308 / 2,864	2.001	125.009	.189	Crushed into irregular shaped pieces and sand.
Do.	Rawlins, Wyoming	2.06×2.02 / 2.01×2.03	Bed / Edge	10,833 / 9,544	2.021	126.069	.217	Broke into large fragments and wedges.
Do.	Left Hand, Colorado	1.99×2.01 / 2.04×1.95	Bed / Edge	11,848 / 13,056	2.394	149.237	.049	Broke suddenly into wedges and small fragments.
Do.	Do. Do.	2.02×1.97 / 2.01×2.04	Bed / Edge	13,300 / 8,841	2.290	142.850	.054	Split into clean, thin pieces.
Do.	Armejo, Conejos Co., Colorado	1.95×1.93 / 2.00×2.01	Bed / Edge	12,019 / 7,814				Broke into small pieces (not satisfactory). do.
Do.	Glencoe, Jefferson Co., Colorado	2.00×2.02 / 2.02×2.02	Bed / Edge	12,733 / 10,778				Snapped suddenly into small pieces and dust.
Do.	Walsenburg, Huerfano County, Colorado	2.00×2.03 / 2.01×2.02	Bed / Edge	5,571 / 5,361				Split into wedges and dust.
Do.	New Gunnison, Gunnison County, Colo.	2.01×2.02 / 2.00×2.02	Bed / Edge	9,903 / 7,153				Broke into wedges and sand.
Tuff	California	1.35×1.43 / 1.32×1.40 / ×1.46	Edge / Bed / Bed	7,460	2.322	145.120	.16	Crushed into small pieces and sand. Held solid to last moment, and then crushed completely to sand. Broke into small wedges and sand.
Sandstone	Middletown, Conn	2	Edge / Bed / Bed	7,262 / 6,050 / 5,550	2.360	148.5	.46	
Do.	Portland, Conn	2	Bed	4,945				
Do.	East Long Meadow, Mass.		Bed	8,812				
Do.	Marquette, Mich	2	Bed / Edge / Bed / Bed	6,165 / 5,550 / 6,223 / 5,240	2.235 / 2.285 / 2.166 / 2.165	142.8 / 148.8 / 135.3 / 135.3	.5 / .8 / .0 / .6	Average of two trials.
Do.	Hinckley, Minn	2	Bed / Edge	17,000 / 14,250	2.629	139.3	.17	Average of three trials.
Do.	Near Fort Snelling, Minn	2	Bed / Edge	20,000 / 9,500	2.221	139.8	.18	Average of two trials.
Do.	Dresbach, Minn	2	Bed / Edge	3,750 / 3,750	1.880	117.5	.4	
Do.	Jordan, Minn	2	Bed / Edge	3,000 / 8,750	1.825	113.1	.8	
Do.	Fond du-Lac, Minn	2	Bed / Edge	5,750 / 4,400	2.245	141.3	.16	
Do.	Jordan, Minn	2	Bed / Edge	4,750 / 3,000	1.901	114.9	.8	
Do.	Dakota, Minn	2	Bed / Edge		1.872	117.	.8	

TABLE SHOWING THE SPECIFIC GRAVITY, STRENGTH PER SQUARE INCH, Etc.—Continued.

Kind of stone.	Locality.	Size of cube. (Inches)	Position.	Strength per square inch. (Pounds)	Specific gravity.	Weight per cubic foot. (Pounds)	Ratio of absorption.	Remarks.
Do.	Taylor's Falls, Minn.	2	{ Bed / Edge }	{ 5,500 / 10,700 }	1.870	117.2		Calcareous sandstone
Do.	Kasota, Minn.	2	Bed	11,675	2.630	164.4		
Do.	do.	2	Edge	6,250	2.630	161.4		
Do.	Frontenac, Minn.	2	Bed	7,775	2.325	145.3		
Do.	do.	2	Edge		2.325	145.3		
Quartzite.	Pipe Stone, Minn.	2	{ Bed / Edge }	{ 27,760 / 27,000 }	2.729	170.6		
Sandstone.	Warrensburgh, Mo.	2	Bed	4,968	2.140	133.7		
Do.	Bellville, N.J.	2	{ Bed / Edge }	{ 11,700 / 10,250 }	2.250	141		Broke suddenly
Do.	Little Falls, N.Y.	2	{ Bed / Edge }	{ 9,850 / 9,150 }	2.250	140.6		
Sandstone.	Haverstraw, N.Y.	2	Bed	4,350	2.130	133.1		
Do.	Hudson River, N.Y.	2	{ Bed }	{ 9,000 / 13,000 }	2.420	151.2		
Do.	Albion, N.Y.	2	Edge	11,482	2.420	151.2		
Do.	do.	2	Bed	13,500	2.130	133.1		
Do.	Haverstraw, N.Y.	2	Edge	11,350	2.410	150.6		
Do.	Medina, N.Y.	2	Bed	4,025	2.390	149.3		Lilac in color
Do.	do.	2	Edge	17,250	2.420	151.1		More purple than last
Do.	Oswego, N.Y.	2	Bed	14,812	2.420	153.0		
Do.	Wadesborough, N.C.	{ 1.98×1.97 / 1.97× / 1×1.97 / 2 }	Bed	{ 17,725 / 6,220 }	2.160	135.2		{ Cracked at 32,000 pounds; crushed at 44,675 pounds.
Do.	do.	2	Edge	8,000	2.157	134.8		
Do.	Vermillion, Ohio.	2	Bed	9,850	2.390	149.3		Average of five trials
Do.	Seneca, Ohio.	2	Edge	7,840	2.390	149.3		
Do.	Cleveland, Ohio.	2	Bed	6,875	2.240	140		
Do.	Marblehead, Ohio.	2	Edge	9,687	2.310	144.4		Rather a chalky limestone
Do.	do.	2	Edge	10,500	2.310	114.4		do.
Do.	Massillon, Ohio.	2	Bed	6,800	2.110	131.8		Average of two trials
Do.	North Amherst, Ohio.	2	Edge	7,010	2.140	133.7		Average of two trials
Do.	do.	2	Bed	6,212	2.175	135.8		Average of two trials

Do	Berea, (1) Ohio	6.03× / 6.52× / 6.03	Bed..	6,510				Very friable, like sugar
Do	Berea, Ohio	2	Bcd.	10,250	2.110	131.9	$\frac{7}{11}$	Average of four trials
Do	...do	2	Bed.	8,222	2.145	134		
Do	Hummelstown, Pa.	6.45× / 6.40× / 6.04	Bed.	12,810				
Do	...do	6.45× / 6.50× / 6.02	End	13,610				Burst suddenly
Do	Bass Island, Wis	2	Bed..	4,850	2.040	127.5	$\frac{7}{11}$	Average of two trials
Do	...do	2	Edge	4,297	2.040	127.5	$\frac{7}{11}$	Average of two trials
Do	Fond du Lac, Wis	2	Bed..	6,237	2.220	138.8	$\frac{7}{11}$	Average of two trials
Cluse.	...do	2	Edge	5,110	2.220	138.8		
Do	Brownville, Me.	1	Bed	29,270				Mean of two trials.
Do	...do	1	Edge	16,750				
Sandstone.	Fairhaven, Vt			12,870				
	Dorchester, New Brunswick.	2	Bed..	9,281				
Do	...do	2	Edge	6,050	2.260	141.3	$\frac{7}{11}$	
Do	Edinburgh (Craigleith), Scotland.	2		12,000				
Do	...do	2	Edge	11,250	2.260	141.3		
Do	Anan, Scotland	6		7,925	2.262	141.3		
Do	Verte Island, Lake Superior.	2		11,342				
Do	Angel Island, Cali			4,574	2.73	170.6	$\frac{7}{11}$	
Do	San Jose, Cali			2,400	2.64	105.0	$\frac{7}{11}$	
Do	Altamount, Cali			1,149	2.68	167.7	$\frac{7}{11}$	
Do	Sespe, Cali			4,122	2.65	165.6		

TABLES SHOWING THE CHEMICAL COMPOSITION OF STONES OF VARIOUS KINDS.

Serpentinous rocks.	Silica.	Magnesia.	Chromic oxide.	Niccolous oxide.	Ferrous oxide.	Manganous oxide.	Alumina.	Water.	Magnetic iron.
Serpentine, near Dublin, Harford County, Md.	40.06	39.02	0.20	0.71	3.43	0.09	1.37	12.10	3.02
Precious serpentine, Easton, Pa	41.55	40.15			Ferric oxide 3.90			13.70	
Serpentine var. Williamsite, Lancaster County, Pa.	45.02	27.75					3.35	13.01	
Serpentine (verdantique marble) Roxbury, Vt	42.60	35.50			8.30	CaCO3 .60		13.00	
Serpentine (verdantique marble) Cavendish, Vt.	43.30	39.55			5.33			11.79	

Limestones and dolomites other than marbles.	Carbonate of lime.	Carbonate of magnesia.	Oxides of iron. Ferric.	Ferrous.	Oxide of aluminum.	Silica and insoluble residue.	Water and loss.	Sulphuric acid.	Chlorides of alkalies. Soda.	Potash.
Limestone, Nauvoo, Ill.	82.48			2.10	7.00	12.30	2.92	0.38	2.65	
Dolomite, Lemont, Ill.	45.83					15.90	6.90			
Do.	42.97	34.30		2.07		21.36		0.21		
Limestone (oolitic), Belford, Ind	96.60	0.13		0.98		0.50	0.96		0.40	0.31
Limestone (oolitic), Spencer, Ind	96.60	0.11		0.01		0.70	0.92		0.32	0.20
Limestone, Bloomington, Ind	95.54	0.19	1.00			0.65	1.57		0.55	0.40
Limestone, North Vernon, Ind.	83.40	0.85	1.00		2.30	1.75	2.66		Trace	1.21
Limestone, Harrison County, Ind. (Stocklager's quarry)	98.10	None	0.18		0.14	0.31	0.62		0.40	0.25
Limestone, Flat Rock Creek, near Saint Paul, Ind	82.71	3.00	1.00		2.40	5.10	1.00		0.50	0.80
Limestone, Greenbury, Ind.	74.20	4.93	2.50		3.70	5.90	0.85		0.60	0.90
Silicious limestone, Putnamville, Ind	63.70	0.33	2.00		1.70	27.50	1.86		1.60	2.60
Magnesian limestone, Anamosa, Iowa	57.32	41.21	0.23			0.72	0.31		0.75	
Magnesian limestone, Le Claire, Iowa	54.23	41.70	0.74			3.33				

Description	Carbonate of lime	Carbonate of magnesia						Alkalies, etc.
Magnesian limestone, Le Grand, Iowa	75.42	20.96		1.08		1.71	0.59	Carbonate of iron 2.02
Magnesian limestone, Stone City, Iowa	57.86	37.29		1.29		0.98		
Limestone (lithographic), Solenhofen, Bavaria	96.24	0.21						
Limestone (oolitic), Bath, England	97.52	2.50		1.20			1.78	
Limestone (oolitic), Portland, England	95.16	1.20		0.60		1.20	1.94	
Limestone (Caen), Aubigney, France	97.60					1.70		
Dolomitic limestone, Minneapolis, Minn. (Weeks & Holscher's quarry).	54.533	36.002	0.90		3.16	16.22	0.375	Soda 1.12 / Potash 1.22
Dolomitic limestone, Minneapolis, Minn. (Foley & Herbert's quarry).	41.880	24.550	4.03			29.93		
Dolomitic limestone, Minneapolis, Minn. (Eastman's quarry).	75.482	6.810		1.70		14.45	1.60	Organic matter 0.80
Argillaceous limestone, Saint Paul, Minn. (A. Rans's quarry).	79.18	6.420	1.63		2.67	13.39		
Dolomitic limestone, Kasota, Minn. (Breckenridge Bros. quarry).	47.004	35.227	1.49			13.85		Soda 0.50 / Potash 0.02
Dolomitic limestone, Kasota, Minn.	49.16	37.53		1.00		13.06		
Dolomitic limestone, Clinton Falls, Minn.	57.08	15.00		1.04		25.51		
Dolomitic limestone, Central Point, Minn.	33.00	18.540	0.33		4.92	39.34		Soda 00.30 / 0.02
Dolomitic limestone, Lanesboro, Minn. (Mill Co.'s quarry).	49.66	42.06	0.37		0.33			Soda 0.68 / 0.15
Dolomitic limestone, Red Wing, Minn. (Sweeney's quarry).	50.68	33.61	0.55		0.37	3.45		Soda 0.24 / 0.02
Dolomitic limestone, Lanesboro, Minn. (Mill Co.'s quarry).	62.14	28.49						
Dolomitic limestone, Stillwater, Minn. (Hersey & Co.'s quarry).	50.22	37.39	0.78	1.05	0.64	7.35		Soda 0.28
Do.	51.50	40.21				8.54		Soda 0.21
Dolomitic limestone, Mantorville, Minn. (Hooke's quarry).	50.20	38.96	1.11	1.11		4.52		Soda 10.6 / 0.12
Dolomite, Winona, Minn.	51.23	41.33	1.77	1.77		6.33		Soda 0.22 / 0.03
Dolomite, Frontenac, Minn.	54.78	42.53	0.36	0.96	0.31	6.32		Soda 0.18
Lime-stone, Fountain, Minn.	86.107	0.470	0.36	1.30		2.93 / 9.89		
Limestone, Point Pleasant, Ohio	79.30	0.01	7.00	7.00		12.00		0.44

TABLES SHOWING THE CHEMICAL COMPOSITION OF STONES OF VARIOUS KINDS.—Continued.

Limestones and dolomites other than marbles.	Carbonate of lime.	Carbonate of magnesia.	Oxides of iron. Ferric.	Oxides of iron. Ferrous.	Oxide of aluminum.	Silica and insoluble residue.	Water and loss.	Sulphuric acid.	Chlorides of alkalies.
Limestone, Dayton, Ohio	92.40	1.10		0.58		1.70	1.08	Soluble silica. 0.90	
Limestone, Xenia, Ohio	84.50	11.16		2.00		2.20			
Magnesian limestone, Marblehead, Ohio	83.20	15.83				0.15			Organic matter. 0.02
Argillaceous dolomite, Yellow Springs, Ohio	51.10	41.12		1.40		5.40	0.80		
Dolomite, Greenfield, Ohio	53.67	42.42	1.30			2.44			
Dolomite, Springfield, Ohio	54.70	44.93		0.20		0.10			

TABLES SHOWING THE CHEMICAL COMPOSITION OF STONES OF VARIOUS KINDS

Limestones and dolomites, marbles.	Carbonate of lime.	Carbonate of magnesia.	Oxides, iron and aluminum.	Insoluble residue.	Carbonate of manganese.	Carbonate of iron.	Loss.
Limestone (white), Talladega County, Ala.	95.25	0.62	1.15	a2.96			
Limestone (blue), Talladega County, Ala.	94.40	0.41	0.75	a4.65			
Dolomite (white), Lee, Mass	54.621	43.932	.365				.610
Dolomite (white), Pleasantville, N.Y.	54.82	45.04	0.23				
Limestone (pink), Nantehala River, North Carolina	94.51	2.12		52.56	0.21	0.60	
Limestone (white), Valley River, North Carolina	97.86	1.29		50.44	0.18	0.23	
Dolomite (white), Valley River, North Carolina	54.10	44.44		50.32	0.52	0.62	
Limestone, Knoxville, Tenn.	98.43	0.30	.31	.38	Sulphur, .014	Organic matter, .0680	.150
Limestone (white statuary), Brandon, Vt.	90.51			.29			.20
Limestone (magnesian), Isle La Motte, Vt.	87.94	4.56	2.60	4.80	Mn O trace		.10
Dolomite, Plymouth, Vt.	53.90	44.7		1.3			
Dolomite, Colchester, Mallett Bay, Vt.	35.31	42.23	12.25	10.30			
Limestone (white), Rutland, Vt.	97.73		.59	1.66			
Limestone (greenish), Rutland, Vt.	85.45			14.55			
Limestone, Sudbury, Vt.	90.70		.30				
Limestone (white), West Rutland, Vt.	98.00	.23		.57			
Limestone (dove colored), Swanton, Vt.	94.68	0.234	1.09	2.39			1.63
Limestone (white), Carrara, Italy	99.236	0.900	1.082	0.16			0.096
Do.	98.765						

a. Siliceous matter.

b. Quartz and silicates.

TABLES SHOWING THE CHEMICAL COMPOSITION OF STONES OF VARIOUS KINDS.—Continued.

Granites.	Silica.	Alumina.	Iron oxide.	Manganese oxide.	Lime.	Magnesia.	Potash.	Soda.	Loss.	Sulphur and copper.
Granite, Monson, Mass. (light)	73.47	15.07	1.15		4.48	.12	0.38	5.59		Trace
Granite, Monson, Mass. (dark)	69.35	18.83	2.00		5.04		3.78	3.07		
Hornblendo granite, East Saint Cloud, Minn	65.12	16.96	4.09		4.77	1.99	2.18			
Hornblende granite, Sank Rapids, Minn	64.13	21.01	0.02		6.00	1.20	1.22	3.31		
Hornblende granite, Beaver Bay, Minn	71.81	13.82	3.82		2.26	0.56	1.02	2.51		
Hornblende granite, East Saint Cloud, Minn	74.43	12.68	3.19		1.28	0.25	2.33	1.55		
Do	74.72	12.30	4.67		1.51	0.25	2.25	1.01		
Do	62.66	19.29	2.08		5.93	3.00	1.62	2.45		
Hornblende granite, Wabab, Minn	78.12	11.14	2.90		.02	Trace	4.48	3.33		
Biotite granite, Raleigh, N C	69.28	17.44		0.16	2.30	0.27	2.76	3.64		
Hornblende biotite granite, Utah	71.78	14.75	1.94	1.09	2.36	0.71	4.80	3.12	0.52	
QUARTZ PORPHYRIES.										
Quartz porphyry, Waterville, N. H	63.63	17.42	5.01	0.23	2.80		5.54	4.52	0.15	
Quartz porphyry "leopardite," Mecklenburgh, N. C.	75.02	14.47	0.88	0.06	1.02		1.01	4.98	0.64	

TABLES SHOWING THE CHEMICAL COMPOSITION OF STONES OF VARIOUS KINDS.

Diabase.	Silica.	Oxides of iron.		Alumina.	Oxide of manganese.	Magnesia.	Soda.	Potash.	Lime.	Phosphoric acid.	Ignition and loss.
		Ferric.	Ferrous.								
Diabase, West Rock, New Haven, Conn.	51.78	3.59	8.25	14.20	0.44	7.63	2.14	0.39	10.70	0.14	0.63
Diabase, Mount Holyoke, Mass	52.66	1.95	9.79	14.14	C 44	6.38	2.56	0.87	9.38		1.00
Diabase, Duluth, Minn	50.43	17.63		23.83		2.46	2.06	0.34	4.79		
Gabbro, Duluth, Minn	48.51	19.34		13.79		4.81	1.67	0.19	8.34		
Diabase, Taylor's Falls, Minn	35.83	48.45				3.12	1.66	0.22	9.35		
Massive labradorite, Beaver Bay, Minn	48.32	35.95				0.25	2.98	0.19	12.05		
Diabase, Jersey City, N. J.	53.13	1.08	9.10	13.74	0.43	8.55	2.30	1.03	9.47		0.90
Diabase, Williamson's Point Pa	50.79	11.28 TiO_2, 0.70		14.19	0.48	7.88	1.89	0.95	9.75	0.15	1.95

TABLES SHOWING THE CHEMICAL COMPOSITION OF STONES OF VARIOUS KINDS.—Continued.

Sandstones and quartzites.	Silica.	Alumina.	Iron oxides.	Manganese oxide.	Lime.	Magnesia.	Potash.	Soda.	Loss.
Sandstone, Flagstaff, Arizona	79.19	3.75			7.76*	3.30			3.26
Sandstone, Armejo, Colo.	80.55	10.58			0.73	0.38			3.27
Sandstone, Glencoe, Colo.	96.85	2.64			0.81	0.08			0.45
Sandstone, Trinidad, Colo.	73.23	16.28		0.30	1.63	0.92			3.24
Sandstone, Oak Creek, Colo.	72.58	15.42			1.48	1.48			2.76
Sandstone, Portland, Conn.	69.94	13.15	2.48		3.09	Trace	8.30	5.43	1.01
Sandstone, Stony Point, Mich.	84.57	5.90	6.48	0.70		0.68	Undetermined	Undetermined	1.92
Sandstone, Portage, Mich.	94.73	0.36	2.64		{ $CaCO_3$ } 0.69	{ $MgCO_3$ } 0.75			0.83
Quartzite, Pipestone, Minn.	84.52	12.33	2.12		.31	Trace	0.11	0.34	2.31
Sandstone, Hinckley, Minn.	94.69	1.06	0.55		.42	0.01	Trace	0.17	
Sandstone, near Fort Snelling, Minn.	97.67	1.31			.41	0.21	0.02	0.15	
Sandstone, Dresbach, Minn.	81.47	8.90			1.90	0.50	4.20	0.30	
Sandstone, Jordan, Minn.	81.19	10.44			.56	0.40	3.60	0.06	
Sandstone, Fond du Lac, Minn.	78.24	10.88	3.83		.95	1.00	1.67	0.06	2.48
Sandstone, Jordan, Minn.	38.41	5.77	1.79		35.87	{ $MgCO_3$ 18.54 / Magnesia 0.30 }	0.12	0.29	
Sandstone, Dakota, Minn	81.55	10.00	1.41		1.15	0.81	1.76	1.03	
Sandstone, Rockville, Mo.	82.00	11.10			0.98		1.20	1.06	1.69
Sandstone, Wadesborough, N. C.	69.28	13.84	3.87		.74	.02	0.24	0.48 / 0.56	
Sandstone, Berea, Ohio	44.40	7.49	1.47		Trace	2.11			1.80
Waverly sandstone, Ohio	91.00	5.20	Trace		0.28	0.28			1.17
Sandstone, Cleveland, Ohio	91.67	6.92	13.44		Trace	0.34			3.30
Waverly sandstone, Piketon, Ohio	73.90	8.56	1.58		.15	0.46		0.45	
Sandstone, Niskowit Bay, Wisconsin	90.86	4.76	1.28		1.40	0.59	1.06		
Sandstone, Annan, Scotland	95.24	.56	3.55		1.88	1.23	Trace		.56
Sandstone, Dorchester, New Brunswick	82.52	7.07		1.42		Trace			3.61

* CO_2, 5.77¾ = 13.11¾ $CaCO_3$.

TABLES SHOWING THE CHEMICAL COMPOSITION OF STONES OF VARIOUS KINDS.—Continued.

Argillites. Clay slates.	Silicic acid.	Titanic acid.	Sulphuric acid.	Alumina.	Ferrous and ferric oxide.	Manganous oxide.	Cobaltous oxide.	Lime.	Magnesia.	Soda.	Potash.	Carbon.	Water.	Iron bisulphide.
Peach Bottom, Md	58.37	Trace	0.22	21.963	10.061			0.30	1.293	1.983			4.09	
Slate, Delta, York County, Pa.	55.88	1.27	0.022	21.849	9.084	0.580	Trace	0.155	1.495	0.450	3.640	1.974	3.385	0.051
Slate, Lancaster County, Pa.	60.32			23.10	7.05				0.87	0.49	3.83		4.08	0.09
Slate	60.50			19.70	7.88			1.12	2.20	2.30	3.18		3.30	
Slate, Llangynog, North Wales	60.150			24.200	{ 1.815 5.837 }				4.278				3.720	
Slate, Llanberis	66.45	0.63		18.38	{ 1.41 1.71 }	.91		2.86	6.29	0.90	0.05	11.30	4.09	
Slate, Nantlle	48.			26.	14.00			4.	8.		3.31	40.92	4.08	
Slate, Bondorf	62.59			16.68	8.42			20.34	2.26					

¹ Carbonic acid.   ² Estimated as argillaceous matter.   ⁴ Tabled as "Carbon and loss."

³ Contained also 1.22 per cent of carbonate of lime and 0.13 per cent of oxide of copper.

APPENDIX II.

PRICES AND COST OF CUTTING.

The prices of stone and the cost of cutting vary with the price of labor and the conditions of the market, hence exact figures can not be given. Those given below are quoted from reliable sources, and will doubtless be found as near correct as possible in a work of this kind. The prices are for the rough stone and at the quarry, ordinary size.

Kinds.	Price per cubic foot.	Cost of dressing per square foot.					Remarks.
		Sawn.	Rubbed.	Pointed.	Ax-hammered.	Bush-hammered or chiseled.	
Granites:							
Common........	$0.35 to $0.75	.....	.....	$0.25 to $0.40	$0.25 to $0.50	$0.40 to $0.75	
Monumental...	.75 to 1.50	.....	.....	.25 to .40	.25 to .50	.40 to .75	
Marbles:							
Statuary.......	7.00 to 9.00	$0.40	$0.00	.25	.50	.75	
Common......	1.50 to 2.50	.40	.90	.25	.50	.75	
Decorative.....	2.00 to 4.00	.40	.90	.25	.50	.75	
Monumental...	4.00 to 5.00	.40	.90	.25	.50	.75	
Tennessee.....	.75 to 3.00	.40	.90	.25	.50	.75	
Sandstones:							
Brown Triassic	1.00 to 2.00	.....	.....	.10 to .15	.30	.....	Extra prices for blocks above 25 cubic feet.
Berea..........	1.00	.....	.....				
N. Y. bluestone	.03 to .10	.....	.....	.15	.....	.25	Per square foot and 2 to 3 inches thick; flagging.
Do..........	.10 to .20						Per square foot and 4 to 8 inches thick; platforms, etc.
Medina........	.60						Building stone.
Limestones......	.50 to .75						
Serpentine, Pennsylvania.	.20 to .40			.10	.15	.15	
Slates..........	2.00 to 3.50						Per square = 100 square feet.

Price-list of Italian marbles.

Quality.	Kind of stone.	Quarry.	Price per cubic foot.	Remarks.
			*Lira.**	
First	Statuary......................	Poggio Silvestro..	35 to 40	Prices reckoned on blocks
Second...	......do	....do	15 to 18	of sufficient size for an
First.....	......do	Bettogli	30 to 35	ordinary statue 5 feet in
Second...	......do	....do	12 to 15	height.
First.....	White or black marble......	Canal Bianco	10	
Do......	......do	Gioja	9. 50	Prices reckoned on blocks
Second...	......do	Ravaccione.......	6 to 6. 50	containing not less than
Third....	......do	Tanti Scritti......	4 to 4. 25	20 cubic feet.
First.....	White veined..............	Vara..............	10. 50	
Second...	......do	Gioja	7	
First.....	Bardiglio	Para..............	8. 50	
Second...	......do	Gioja.............	6. 50	
First.....	Bardiglio, veined	Serravezza........	8. 75	
Second...	......do	....do	7. 25	
First.....	Portor, black and gold......	Spezia.............	10. 50	
Do.....	Red mixed...................	Levanto............	10. 50	
Do.....	Parmazo...................	Miseglia...........	12	
	......do	Pescina...........	12	Prices of all of these de-
	......do	Bocca del Frobbi..	12	pend upon the sizes of
	Yellow	Sienna............	18 to 20	the pieces and the
	Portor	Monte d'Arma....	11	beauty of the veining.
	Black......................	Colonnata	10. 50	
	Breccia	Gragnana..........	Exceptional.	
	Yellow	....do	....do	
	Green (serpentine)..........	Garfagnana........	....do	
	......do	Genoa ....'..	....do	
	Breccia....................	Serravezza........	....do	
	Yellow	Verona............	....do	
	Red........................	Castel Poggio.....	7	

*A lira equals 19.3 cents American money.

NOTE.—For this list of quarries and prices we are indebted to Hon. William P. Rice, United State consul at Leghorn, Italy.

APPENDIX III.

LIST OF SOME OF THE MORE IMPORTANT STONE STRUCTURES OF THE UNITED STATES.

Locality.	Structure.	Material.	Date of erection.
Akron, Ohio	Memorial Chapel	Sandstone, Marietta, Ohio	
Albany, N. Y.	State Capitol	Granite, Hallowell, Me. (in great part).	1863-'82
	City Hall	Granite, Millford, Mass	
	United States court and post-office building.	Granite, Maine	1884
Augusta, Me	State Capitol	Granite, Hallowell, Me	1829-'32
	Asylum for the Insane	......do	1837-'40
	United States Arsenal	......do.	1828
Atlanta, Ga	United States post-office and court-house.	Granite, Vt	1880
Baltimore, Md	Eutaw Place Baptist Church	White marble (dolomite), Texas and Cockeysville, Md.	
	Brown Memorial Presbyterian Church.	......do	
	Franklin Street Presbyterian Church.	......do	
	City Hall	......do	
	Peabody Institute	......do	
	First Presbyterian Church	Sandstone, New Brunswick, N. J.	
	City Prison	Gneiss, Jones's Falls, Md	
	Catholic Cathedral	Gneiss, Ellicott City, Md	1806
Bangor, Me	Post-office and custom-house	Granite, Frankfort, Me	1855
Boston, Mass	King's Chapel	Granite (bowlders)	1749-'54
	United States custom-house	Granite, Quincy, Mass	1837.'48
	United States court-house	......do	1830-'31
	Masonic Temple	......do	1828-'29
	St. Paul's Church	......do	1820
	Merchants' Exchange	......do	1842
	Mount Vernon Church	......do	
	Unitarian Church, Jamaica Plains	......do	
	Bowdoin Square Baptist Church	......do	
	Bunker Hill Monument	......do	1825-'42
	United States post-office	Granite, Cape Ann, Mass	1869-'82
	Boston Water-Works	......do	
	St. Vincent de Paul Church	......do	
	Herald Building	Granite, Concord, N. H	
	Transcript Building	......do	
	Advertiser Building	......do	
	Massachusetts General Hospital	Granite, Westford, Mass	1818-'21
	Massachusetts General Hospital (addition).	......do	1846
	Equitable Insurance Company's building.	Granite, Hallowell, Me	
	Odd Fellows' Memorial Hall (in part).	......do	
	Parker House, on School street	Marble, Rutland, Vt	1854
	St. Cloud Hotel	......do	
	Hotel Dartmouth	......do	
	Hotel Vendome (old part)	Marble, Italy	
	New York Mutual Life Insurance Company's building.	Marble (dolomite), Tuckahoe, N. Y.	
	Hotel Vendome (new part)	......do	
	Hotel Pelham	Red sandstone, Portland, Conn., and New Jersey.	
	Second Unitarian Church	Red sandstone, Newark, N. J	
	Arlington Street Church	Red sandstone, Belleville and Little Falls, N. J	
	Young Men's Christian Union, Boylston street.	Red sandstone, Bay View, New Brunswick.	
	Young Men's Christian Union	Sandstone, Amherst, Ohio	

LIST OF SOME OF THE MORE IMPORTANT STONE STRUCTURES OF THE UNITED STATES—Continued.

Locality.	Structure.	Material.	Date of erection.
Boston, Mass........	Harvard College Building, Arch street.	Sandstone, Amherst, Ohio....—..	....
	First Church, Marlborough and Berkeley streets.	Conglomerate, Roxbury, Mass...—	....
	Brattle Square Church.............	.....do.......................	....
	Central Congregational Church..	.....do.......................	....
	Emanuel Church, Newbury street.	.....do.......................	....
	New Old South Church........	.....do.......................	....
	Second Universalist Church......	.....do.......................	....
	Tremont Street Methodist Episcopal Church.	.....do.......................	....
	Cathedral of the Holy Cross	..... do.......................	....
	St. James (Episcopal) Church....	.....do.......................	....
	St. Peter's Church (Dorchester)...	..... do.......................	....
	Trinity Church.............	Granite, Dedham, Mass..........	....
Brooklyn, N. Y	Academy of Design, Montague street.	Brown sandstone, Portland, Conn..	....
Cambridge, Mass	Soldiers' Monument	Granite, Mason, N. H......	....
Chicago, Ill	Court-house	Dolomite, Lemont, Ill..............	....
	......do	{Granite, Fox Island, Me. {Oolitic limestone, Bedford, Ind	....
	Custom-house and post-office building.	Sandstone, Freestone, Ohio........	1880
	Chamber of Commerce...........	Granite, Fox Island and Hallowell, Me.	....
	Palmer House	Sandstone, Amherst, Ohio........	....
	Grand Pacific Hotel	.....do.......................	....
	St. Paul Universalist Church....	Dolomite, Lemont, Ill.............	....
	Union League Club house.......	Brown sandstone, Springfield, Mass.	....
	Central Music Hall	Dolomite, Lemont, Ill.............	....
Columbia, S. C	State House	Granite, near Columbia, S. C......	....
	Post-office and court-house	Granite, Winnsborough, S. C	....
Denver, Colo	Windsor Hotel	Rhyolite-tuff, Douglas County, Colo.	....
	Union Depot	.....do.......................	....
	Union Pacific Freight Depot......	.....do.......................	....
	Rio Grande Depot	.....do.......................	....
Denver, Colo...	State capitol building.	Sandstone, Gunnison, Colo........	1886
Hoboken, N. J.......	Stevens Institute building.......	Diabase, Jersey City..............	....
Houghton, Mich.....	State Mining School buildings....	Sandstone, Portage Entry, Mich..	....
Indianapolis, Ind....	Court House......................	Bedford Oolite.	....
	State House......................	.....do.......................	....
	St. Patrick's Cathedral.	..... do.......................	....
Jersey City, N. J	Court House......................	Diabase, Jersey City.......	....
Lansing, Mich.......	State capitol building.............	Sandstone, Amherst, Ohio...	....
Louisville, Ky.......	U. S. Custom House.	Bedford Oolite...................	....
Malden, Mass........	Converse Memorial Library	Sandstone, East Long Meadow, Mass.	....
Middletown, Conn ...	Wesleyan University buildings..	Brown sandstone, Portland, Conn..	....
Minneapolis, Minn ..	Washburne Flouring Mills........	Magnesian limestone, Minneapolis, Minn.	....
	University of Minnesota............	..... do.......................	....
	Universalist Church..............	......do.......................	1873-'85
	City hall.	......do.......................	....
	Westminister Presbyterian Church.	Brown sandstone, Fond du Lac, Minn.	1881-'83
Mobile, Ala..........	Custom-House....................	Granite, Quincy, Mass............	1858
Nashville, Tenn	......do	Oolitic limestone, Bowling Green, Ky.	1883
	State capitol	Limestone near Nashville, Tenn...	....
Newark, N. J	Custom-house and post-office building.	Sandstone, Little Falls, N. J......	1859
	County court-house...............	.....do.......................	....
New Orleans, La	Custom-house....................	Granite, Quincy, Mass............	1872
	Monument to General Robert E. Lee.	Granite, Georgia.................	....
New York City......	Columbia College	Gray marble, Knoxville, Tenn.....	....
		Red sandstone, Potsdam, N. Y	....
	Trinity Church, Broadway and Wall street.	Brown sandstone, Little Falls, N.J.	....
	Lenox Library, Fifth avenue and Seventieth street.	Limestone, Lockport, N. Y........	....
	Hospital, Sailors' Snug Harbor, Staten Island.	Granite, Spruce Head, Me.........	....
	Ludlow street jail	Granite, Hallowell, Me............	....

LIST OF SOME OF THE MORE IMPORTANT STONE STRUCTURES OF THE
UNITED STATES—Continued.

Locality.	Structure.	Material,	Date of erection.
	Halls of Justice or "Tombs"	.\....do.......................	....
	Seventh Regiment armory........	Granite, Round Pond, Me...........	....
	Metropolitan Museum of Art.....	Granite, Mt. Desert, Me	....
	New York post-office	Granite, Dix Island, Me	1883
	Court-house in City Hall Park....	.....do..........................	....
	Astor House	Granite, Quincy, Mass	....
	Reformed C h u r c h, La Fayette Place.	.....do..........................	....
	Egyptian obelisk in Central Park .	Hornblende granite, Egypt	....
New York City.....	St. Patrick's Cathedral (in part)..	Dolomite (marble), Lee, Mass.....	....
	Old city hall, east, south, and west fronts.	Dolomite (marble), West Stockbridge, Mass.	....
	Treasury building, Wall street ...	.....do	....
	St. Patrick's Cathedral (in part)..	Dolomite (marble), Tuckahoe, N.Y.	....
	Stock Exchange	.....do	....
	St. Patrick's Cathedral (in part)..	"Snowflake" marble (dolomite), Pleasantville, N. Y.	....
	Union Dime Savings Bank........	Marble (dolomite), Pleasantville, N. Y.	....
	Fortifications, Fort Richmond....	Granite, Dix Island, Me	....
	Fortifications, Fort Lafayette....	Brown sandstone, New Jersey...	....
	Fortifications at Willets Point ...	Granite, Spruce Head, Me	....
	Fortifications at Governor's Island.	.....do..........................	....
	Fortifications at Bedloe's Island..	.....do..........................	....
	Fortifications at Ellis Island......	.....do..........................	....
	Fortifications, Fort S c h u y l e r, Throgg's Neck.	Gneiss	....
	Fortifications, Fort Wadsworth, Staten Island.	Granite, Maine...................	....
	Fortifications, Fort Hamilton.....	.....do..........................	....
	Fortifications, Fort Diamond....	.....do..........................	....
New York City and Brooklyn.	New York and Brooklyn bridge.	Granite, Frankfort, Me.; Concord, N. H.; Spruce Head, Me.; Cape Ann, Mass.; Hurricane Island, Me.; Westerly, R. I.; East Bluehill, Me.; Stony Creek, Conn.; Mt. Desert Island, Me.; Chanceburgh, N. J. Limestone, Rondout, N. Y.; Kingston, N. Y.; Isle La Motte, Lake Champlain; Willsborough Point, Lake Champlain; near Catskill, N. Y.	....
Philadelphia, Pa, ...	Girard Bank...................	Limestone (marble), Montgomery County, Pa.	1798
	United States custom-house	.....do..........................	1819
	United States mint...............	.....do..........................	1829
	United States Naval Asylum	.....do..........................	1830
	Merchants' Exchange	.....do..........................	1832
	Girard College........	.....do..........................	1833
	Philadelphia National Bank	Granite, Quincy, Mass	1850-'60
	First National Bank.............	... do...........................	1865
	Now Masonic Temple	Granite, Fox Island, Me.; Cape Ann, Mass.	1872
	New Post-Office...................	Granite, Dix Island, Me.; Richmond, Va.	1885
	St. Mark's Protestant Episcopal Church.	Sandstone, Portland, Conn........	1849
	Bank of Commerce	.....do..........................	1850
	Bank of North America	.....do..........................	1850
	Holy Trinity Episcopal Church ..	.....do..........................	1857
	Fifth Baptist Church.............	.....do..........................	1863
	New city buildings	Dolomite (marble), Lee Mass	...
	University of Pennsylvania	Serpentine, Chester County, Pa...	1871
	Memorial Baptist Church.........	.....do..........................	1874
	Holy Communion Church	.....do..........................	1875
	Academy of Natural Sciences	......do	1876
	Young Men's Christian Association.	Sandstone, Ohio..................	1868
Portland, Me	Forts Preble, Scammel, and Gorges	Granite, Mount Waldo, Biddeford, and Spruce Head, Me.	....
	Post-office	Crystalline limestone (marble), Vermont.	1872

LIST OF SOME OF THE MORE IMPORTANT STONE STRUCTURES OF THE
UNITED STATES—Continued.

Locality.	Structure.	Material.	Date of erection.
	Custom-house...................	Granite, Hallowell, Me., Concord, N. H.	1872
Providence, R. I.....	City hall	Granite, Hurricane Island, Me.; Westerly, R. I., and Concord, N. H.	....
	Soldiers' and sailors' monument ..	Granite, Westerly, R. I...........	....
	Post-office and custom-house......	Granite, Quincy, Mass	1858
	Roger Williams's monument......	Granite, Westerly, R. I	....
	New Catholic cathedral..........	Sandstone, Portland, Conn.......	....
	Grace Church....................	Sandstone, Little Falls, N. J.....	....
	First Congregational Church	Granite, Smithfield, R. I	....
Saint Paul, Minn.....	Catholic cathedral	Magnesian limestone, Saint Paul, Minn.	....
	Unitarian church.	....do...........................	....
	St. Paul's Episcopal church.......	Magnesian limestone, Kasota, Minn.	1873-'74
	United States custom-house and post-office.	....do...........................	1872
	Adams school....................	....do...........................	....
	Franklin school.................	....do...........................	....
	County jail	....do...........................	....
Salt Lake City, Utah.	Assembly house	Granite, Little Cottonwood Cañon, Utah.	....
	New Mormon Temple.............	....do...........................	....
San Francisco, Cal...	Bank of California...............	Blue sandstone, Angel Island, San Francisco Bay.	1865
	United States mint	Sandstone, New Castle Island, Gulf of Georgia, British Columbia.	1874
Savannah, Ga........	Presbyterian church.............	Granite, Quincy, Mass............	....
Trenton, N. J	Custom-house	....do...........................	1852
	State capitol	Sandstone, Trenton, N. J.........	....
Washington, D. C....	State prison	....do...........................	....
	Executive Mansion	Sandstone, Acquia Creek	....
	Treasury Building, old portion....	....do............................	1836 '41
	Treasury Building, new portion...	Granite, Dix Island, Maine	1855
	Patent Office Building, old portion.	Sandstone, Acquia Creek, Va	1837-'42
	Patent Office Building, extension.	Dolomite (marble), Cockeysville, Md.	1849-'64
	Chapel in Oak Hill Cemetery.....	Mica schist, near Washington ...	....
	Georgetown College (new building.)	....do..........	....
	Cabin John's Bridge, parapets and coping.	Sandstone, Seneca Creek, Md....	1848-'55
	Washington Monument, exterior, in part.	Dolomite (marble), Lee, Mass..	1848-'84
	Washington Monument, exterior.	Dolomite (marble), Cockeysville, Md.	....
	Washington Monument, interior..	Mica schist, near Washington ; granite, Massachusetts and Maine.	....
	General Post-Office, old portion ..	Dolomite (marble), West Chester, N. Y.	1839
	General Post-Office, extension....	Dolomite (marble), Cockeysville, Md.	1855
	United States Capitol, old portion.	Sandstone, Acquia Creek	1793
	United States Capitol, extension..	Dolomite (marble), Lee, Mass ...	1851-'65
	United States Capitol, extension, columns.	Dolomite (marble), Cockeysville, Md.	....
	Smithsonian Institution	Sandstone, Seneca Creek, Md	1847-'56
	St. Dominick's Church	Gneiss, Port Deposit, Md	....
	Corcoran Art Gallery (in part) ...	Sandstone, Belleville, N. J	....
	State, War, and Navy Building.	Basement and sub-basement granite, Maine ; superstructure granite, near Richmond, Va.	1871-'86
	Butler house, Capitol Hill........	Granite, Cape Ann, Mass	....
	Congressional Library building...	Granite, Concord, N. H..........	Begun ...1890

APPENDIX IV.

BIBLIOGRAPHY OF WORKS ON BUILDING STONE.

The following list includes all the principal works on the subject of building stone which have come under the writer's notice. It does not include isolated and special papers which have appeared from time to time in various journals and periodicals, or State geological reports. Such, when containing matter of sufficient importance, have been mentioned in the text and reference given in the foot-notes. The list is arranged alphabetically by authors.

BLUM, Dr. J. REINHARD. Lithurgik oder Mineralien und Felsarten nach ihrer Anwendung in ökonomischer, artistischer und technischer Hinsicht systematisch abgehandelt. Stuttgart, 1840.

BÖHME, Dr. Die Festigkeit der Baumaterialien. Resultate der Untersuchungen in der Station zur Prüfung der Festigkeit von Bausteinen an der königlichen Gewerbe-Akademie zu Berlin, etc. Berlin, 1876.

BURGOYNE, Sir JOHN. Rudimentary Treatise on the Blasting and Quarrying of Stone. London: J. Wale, 1852.

BURNHAM, S. M. History and Uses of Limestone and Marbles. Illustrated, with colored plates. Boston: S. E. Cassino & Co., 1883.

CHATEAU, THÉODORE. Technologie du Bâtiment ou Étude Complète des Matériaux de toute Espèce employés dans les constructions, etc. 2. éd. Paris, 1880.

DAVIES, D. C. Slate and Slate Quarrying. London: Crosby, Lockwood & Co., 1878.

DELESSE, A. Matériaux de Construction de l'Exposition Universelle de 1855. Paris, 1856.

DOBSON, EDWARD. Masonry and Stone-cutting. Weale's Rudimentary series. London: Crosby, Lockwood & Co., 1873.

428

GERSTENBERGK, HEINRICH VON. Katechismus der Baumaterialkunde, etc. Berlin, 1868.

GOTTGETREU, RUDOLPH. Physische und Chemische Beschaffenheit der Baumaterialien. 2 vols. Berlin, 1880–'81. Verlag von Julius Springer.

GRUEBER, BERNHARD. Die Baumaterialien-Lehre. Berlin, 1863. Verlag von Ernst & Korn.

GWILT, JOSEPH. An Encyclopedia of Architecture. London, 1851.

HALL, Prof. JAMES. Report on Building Stones.

HARRIS, GEORGE F. Granite and our Granite Industries. London: Crosby, Lockwood & Son, 1888.

HARTMANN, Dr. CARL. Vollständiges Handbuch der Steinarbeiten, etc. Weimar, 1862.

HAUENSCHILD, HANS. Katechismus der Baumaterialien. Wien: Lehmann & Wentzel, 1879.

HULL, EDWARD. A Treatise on the Building and Ornamental Stones of Great Britain and Foreign Countries. London: Macmillan & Co., 1872.

KERSTEN, E. Die Baumaterialienkunde, etc. Leipzig (not dated). Verlag von Eduard Hahnel.

KÖLLSCH, CARL. Die Baumaterialienkunde für ausführende Bautechniker und für Studirende der Bauwissenschaft. Schwetschke & Sohn. Bruhn, 1861.

KUNZ, GEORGE F. Gems and Precious Stones of North America. Scientific Publishing Company, New York. 1890.

MALÉCOT, LÉON. Matériaux de Construction employés en Belgique. Bruxelles & Liége, 1866.

NEWBERRY, J. S. Building and Ornamental Stones. Report of Judges, Group I, U. S. International Exposition, 1876, Vol. III. Washington, 1880.

Notes on Building Construction. Part III. Materials. (South Kensington Educational Series). London, Oxford, and Cambridge, 1879.

SCHLEGEL, CARL FRIEDRICH. Die Lehre von den Baumaterialien und den Arbeiten der Maurer. Leipzig: Verlag von Heinrich Matthes, 1857.

SCHMIDT, OTTO. Die Baumaterialien. Berlin, 1881. Verlag von Theodor Hofmann.

SMOCK, JOHN C. Building Stone in the State of New York. Bulletin No. 3, New York State Museum of Natural History, March 1888, 8vo, 152 pp.

Report on the Building Stones of the United States, and Statistics of the Quarry Industry for 1880. Vol. X. Report of the Tenth Census of the United States. Washington: Government Printing Office, 1884.

THURSTON, R. H. Materials of Construction. New York: Wiley & Sons, 1885.

VIOLET, ADOLPH. Les Marbres et les Machines à travailler le marbre. (Rapports sur l'Exposition de 1878, XXVIII.) Paris, 1879.

VISSER, J. E.   Die Baumaterialien.   Handbuch für Architecten, etc.   Emden, 1861.

WEBBER, MARTIN.   Das Schleifen, Poliren, Färben und künstlerische Verzieren des Marmors.   Weimar, 1878.   Bernhard Friedrich Voigt.

WENCK, Dr. JULIUS.   Die Lehre von den Baumaterialien, etc.   Berlin, 1863.

The works mentioned below bear upon the subject only indirectly. They are given up largely to metals and timber.

ANDERSON, JOHN.   The Strength of Materials and Structures.   London: Longmans, Green & Co., 1880.

BARLOW, PETER.   A Treatise on the Strength of Materials, etc.   New Edition; revised.   London: Lockwood & Co.   1867.

BÖHME, Dr.   Die Festigkeit der Baumaterialien.   Berlin, 1876.

GILLMORE, L. A.   Notes on the Compressive Resistance of Freestones, Brick Piers, Hydraulic Cement, Mortars and Concretes.   New York, Wiley & Sons, 1888.

MORIN, ARTHUR.   Resistance des Matériaux.   Paris: L. Hachette & Co., 1862.

APPENDIX V.

Æolian rocks. Fragmental rocks, composed of wind-drifted materials. The " drift sand rock," the common building-stone of Bermuda, is a good example.

Argillacecus. Containing clayey matter.

Ashlar masonry. Cut stone laid in continuous courses.

Bardiglio. This is a favorite Italian marble obtained on Montalto, on the southern borders of Tuscany. It is a gray or bluish color, traversed by dark veins. In some specimens the veining assumes the appearance of flowers, when it is known as Bardiglio fiorito. The name is now commonly applied to any marble having this color and veining.

Bastard granite. A somewhat indefinite name given by quarrymen to gneissic or schistose rocks, resembling granites in a general way, but differing in structure. The name is frequently applied by quarrymen to any vein or dike rock occurring in a granite quarry.

Bird's-eye-marble. A term used in Iowa to designate a fossil coral (Acervularia davidsoni), and used for making small ornaments.

Bituminous. Containing bitumen.

Breast. The face or wall of a quarry is sometimes called by this name.

Breccias. Fragmental stones, the Individual particles of which are large and angular in form.

Bluestone. In Maryland a gray gneiss ; in Ohio, a gray sandstone ; in the District of Columbia a mica schist ; in New York a blue-gray sandstone ; in Pennsylvania a blue-gray sandstone. A popular term ; not sufficiently definite to be of value.

Butt. The butt of a slate quarry is where the overlying rock comes in contact with an inclined stratum of slate rock.

Calcareous. Containing lime.

Cavernous. Containing irregular cavities or pores, due in most cases to the removal of some mineral, or in limestones of a fossil.

Cellular or **vesicular.** Containing cells or vesicles. This structure is very

431

common in recent eruptive rocks, especially the glassy forms. Sometimes the stone contains so many cells that it will float on water, as is
the case with common pumice. These cells are in many cases subsequently filled with other minerals, and the rock is then called amygdaloidal. The Brighton melaphyr is the best example of amygdaloidal
structure found in our building stones.

Choncoidal fracture. When the surfaces of a chip broken off by a hammer
are curved like a bivalve mollusk the stone is said to have a choncoidal
fracture. Compact stones, like lithographic limestones, obsidians, and
flints, usually break in this manner.

Clay-holes. Cavities in stone which are usually filled with fine sand or clayey
material often of a lighter color than the stone itself, and so loosely
coherent as to fall away immediately or to weather out on exposure.
They are especially prevalent in many of our Triassic sandstones, and,
besides being unsightly, are elements of weakness and should always be
avoided.

Concretionary. Made of concretions, or rounded particles formed by the col-
lecting of mineral matter around some centre so as to form a rounded
mass composed of concentric layers like the coatings of an onion. When
the concretions are small, like the roe of a fish, the structure is called
oölitic, or if large as a pea, *pisolitic*. The best examples of this structure in our building stones are the oölitic limestones of Bedford, Indiana, and other places. A rare structure in crystalline rocks.

Conglomerates. Fragmental stones composed of large, rounded fragments.
(See p. 248.)

Coquina. The Spanish name for a shell limestone which occurs abundantly in
Florida, and composed simply of a mass of shells cemented together.
(See p. 123.)

Coral limestone. A rock composed of fragments of corals.

Crystalline. Consisting wholly of crystals or crystalline particles, *not fragmental*. Rocks which like granite or crystalline limestone are made up
wholly of crystalline grains are called *crystalline-granular* or *granular-
crystalline* rocks. The term *micro-crystalline* and *crypto-crystalline* are
often applied to rocks in which the individual particles are too small to
be readily distinguished by the unaided eye. Such rocks are sometimes
called *compact*, a term which is also applied to fragmental rocks of similar texture.

Curb. A flat piece of stone placed vertically, bounding the street edges of
sidewalks.

Diabase. An eruptive rock composed essentially of a plagioclase feldspar and
augite. (See p. 228.)

Dikes (or **dykes**). Masses of igneous rocks which have been forced up from below in a molten condition to fill fractures or fissures in the earth's crust. Such are also called trap-rocks. The diabases and a variety of eruptive rocks frequently occur in the form of dikes.

Diorite. An eruptive rock composed essentially of a plagioclase, feldspar and hornblende. (See p. 239.)

Dip. The slope or pitch of the strata, or the angle which the layers make with the plane of the horizon.

Dolomite. A stone composed of mixed calcium and magnesium carbonates. (See p. 83.)

A "Dry." A natural seam usually invisible when the rock is freshly quarried, but which is brought out on exposure to weather or sometimes during the process of cutting. A very serious defect in many stones.

Escarpment. A nearly vertical natural face of rock or ledge.

Feldspathic. Containing feldspar.

Ferruginous. Containing iron oxides.

Fibrous. Having a structure as though made up of bundles of distinct fibres. This structure is not found in any building stone, but is common in some forms of gypsum and of calcite, which are used for making small ornaments.

Flagstone. Any kind of a stone which separates naturally into thin tabular plates suitable for pavements and curbing. Especially applicable to sandstones and schists.

Flint. Quartz in any kind of rock is commonly known to quarrymen as flint. True flint is amorphous silica, occurring in nodular form in chalk beds.

Foliated or schistose. Terms applied to rocks which, like gneiss and schist, have their constituents arranged in more or less definite nearly parallel planes.

Fragmental or clastic. Terms which are applied to rocks composed of fragments, like ordinary sandstone. When the fragments are the size of a pea or larger, and rounded in form, the structure is called *conglomerated*, or if the particles are angular, *brecciated*.

Freestone. This is a term which has been applied to stones that work freely in any direction. Especially applied to sandstones and limestones. A term of no special value, as it is too indefinite.

Gneiss. A rock of the composition of granite but in which the ingredients are arranged in more or less parallel layers. (See p. 244.)

Gneissoid. Like gneiss.

Grain. The direction in a rock at right angles with the rift. (See p. 39.)

Granite. A rock consisting of quartz, orthoclase, and mica or other accessory minerals. In the stone-cutter's nomenclature no distinction is made

between the varieties ; all stones which are hard, granular, and crystallized are called granite. (See p. 175.)

Granitoid. Thoroughly crystalline and massive, like granite.

Granular. A term applied to rocks composed of distinct grains, whether fragmental and water worn or crystalline.

Greenstone or **Grünstein.** A term formerly used to designate certain basic
eruptive rocks occurring in the form of dikes. Through mistaken
notions regarding their true nature and from a general similarity in their
appearance the name was made to include a variety of compact, dark-
greenish or nearly black rocks, which microscopic examination has shown
to be principally diabase and diorite.

Grit. Any sharp, gritty sandstone or schist used as a whetstone or hone.

Grub-saw. A saw made from a notched blade of thin iron, and provided with
a wooden back. Used with sand for sawing stone by hand power. (See
Plate XI.)

Guys. Ropes or chains used to prevent anything from swinging or moving
about.

Hackly fracture. A term applied when the surfaces of a fracture are rough
and jagged.

Joints. Divisional planes which divide the rock in the quarry into natural
blocks. There are usually two or three nearly parallel series called by
quarrymen end joints, back joints, and bottom joints, according to their
position. (See p. 316.)

Ledge. Any natural solid body of rock.

Lewis hole. The Lewis * hole consists of a series of two or more holes drilled
as closely together as possible, and then connected by knocking out the
thin partition between them, forming thus one wide hole, having its
greatest diameter in a plane with the desired rift. Blasts from such
holes are wedge-like in their action, and by means of them larger and
better-shaped blocks can be taken out than would otherwise be possible.
This style of hole is said † to have been devised by a Mr. Joseph Richards, of Quincy, though at about what date we are not informed. This
same gentleman was also the inventor of the bush hammer, which, however, when first patented, about 1831, consisted of a solid piece, instead
of several pieces bolted together as now.

Limestone. Under this term almost all the calcareous quarried rocks, whether
fragmental or crystalline, are classified. (See p. 78.)

Liver rock. This term is applied to that variety of the Ohio sandstone which

---

* This word is spelled by some Louis.

† Potter's History of Quincy, Massachusetts.

breaks or cuts as readily in one direction as in another. In other words, the working of the stone is not affected by stratification.

Lyonaise marble. A local term applied to marbles which are composed of a mixture of red and white colors, as those of Mallet's Bay, Vermont.

Marble. Any limestone or dolomite capable of being polished and suited for ornamental work.

Massive ; unstratified. Having no definite arrangement in layers or strata, but the various ingredients being thoroughly commingled, as in granite and diabase.

Nigger head. (1) The black concretionary nodules found in granite ;

(2) Any hard, dark, colored rock weathering out into rounded nodules or bowlders ;

(3) Slaty rock associated with sandstone. A quarryman's term.

Oolite. A stone composed of small globules resembling the roe of a fish.

Ophiocalcite, ophiolite, or ophite. A mixture of serpentine and limestone or dolomite. (See p. 53.)

Perch. In Philadelphia, 22 cubic feet are called a perch. A perch of masonry. contains 24¾ cubic feet, 16½ x 1½ x 1. It is usually taken at 25 cubic feet. The term is falling into disuse.

Plucky. A term often used by stone-cutters to designate stones which under the chisel break away in irregularly conchoidal chips, and which are therefore difficult to trim to a line or to bring to a perfect surface. Common in compact and impure limestones.

Porphyry. Any stone composed of an extremely fine ground mass in which larger crystals are developed. (See p. 217.)

Porphyritic. When a rock consists of a compact or fine and evenly crystalline groundmass, throughout which are scattered larger crystals, usually of feldspar, the structure is said to be porphyritic. This structure is quite common in granite, but is not particularly noticeable, owing to the slight contrast in color between the larger crystals and the finer groundmass. It is most noticeable in such rocks as the felsites, in which, as is the case with some of the " porphyries" of eastern Massachusetts, the groundmass is exceedingly dense and compact and of a black or red color, while the large feldspar crystals are white and stand out in very marked contrast. This structure is so striking in appearance that rocks possessing it in any marked degree are popularly called porphyries whatever may be their mineral composition. The term porphyry is said to have been originally applied to certain kinds of igneous rocks of a reddish or purple color, such as the celebrated red porphyry or "roseo antico" of Egypt. The word is now used by the best authorities almost wholly in its adjective sense, since any rock may possess this structure whatever its origin or composition may be.*

Putty powder, or polishing putty, is a fine whitish powder, consisting in the commercial form of about equal parts oxide of tin and lead. Used in polishing stone and glass.

Quarry. Any opening in a ledge for taking out stone.

Quarry Water. All rocks when first taken from the quarry contain more or less water, which evaporates on exposure, leaving the stone considerably harder. In sandstones this quarry water is considered by Newberry to be a solution of silica ("Report of Judges," Group I. p. 127). Its composition probably varies greatly in different classes of rocks. See p. 363.

Rhyolite. A post-Tertiary volcanic rock of the composition of granite. See p. 221.

Rift. The direction in a rock parallel to the lamination or foliation, and along which it splits with greatest ease.

Rubberstone. A sharp-gritted Ohio or Indiana sandstone used for sharpening shoe-knives ; also called a shoe-stone.

Rubble masonry. Rough, unsquared stone laid in irregular courses.

Saccharoidal. Having a grain and structure like that of loaf sugar. Common in crystalline limestone.

Salt veins. A term applied by the quarrymen to the coarse granite veins from 2 inches to 2 or more feet thick, and which are found intersecting granites and older crystalline rocks.

Scab. A local term used in certain sandstone quarries in Iowa. The stone is very massive and is broken from the quarry in irregular lumps by blasting. These lumps are then trimmed down to a shape approximately rectangular by means of heavy picks. This process is denominated *scabbing.*

Sap. The term originated from imagined analogy between the decomposed layer and the sap wood of trees. A term applied to the stained and worthless portions of the stone extending inward from the joint.

Sculp. To sculp slate is to break up the large blocks into long slabs, suitable to split.

Segregated. A term applied to the veins and nodular masses of finer or coarser texture that have formed in granite and other crystalline rocks ; as for example, the black patches in granite.

Serpentine. A rock composed of hydrous magnesia silicate. (See p. 53.)

Shell limestone. Rock composed of consolidated shells.

---

* Hull, " Building and Ornamental Stones," p. 75.

Siliceous. Containing silica.

Spalls. This is a term which is used quite generally by stone-cutters to denote the chips and other waste material cut from a block in process of dressing.

Spider-web. A term applied to the wavy lines in the Ohio sandstones, and which are caused by stains of iron oxide. Frequently seen in sawed stones, especially where the lamination is slightly oblique or irregular. It is very like the grain of wood which shows in a planed board. (See p. 277.)

Split rock. This term applies to those rocks possessing tabular structure, or which cleave easily in the lines of lamination, and are consequently applicable to the preparation of flagging and for curbstones.

Stalactite or Stalagmite marble. This is a marble which is formed by the deposit of lime carbonates from waters percolating into cavities or caves.

Strata. Layers or beds of rock of the same kind lying one upon another.

Stratified; bedded. Composed of layers or beds lying parallel to one another, as is so frequently seen in sandstone and limestone. When the strata are fine and leaf-like the structure is called laminated or shaly.

Streaked. Having some of the mineral constituents so arranged as to give the rock a striped or streaked appearance. In the eruptive rocks this structure is often produced by the flowing of the mass in a partially cooled condition. It is best seen in obsidian, rhyolite and quartz porphyries.

Stock. The useful rock taken from a quarry.

Strike. The direction in strata at right angles to the dip, or the course of a horizontal line on the surface of inclined beds.

Syenite. A granular massive rock with the structure of a granite, but containing no quartz. (See p. 223.)

Trachyte. A post-Tertiary volcanic rock of the composition of syenite. (See p. 226.)

Trap or trap-rock. (See Dikes and Greenstone.) The name applies to the manner in which a rock occurs, and is not itself a name of specific value.

Travertine. A calcareous rock deposited by water from solution, and which was used as a building stone in Rome. (See text, p. 116.)

Verde antique. Antique green. A rock composed of a mixture of serpentine and limestone. (See p. 54.)

Vitreous or glassy. These terms are applied to rocks that have a structure like glass, as obsidian. Rocks of this type are at present little used for any kind of work.

INDEX.

439

.

www.ingramcontent.com/pod-product-compliance
Lightning Source LLC
Chambersburg PA
CBHW031813270326
41932CB00008B/401